Ivo Van Horebeek Johan Lewi

Algebraic Specifications in Software Engineering

An Introduction

With 240 Figures

Springer-Verlag Berlin Heidelberg New York
London Paris Tokyo Hong Kong

Ivo Van Horebeek
Johan Lewi

Katholieke Universiteit Leuven
Department of Computer Science
Celestijnenlaan 200 A
B-3030 Leuven/Heverlee, Belgium

ISBN-13: 978-3-642-75032-8   e-ISBN-13: 978-3-642-75030-4
DOI: 10.1007/978-3-642-75030-4

Library of Congress Cataloging-in-Publication Data
Horebeek, Ivo van, 1959- Algebraic specifications in software engineering: an introduction
Ivo van Horebeek, Johan Lewi. p. cm.
Includes bibliographical references.

1. Software engineering. 2. Abstract data types (Computer science) I. Lewi, Johan. II. Title.
QA76.758.H67 1989 005.1'01'5102--dc20 89-26115

Offsetprinting: Weihert-Druck GmbH, Darmstadt
Binding: J. Schäffer GmbH & Co. KG, Grünstadt
2145/3140–543210

To Lutgarde and Dany

Preface

"I prefer to view formal methods as tools,
the use of which might be helpful."
E. W. Dijkstra

Algebraic specifications are about to be accepted by industry. Many projects in which algebraic specifications have been used as a design tool have been carried out. What prevents algebraic specifications from breaking through is the absence of introductory descriptions and tools supporting the construction of algebraic specifications. On the one hand, interest from industry will stimulate people to make introductions and tools, whereas on the other hand the existence of introductions and tools will stimulate industry to use algebraic specifications. This book should be seen as a contribution towards creating this virtuous circle. The book will be of interest to software designers and programmers. It can also be used as material for an introductory course on algebraic specifications and software engineering at undergraduate or graduate level.

Nowadays, there is general agreement that in large software projects appropriate specifications are a must in order to obtain quality software. Informal specifications alone are certainly not appropriate because they are incomplete, inconsistent, inaccurate and ambiguous and they rapidly become bulky and therefore useless. The only way to overcome this problem is to use *formal specifications*. An important remark here is that a specification formalism (language) alone is not sufficient. What is also needed is a design method to write specifications in that formalism.

Formal specifications (languages and methods) are a *promising* topic within software engineering. They play the role of a contract between implementors and customers. They are useful as program documentation of the abstractions being made during the design phase. They serve as a mechanism for generating questions about design decisions and intrinsic properties of the software system, thus improving understanding between implementors and customers. Formal specifications form the starting-point for verifications and validations. Finally, they enable rapid prototyping. Three important categories of formal specifications are: pre- and post-conditions, denotational semantics, and algebraic specifications. Our belief is that in software design these formalisms are not competitors and that each formalism must be used where it is most appropriate. This book centres around algebraic specifications.

Formal specifications in the design of large software are a *challenging* topic because a number of psychological barriers have to be broken. Formal specifications often have a bad reputation among designers and implementors in industry. Formal often stands for "How do we make the simple cases intricate?" and "How do we give a program a scientific and academic gloss so that it looks mysterious for others?". First of all, these people are hardly to be blamed since very little has been done on the diffusion of the practical (software engineering) aspects of the theoretical results. Most literature on formal specifications is of a theoretical nature and is inaccessible for most practitioners.

In order to bridge the gap between theory and practice, there is a need for good introductions. Writing such an introduction for one particular class of specifications, namely algebraic specifications, is the aim of this book. In this book we (1) show the benefits from using algebraic specifications, (2) present an algebraic specification language and a method to use this language, (3) explain the underlying mathematical foundations of algebraic specifications and the consequences of the theory for the practitioner, and (4) present not only small examples but also case studies of a reasonable complexity.

The practitioner who expects just a number of recipes to construct formal specifications will be disappointed while reading this book. It is our strong belief that learning to use formal specifications is first of all a matter of *education* rather than *training*. The process of constructing algebraic specifications (and formal specifications in general) can only be successful if one has at one's disposal a minimal knowledge of the underlying mathematical foundations. This knowledge is necessary to be aware of what precisely one is doing when writing algebraic specifications.

In our book an attempt is made to integrate the mathematical foundations and the engineering aspects of algebraic specifications. The theoretical concepts are the starting-point for the design of a practical specification language. The impact of traditional principles of software engineering and advanced features of current high level programming languages on the development of the specification language is discussed. The main characteristic of the language is that it enables the design of constructive specifications; this is useful for rapid prototyping. Other important characteristics of the strongly typed specification language are its module mechanism and its general parameterization concept. Finally, the language contains an elegant notation supporting an explicit error detection and error handling method. Many case studies have been carried out, including an industrial specification of a call handling system (PABX). These case studies show that an algebraic specification as a formalism is not sufficient. It must be accompanied by a design method. The design method used for the PABX is object-oriented. In this book a contribution is made to abstract implementations as well. Finally, programming environments and rapid prototyping supporting the construction of algebraic specifications are briefly discussed.

Acknowledgements

Part of this research has been supported by Bell Telephone Alcatel in the context of a joint project between the Research Centre of Bell Telephone and the Department of Computer Science of the Katholieke Universiteit Leuven.

Our research group is greatly indebted to W. Van Puymbroeck, J. De Man and L. Duponcheel (Bell Telephone, Antwerp) and P.-Y. Schobbens (Université Catholique de Louvain) for many interesting brainstorming sessions about algebraic specifications and software engineering. We would also like to thank J. Jacobs (Bell Telephone, Geel) for his support that made the specification of the PABX possible.

It is also a great pleasure to thank our colleagues E. Bevers, E. Van Gestel, E. Devriendt and B. Vergauwen for the fruitful collaboration and their helpful criticism. All members of our department merit special mention for their encouragement and assistance.

It is impossible to list exhaustively all people who have contributed to this book. Special mention must be made to the students we collaborated with in the context of their graduate theses and to the many students who made helpful comments on parts of this text that have been used in a course on formal specifications. Finally, we offer our warmest thanks to our wives Lutgarde and Dany for their patience and encouragement throughout the long writing period and for their help in proofreading the manuscript.

Leuven, July 1989   I. Van Horebeek
                                     J. Lewi

Contents

"Begin at the beginning." the King said very gravely,
"and go on till you come to the end; then stop."
'Alice in Wonderland', Lewis Carroll

1. Introduction   1

  1.1   Software Engineering   1
  1.2   Software Life Cycle   2
  1.3   Abstract Data Types and Specifications 3
  1.4   Why Specifications ?   4
  1.5   Why Formal Specifications ?   5
  1.6   Algebraic Specifications, an Intuitive Approach   7
  1.7   Survey   10
  1.8   Historical Remarks on Algebraic Specifications   12

2. Abstract Data Types as Initial Algebras   14

  2.1   Many-Sorted Algebra, Signature and Graphical Notation   15
  2.2   Homomorphism and Isomorphism   20
  2.3   Variable-Free Termlanguage   23
  2.4   Word Algebra   24
  2.5   Signature, Variety and Termalgebra   26
  2.6   Signature and Initial Algebra   26
  2.7   Abstract Data Types Defined by a Signature   27
  2.8   Termlanguage   27
  2.9   Substitution and Ground Substitution   28
  2.10 Assignment   29
  2.11 Axioms and Presentation   30
  2.12 Presentation, Variety and Termalgebra   32
  2.13 Equational Reasoning   32
  2.14 Presentation and Initial Algebra   35
  2.15 Abstract Data Types Defined by a Presentation   38
  2.16 Examples   38
  2.17 Induction   43
  2.18 Hidden Operations and Sorts   55
  2.19 Bibliographic Notes   58

3. An Algebraic Specification Language   66

  3.1   Modularity   68
       3.1.1   Modules   68
       3.1.2   Import and Export Clauses   71
       3.1.3   Export of the Import   73
  3.2   Hierarchical Specifications   74
  3.3   Notational Extensions   76
       3.3.1   Ifthenelse Construct   76
       3.3.2   Mixfix Notations   78
       3.3.3   Conditional Axioms   80
       3.3.4   Case Constructs   81
       3.3.5   Let Constructs   82
       3.3.6   Qualified Names and Renaming   84
  3.4   Parameterized Specifications   85
       3.4.1   Parameter Morphisms   90
       3.4.2   Instantiations   91
       3.4.3   Requirements and Induction   93
       3.4.4   Remarks on Hierarchical Constraints   94
       3.4.5   Renaming and Qualified Names   99
       3.4.6   Partial Instantiations   101
       3.4.7   Parameterized Parameter Passing   103
       3.4.8   Parameterizing Requirements   107
  3.5   Clusters   111
  3.6   Bibliographic Notes   114

4. Constructive Specifications   120

  4.1   Simple Example   121
  4.2   Constructive Specifications   123
  4.3   Theorems   125
  4.4   Equality Operation   128
  4.5   Example   129
  4.6   Constructor Axioms   130
  4.7   Semi-Constructive Specifications   134
  4.8   Inconsistency   139
  4.9   On Constructing Requirements   140
  4.10 Claiming Modules   151
  4.11 The Cartesian Product of Sorts   155
  4.12 Constructivity and Abstraction   157
  4.13 Bibliographic Notes   159

5. A Case Study : the Ferry Problem   164

5.1   Informal Description of the Ferry Problem   165
5.2   Formal Specification of the Ferry Problem   166
5.3   The Farmer, the Wolf, the Goat and the Cabbage   169
5.4   The Missionaries and the Cannibals   171
5.5   Specification of a Search Strategy   173
5.6   Conclusion   175

6. A Case Study : the Mini-PABX   176

6.1   Object-Oriented Design Method   177
6.2   Modularity   180
6.3   The Abstract Data Type Phone   182
6.4   Error Handling   184
6.5   The Abstract Data Type Mini-PABX   184
6.6   The Scheduling of the Messages   187
6.7   Skeleton of the Mini-PABX   188
6.8   A Two-Party Voice Call   189
        6.8.1   The Module Phone   190
        6.8.2   The Module PhoneMessages   191
        6.8.3   The Module NextPhone   196
        6.8.4   The Module OutPhone   197
6.9   Enquiry Call   198
        6.9.1   The Module Phone   199
        6.9.2   The Module PhoneMessages   201
        6.9.3   The Module NextPhone   205
        6.9.4   The Module OutPhone   206
6.10   User Actions   206
        6.10.1 The Module PhoneMessages   207
        6.10.2 The Module NextPhone   208
        6.10.3 The Module OutPhone   210
6.11   Conclusion   212

7. Error Handling   215

7.1   The Need for an Error Handling System   216
7.2   Safety Functions   220
7.3   Safety and Unsafety Markers   221
7.4   Method of Error Specification   224
7.5   Safety Conditions   227
7.6   Miscellanies   238
7.7   Bibliographic Notes   243

8. Abstract Implementations   246

    8.1   Example of the Stacks   250
    8.2   Concepts of Abstract Implementations   254
        8.2.1   Data Representation Part of $\downarrow$A   256
        8.2.2   Procedure Implementation Part of $\downarrow$A   257
        8.2.3   Representation Function   258
        8.2.4   Implementation Invariant   262
        8.2.5   Abstraction Function   265
        8.2.6   Equivalence Relation   268
        8.2.7   A Multi-Step Implementation Method   270
    8.3   Implementation Constraints   271
    8.4   Example: Scheme of Stacks   278
    8.5   Example: Scheme of Symbol Tables   287
    8.6   Properties and Relations   295
    8.7   Bibliographic Notes   304

Conclusions   309

Appendix A : Syntax   318

Appendix B : Rapid Prototyping, the Mini-PABX   323

Bibliography   327

Index   343

1. Introduction

> "A problem well defined is half solved."
> *old adage*

1.1 Software Engineering

The aim of software engineering is to construct software of high quality. By software we mean large programs. Most design and programming techniques directed towards the development of small programs cannot simply be generalized to be applicable to large scale software development. Qualities, sometimes called software engineering criteria, are divided into two categories: external and internal qualities. The external qualities we are particularly interested in are correctness, robustness, extendibility, reusability and efficiency. The internal qualities dealt with in this book are modularity and continuity. Each of these qualities is now briefly discussed. More detailed discussions can be found in literature. Some of the many authors dealing with the construction of quality software are [Boehm78, De Remer76, Parnas72b, Meyer88, Liskov86, Jackson75, Jackson83].

Correctness or *reliability* is the ability of a software system to perform its services as defined by its requirements definition and specification.

Robustness is the ability of a software system to continue to behave reasonably even in abnormal situations.

Extendibility is the ease with which a software system can be adapted to changes of its requirements definition and specification.

Reusability is the ability of software modules to be reused as components to construct new software for other applications.

Efficiency is the ability of software to make good use of hardware resources and operating system services.

Modularity is the property of software to be divided into more or less autonomous components connected with a coherent and simple interface. Modularity is not only important at the implementation (program) level but also at the design (specification) level. At the implementation level, examples of modules are procedures, data, data types, iterators and processes. Procedures are often called actions, subroutines, functions and subprograms. Data types are known as packages in Ada [Ada83], classes in

1. Introduction

1.1 Software Engineering

phases of the life cycle. Secondly, the maintenance phase covers not only repairing activities of errors but also any changes due to the evolution of the software system before and after the program has been released. Maintenance usually involves many iterations over the other phases. Following [Boehm76, Lientz80], maintenance costs cover approximately 50–75 % of the total cost of software. One of the key benefits from using formal specifications is the detection of design errors in an early stage of the software development. Structuring the formal specification into the appropriate modules will make software easier to modify. In this way, maintenance can be kept under control, avoiding an abrupt increase of the program entropy whenever changes have to be made in the requirements definition and specification.

1.3 Abstract Data Types and Specifications

In literature a number of techniques to construct quality software can be found. By quality software we mean software that meets the software engineering criteria or more exactly a trade-off between these criteria, since some of these criteria are in conflict. Examples of such software engineering techniques are Jackson's system development [Jackson83], Yourdon's structured design [Yourdon79] and structured analysis [De Marco78]. All these methods have one important aspect in common: software is structured around data rather than around functions. The reason for this choice is that functions are not the most stable part of a system. Structuring around data yields systems with a higher degree of continuity and reusability. The key point in structured design of software systems is to look for abstract data types, abbreviated ADTs in the sequel. Roughly speaking, a specification of an ADT describes a class of data structures by listing the services available on the data structures, together with the intrinsic properties of these services.

By specifying an ADT, we do not care *how* a data structure is actually represented or *how* each operation is implemented. What matters is *what* the data structure signifies at the level of a customer who wants to make instantiations (individual data structures) of the data type for further use in his program. To illustrate the concept of ADT, let us take the class of stacks of natural numbers, called Stack. The specification of Stack will list the services newstack, push, isnewstack, pop and top. Furthermore, given an object of type Stack, it describes how these services must be called for that object and it describes the intrinsic properties of these services. An example of such a property for Stack is pop(push(s, n)) == s;

where s is any Stack object and n is any natural number. This property simply expresses that pushing a natural number n on a stack s, followed by popping the resulting stack, yields the original stack s. The identifiers s and n are variables ranging over instantiations (objects) of types Stack and Nat respectively.

Writing specifications of ADTs is an activity that is located in the design phase of the software life cycle. Specifications are designed in a modular way. Roughly speaking, with each specification module in the design phase corresponds a program module in the implementation phase. Specification modules, unlike program modules, make abstraction of all irrelevant details of data representation and procedure implementation. An important remark is that finding the appropriate set of specification modules is not always an easy job. The choice of the modules must be such that complexity of the module interfaces is minimal and that continuity of the software system is maximal. Mostly, a trade-off between these criteria has to be strived for.

1.4 Why Specifications ?

A specification may serve different purposes.

- Specifications are obviously used for program documentation. They describe the abstractions being made.

- Specifications serve as a mechanism for generating questions. The construction of specifications forces the designers to think about the requirements definition and the intrinsic properties and functionalities of the software system to be designed. In this way the construction of specifications helps the designers to better understand these requirements and to detect design inconsistencies, incompleteness and ambiguities in an early stage of software development. Such a better understanding is already an important benefit from the specification activity.

- A specification can be considered as a kind of contract between the designers of a program and its customers. It describes the obligations and rights of both parties. A specification binds customers and designers by expressing the conditions under which the services of a module are legitimate and by defining the results when calling these services.

• Specifications are a powerful tool in the development of a program
  (module) during its software life cycle. The presence of a good
  specification helps not only designers, but also implementors and
  maintainers. The modularity of the specification must be reflected in
  the modularity of the program. A specification serves as a blueprint
  for the implementation phase, where a program is written in some
  executable language. In most software projects, the language used is of
  an imperative nature. Unlike specifications, programs deal with
  implementational details as memory representation (such as arrays,
  records, variant records, linked lists), memory management (such as
  dispose in Pascal, free in PL1 and unchecked deallocation in Ada) and
  efficient (in time and space) coding of the system services.

  Writing a specification must not be seen as a separate phase in the
  construction of software. Also, specifications must be adapted each
  time modifications are introduced in any of the other phases of the
  software life cycle. Especially, specifications have to be updated during
  the maintenance phase taking into account the evolution of the software
  system.

• With regard to program validation, specifications may be very helpful
  to collect test cases to form a validation suite for the software system.

1.5 Why Formal Specifications ?

Specifications must be at the same time compact, complete, consistent,
precise and unambiguous. From experience, it has turned out that a
natural language is not a good candidate as a specification language. In
industry, a lot of effort has been devoted to writing informal specifications
for software systems, but little or no attention is paid to these
specifications when they are badly needed, i.e. during maintenance of the
software. Why is it so ? Specifications in a natural language rapidly
become bulky, even to such an extent that nobody has the courage to dig
into them. Moreover, such specifications are at many places inaccurate,
incomplete and ambiguous. It must be very discouraging to discover after
a long search that the answer can only be obtained by running the system
with the appropriate input data. The tragedy in software development is
that once a program modification is made without adapting the
corresponding specification, the whole specification becomes obsolete for
the rest of the software life cycle and the whole specification effort is lost.
Having a non-existent or an obsolete specification is the reason why there
exist so many software systems the behaviour of which nobody can

exactly derive in a reasonable lapse of time. It also explains the many situations where services of software systems are marketed and advertised that in reality do not exist. Notice that running the program with the appropriate input can only give partial answers to questions about the system behaviour.

We do not assert that informal specifications are useless. They may be very useful as a first introduction to a software system and as comment to enhance the readability of the formal specifications. Formal and informal specifications must not be regarded as competitive but rather as complementary.

Formal specifications, unlike informal ones, enable the designer to use *rigorous mathematical reasoning*. Properties of the specification (and thus of the program to be constructed at a later stage) can be proved to be true just as theorems can be proved in mathematics. In this way, design errors (e.g., inconsistencies and incompleteness) can be detected in an early stage of the development. Another aspect of mathematical reasoning with formal specifications is the ability to verify formally that the implementation (program) satisfies its specification. Both aspects of mathematical reasoning have to do with what is called *program correctness proofs*.

There is an intensive debate around rigorous mathematical reasoning. Algebraic specifications enable the designer to prove certain properties of his design and to prove that the implementation (program) meets its specification. We must admit that this is easier said than done. Most examples in literature apply proof techniques to small examples. For large software, correctness proofs would require practical tools such as intelligent theorem provers. Unfortunately, automatic theorem proving for large software is still beyond today's program proving technology. However correctness proofs of parts of the system and verification of some of the properties are feasible. The general rule is to prove and verify as much as possible. It is a well-known fact that correctness proofs and verification show the absence of errors, whereas testing only indicates the presence of errors for some sample input of the system.

Formal specifications that are constructive, can be directly executed, although with poor performance. Then, formal specifications are used in a process called *rapid prototyping*. With constructive formal specifications, one is able to design top-down, to verify top-down and even to test top-down. The notion of top-down means here that the specification is treated before any instruction of the implementation has been written. A benefit from making constructive formal specifications that certainly will interest the practitioner, is that this kind of rapid prototyping enables designers and customers to get user feedback and hands-on experience with the software system before the implementation already gets started. In this way, design errors due to misunderstandings between designers and customers, and lack of understanding of the service mechanisms to be provided by the system can be detected and corrected at an early stage. With the concepts of constructive formal specifications and direct implementation, the boundaries between specifications and implementations are not very sharp. Both specifications and implementations are in fact programs, but the former are of a more abstract level than the latter. Moreover, in the life cycle of a software system there may be more than two levels of abstraction. A module may serve as a specification for the lower level and at the same time as an implementation for the higher one.

Many specification formalisms can be found in literature [Milgrom88]. In the *axiomatic method*, the behaviour of a program is characterized by pre- and post-conditions. Its pioneers are Floyd, Hoare and Dijkstra [Floyd67, Hoare72, Dijkstra76]. Another well-known formalism is *denotational semantics* [Stoy77, Gordon79]. Especially the use of high order functions is very useful to describe the powerful control structures of programming languages. Since the mid seventies, a new formalism based on the concept of abstract data types has been developed. As many-sorted algebras are the underlying mathematical model, such specifications are called *algebraic specifications*. In this book, we will only concentrate on algebraic specifications.

1.6 Algebraic Specifications, an Intuitive Approach

Recall that an ADT is a class of data structures described by an external view, i.e. available services and properties of these services. An algebraic specification is a mathematical description of such an ADT. As an introduction, we now intuitively discuss the abstract data type Stack, formally described by the algebraic specification shown in Fig. 1/2. A more elaborate discussion of this example will be given in the following chapters.

The *sort(s)* part lists the names of the abstract data types being described. In this example there is only one type, namely Stack. The *operations* part lists the services available on instances of the type Stack and syntactically describes how they have to be called. These parts are

```
sort Stack;
operations
   newstack: -> Stack;
   push: Stack * Nat -> Stack;
   isnewstack: Stack -> Bool;
   pop: Stack -> Stack;
   top: Stack -> Nat;
declare s: Stack;   n: Nat;
axioms
   isnewstack( newstack ) == true;
   isnewstack( push( s, n ) ) == false;
   pop( newstack ) == newstack;
   pop( push( s, n ) ) == s;
   top( newstack ) == zero;
   top( push( s, n ) ) == n;
```

Fig. 1/2

called the *signature* of the algebraic specification. As an example,

   push: Stack * Nat -> Stack;

means that push is a function with two arguments, of respective types Stack and Nat, and yields a result of type Stack. Notice that newstack is a nullary function, i.e. has no arguments, and yields a result of type Stack. It is also called a constant. The term function here is used in the mathematical sense, not in the context of programming. So, functions in algebraic specification have no side-effects. In our example, push takes as arguments a stack s and a natural number n and produces a new stack which is identical to the input stack except for one more element on its top. Side-effects will be introduced at the implementation stage, when efficient programs for the services available on stacks are written. Implementing the algebraic specification, we usually do not want to copy the input stack for every call of push. The service push will be implemented as a procedure with the Stack parameter as a call by variable (sometimes termed call by reference). The side-effect of calling push consists in the direct modification of the input parameter of type Stack. Algebraic specifications are some sort of functional specifications. By systematically avoiding any kind of side-effects, properties of the abstract data type can be expressed in a simple and rigorous way. For the algebraic specifications, these properties will have the form of axioms (as explained later) and theorems (see Section 4.3).

   The *axioms* part formally describes the semantic properties of the algebraic specification. So far, the specification applies to any data structure with services described by functions with the same signature, such as queues and lists. The axioms will restrict the specification towards stacks by listing the fundamental properties of stacks. One of these properties is described by the axiom

pop(push(s, n)) == s;

This axiom was explained in Section 1.3. Another axiom is

isnewstack(newstack) == true;

expressing that the function isnewstack applied to a newly created stack yields true, whereby true is a nullary function of the boolean values imported from another algebraic specification module. Import and export of algebraic specification modules and module dependency will be covered in Section 3.1. The variable n ranges over the set Nat of natural numbers, whose ADT is also defined elsewhere. As a last example, consider the axioms

pop(newstack) == newstack;
top(newstack) == zero;

This is a naive but correct specification of what happens when one pops an empty stack or takes the top element of an empty stack. Stack is specified in this way only to avoid the discussion of abnormal (exceptional) cases at this early stage. What we want is that the action pop applied to an empty stack yields some kind of erroneous stack and that the action top applied to an empty stack yields an erroneous natural number. We also want to decide whether further actions on an erroneous stack will keep the stack in its error state or transform the erroneous state back into a normal state. This latter process is called *error recovery*. Also more than one kind of erroneous stack will be possible to model, e.g., overflow and underflow of stacks. Error handling and error recovery will be thoroughly discussed in Chapter 7.

The algebraic specification of Stack expresses only the essential properties of the Stack services without overspecifying. It makes abstraction from any Stack representation and service implementation details. It is overspecification that makes verification and rigorous reasoning difficult. Algebraic specifications provide a computational model with ADTs. As an example of such computations, consider the following expressions

declare s1, s2: Stack;   n: Nat;
s1:= pop(push(push(newstack, 5), 7));
s2:= push(push(push(newstack, 0), top(s1)), 4);
n:= top (pop(pop(s2)));

By applying the axioms, successive simplifications may be performed.
These algebraic simplifications can be carried out mechanically. After
these simplifications have been carried out, the above expressions become:

s1:= push(newstack, 5);
top(s1):= 5;
s2:= push(push(push(newstack, 0), 5), 4);
n:= 0;

This kind of symbolic computation is heavily related to concepts such as
constructivity, term rewriting and rapid prototyping.

Furthermore, the book deals with a number of important design issues
centred around specifications in general and algebraic specifications in
particular. Some of the issues are constructivity versus non-
constructivity, modularity, abstraction by parameterization, rigorous
reasoning, error detection, error recovery and abstract implementations.

1.7 Survey

Chapter 2 discusses the *mathematical foundations* of algebraic
specifications. ADTs are defined as many-sorted initial algebras. Due to
these underlying mathematical concepts, algebraic specifications can be
made accurate and unambiguous. They enable us to give a well-defined
and implementation-independent meaning to an ADT. It is not our
intention, however, to go deeply into mathematics. We are especially
interested in the engineering aspects of formal specifications. The
mathematical concepts are informally described and illustrated by many
examples. Rigorous reasoning is obtained by equational reasoning and by
induction. The power of the algebraic specification method is increased by
using hidden functions, which can also be used as auxiliary functions.

Chapter 3 deals with *principles of software engineering*. These
principles are incorporated into the mathematical notation developed in
Chapter 2, in order to obtain a practical specification language.
Programming in this language results in modular, reliable, readable and
reusable specifications. A technique of hierarchical specifications is

proposed, providing us with a modular specification method. Import and export clauses in modules form the interfaces between the modules and provide additional safety. The readability is enhanced by notational extensions. Another important feature is the possibility of parameterized specifications, resulting in more reusable and readable specifications. Also parameterized parameter passing is allowed.

In Chapter 4 we restrict the specifications to *constructive* and *semi-constructive* ones in order to enable rapid prototyping. In this way, a style of specifying is proposed distinguishing between data and procedural abstraction. By introducing constraints that can be checked in a mechanical way, the chance of writing erroneous specifications can be reduced considerably. The specification will be considered as the input for a term rewriting system.

In Chapter 5 a non-trivial case study, called the *ferry problem*, is discussed. This ferry problem is a generalization of the riddle of the farmer, the wolf, the goat and the cabbage. It is a nice example of abstraction by parameterization. A distinction will be made between the specification of the problem on the one hand (the *what*) and the specification of an implementation on the other hand (the *how*).

One of the most challenging case studies we made is the formal specification of a substantial part of a call handling system, the *ITT 5400 BCS* [Bell85b]. In the specification abstraction is made from technical information about the ITT 5400 BCS (e.g., a user needs not to know it is based on a 16-bit micro-processor). Because of the considerable length of this industrial case study, we extracted for Chapter 6 a *mini-PABX*. This mini-PABX provides the two-party voice calls and the enquiry feature of the ITT 5400 BCS. The specification of the mini-PABX is based on an object-oriented design method. The resulting specification is highly modular and adaptable and therefore more readable.

An explicit *error detection and error handling mechanism* for an algebraic specification language is described in Chapter 7. An elegant notation, directly supporting this error handling method, is introduced in a many-sorted initial algebra framework. Firstly, a safety function is provided for every sort. This function characterizes each object as being safe or unsafe. Secondly, axioms may contain markers that indicate to which kind of objects the axioms are applicable. The proposed notation is a trade-off between readability and capability to handle a large class of error situations. A major point is that the presented description of error handling promotes a two-step design method of algebraic specifications. In a first step the specification is given with error detection only, in a second step error handling is superimposed.

Chapter 8 treats a top-down implementation method for (semi-) constructive specifications of data types, called *abstract implementations*. First, a high level specification of the data type is produced in which abstraction is made from all irrelevant details, only the relevant properties are described. Next, an implementation for the specification can be constructed using specifications of other data types. In turn these specifications can be provided with implementations, and so on. If (semi-) constructive specifications are used, each level can be tested (rapid prototyping) before it is implemented. Furthermore, each level can be verified to be correct before it is implemented.

Appendix A contains the complete ECF syntax of the presented specification language. An example of rapid prototyping, concerning the specification of the mini-PABX of Chapter 6, can be found in Appendix B. Finally, an index of technical terms and a bibliography are given.

Most chapters conclude with a survey of the literature. A lot of articles providing further information on underlying mathematical theories, proofs and examples, are referred to. An exhaustive bibliography on algebraic software specifications can be found in [Klaeren85, Schobbens89].

1.8 Historical Remarks on Algebraic Specifications

The pioneers of algebraic specifications are Zilles [Zilles74], Guttag [Guttag75] and the ADJ group [Goguen74] consisting of Goguen, Thatcher, Wagner and Wright. They all considered a software module representing an ADT as a many-sorted algebra. The basic argument for the algebraic approach is that such a software module has exactly the same structure as an algebra: the various sorts of data involved form sets and the operations of interest are functions among these sets [Meseguer85a].

During the last years, many different algebraic models have been proposed. The ADJ group [Goguen78] presented the theory of the (many-sorted) initial algebras. Final algebra semantics were discussed, e.g., in [Wand79]. The idea of behavioural equivalence was introduced by [Giarratana76]. The Munich CIP-group [Partsch78, CIP85] took the class of all algebras fitting to a given specification as its semantics. The central idea of Sannella and Tarlecki [Sannella85b] is based on the fact that much work on algebraic specifications can be done independently of the particular logical system on which the specification formalism is based.

The first specification language based on algebraic specifications was CLEAR [Burstall77], where, among others, the concept of parameterized specifications was incorporated. Since then many other algebraic specification languages have been developed. The most popular ones are ACT ONE [Ehrig85] and the OBJ family [Goguen79, Goguen83, Goguen84c, Futatsugi85], both based on many-sorted initial algebras. Algebraic specification languages may be considered as strongly-typed functional languages like Hope [Burstall80] or as rewrite rule languages [Huet80].

Topics about algebraic specifications discussed in literature include correctness, theorem proving, parameterizing, error handling and abstract implementations. Important work on power and limits of algebraic specifications is contained in [Majster77, Thatcher78, Bergstra81]. A combination of initial algebra semantics with Horn clause logic resulted in Eqlog [Goguen84d] and LPG [Bert86, Declerfayt89].

Algebraic specification techniques and languages have been successfully applied to the specification of systems ranging from basic data types as stacks and natural numbers [Guttag78a] to highly sophisticated software systems as a graphical programming language [Mallgren82] and the Unix file system [Bidoit87]. Algebraic specification techniques are used in the wide spectrum language CIP [CIP85], which allows the derivation of correct software from formal requirements via design specifications down to a machine-oriented level using jumps and pointers. Another wide spectrum language that has an algebraic kernel is Larch [Guttag85]. At the moment, many researchers all over the world are involved in research in the field of algebraic specifications. Many Esprit Projects, e.g., Gipe and Meteor [Bergstra87], are covering topics related to algebraic specifications.

More historical information about algebraic specifications can be found in [Kutzler83, Ehrig85, Futatsugi85].

2. Abstract Data Types as Initial Algebras

> "Use theory to provide insight, use common sense and intuition
> where it is suitable, but fall back on the formal theory
> for support when difficulties and complexities arise."
>
> *David Gries*

Because software is structured around data rather than around services of
a system, abstract data types (ADTs) play a central role in the search for
an appropriate structure of modularity during the design phase of the
software life cycle. Intuitively speaking, an ADT is characterized by a set
of data structures together with a number of services (functions) available
on these data structures. To deal with ADTs in a rigorous way, we first
model ADTs by means of algebras. Many algebraic models can be chosen
as underlying mathematical foundation. In this book, the *initial* model is
used. It is one of the most widespread models in literature. Other models
will be briefly discussed in Section 2.19. As an algebra may define several
abstract data types (called sorts), the term *many-sorted initial algebra* is
used. A description (notation) of an algebra, e.g., of a many-sorted initial
algebra, is called an *algebraic specification*.

In this chapter a clear distinction is made between abstract elements, i.e.
elements of many-sorted initial algebras, and concrete notations, i.e.
elements of algebraic specifications. For this purpose, cloudlets are used to
mark abstract elements. Such a distinction may seem to be a bit tedious,
but from our didactic experience we have learned that it avoids a lot of
confusion and that without such a distinction many students are not able
to express themselves clearly during discussion sessions on algebraic
specifications.

The main reason why we are so interested in modelling ADTs by
mathematical objects (in our case many-sorted initial algebras) is that we
can profit from *rigorous reasoning* as defined for these objects. Rigorous
reasoning on algebraic specifications is based on two important techniques
called *equational reasoning* and *induction*. Both techniques enable the
designer to derive theorems from his algebraic specification. These
theorems then represent properties of the algebraic specification and of the
software system described by it. The fact that such a theorem has been
derived implies that the property it represents has been proved to be true.

The attentive reader may notice that at this point no mention is made of
constructivity (see Chapter 4) in algebraic specifications. The reason why
we do so is that a non-constructive specification is often more natural and

is of a higher level of abstraction than a constructive one. Such a non-constructive specification can then be considered as a first step in the specification phase, from which a constructive version can be derived in a second step.

Due to the mathematical foundation of the chosen model, namely many-sorted initial algebras, designers are able to give well-defined and implementation-independent meanings to ADTs. Due to this mathematical framework, algebraic specifications can be made accurate and unambiguous. To make the reader familiar with accuracy and unambiguity aspects of algebraic specifications, clear definitions of concepts and an appropriate terminology for these concepts are introduced in this chapter. Our intention is not to go into all the details of the mathematical machinery. The concepts are described informally and illustrated by many examples. No proofs are included in the text, but many references to literature are given in a systematic way, where a more mathematical treatment on the subject can be found.

2.1 Many-Sorted Algebra, Signature and Graphical Notation

A *many-sorted algebra* is an abstract structure consisting of a family of sets of objects and a number of functions whose arguments and results belong to these sets.

The structure of stacks of natural numbers is a simple example: the structure consists of the set of stacks, the set of natural numbers, the set of booleans, and the functions push, pop, top, isnewstack and succ.

In order to enable communication, a suitable notation for an algebra is required. Such a notation is called a *signature*. A signature introduces names for the sets of objects of the algebra. These names are called the *sorts* or *types* of the corresponding objects. Objects and functions of the algebra too can be given a name by the signature. Such named objects and named functions are respectively called *nullary* and *nonnullary operations*.

As an example, Fig. 2/1 shows a signature denoting the many-sorted algebra of stacks of natural numbers. A stack is a storage device where items are stored by the operation push. We only have direct access to the topmost (i.e. last stored) item, by means of the operation top. Access to lower items is only possible by first removing from the top one by one all items above the item to be accessed. Removing the item on top of the stack is done by the operation pop. This access mode is expressed by the principle *last in - first out*, which means that items stored last must be removed first. This access mode is very common in computer science. It is used, e.g., in the evaluation of expressions.

```
sorts Stack; Nat; Bool;
operations
    true, false: -> Bool;
    zero: -> Nat;
    succ: Nat -> Nat;
    newstack: -> Stack;
    push: Stack * Nat -> Stack;
    isnewstack: Stack -> Bool;
    pop: Stack -> Stack;
    top: Stack -> Nat;
```

Fig. 2/1

The sort names of the sets of objects follow the keyword **sorts** in the signature; their order is irrelevant. After the keyword **operations** follow the syntactic definitions of the operations in an arbitrary order. The syntactic definition of a nullary operation consists of its operation name and its *rank*, i.e. the sort of the nullary operation. The syntactic definition of a nonnullary operation consists of its operation name together with its *rank*, i.e. the sort names of its domain and range. Remember that nullary operations denote objects, whereas nonnullary operations denote functions in the many-sorted algebra.

In the example of Fig. 2/1 the sets of objects are called Stack, Nat and Bool. The names true and false denote objects of the set Bool, zero denotes an object of the set Nat and succ denotes a function with rank Nat -> Nat, meaning that the denoted function has a natural number as argument and yields a natural number as result. Furthermore, newstack denotes an object of the set Stack, push is a function with rank Stack * Nat -> Stack and isnewstack is a function with rank Stack -> Bool. Finally, the domain and range of pop are Stack. So is the domain of top, but its range is the set of natural numbers.

The relationship between signature and algebra can be illustrated by means of a diagram. As an example, the signature of Fig. 2/1 denotes the algebra of stacks of natural numbers as shown in Fig. 2/2. This relationship is indicated by the *denotation function* δ.

The left part of the diagram consists of names within the signature, whereas the right part contains an algebra, whose elements (objects and functions) form the abstract world. An abstract element is represented by a cloudlet containing a name (or names) that is one possible representation of the element, e.g., 'false'. Cloudlets are used to indicate that we deal

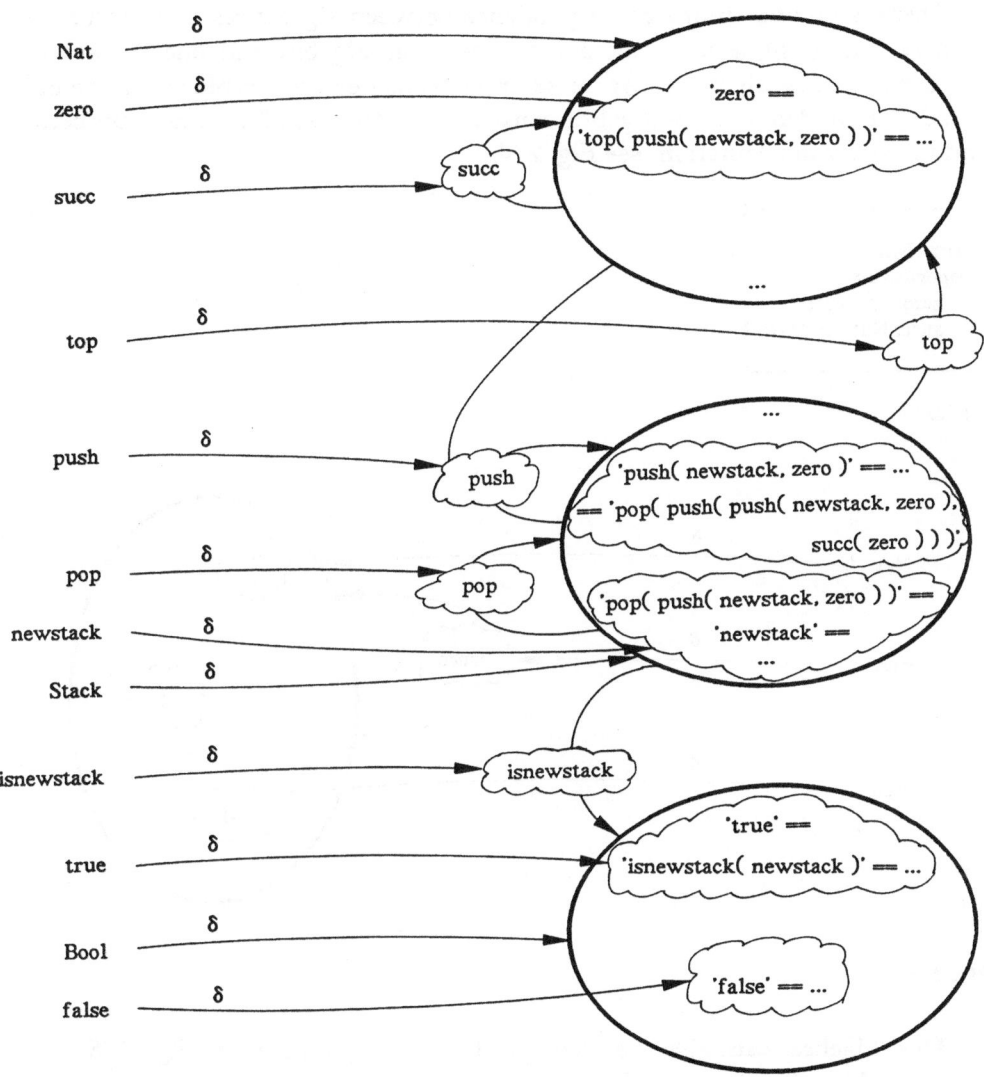

Fig. 2/2

with abstract elements, which strictly speaking cannot be represented. The sets of objects are represented by ovals. One(or more)-tailed arrows represent functions.

Notice that, in Fig. 2/2, we have given only one of the many possible definitions of the denotation function to map the given signature on the algebra of stacks of natural numbers. It would be equally possible for true to denote 'false'. Furthermore, it would be equally possible to map the same signature on the algebra of queues of natural numbers or lists of natural numbers.

There is no one-to-one correspondence between signatures and algebras. Clearly, many signatures can denote one same algebra and one signature can denote many algebras. As an example, consider the simple signature of Fig. 2/3 that denotes the algebra consisting of the set of natural numbers and the successor function, see Fig. 2/4.

```
sort Nat;
operations
  zero: -> Nat;
  succ: Nat -> Nat;
```

Fig. 2/3

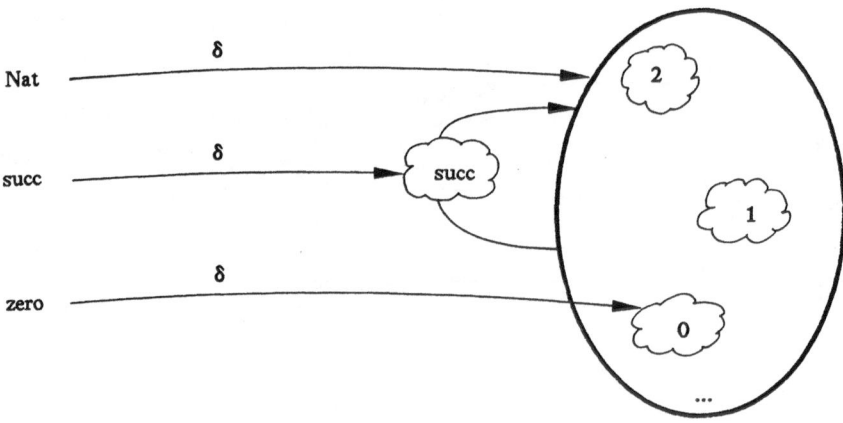

Fig. 2/4

This algebra can also be denoted by the signature of Fig. 2/5, as illustrated by the diagram of Fig. 2/6.

```
sort N;
operations
  start: -> N;
  next: N -> N;
```

Fig. 2/5

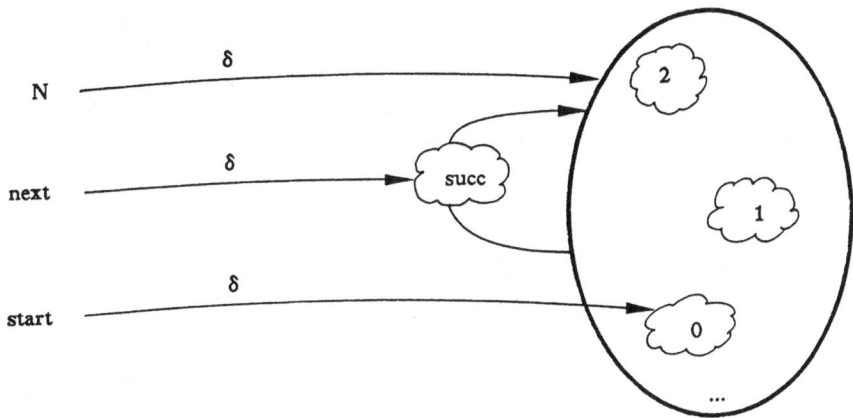

Fig. 2/6

The signature of Fig. 2/5 can also denote the algebra consisting of a singleton and the identity function, see Fig. 2/7.

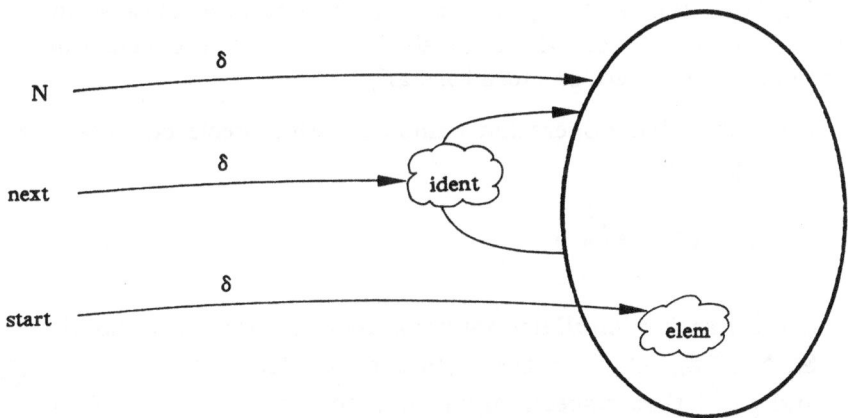

Fig. 2/7

The signature of Fig. 2/5 can also denote the algebra consisting of the set of integers and the successor function, see Fig. 2/8.

Because each signature can denote many different algebras in many different ways, we will develop a mathematical framework that enables us to associate a unique algebra with each signature; in fact it will only be unique up to an isomorphism.

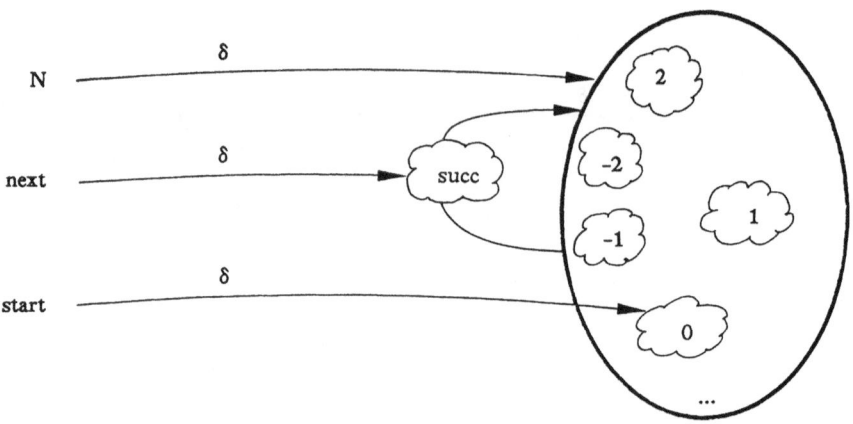

Fig. 2/8

2.2 Homomorphism and Isomorphism

Consider two algebras A and B denoted by the same signature that has S_1, S_2, ... and S_m as sorts. A *homomorphism* from A to B with respect to the given signature is a family of mappings $\{ f_1, f_2, ..., f_m \}$ in which f_j is a mapping from the set $\delta_A.S_j$ of objects of sort S_j in algebra A onto the set $\delta_B.S_j$ of objects of sort S_j in algebra B, so that the behaviour of the operations is preserved, or more formally

1. for each nullary operation name s_i, with s_i declared as $s_i: \ ->\ S_{i_j}$ in the signature:

$$f_{i_j}(\ \delta_A.s_i \ ) = \delta_B.s_i$$

2. and for each nonnullary operation name s_i, with s_i declared as $s_i: S_{i_1} *$ $S_{i_2} * ... * S_{i_k} -> S_{i_j}$ in the signature, and for all objects $\boxed{t_1}$, $\boxed{t_2}$, ... and $\boxed{t_k}$ that respectively belong to the sets $\delta_A.S_{i_1}$, $\delta_A.S_{i_2}$, ... and $\delta_A.S_{i_k}$:

$$f_{i_j}(\ (\ \delta_A.s_i \ ) (\boxed{t_1}, \boxed{t_2}, ..., \boxed{t_k}) \ ) =$$

$$(\ \delta_B.s_i \ ) (\ f_{i_1}(\boxed{t_1}), f_{i_2}(\boxed{t_2}), ..., f_{i_k}(\boxed{t_k}) \ )$$

An *isomorphism* is a bijective homomorphism (i.e. a homomorphism so that each f_j is bijective).

As an example consider the signature of Fig. 2/3 and two algebras NAT and MOD2. NAT consists of the set of natural numbers and the successor function, see Fig. 2/4. MOD2 consists of the set of numbers modulo 2 and the addition–modulo–2 function denoted by add_2, see Fig. 2/9.

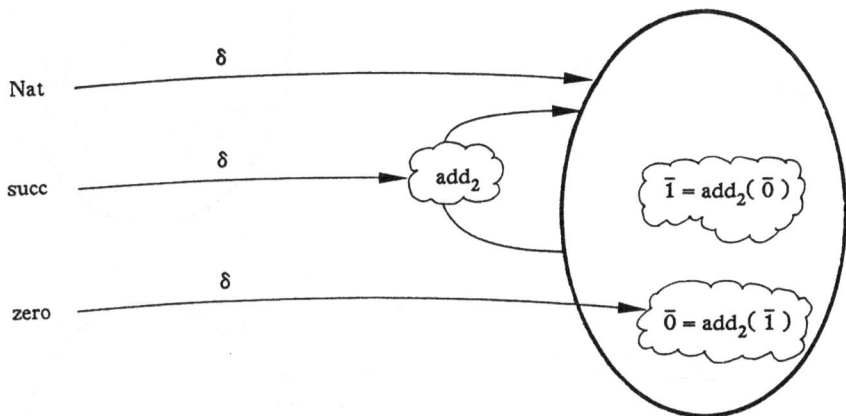

Fig. 2/9

Consider the following mapping f from NAT onto MOD2:

$$f: \{ \textcircled{0}, \textcircled{1}, \textcircled{2}, \ldots \} \rightarrow \{ \overline{0}, \overline{1} \} \quad \text{with } f(\textcircled{2n}) = \overline{0}$$

$$\text{and } f(\textcircled{2n+1}) = \overline{1}$$

{f} is an homomorphism, see Fig. 2/10, because

- $f(\delta_{NAT}.\text{zero}) = f(\textcircled{0}) = \overline{0} = \delta_{MOD2}.\text{zero}$
- $f((\delta_{NAT}.\text{succ})(\textcircled{2n})) = f(\textcircled{2n+1}) = \overline{1} =$

$$\textcircled{add_2}(\overline{0}) = (\delta_{MOD2}.\text{succ})(f(\textcircled{2n}))$$

- $f((\delta_{NAT}.\text{succ})(\textcircled{2n+1})) = f(\textcircled{2n+2}) = \overline{0} =$

$$\textcircled{add_2}(\overline{1}) = (\delta_{MOD2}.\text{succ})(f(\textcircled{2n+1}))$$

Notice that no homomorphism exists from MOD2 to NAT.

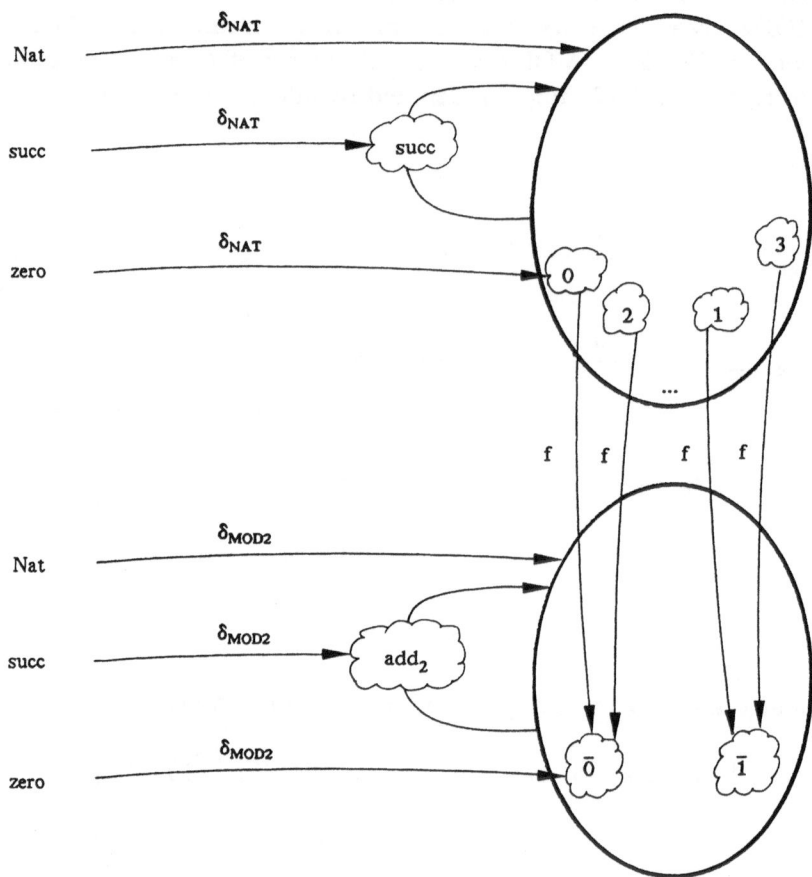

Fig. 2/10

We will now give an example of an isomorphism. Consider the signature of Fig. 2/3, denoting the algebra that consists of the set of Arabic numerals and the successor function. The set of binary numerals and the binary successor function form another algebra denoted by the same signature. A unique isomorphism between these two algebras exists, see Fig. 2/11.

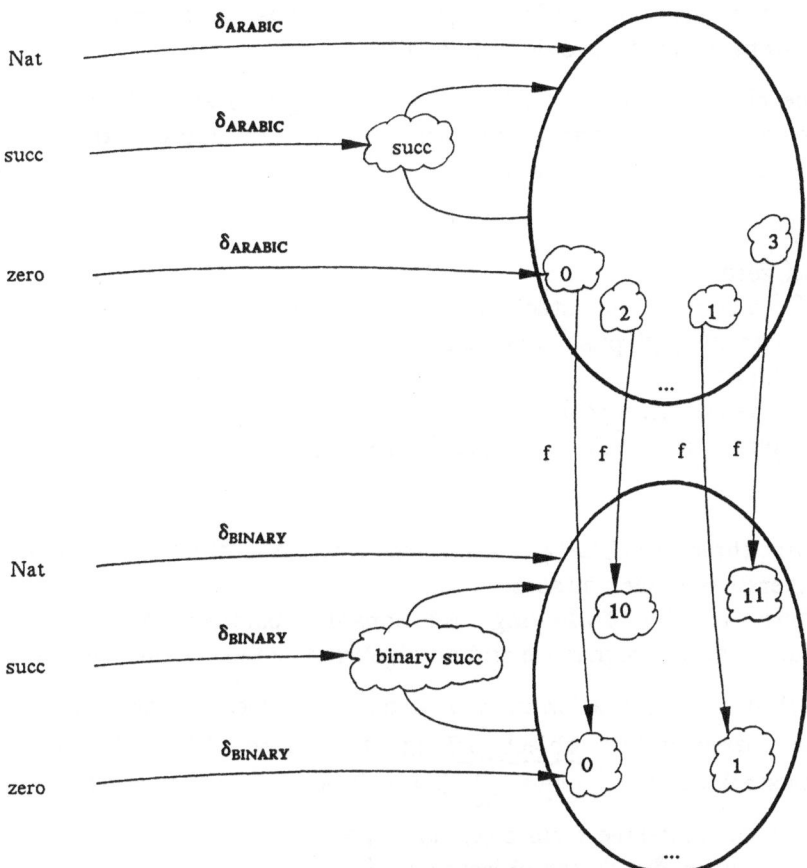

Fig. 2/11

2.3 Variable–Free Termlanguage

Consider a signature with sort names S_1, S_2, ... and S_m, and with a number of operation names, each with a given rank. This signature defines a language, called *variable-free termlanguage*, in the following recursive way:

- Each nullary operation name s_i, with s_i declared as $s_i: -> S_{i_j}$ in the signature, belongs to the language. Its sort is S_{i_j}.

- For each nonnullary operation name s_i, with s_i declared as $s_i: S_{i_1} * S_{i_2} * ... * S_{i_k} -> S_{i_j}$ in the signature, we have that if t_1, t_2, ... and t_k belong to the language and their sorts are respectively S_{i_1}, S_{i_2}, ... and S_{i_k}, then $s_i(t_1, t_2, ...,t_k)$ is also an element of the language. Its sort is S_{i_j}.

- Every element of the language must be constructed in a finite number of steps using the previous two rules.

The elements of a variable–free termlanguage are called *variable–free terms* or *constant terms*. The variable–free termlanguage defined by the signature of Fig. 2/1, contains:

```
zero
succ( zero )
top( push( push( newstack, succ( zero ) ) ), zero ) )
isnewstack( pop( push( newstack, zero ) ) )
newstack
push( newstack, zero )
pop( push( newstack, succ( succ( zero ) ) ) )
. . .
```

The first three variable–free terms are of sort Nat, the fourth has Bool, and the others have Stack as sort.

There is the following relationship between the variable–free termlanguage of a signature and an algebra denoted by the signature:

- Each nullary operation name s_i denotes an object. If the sort of s_i is S_{i_j}, the corresponding object belongs to the set $\delta.S_{i_j}$. As an example, newstack denotes `'newstack'`, which belongs to the set $\delta.Stack$.

- Each variable–free term $s_i(t_1, t_2, ..., t_k)$ denotes the result of applying the function $\delta.s_i$ to the objects $\delta.t_1, \delta.t_2, ...$ and $\delta.t_k$. If the sort of $s_i(t_1, t_2, ..., t_k)$ is S_{i_j}, the denoted object belongs to the set $\delta.S_{i_j}$. As an example, push(newstack, zero) denotes `'push(newstack, zero)'`, which belongs to the set $\delta.Stack$.

Variable–free terms may be added to the left parts of the diagrams.

2.4 Word Algebra

A particularly interesting algebra denoted by a signature is its word algebra. A *word algebra* is an algebra in which the objects of the set $\delta.S_j$ are the variable–free or constant terms of sort S_j, considered as character strings, and in which the functions are string combinators that build larger strings from smaller ones; furthermore every variable–free term denotes the object derived from itself. Given the signature of Fig. 2/1, its word algebra is shown in Fig. 2/12.

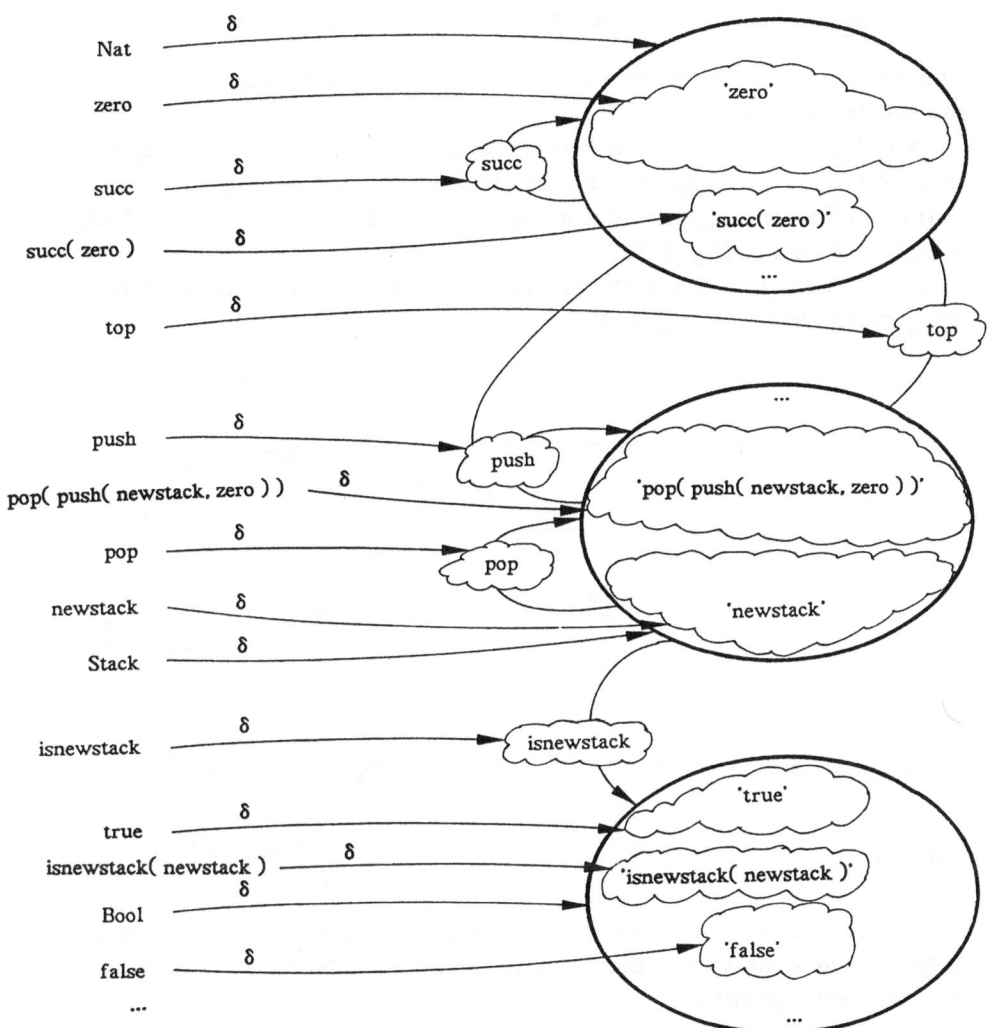

Fig. 2/12

Notice that a variable-free termlanguage, although it has been derived from a signature, which is a syntactic notation, defines an algebra that belongs to the abstract world.

We could write the variable-free terms in postfix notation or represent them by trees instead of strings. All these word algebras are isomorphic. When we refer to *the* word algebra, we actually mean any of these isomorphic algebras.

2.5 Signature, Variety and Termalgebra

The *variety* over a signature is the set of all possible algebras denoted by that given signature.

An algebra denoted by a signature is a *termalgebra* of the signature if each object of the algebra can be denoted by a variable-free term. An example of a termalgebra of the signature of Fig. 2/1 is its word algebra, which is shown in Fig. 2/12.

Let us now use the signature of Fig. 2/3 to denote the algebra of the integers, as shown in Fig. 2/13.

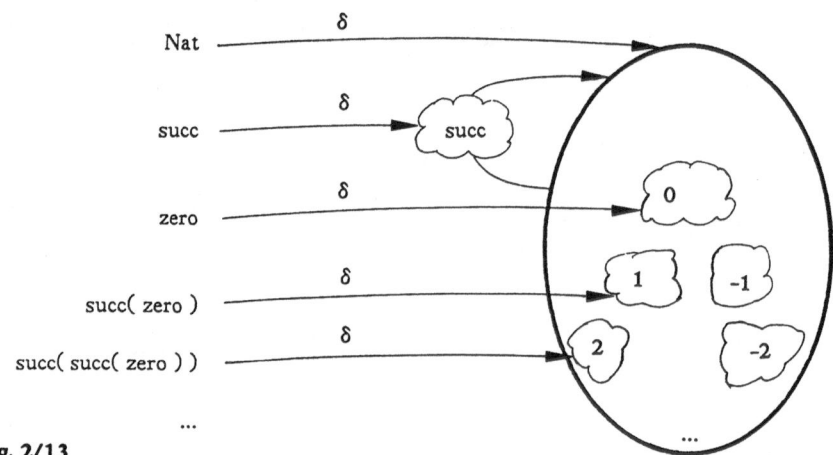

Fig. 2/13

Notice that the negative integers cannot be denoted by a variable-free term of the signature. Therefore, the denoted algebra is not a termalgebra of the given signature.

2.6 Signature and Initial Algebra

A *category* of algebras over a signature is a set of algebras denoted by the signature, together with a number of homomorphisms between these algebras including the identity homomorphisms.

An algebra I is *initial* in a category C of algebras over a signature, if and only if I belongs to C and for each algebra A in C, a unique homomorphism in C from I to A does exist. It can easily be shown that if I and I' are both initial algebras in the same category, they are isomorphic [Goguen78, Ehrig85]. When we refer to *the* initial algebra, we actually mean any of these isomorphic algebras.

Convention: whenever we use the term category over a signature without specifying which category is meant, we mean the variety over the signature together with all possible homomorphisms.

The initial algebra of the category over a signature always exists [Goguen78, Meseguer85a, Ehrig85]. Indeed, the word algebra of a signature is the initial algebra of its category.

2.7 Abstract Data Types Defined by a Signature

The *abstract data types* defined by a signature are the sets of objects $\delta.S_j$ together with the functions $\delta.s_i$ defined on these sets, of the initial algebra of the category over the signature. The data types are called abstract because they are defined up to an isomorphism. Because of the mathematical notion of algebras, abstraction is made from data representations and only fundamental properties of objects and functions are considered. Concrete representations and implementations of objects and functions are irrelevant at this level of specification.

Until now, we have developed a mathematical framework in which each variable-free term denotes a different object of the abstract data types. This framework, as explained so far, is not powerful enough for most abstract data types currently used in software systems. Therefore, we will introduce the notion of axiom so that different variable-free terms can denote the same object.

2.8 Termlanguage

Consider the signature consisting of the sort names S_1, S_2, ... and S_m, and a number of operation names each with a given rank. Furthermore, for each sort S_j a set of unique names $\{ x_{j_1}, x_{j_2}, ..., x_{j_n} \}$, called *variables* of sort S_j, is given. The *termlanguage* of the signature with respect to the sets of variables is defined in the following recursive way:

- Each variable x_{j_h} of sort S_j belongs to the language.

- Each nullary operation name s_i, with s_i declared as s_i: -> S_{i_j} in the signature, belongs to the language. Its sort is S_{i_j}.

- For each nonnullary operation name s_i, with s_i declared as s_i: S_{i_1} * S_{i_2} * ... * S_{i_k} -> S_{i_j} in the signature, if t_1, t_2, ... and t_k belong to the language and their sorts are respectively S_{i_1}, S_{i_2}, ... and S_{i_k}, then $s_i(t_1, t_2, ..., t_k)$ is also an element of the language. Its sort is S_{i_j}.

- Every element of the language must be constructed in a finite number of steps using the previous three rules.

The elements of a termlanguage are called *terms*. The termlanguage defined by the signature of Fig. 2/1, with respect to the set of variables $\{n_1\}$ of sort Nat, the set of variables { stack$_1$, stack$_2$ } of sort Stack and the empty set of variables of sort Bool contains the following terms:

zero
succ(succ(n_1))
top(push(stack$_1$, n_1))
push(pop(stack$_1$), zero)
pop(push(stack$_1$, top(push(stack$_2$, n_1))))
isnewstack(push(stack$_2$, n_1))
. . .

The first three terms are of sort Nat, the next two have Stack and the last term has Bool as sort.

2.9 Substitution and Ground Substitution

Assume that a signature together with sets of variables are given. A *substitution* σ is a family of mappings { σ_1, σ_2, ..., σ_m } in which σ_j is a mapping from the set of variables of sort S_j onto the set of terms of sort S_j. A *ground substitution* is a substitution in which each variable is mapped onto a variable-free term.

Given a signature, sets of variables and a corresponding substitution, application of the substitution to an arbitrary term results in a new term obtained by simultaneously replacing all the variables by the terms as specified by the substitution.

Consider the signature of Fig. 2/1, the sets of variables of sort Nat, Stack and Bool, respectively { n_1 }, { stack$_1$ } and { }, and consider the substitution { { (n_1, zero) }, { (stack$_1$, push(newstack, n_1)) }, { } }. By applying the substitution, the term top(stack$_1$) is transformed into the term top(push(newstack, n_1)), and the term pop(push(stack$_1$, n_1)) is transformed into the term pop(push(push(newstack, n_1), zero)).

2.10 Assignment

Given a signature denoting an algebra and given a set of variables for each
sort S_j. An *assignment* is a family (set) of mappings $\{ \theta_1, \theta_2, ..., \theta_m \}$ in
which θ_j is a mapping from the set of variables of sort S_j onto the set $\delta.S_j$.
An assignment for the signature of Fig. 2/1 denoting the algebra of stacks
of natural numbers as shown in Fig. 2/2, and for $\{ n_1 \}$, $\{ stack_1 \}$ and $\{ \}$
as sets of variables of the sorts Nat, Stack and Bool, may be $\{ \{ (n_1,$
'zero' $)) \}, \{ (stack_1,$ 'push(newstack, zero)' $)) \}, \{ \} \}$.

An assignment may be interpreted as an extension of the denotation
function for variables. As a result, the denotation function is then defined
over terms. Given a signature denoting an algebra and given a set of
variables for each sort S_j together with an assignment, terms denote objects
in the following way, see Fig. 2/14:

- Each nullary operation name s_i of sort S_{i_j} denotes the object $\delta.s_i$ of $\delta.S_{i_j}$,
  e.g., newstack denotes 'newstack' in δ.Stack.

- Each variable of sort S_j denotes the object of $\delta.S_j$ as specified by the
  assignment, e.g., n_1 denotes 'zero' of δ.Nat.

- Each term $s_i(t_1, t_2, ..., t_k)$ of sort S_{i_j} denotes the result of applying the
  function $\delta.s_i$ on the objects $\delta.t_1, \delta.t_2, ...$ and $\delta.t_k$. The result belongs to
  $\delta.S_{i_j}$, e.g., push(newstack, n_1) denotes 'push(newstack, zero)' of
  δ.Stack.

Every ground substitution implicitly defines an assignment. The
ground substitution

$$\{ \{ (n_1, zero) \}, \{ (stack_1, push(newstack, zero)) \}, \{ \} \}$$

implicitly defines the assignment given above.

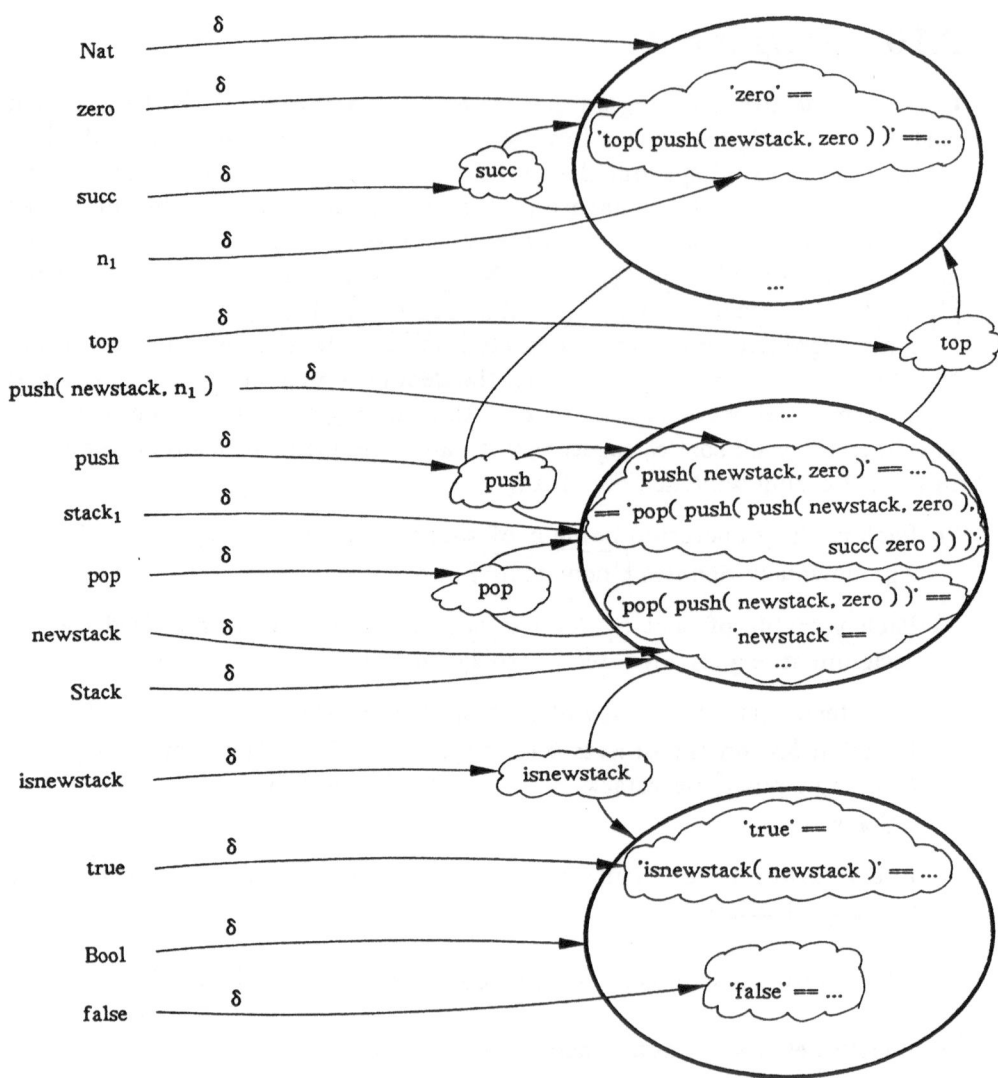

Fig. 2/14

2.11 Axioms and Presentation

A *presentation* is a signature extended by means of axioms. An *axiom* consists of a number of sets of variables (at most one set of variables for each sort of the signature) and two terms of the same sort belonging to the termlanguage of the signature with respect to the sets of variables. In most presentations all axioms have the same sets of variables because the variables need not occur in the constituent terms of every axiom. An example of a presentation is given in Fig. 2/15.

```
sorts Stack; Nat; Bool;
operations
   true, false: -> Bool;
   zero: -> Nat;
   succ: Nat -> Nat;
   newstack: -> Stack;
   push: Stack * Nat -> Stack;
   isnewstack: Stack -> Bool;
   pop: Stack -> Stack;
   top: Stack -> Nat;
declare s: Stack;   n: Nat;
axioms
   isnewstack( newstack ) == true;        -- 1 --
   isnewstack( push( s, n ) ) == false;   -- 2 --
   pop( newstack ) == newstack;           -- 3 --
   pop( push( s, n ) ) == s;              -- 4 --
   top( newstack ) == zero;               -- 5 --
   top( push( s, n ) ) == n;              -- 6 --
```

Fig. 2/15

In Fig. 2/15 the variables are common to all axioms. After the keyword **declare** the variables are listed with their sort. The axioms follow the keyword **axioms**. Neither the order of the variables nor the order of the axioms is relevant. If the axioms have distinct sets of variables, a declaration part must be given for each axiom. In order to avoid confusion, a variable that is declared in several declaration parts, will always be declared of the same sort.

It is obvious that error treatment is a very important issue from a software engineering viewpoint. A thorough treatment of error detection and error handling will be given in Chapter 7. Meanwhile the exceptional situations are treated in a naive way. In our Stack example, the top of an empty stack yields zero and the pop of an empty stack gives the empty stack back.

An algebra is *denoted by a presentation* if it is denoted by the signature of the presentation. An algebra denoted by a presentation *satisfies* the axioms of its presentation if for each axiom the two constituent terms denote the same object of the algebra for each possible assignment.

2.12 Presentation, Variety and Termalgebra

The *variety* over a given presentation is the set of all possible algebras denoted by the presentation and satisfying the axioms of the presentation. An example of an algebra belonging to the variety over the presentation of Fig. 2/15 was given in Fig. 2/2.

A *termalgebra* of a presentation is an algebra denoted by the presentation in which each object can be denoted by a variable-free term of the presentation.

2.13 Equational Reasoning

Equational reasoning is one of the techniques that enable the software designer to use so-called *rigorous mathematical reasoning* (another technique is induction, see Section 2.17). Properties of the specification of software can be proved to be true, even before the implementation has been started. Such proofs of properties are very similar to proofs of theorems in mathematics. Proofs about specifications of programs serve two purposes. They constitute the program documentation by excellence and they enhance software correctness and reliability.

Given a presentation, *equational reasoning* is the process of deriving new axioms by applying the following rules [Goguen81, Meseguer85a, Meseguer85b]:

- *Reflexivity:* if t is a term of the presentation,

  declare <declaration part>
  axiom
    t == t;

  is derivable by reflexivity if the variables used in the term t are listed in the declaration part.

- *Symmetry:* if the axiom

  declare <declaration part>
  axiom
    t_1 == t_2;

  is given or derivable, then

    declare <declaration part>
    axiom
      $t_2 == t_1$;

is derivable.

- *Transitivity:* if the axioms

    declare <declaration part>
    axioms
      $t_1 == t_2$;
      $t_2 == t_3$;

are given or derivable, then

    declare <declaration part>
    axiom
      $t_1 == t_3$;

is derivable.

- *Substitutivity:* if the axioms

    declare x: S_j;   <declaration part 1>
    axiom
      $t_1 == t_2$;
    declare <declaration part 2>
    axiom
      $t_3 == t_4$;

are given or derivable, with t_3 and t_4 being of sort S_j, then

    declare <declaration part 1>   <declaration part 2>
    axiom
      $t_5 == t_6$;

is derivable, with t_5 being the result of applying the substitution $\{\{(x, t_3)\}\}$ to t_1 and with t_6 being the result of applying the substitution $\{\{(x, t_4)\}\}$ to t_2.

- *Abstraction:* if the axiom

    declare <declaration part>
    axiom
      $t_1 == t_2$;

is given or derivable, x is a variable of sort S_j and x is not declared in the declaration part, then

    declare x: S_j;   <declaration part>
    axiom
      $t_1 == t_2$;

is derivable.

- *Concretion:* if the axiom

    declare x: S_j;   <declaration part>
    axiom
      $t_1 == t_2$;

is given or derivable, the set of variable-free terms of sort S_j is not empty and x does not appear in t_1 nor t_2, then

    declare <declaration part>
    axiom
      $t_1 == t_2$;

is derivable.

Given a presentation, deriving new axioms by equational reasoning always yields axioms that are satisfied by all algebras of the variety over the presentation [Meseguer85a, Ehrig85]. A second important property is that every axiom satisfied by all algebras of the variety over the presentation can be deduced using these rules [Meseguer85a, Ehrig85].

Example of the Stacks

A derivable axiom is

    declare s: Stack;   n: Nat;
    axiom
      push(s, n) == push(s, top(push(s, n)));   -- 0' --

To prove this, we first apply reflexivity obtaining

    declare s: Stack;   n: Nat;
    axiom
      push(s, n) == push(s, n);   -- 1' --

The symmetry property transforms axiom 6 of Fig. 2/15 into

declare s: Stack;   n: Nat;
axiom
   n == top(push(s, n));   -- 2˙ --

Substitutivity for the variable n of axiom 1˙ by axiom 2˙ yields axiom 0˙.

Notice that the axioms of the presentation define a family of equality relations between the variable-free terms. Each equality relation defines the equality between the variable-free or constant terms of a given sort: two variable-free terms are equal if and only if they can be the constituent terms of an axiom with empty sets of variables derived by equational reasoning. These equality relations are equivalence relations, i.e. relations that are reflexive, symmetric and transitive. E.g., the equality relation for sort Stack defined by the axioms of Fig. 2/15 implies that the following variable-free terms are equal:

newstack
pop(newstack)
pop(push(newstack, zero))
pop(push(newstack, top(newstack)))
pop(pop(push(push(newstack, succ(zero)), zero)))

The equality relations defined by the axioms of a presentation are even congruence relations: if s_i has been declared as $s_i: S_{i_1} * S_{i_2} * ... * S_{i_k} -> S_{i_j}$ in the presentation and if $t_1 == u_1$, $t_2 == u_2$, ... and $t_k == u_k$ with t_1 and u_1, t_2 and u_2, ... and t_k and u_k variable-free terms of sorts S_{i_1}, S_{i_2}, ... and S_{i_k} respectively, then $s_i(t_1, t_2, ..., t_k) == s_i(u_1, u_2, ..., u_k)$.

2.14 Presentation and Initial Algebra

A *category* of algebras over a given presentation is a set of algebras denoted by the presentation, together with a number of homomorphisms between these algebras including the identity homomorphisms. A frequently used category is the variety over a presentation, together with all possible homomorphisms between the algebras of this variety.

An algebra I is *initial* in a category C of algebras over a presentation, if and only if I belongs to C and for each algebra A in C, a unique homomorphism from I to A does exist. If the initial algebra exists, it is uniquely determined up to an isomorphism [Goguen78, Ehrig85].

Convention: whenever we use the term category over a presentation without specifying which category is meant, we mean the variety over the presentation together with all possible homomorphisms.

How can the initial algebra of the category over a presentation be found? Consider the word algebra of the signature of a given presentation (the word algebra of the presentation for short) together with the equality relations defined by its axioms (see previous section). The equality relations are congruence relations that partition each set $\delta.S_j$ (of variable-free terms of sort S_j) into a number of congruence classes of sort S_j. The classes of sort S_j are the objects of the set $\delta.S_j$ in a new algebra, called *quotient algebra* of the presentation. Each function of the given word algebra corresponds to a function in the quotient algebra. If the function $\delta.s_i$, with s_i declared as $s_i: S_{i_1} * S_{i_2} * \ldots * S_{i_k} \rightarrow S_{i_j}$ in the presentation, maps the arguments $\delta.t_1$, $\delta.t_2$, $\ldots$ and $\delta.t_k$ to $\delta.s_i(\, t_1,\ t_2,\ \ldots,\ t_k\,)$ in the word algebra with t_1, t_2, $\ldots$ and t_k being variable-free terms of sorts S_{i_1}, S_{i_2}, $\ldots$ and S_{i_k} respectively, then the corresponding function maps the arguments C_1, C_2, $\ldots$ and C_k to C with C_1, C_2, $\ldots$, C_k and C being the congruence classes to which $\delta.t_1$, $\delta.t_2$, $\ldots$, $\delta.t_k$ and $\delta.s_i(\, t_1,\ t_2,\ \ldots,\ t_k\,)$ respectively belong.

The initial algebra of the category over a presentation is the quotient algebra of the word algebra of the presentation for the equality relations defined by the axioms [Goguen78, Ehrig85].

We will illustrate this algorithm by the example of Fig. 2/15. The word algebra was shown in Fig. 2/12. This word algebra does not belong to the variety over the given presentation (Fig. 2/15) because none of the axioms is satisfied. The equality relations defined by the axioms divide the sets of objects into classes as shown in Fig. 2/16.

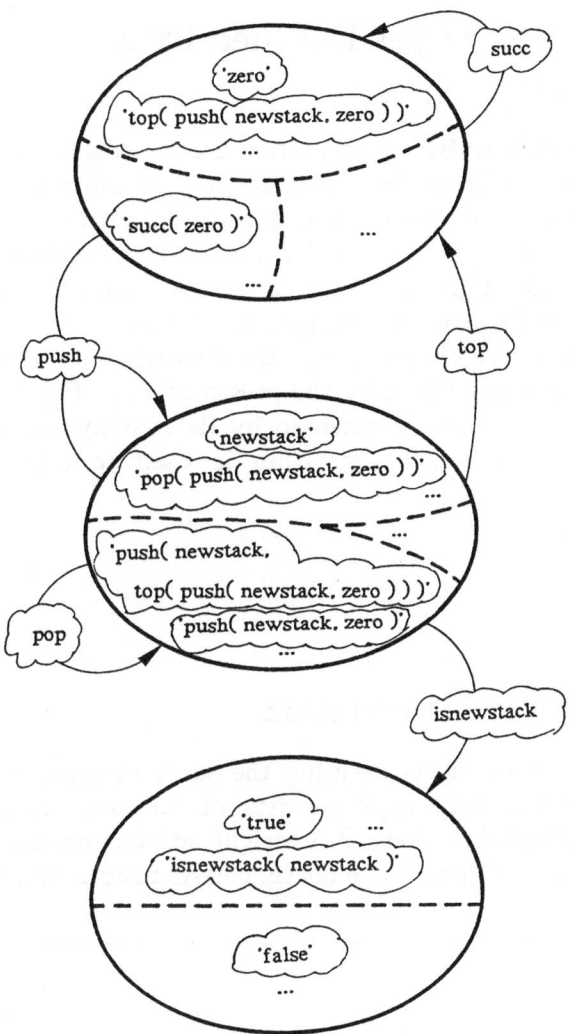

Fig. 2/16

If the classes of sort S_j are considered as the objects of the set $\delta.S_j$ upon which corresponding functions are defined, we obtain the quotient algebra of the word algebra for the equality relations defined by the axioms, see Fig. 2/2. This quotient algebra belongs to the variety over the presentation, because it satisfies the axioms. It can be proved that it is the initial algebra of the variety [Goguen78, Ehrig85].

2.15 Abstract Data Types Defined by a Presentation

The *abstract data types* defined by a presentation are the sets of objects $\delta.S_j$ together with the functions $\delta.s_i$ defined on these sets, of the initial algebra of the category over the presentation. The data types are called abstract because they are defined up to an isomorphism. Because of the mathematical notion of algebras, abstraction is made from data representations and only fundamental properties of objects and functions are taken into account. If we consider, e.g., the abstract data type of the stacks of natural numbers as defined by the presentation of Fig. 2/15, it is irrelevant whether the stacks are represented by lists, arrays or anything else, neither is it relevant which algorithm is used to calculate the functions.

2.16 Examples

The Abstract Data Type Orientation

Fig. 2/17 shows two presentations defining the same abstract data type Orientation. The abstract data type consists of the set δ.Orientation together with the functions δ.turnleft, δ.turnright and δ.opposite. The set δ.Orientation contains four objects, i.e. δ.north, δ.east, δ.south and δ.west.

```
sort Orientation;
operations
   north, east, south, west: -> Orientation;
   turnleft, turnright, opposite: Orientation -> Orientation;
declare or: Orientation;
axioms
   turnleft( north ) == west;                    turnleft( east ) == north;
   turnleft( south ) == east;                    turnleft( west ) == south;
   turnright( turnleft( or ) ) == or;
   turnleft( turnleft( or ) ) == opposite( or );

sort Orientation;
operations
   north, east, south, west: -> Orientation;
   turnleft, turnright, opposite: Orientation -> Orientation;
```

axioms
  turnleft(north) == west;   turnleft(east) == north;
  turnleft(south) == east;   turnleft(west) == south;
  turnright(north) == east;   turnright(east) == south;
  turnright(south) == west;   turnright(west) == north;
  opposite(north) == south;   opposite(east) == west;
  opposite(south) == north;   opposite(west) == east;

Fig. 2/17

Each of the axioms of one presentation is derivable from the axioms of the other one using equational reasoning and induction (see Section 2.17). Notice that the first presentation is shorter but the second one is more constructive, i.e. it is easier to derive an implementation (program) from it. Constructivity will be treated in Chapter 4.

Unbounded Arrays of Boolean Values

In Fig. 2/18 a presentation is given defining the abstract data types of the boolean values, the natural numbers and the unbounded arrays of boolean values with natural numbers as indices.

```
sorts Array; Nat; Bool;
operations
  true, false: -> Bool;
  ifthenelse: Bool * Bool * Bool -> Bool;

  zero: -> Nat;
  succ: Nat -> Nat;
  equal: Nat * Nat -> Bool;

  empty: -> Array;
  assign: Array * Bool * Nat -> Array;
  read: Array * Nat -> Bool;  .
declare
  b, b₁, b₂: Bool;   n, n₁, n₂: Nat;   ar: Array;
axioms
  ifthenelse( true, b₁, b₂ ) == b₁;
  ifthenelse( false, b₁, b₂ ) == b₂;

  equal( succ( n₁ ), succ( n₂ ) ) == equal( n₁, n₂ );
  equal( zero, succ( n ) ) == false;
  equal( succ( n ), zero ) == false;
  equal( zero, zero ) == true;

  read( empty, n ) == true;
  read( assign( ar, b, n₁ ), n₂ ) ==
    ifthenelse( equal( n₁, n₂ ), b, read( ar, n₂ ) );
```

Fig. 2/18

The abstract data types defined by the above presentation consist of the sets δ.Bool, δ.Nat and δ.Array, and the functions δ.ifthenelse, δ.succ, δ.equal, δ.assign and δ.read. Notice that if the operations had other names, e.g., true was called waar and false was called onwaar, we would still have the same abstract data types because an abstract data type is defined up to an isomorphism. From the axioms defined for the operation read we can deduce that a newly created unbounded array is initialized with true. So, reading a value on a given index of an unbounded array will always yield the value true, if there has never been an assignment of a value on that index. In Chapter 3, where we deal with (algebraic specification) language aspects, we will introduce language-defined operations for ifthenelse and equal.

The Farmer, the Wolf, the Goat and the Cabbage

An example coming from the field of artificial intelligence is the problem of the farmer, the wolf, the goat and the cabbage crossing a river. A farmer, a wolf, a goat and a cabbage want to cross a river but they can only dispose of one boat. The farmer can cross the river but he can only carry one passenger at most. When the farmer is absent, the wolf may eat the goat or the goat may eat the cabbage. So the problem of how to cross the river safely arises.

A specification is given in Fig. 2/19. This specification describes a solution (the *what*) without giving an implementation (algorithm) to find this solution (the *how*).

The wolf, the goat and the cabbage form the objects of sort Thing. The farmer and the boat are not explicitly defined in the specification since we assume that crossing the river without the boat is impossible and that the boat can only move from one bank to the other one if it is navigated by the farmer. Sequences of moves are modelled by objects of sort MoveSeq. An example of such an object is cross(transport(start, goat)). This object can be interpreted as follows: (1) initially all things, the farmer and the boat are at one of two banks, say bank A; (2) the farmer crosses the river together with the goat (3) finally, the farmer leaves the goat at bank B and crosses the river all alone. The situation after the sequence of moves is as follows: the farmer, the wolf, the cabbage and the boat are at bank A whereas the goat is at bank B. Clearly, there are an infinite number of move sequences. Only those move sequences for which the operation issolution yields true, are a solution of the given problem. The operation issolution is defined in terms of the operations samebank, otherbank, over, allover, possible, dangerous, unsafe and safe.

Notice that comments are inserted in the specification. A comment starts with two adjacent hyphens and extends to the end of the line or two adjacent hyphens, whatever comes first.

sorts MoveSeq; Thing; Bool;
operations

true, false: -> Bool;
not: Bool -> Bool;
and, or: Bool * Bool -> Bool;
if: Bool * Bool * Bool -> Bool;

wolf, goat, cabbage: -> Thing;
eq: Thing * Thing -> Bool;
  -- equality function for things

start: -> MoveSeq;
  -- the farmer, the wolf, the goat, the cabbage and the boat are at the same bank;
  -- which of the two banks is irrelevant
cross: MoveSeq -> MoveSeq;
  -- the farmer crosses the river alone
transport: MoveSeq * Thing -> MoveSeq;
  -- the farmer transports either the wolf, the goat or the cabbage

samebank: MoveSeq * Thing -> Bool;
  -- samebank indicates whether, after executing a sequence of movements,
  -- a Thing is at the same bank of the river as the farmer
otherbank: MoveSeq * Thing -> Bool;
  -- the negation of samebank
over: MoveSeq -> Bool;
  -- indicates whether the farmer, after the execution of a sequence of movements,
  -- is at the bank he wants to arrive at
allover: MoveSeq -> Bool;
  -- indicates whether, after the execution of a sequence of movements, the farmer, the
  -- wolf, the goat and the cabbage arrive at the bank the farmer wants them to be at
possible: MoveSeq -> Bool;
  -- indicates whether a sequence of movements is possible; the farmer can
  -- only transport a thing from a bank if that thing is present at that bank
dangerous: MoveSeq -> Bool;
  -- indicates whether the wolf may eat the goat or the goat may eat the
  -- cabbage after the execution of a sequence of movements
unsafe: MoveSeq -> Bool;
  -- indicates whether the wolf may have eaten the goat or the goat may have eaten
  -- the cabbage during or after the execution of a sequence of movements
safe: MoveSeq -> Bool;
  -- the negation of unsafe
issolution: MoveSeq -> Bool;
  -- indicates whether a sequence of movements is a solution of the given problem

declare b, b_1, b_2: Bool;
th, th_1, th_2: Thing;
ms: MoveSeq;

axioms
not(true) == false;   not(false) == true;
and(true, b) == b;   and(false, b) == false;
or(true, b) == true;   or(false, b) == b;
if(true, b_1, b_2) == b_1;   if(false, b_1, b_2) == b_2;

eq(wolf, goat) == false;   eq(goat, cabbage) == false;

```
eq( wolf, cabbage ) == false;    eq( th₁, th₂ ) == eq( th₂, th₁ );
eq( th, th ) == true;

samebank( start, th ) == true;
samebank( cross( ms ), th ) == not( samebank( ms, th ) );
samebank( transport( ms, th₁ ), th₂ ) ==
  if( eq( th₁, th₂ ),
    -- then --  true,
    -- else --  not( samebank( ms, th₂ ) ) );
otherbank( ms, th ) == not( samebank( ms, th ) );
over( start ) == false;
over( cross( ms ) ) == not( over( ms ) );
over( transport( ms, th ) ) == not( over( ms ) );
allover( ms ) == and( and( and(
  over( ms ),
  samebank( ms, wolf ) ),
  samebank( ms, goat ) ),
  samebank( ms, cabbage ) );
possible( start ) == true;
possible( cross( ms ) ) == possible( ms );
possible( transport( ms, th ) ) == and(
  samebank( ms, th ),
  possible( ms ) );
dangerous( ms ) == or(
  and(
    otherbank( ms, wolf ),
    otherbank( ms, goat ) ),
  and(
    otherbank( ms, goat ),
    otherbank( ms, cabbage ) ) );
unsafe( start ) == dangerous( start );
unsafe( cross( ms ) ) == or(
  dangerous( cross( ms ) ),
  unsafe( ms ) );
unsafe( transport( ms, th ) ) == or(
  dangerous( transport( ms, th ) ),
  unsafe( ms ) );
safe( ms ) == not( unsafe( ms ) );
issolution( ms ) == and( and(
  possible( ms ),
  safe( ms ) ),
  allover( ms ) );
```

Fig. 2/19

Notice that both the operations and the axioms parts have been divided
into three subparts. There is one subpart for each sort. This kind of
modularity, which is still implicit, will be made explicit later when we
deal with algebraic specification language aspects in Chapter 3.

2.17 Induction

Like equational reasoning, *induction* is a mathematical technique that can
be used to derive new axioms from a given presentation. Axioms derivable
by equational reasoning are satisfied by every algebra of the variety over
the presentation. Axioms derivable by induction will be satisfied by every
termalgebra of the variety over the given presentation, and consequently
by the initial algebra too. As equational reasoning, induction is a very
important technique to prove theorems of abstract data types.

A mathematical (but rather tedious) definition of induction can be
found in [Boyer79]. The main idea behind induction is that one assumes
instances of the property being proved during its own proof. One of the
hardest problems in discovering an inductive proof is finding an
appropriate induction scheme that is complete and sound.

Example of the Integers

```
sort Z;
operations
  zero: -> Z;
  succ: Z -> Z;
  pre: Z -> Z;
  add: Z * Z -> Z;
declare i, j: Z;
axioms
  pre( succ( i ) ) == i;                    -- 1 --
  succ( pre( i ) ) == i;                    -- 2 --
  add( zero, i ) == i;                      -- 3 --
  add( succ( i ), j ) == succ( add( i, j ) );  -- 4 --
  add( pre( i ), j ) == pre( add( i, j ) );    -- 5 --
```

Fig. 2/20

The presentation of Fig. 2/20 defines the abstract data type of the
integers including the successor, predecessor and addition functions. An
axiom derivable by induction is the commutativity of the addition:

declare i, j: Z;
axiom
    add(j, i) == add(i, j);   -- 0' --

It is provable by induction over j as well as over i. We will demonstrate it by induction over j. For each termalgebra of the presentation, each object can be denoted by a variable-free term consisting of the operation names zero, succ and pre only. This will be proved by induction, further on.

    To prove axiom 0', we have to prove the induction base

declare i: Z;
axiom
    add(zero, i) == add(i, zero);   -- 1' --

and given the induction hypothesis

declare i, j': Z;
axiom
    add(j', i) == add(i, j');   -- 2' --

we have to prove the induction conclusions

declare i, j': Z;
axioms
    add(succ(j'), i) == add(i, succ(j'));   -- 3' --
    add(pre(j'), i) == add(i, pre(j'));   -- 4' --

If axiom 0' is written in the form F(j, i), we can use the following induction scheme:

	F(zero, i)
F(j', i) =>	F(succ(j'), i)
F(j', i) =>	F(pre(j'), i)

Using axiom 3 of Fig. 2/20, we can rewrite axiom 1' as:

declare i: Z;
axiom
    i == add(i, zero);   -- 1.0' --

This axiom can be proved by induction over i. As already mentioned, for each termalgebra each object can be denoted by a variable-free term consisting of the operation names zero, succ and pre only.
We have to prove the induction base

axiom
  zero == add(zero, zero);   -- 1.1' --

and given the induction hypothesis

declare i': Z;
axiom
  i' == add(i', zero);   -- 1.2' --

we have to prove the induction conclusions

declare i': Z;
axioms
  succ(i') == add(succ(i'), zero);   -- 1.3' --
  pre(i') == add(pre(i'), zero);   -- 1.4' --

If axiom 1.0' is denoted as G(i), we can use the following induction
scheme;

$$
\begin{array}{ll}
 & G(\text{ zero }) \\
G(\text{ i' }) => & G(\text{ succ}(\text{ i' })) \\
G(\text{ i' }) => & G(\text{ pre}(\text{ i' }))
\end{array}
$$

Axiom 1.1' can be derived from axiom 3 of Fig. 2/20.
Using axiom 4 of Fig. 2/20, axiom 1.3' can be transformed into

declare i': Z;
axiom
  succ(i') == succ(add(i', zero));

Using the induction hypothesis 1.2', the right-hand side can be transformed
into the left-hand side.
Axiom 1.4' can be transformed using axiom 5 of Fig. 2/20 into

declare i': Z;
axiom
  pre(i') == pre(add(i', zero));

Using the induction hypothesis 1.2', the right-hand side can be transformed
into the left-hand side. This proves axiom 1'.
The first induction conclusion:

declare i, j': Z;
axiom
  add(succ(j'), i) == add(i, succ(j'));   -- 3' --

can be transformed into

declare i, j': Z;
axiom
  succ(add(j', i)) == add(i, succ(j'));

by using axiom 4 of Fig. 2/20. Using the induction hypothesis 2', it can be transformed into

declare i, j': Z;
axiom
  succ(add(i, j')) == add(i, succ(j'));   -- 3.0' --

This axiom can be proved by induction over i. As already mentioned, for each termalgebra each object can be denoted by a variable-free term consisting of the operation names zero, succ and pre only.
We have to prove the induction base

declare j': Z;
axiom
  `succ(add(zero, j')) == add(zero, succ(j'));   -- 3.1' --

and given the induction hypothesis

declare i', j': Z;
axiom
  succ(add(i', j')) == add(i', succ(j'));   -- 3.2' --

we have to prove the induction conclusions

declare i', j': Z;
axioms
  succ(add(succ(i'), j')) == add(succ(i'), succ(j'));   -- 3.3' --
  succ(add(pre(i'), j')) == add(pre(i'), succ(j'));   -- 3.4' --

If axiom 3.0' is denoted as H(i, j'), we can use the following induction scheme:

	H(zero, j')
H(i', j') =>	H(succ(i'), j')
H(i', j') =>	H(pre(i'), j')

Using axiom 3 of Fig. 2/20 the left as well as the right-hand side of 3.1' can be transformed into

  succ(j')

Axiom 3.3' can be transformed into

declare i', j': Z;
axiom
  succ(succ(add(i', j'))) == succ(add(i', succ(j')));

by using axiom 4 of Fig. 2/20. Using the induction hypothesis 3.2' the left-hand side can be transformed into the right-hand side.
Axiom 3.4' can be transformed into

declare i', j': Z;
axiom
  succ(pre(add(i', j'))) == pre(add(i', succ(j')));

by using the last axiom of Fig. 2/20. Using the induction hypothesis 3.2', it can be transformed into

declare i', j': Z;
axiom
  succ(pre(add(i', j'))) == pre(succ(add(i', j')));

which can be proved by using axioms 1 and 2 of Fig. 2/20. This deduction proves induction conclusion 3'.
The proof of induction conclusion 4' is completely analogous to that of 3'.

We still have to prove that for each termalgebra of the given presentation, each object can be denoted by a variable–free term consisting of the operation names zero, succ and pre only, i.e. the operation names zero, succ and pre provide us with a system of canonical forms. We will even prove that each object of such an algebra can be denoted by

1. either the term zero;

2. or a variable–free term consisting of the operation names zero and succ only; if the variable–free term contains n occurrences of the operation name succ, it will be written as $succ^n($ zero $)$ with $n > 0$;

3. or a variable–free term consisting of the operation names zero and pre only; if the variable–free term contains n occurrences of the operation name pre, it will be written as $pre^n($ zero $)$ with $n > 0$.

This property will be written in the form F(x), where x stands for an arbitrary object of the termalgebra. We use the following induction scheme:

	F(zero)	-- a --
F(x') =>	F(succ(x'))	-- b --
F(x') =>	F(pre(x'))	-- c --
F(x') and F(y') =>	F(add(x', y'))	-- d --

Case a is trivial. Cases b and c are proved respectively using axioms 2 and 1 of Fig. 2/20. Before proving case d, we first prove some useful lemmas.

declare i: Z;
axiom
    add($succ^n$(zero), i) == $succ^n$(i);   -- with n $\geqslant$ 0   lemma 1

Lemma 1 can be proved by a simple induction over n. The induction base (n = 0) is identical to axiom 3 of Fig. 2/20. If the induction hypothesis

declare i: Z;
axiom
    add($succ^{n'}$(zero), i) == $succ^{n'}$(i);

is true, we still have to prove that

declare i: Z;
axiom
    add($succ^{n'+1}$(zero), i) == $succ^{n'+1}$(i);

The above axiom can be written as

declare i: Z;
axiom
    add(succ($succ^{n'}$(zero)), i) == succ($succ^{n'}$(i));

which can be transformed to

declare i: Z;
axiom
    succ(add($succ^{n'}$(zero), i)) == succ($succ^{n'}$(i));

using axiom 4 of Fig. 2/20. The above axiom can be proved using the induction hypothesis.

The proof of the following lemma is analogous.

declare i: Z;
axiom
    add(pre^n(zero), i) == pre^n(i);   -- with n $\geqslant$ 0   lemma 2

Lemma 3 is

> **declare** i: Z;
> **axiom**
> $succ^n(\ pre^n(\ i\ )\ ) == i$;   -- with n $\geqslant$ 0   lemma 3

The induction base (n = 0) is trivial. If the induction hypothesis

> **declare** i: Z;
> **axiom**
> $succ^{n'}(\ pre^{n'}(\ i\ )\ ) == i$;

is true, we have to prove the induction hypothesis

> **declare** i: Z;
> **axiom**
> $succ^{n'+1}(\ pre^{n'+1}(\ i\ )\ ) == i$;

which can be written as

> **declare** i: Z;
> **axiom**
> $succ(\ succ^{n'}(\ pre^{n'}(\ pre(\ i\ )\ )\ )\ ) == i$;

The above axiom can be proved using the induction hypothesis and axiom 2 of Fig. 2/20.

The proof of lemma 4 is analogous.

> **declare** i: Z;
> **axiom**
> $pre^n(\ succ^n(\ i\ )\ ) == i$;   -- with n $\geqslant$ 0   lemma 4

We still have to prove case d.

$$F(\ x'\ )\ \text{and}\ F(\ y'\ ) => \quad F(\ add(\ x', y'\ )\ ) \quad \boxed{\text{-- d --}}$$

The induction hypothesis expresses that x' can be written as zero, as $succ^n(\ zero\ )$ or as $pre^n(\ zero\ )$ with n > 0. We consider these three situations.

1. x' can be written as zero. The right-hand side of case d becomes $F(\ add(\ zero, y'\ )\ )$ which can be transformed, using axiom 3 of Fig.

2/20, to $F(y')$ which is part of the induction hypothesis.

2. x' can be written as $succ^n(zero)$ with $n > 0$. Applying lemma 1 yields as right-hand side of case d $F(succ^n(y'))$. As $F(y')$ is valid, y' can be written as zero, $succ^m(zero)$ or as $pre^m(zero)$ with $m > 0$. If y' can be written as zero or $succ^m(zero)$, $F(succ^n(y'))$ is obvious valid. If y' can be written as $pre^m(zero)$, we have three possibilities:

$n < m$: The right-hand side may be written as

$$F(succ^n(pre^n(pre^{m-n}(zero))))$$

which can be proved using lemma 3.

$n = m$: Using lemma 3 we obtain $F(zero)$, which is valid.

$n > m$: The right-hand side may be written as

$$F(succ^{n-m}(succ^m(pre^m(zero))))$$

which can be proved using lemma 3.

3. x' can be written as $pre^n(zero)$. The proof is analogous to that of the previous situation.

In Chapter 4 constructive specifications will be defined for which a system of canonical forms (terms built up of constructors only) is designated by the designer of the specification.

Counter-Example

The variety over the presentation of Fig. 2/20 contains the following algebra [Huet80], see Fig. 2/21. The set of objects of the algebra is the union of the set of blue integers $\{i_{blue}\}$ and the set of red integers $\{i_{red}\}$, with i standing for an integer. The functions of the algebra are $\{pre\}$, $\{succ\}$ and $\{+\}$. Their meaning is intuitively described as follows

$$\{pre\}(\{i_{blue}\}) = \{(i-1)_{blue}\}$$

$$\{pre\}(\{i_{red}\}) = \{(i-1)_{red}\}$$

$$\{succ\}(\{i_{blue}\}) = \{(i+1)_{blue}\}$$

$$\{succ\}(\{i_{red}\}) = \{(i+1)_{red}\}$$

$$\{i_{blue}\} \overset{\circ}{(+)} \{j_{blue}\} = \{(i+j)_{blue}\}$$

$$\{i_{red}\} (+) \{j_{red}\} = \{(i+j)_{red}\}$$

$$\{i_{blue}\} (+) \{j_{red}\} = \{(i+j)_{red}\}$$

$$\{i_{red}\} (+) \{j_{blue}\} = \{(i+j)_{blue}\}$$

The nullary operation zero denotes $\{0_{blue}\}$.

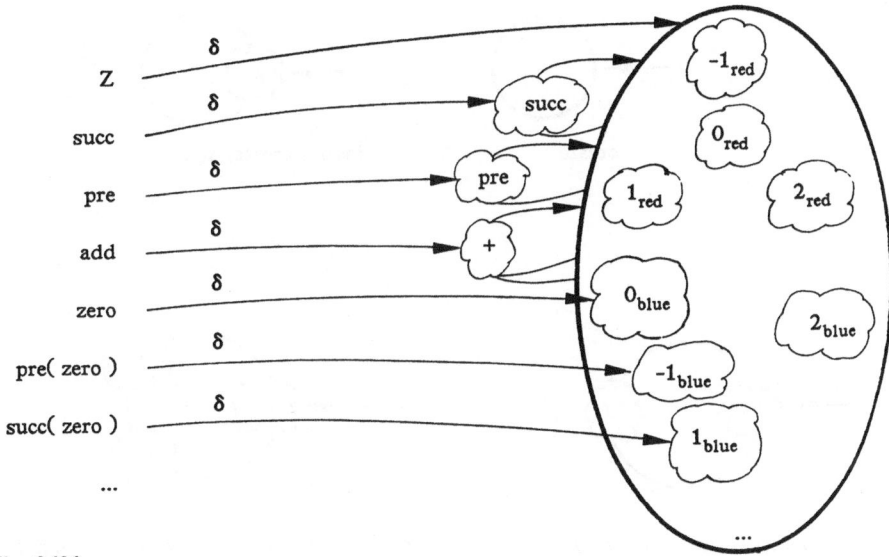

Fig. 2/21

This algebra does not satisfy the derived axiom $0^{\cdot}$:

$$\{i_{blue}\} (+) \{j_{red}\} = \{(i+j)_{red}\} \neq \{(j+i)_{blue}\} = \{j_{red}\} (+) \{i_{blue}\}$$

This algebra is not a termalgebra of the variety over the given presentation. Therefore axioms derived by induction are not always satisfied by this algebra.

Example of the Circular Lists

A somewhat richer example is the Circularlist [Guttag78a]. This data type has seven operations. The operations create, insert, delete, value and isempty have analogous operations as in type Stack. The operations right and join introduce additional complexity by allowing us to rotate the list of stored elements and to join two lists into one. The presentation is given in Fig. 2/25. An informal description is given in the next paragraph.

Every circular list can be denoted by a variable-free term consisting of the Circularlist operation names create and insert (and Nat operation names) only. We can represent circular lists in a graphical way, see Fig. 2/22. The arrow refers to the last inserted natural number.

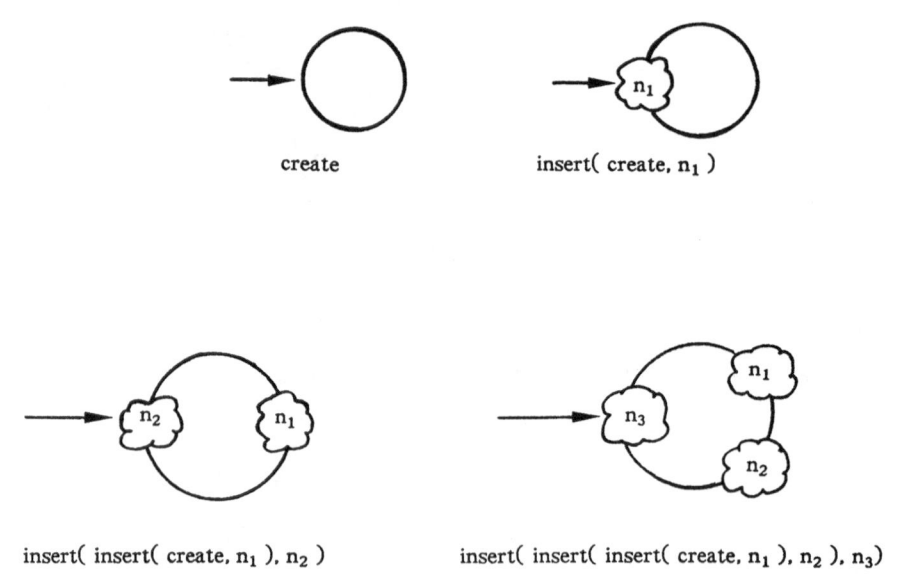

create   insert(create, n_1)

insert(insert(create, n_1), n_2)   insert(insert(insert(create, n_1), n_2), n_3)

Fig. 2/22

The operation isempty indicates whether a circular list is empty. The operation value returns the last inserted natural number. The operation delete deletes the last inserted natural number from a circular list. The operation right rotates the list of stored elements as shown in Fig. 2/23.

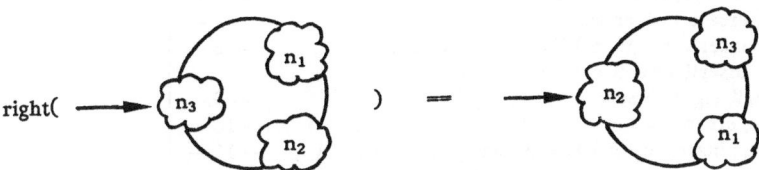

Fig. 2/23

The operation join joins two lists into one as illustrated in Fig. 2/24.

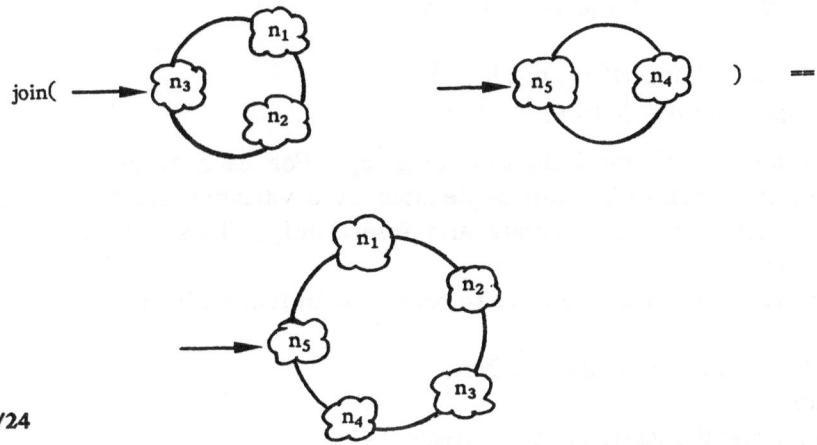

Fig. 2/24

```
sorts Circularlist; Nat; Bool;
operations
  zero: -> Nat;
  succ: Nat -> Nat;

  true, false: -> Bool;

  create: -> Circularlist;
  insert: Circularlist * Nat -> Circularlist;
  isempty: Circularlist -> Bool;
  delete, right: Circularlist -> Circularlist;
  value: Circularlist -> Nat;
  join: Circularlist * Circularlist -> Circularlist;
declare c, c₁, c₂: Circularlist;   n, n₁, n₂: Nat
axioms
  isempty( create ) == true;                           -- 1 --
  isempty( insert( c, n ) ) == false;                  -- 2 --
  delete( create ) == create;                          -- 3 --
  delete( insert( c, n ) ) == c;                       -- 4 --
```

```
value( create ) == zero;                                    -- 5 --
value( insert( c, n ) ) == n;                               -- 6 --
right( create ) == create;                                  -- 7 --
right( insert( create, n ) ) == insert( create, n );        -- 8 --
right( insert( insert( c, n₁ ), n₂ ) ) ==
    insert( right( insert( c, n₂ ) ), n₁ );                 -- 9 --
join( c, create ) == c;                                     -- 10 --
join( c₁, insert( c₂, n ) ) == insert( join( c₁, c₂ ), n ); -- 11 --
```

Fig. 2/25

For every termalgebra of the presentation the following theorem can be proved by induction:

declare c_1, c_2: Circularlist; n: Nat;
axiom
   join(right(insert(c_1, n)), c_2) ==
      right(insert(join(c_1, c_2), n));   -- 0' --

It can be proved by induction over c_2. For each termalgebra of the presentation each object can be denoted by a variable-free term consisting of the operation names create and insert only. This can be proved by induction.

To prove axiom 0', we have to prove the induction base

declare c_1: Circularlist; n: Nat;
axiom
   join(right(insert(c_1, n)), create) ==
      right(insert(join(c_1, create), n));   -- 1' --

and, given the induction hypothesis

declare c_1, c_2': Circularlist; n: Nat;
axiom
   join(right(insert(c_1, n)), c_2') ==
      right(insert(join(c_1, c_2'), n));   -- 2' --

we have to prove the induction conclusion

declare c_1, c_2': Circularlist; n, m: Nat;
axiom
   join(right(insert(c_1, n)), insert(c_2', m)) ==
      right(insert(join(c_1, insert(c_2', m)), n));   -- 3' --

If axiom 0' is denoted as F(c_1, n, c_2), we have the following *induction scheme*.

$$
\boxed{F(c_1, n, c_2') => \quad \begin{array}{l} F(c_1, n, \text{create}) \\ F(c_1, n, \text{insert}(c_2', m)) \end{array}}
$$

The induction base 1' can be proved by equational reasoning using axiom 10 of Fig. 2/25.

The induction conclusion 3' can be proved by equational reasoning using axioms 9 and 11 of Fig. 2/25 and using the induction hypothesis.

2.18 Hidden Operations and Sorts

The readability of specifications can often be enhanced by using auxiliary operations or auxiliary sets of objects, respectively called *hidden operations* and *hidden sorts*. The *abstract data types* defined by a presentation consist of the sets of objects $\delta.S_j$ together with the functions $\delta.s_i$ between these sets, of the initial algebra of the category over the presentation, with exclusion of hidden sorts and hidden operations. Examples of hidden operations have already been given, e.g., the auxiliary operation allover in Fig. 2/19.

Hidden operations and hidden sorts can not only be useful, they can even be necessary. Without hidden operations and hidden sorts, many abstract data types would require an infinite number of axioms. The peekstack [Thatcher78, Nolan79] is such a data type that cannot be specified without hidden operations.

Example of the Peekstacks

A peekstack is a stack that has a window. This window can cover any item of the peekstack or it can disappear. By means of the operation return the window covers the top of the peekstack. The operation return on the empty peekstack has no effect. The window can be moved downwards using the operation down. If the window covers the bottom item of the peekstack and the operation down is executed, the window will disappear. If the window has disappeared, the execution of the operation down is not allowed. Only the item covered by the window can be accessed by the operation read. If the window has disappeared, the operation read will return an error item. The window of the empty peekstack will always disappear. The execution of the operation push is only allowed if the window covers the top of the peekstack or if the peekstack is empty (otherwise the erroneous peekstack err is obtained). The new item will be added on top of the peekstack and the window will cover the new top. The execution of the operation pop is only allowed if the peekstack is not empty and if the window covers the top of the peekstack (otherwise the erroneous peekstack err is obtained). The top item will be removed from the peekstack and the window will cover the new top or will disappear if the peekstack becomes empty.

It can be proved that the peekstack requires an infinite number of axioms if no hidden operations are used [Thatcher78]. This requirement can be intuitively understood by looking at the axioms of Fig. 2/26.

---

declare s: Peekstack;   it, it_1, it_2, it_3: Item;
axioms
  read(push(s, it)) == it;
  read(down(push(push(s, it_1), it_2))) == it_1;
  read(down(down(push(push(push(s, it_1), it_2), ti_3)))) == it_1;
  . . .

Fig. 2/26

The introduction of a hidden operation shove is sufficient for the construction of a finite axiom system to specify non-erroneous peekstacks. The operation shove has the effect of adding an item on top of the peekstack irrespectively of the current position of the window, which remains at the same position. A specification of the peekstack is given in Fig. 2/27. For reasons of error handling, the auxiliary operations safePeekstack and ifthenelse are introduced. The operation safePeekstack yields false if its argument is an erroneous peekstack. The topic of error handling will be thoroughly discussed in Chapter 7.

---

sorts Item; Peekstack;

operations
  error: -> Item;
  . . .

  newstack: -> Peekstack;
  push: Peekstack * Item -> Peekstack;
  shove: Peekstack * Item -> Peekstack;   -- hidden operation --

---

```
-- Every non-erroneous peekstack can be written as
--   shove( ... shove( push( ... push( newstack, i₁ ) ..., i_j ), i_k ) ..., i_z )
-- with possibly no occurrences of the operation shove
-- (i.e. the top of the peekstack is covered by the window, if any)
-- and/or no occurrences of the operation push
-- (i.e. the window has disappeared).
-- i_j is covered by the window, if any.
```

err: -> Peekstack;
safePeekstack: Peekstack -> Bool;
pop: Peekstack -> Peekstack;
read: Peekstack -> Item;
return: Peekstack -> Peekstack;
down: Peekstack -> Peekstack;

true, false: -> Bool;
ifthenelse: Bool * Peekstack * Peekstack -> Peekstack;

declare s, s_1, s_2: Peekstack;   it, it_1, it_2: Item;
axioms
  push(err, it) == err;
  push(shove(s, it_1), it_2) == err;

  shove(err, it) == err;

  safePeekstack(newstack) == true;
  safePeekstack(push(newstack, it)) == true;
  safePeekstack(push(push(s, it_1), it_2)) == safePeekstack(push(s, it_1));
  safePeekstack(push(shove(s, it_1), it_2)) == false;
  safePeekstack(push(err, it)) == false;
  safePeekstack(shove(s, it)) == safePeekstack(s);

  pop(newstack) == err;
  pop(push(s, it)) == ifthenelse(safePeekstack(push(s, it)),
    -- then -- s,
    -- else -- err);
  pop(shove(s, it)) == err;
  pop(err) == err;

  read(newstack) == error;
  read(push(s, it)) == ifthenelse(safePeekstack(push(s, it)),
    -- then -- it,
    -- else -- error);
  read(shove(s, it)) == read(s);
  read(err) == error;

  return(newstack) == newstack;
  return(push(s, it)) == push(s, it);
  return(shove(s, it)) == push(return(s), it);
  return(err) == err;

  down(newstack) == err;
  down(push(s, it)) == ifthenelse(safePeekstack(push(s, it)),
    -- then -- shove(s, it),
    -- else -- err);
  down(shove(s, it)) == shove(down(s), it);
  down(err) == err;

  ifthenelse(true, s_1, s_2) == s_1;
  ifthenelse(false, s_1, s_2) == s_2;

Fig. 2/27

2.19 Bibliographic Notes

The fundamental ideas of one-sorted algebras go back to Birkhoff [Birkhoff38], Cohn [Cohn65] and Graetzer [Graetzer68], in which they are called *universal algebras*. Sometimes they are called *homogeneous algebras* [Guttag78c].

The pioneers of many-sorted algebras (originally called *heterogeneous algebras*) are Higgins [Higgins63], and Birkhoff and Lipson [Birkhoff70], who generalized the ideas of one-sorted algebras.

The idea of defining algebras in terms of operations and axioms was picked up by Zilles and Liskov to specify abstract data types like stacks, queues and strings by algebraic specifications [Zilles74, Liskov74]. Goguen [Goguen74] applied the basic principle of many-sorted initial algebras to the denotational semantics of context-free languages.

The group consisting of Goguen, Thatcher, Wagner and Wright (later occasionally also Bloom, Ehrig and Kreowski) is sometimes referred to as the ADJ group.

Many interesting papers on many-sorted algebras can be found in literature. The publications of Burstall and Goguen [Burstall82] and Goovaerts and Van Puymbroeck [Goovaerts83] are very readable texts for non-mathematicians. Many small examples of algebraic specifications can be found in [Guttag78a]. A more mathematically-oriented article is the famous work of Goguen [Goguen78]. Among others the following properties are proved there:

- If the algebras A and B are both initial in a category C of algebras over a presentation, then A and B are isomorphic. If A and B belong to a category C of algebras over a presentation, if A is initial in C and if A and B are isomorphic, then B is initial in C.

- The initial algebra of the variety over a presentation is the quotient algebra of the word algebra (of the presentation) for the equality relations defined by the axioms.

Initial algebras are often characterized by their properties of having *no junk* and having *no confusion* [Burstall82, Futatsugi85]. Having no junk means that each object of the algebra can be denoted by at least one variable-free term, i.e. the algebra is a termalgebra. Having no confusion means that two variable-free terms denote the same object if they can be proved to be equal by equational reasoning from the given axioms. A termalgebra is often called *reachable* [Sannella85a]. A termalgebra is called *generated* by Ehrig and Mahr [Ehrig85]. They call an algebra of a category *typical* when two variable-free terms denote the same object if and only if this can be proved by equational reasoning. A generated and typical algebra is always initial. The initial algebra of the variety of the presentation is always generated and typical [Ehrig85].

In literature, axioms are also called *equations, laws* or *identities*, and the terms are sometimes called *expressions* or *formulas*. An *interpretation* is a synonym for an assignment. Given an algebra with its presentation and an assignment, the object denoted by a term is sometimes called the *evaluation* of the term in the given algebra [Goovaerts83]. In [Goguen78] a presentation only consists of a set of axioms over a given signature. The set of all axioms derivable by equational reasoning from a given set of axioms is called the *closure* of the given set; a set of axioms forming its own closure is called *closed* [Burstall82]. If the axioms of a presentation are closed, the presentation is called a *theory* [Burstall82]. Because in most cases the closure is an infinite set, a theory is usually used as a synonym for a presentation [Burstall77]. The sets of objects are usually called *carriers* [Goguen78], in [Guttag78c] they are called *phyla* and the phylum one is interested in, is called the *type of interest* (TOI). In [Goguen78] a word algebra is also called a *Herbrand universe*.

[Wirsing82, Laut83] also consider algebras containing *partial functions*. Partial functions however can be made total by adding error elements to the sets of objects.

The notion of initiality is well-known in category theory and initial algebras can be seen as a special case of *free algebras*. Information about category theory is available in [Hilton74, Goldblatt79, Ehrig85].

Equational Reasoning

A survey of equational reasoning can be found in [Huet80, Ehrig85, Lescanne85]. A well-known problem is to find an algorithm that for any presentation can check whether two terms are equal by equational reasoning. This problem is called the *word problem*. It has been proved that the word problem is undecidable [Tarski68, McNulty76, Evans78]. A partial solution is the *Knuth-Bendix algorithm* [Knuth67], which does not always terminate. The ideas of the Knuth-Bendix algorithm have been generalized to the *critical pair completion* method [Buchberger85].

The rules of equational reasoning were originally designed for one-sorted algebras. One-sorted algebras need only rules for reflexivity, symmetry, transitivity and substitutivity. For many-sorted algebras two new rules, the abstraction and concretion rules, have been added to avoid unsound deductions for abstract data types having empty sets of objects. The following example comes from [Meseguer85a].

```
sorts A; B;
```

```
operations
  t, f: -> B;
  not: B -> B;
  and, or: B * B -> B;
  foo: A -> B;
declare a: A;   b: B;
axioms
  not( t ) == f;
  not( f ) == t;
  or( b, not( b ) ) == t;
  and( b, not( b ) ) == f;
  or( b, b ) == b;
  and( b, b ) == b;
  foo( a ) == not( foo( a ) );
```

Fig. 2/28

The rules of one-sorted equational reasoning give

$$t == or(\ foo(\ a\ ),\ not(\ foo(\ a\ )\ )\ ) == or(\ foo(\ a\ ),\ foo(\ a\ )\ ) == foo(\ a\ ) ==$$
$$and(\ foo(\ a\ ),\ foo(\ a\ )\ ) == and(\ foo(\ a\ ),\ not(\ foo(\ a\ )\ )\ ) == f$$

If these rules of deduction were sound, then the axiom t == f should be satisfied by every algebra of the variety over the presentation. But there is an algebra belonging to the variety over the presentation in which the axiom is not satisfied. It is the algebra consisting of the boolean values and an empty set δ.A. It is obvious that this algebra satisfies the axioms of Fig. 2/28, although true ≠ false.

A first rigorous treatment of equational reasoning for many-sorted algebras was given in [Goguen81]. Using these deduction rules (see Section 2.13) we can only derive for the specification of Fig. 2/28

```
declare a: A;
axiom
  t == f;
```

But we cannot derive

```
axiom
  t == f;
```

because the concretion rule cannot be applied.

In Section 2.13 equational reasoning was based on the reflexivity, symmetry, transitivity, substitutivity, abstraction and concretion rules. It is possible to use alternative sets of equational rules that are equivalent to the given one, see Chapter 5 in [Ehrig85]. In the same chapter the strong relationship between equational reasoning and term rewriting is thoroughly discussed.

Induction

Many formal definitions of induction can be found in literature. The most general (but rather tedious) definition we have found, is given in [Boyer79] for LISP programs. The correctness of proving by induction is also considered there. Many heuristic rules are given in [Boyer79] to find an appropriate induction scheme that is complete and sound. The rules are based on the natural relation between recursion and induction. In [Bevers85], these ideas have been specifically applied on algebraic specifications.

The Knuth-Bendix algorithm, which was mentioned earlier, can not only be used for equational reasoning but also for proving by induction. Using this algorithm is sometimes called *induction without induction* or *inductionless induction* [Goguen80, Musser80, Huet82].

Graphical Notation

The graphical notation we used in this chapter is based on [Lewi86], where a similar notation for the semantic description of algorithmic languages is used. Another graphical notation can be found in [Goguen78]. An example of such notation for the presentation of Fig. 2/15 is given in Fig. 2/29. The main difference is that in our graphical notation the algebra (semantic part) is pictured, while in [Goguen78] the signature (syntactic part) is pictured.

Hidden Operations and Sorts

The use of hidden operations was the subject of an interesting discussion ending with the conclusion that hidden operations strictly increase the expressive power of algebraic specifications [Ehrig85]. By using hidden operations, we are able to specify any computable total function, and some non-computable total functions too [Ehrig85]. Other examples of hidden operations can be found in [Laut83], where the Pascal file type is specified. An example of a hidden sort can be found in [Mallgren82], where it is used for correctness proofs.

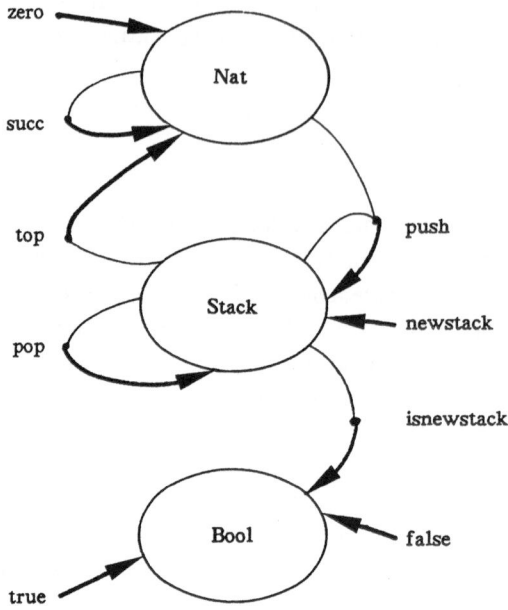

zero

Nat

succ

top   push

Stack   newstack

pop

isnewstack

Bool   false

true

Fig. 2/29

Initial Versus Final Algebras

In this chapter the mathematical model on which abstract data types have
been based, is the initial algebra. Another frequently used mathematical
model is the *final algebra*. Roughly speaking, the initial algebra defined by
a presentation is the termalgebra satisfying the given axioms that has the
greatest possible number of objects, whereas the final algebra is the
termalgebra satisfying the given axioms that has the smallest possible
number of objects. Obviously, between these two extreme algebras, there
can be a wide spectrum of algebras.

The basic philosophy of initial semantics is that two variable–free terms
denote a different object unless it can be proved from the given axioms
that they denote the same object. The basic philosophy of final semantics
is that two variable–free terms (of the same sort) denote the same object
unless it can be proved from the given axioms that they denote a different
object.

The difference between initial and final algebras will be illustrated by
the presentation of Fig. 2/30. We assume that the abstract data type of
boolean values including an ifthenelse function and the abstract data type
of natural numbers including an equality function have been defined.

```
sort X;
operations
  empty: -> X;
  insert: Nat * X -> X;
  isin: Nat * X -> Bool;
declare n, n₁, n₂: Nat;   x: X;
axioms
  insert( n₁, insert( n₂, x ) ) == insert( n₂, insert( n₁, x ) );
  isin( n, empty ) == false;
  isin( n₁, insert( n₂, x ) ) ==
    ifthenelse( eq( n₁, n₂ ),
      -- then -- true,
      -- else -- isin( n₁, x ) );
```

Fig. 2/30

The initial algebra of this presentation is the bag of natural numbers with the functions insert and isin. The first axiom expresses that the order of insertion is irrelevant. The two other axioms define the function isin. The number of times a natural number has been inserted, is relevant. Two bags are different if and only if at least one natural number has been inserted a different number of times.

The final algebra of this presentation is the set of natural numbers with the functions insert and isin. Two sets are equal unless the function isin gives a different result, i.e. one set contains a natural number that is not included in the other set. The first axiom is redundant, it can be deleted without changing the final semantics.

Sometimes initial and final semantics are both used in a hierarchy of specifications [Goovaerts83]. Such hierarchy starts with initial semantics. Each level of the hierarchy has to preserve the structure of the previously defined abstract data types, otherwise the specification is *inconsistent* or not *sufficiently complete*. If only final semantics are used, an abstract data type (usually Bool, e.g., [Hornung80]) must be predefined, otherwise all sets of objects will degenerate into empty sets or singletons. However, this predefined abstract data type cannot be specified using final semantics only.

An important reason why initial semantics are more frequently used in literature, is that algebraic specifications based on initial algebras can, in general, easier be made constructive, thus enabling rapid prototyping. Some abstract data types however are more naturally specified in terms of a final algebra [Goovaerts83].

A mathematical definition of final algebras can be found in [Wand79, Kamin80, Bergstra83]. An algebra F is final in a category C of algebras over a presentation if and only if F belongs to C and for each algebra A in

C, a unique homomorphism in C from A to F does exist. In [Hornung80, Wirsing82] final algebras are called *terminal algebras*. Some examples in [Guttag86] are based on final semantics, others are based on behavioural equivalence.

Isomorphisms Versus Behavioural Equivalence

Roughly speaking, we may say that two algebras belonging to the variety over a given presentation, are *behaviourally equivalent* with respect to a set of *observable sorts* if it is not possible to distinguish them by evaluating terms of an observable sort [Sannella85a, Sannella87]. Notice that the evaluated terms can have proper subterms of a sort that is not observable. Usually, the initial algebra of a presentation is taken, and this algebra is generalized to the class of algebras that belong to the variety over the given presentation and that are behaviourly equivalent to the initial one with respect to the observable sorts. Abstract in abstract data types now means abstract up to behavioural equivalence instead of up to isomorphism. This form of abstraction is called *behavioural abstraction* [Sannella85a].

Again consider the presentation of Fig. 2/30. Using the previous definition, the initial algebra (bag) and the final algebra (set) are behaviourally equivalent with respect to {Bool}.

One of the first articles on behavioural equivalence was [Giarratana76]. Guttag used behavioural equivalence in [Guttag77, Guttag78b]. [Sannella85a] called it *observational equivalence*. The examples given in [Guttag78a] seem to be based on behavioural equivalence.

In [Meseguer85a] abstract data types with abstract in the sense of up to behavioural equivalence are called *abstract machines*. A sharp distinction is made between abstract data types, which are just algebras, e.g., initial or final algebras, and abstract machines, which are behavioural equivalent with respect to the *visible sorts*, i.e. observable sorts.

A typical example of an abstract data type is that of the integers, which consists of objects, i.e. integers, and of functions defined upon them, e.g., addition and subtraction. A typical example of an abstract machine is a software module in the sense of [Parnas72a]. Such a module specifies only the behaviour and not the different data structures, which are considered as implementation details. Algebras that represent different abstract data types, i.e. are not isomorphic, may represent the same abstract machine, i.e. may be behaviourally equivalent. E.g., the initial and final algebra of Fig. 2/30 represent different abstract data types (bag and set) but they represent the same abstract machine with respect to {Bool}. This abstract machine may even be represented by an algebra (of the variety of the presentation of Fig. 2/30) that is not a termalgebra, as long as this algebra is behaviourally equivalent to bag and set.

Notice that abstract machines generalize the idea of abstract data types since in case all sorts are visible two machines are equivalent if and only if they are isomorphic, i.e. abstract machines become abstract data types if all sorts become visible [Meseguer85a].

The price to be paid for this generalization is a higher complexity in rigorous reasoning because two machines that are behaviourally equivalent need not be isomorphic. An axiom that is satisfied by an algebra need not be satisfied by another algebra that is behaviourally equivalent to the first one. E.g., the axiom

$$\text{insert}(n_1, \text{insert}(n_1, x)) == \text{insert}(n_1, x);$$

is satisfied by the final but not by the initial algebra of Fig. 2/30. However, both algebras are behaviourally equivalent with respect to {Bool}, as mentioned above.

3. An Algebraic Specification Language

> "The metalanguage of a formal definition must not become
> a language known to only the priests of the cult. Tempering science
> with magic is a sure way to return to the Dark Ages."
>
> *M. Marcotty*

In Chapter 2 we dealt with the mathematical foundations of algebraic specifications. These foundations are important for gaining insight into the underlying concepts of the specification formalism. From these foundations it became clear that, unlike informal specifications, algebraic specifications can be made in a precise and unambiguous way.

To illustrate these underlying concepts, a simple notation for algebraic specifications was used. Such a notation is quite satisfactory to describe small examples. In this chapter the emphasis is put on the development of large software. Then, the simple notation used in Chapter 2 is inappropriate. What we need in the first place is a linguistic support to express modularity of software design to reduce complexity. This leads to the introduction of the notion of *module*. Such modules contain import and export clauses to express the interfaces between modules, also called *intermodule dependency*, and to provide additional safety. Modules with import and export clauses are analogous to what is available in traditional high level programming languages as Ada, Modula-2 and Clu.

Another important reason why the simple notation used in Chapter 2 is inappropriate is the absence of any form of parameterization. The algebraic specification language we propose in this chapter provides a high degree of parameterization. We believe that specification by abstraction and specification by parameterization are both powerful means to design modular and reusable software. An important aspect of parameterization in algebraic specifications is that the requirements of the interfaces (between formal and actual parameters) are not only of a syntactic nature, but also of a semantic one. This is in sharp contrast with parameterization in conventional programming languages as Ada and Clu, where semantic requirements can only be expressed in the form of program comment. Incorporation of semantic requirements within the algebraic specification language enhances software robustness. Another motivation for introducing parameterized specifications is the treatment of incomplete specifications in which some design decisions are delayed. Such design features can be treated as parameters of the specification. In this way a design can be made top-down.

Modules and their intermodule dependency form a graph. Hierarchical specifications are a special case. Hierarchical specifications can be built bottom-up. Starting from the primitive modules, new modules can be constructed that use (via import clauses) these primitive modules as building blocks and so on. To maximize the profits of hierarchical specifications, each level of the hierarchy must meet some constraints, called *hierarchical constraints*, to preserve the structure of the previous levels. Hierarchical constraints can be mechanically verified, enhancing software reliability.

To enhance readability, we introduce a number of notational extensions such as ifthenelse, case and let constructs. In our specification language prefix, infix, postfix as well as mixfix notations are allowed as long as the notation does not give rise to conflicts. Also overloading of operation names is permitted. Other notational extensions are the use of qualified names and renaming facilities. These naming and renaming facilities are useful to realize the principle of reusability in software development without being forced always to use the same names. Moreover, these facilities are needed to avoid name conflicts.

Syntax Notation

The syntax of the algebraic specification language* is described using a modified version of Backus-Naur Form. Syntactic categories are represented by names possibly containing blanks. A nonterminal category is defined in terms of other categories by a kind of equation known as production rule. Categories that cannot be decomposed further are called terminal. The name of a nonterminal category is enclosed by < and >. The name of a terminal category is enclosed by ". A production rule consists of the name of the (nonterminal) category being defined followed by the symbol = and its defining sequence. Other symbols used are vertical bars that separate alternatives, square brackets that enclose optional items, a plus following an item to indicate that the item must appear once or many times, and a star following an item to indicate that the item may be omitted, appear once or be repeated many times. The plus

---

* Although a detailed description of the proposed algebraic specification language will be given, this text is not intended as a reference manual. Detailed information about, e.g., the lexical structure is not given.

and the star have the highest priority whereas sequencing has the lowest one. Parentheses may be used to change priorities.

3.1 Modularity

3.1.1 Modules

Sorts, operations, declarations and/or axioms that logically belong together, are grouped into a *module*. A *specification* is built up of a number of modules. A specification has the following syntactic form:

<specification> = (<module>)+

<module> =
  "module" [<module name>] ";"
    [<import clause>]
    [<sorts part>]
    [<operations part>]
    [<declarations part>]
    [<axioms part>]
  "end" "module" [<module name>] ";"

<import clause> =
  "import" "all" "from" <module name list> ";"

<module name list> = <module name> ("," <module name>)*

<sorts part> =
  ("sort" | "sorts") (<sort name > ";")+

Usually, each module contains at most one sort. A module has the same syntax as a presentation except for the enclosing keywords, the module name and the import clause (if any). The *import clause* of a module M enumerates the names of all other modules M_1, M_2, ..., M_m from which M uses sorts and operations. These modules are called the *directly imported* modules of M. The directly and indirectly imported modules of M_1, M_2, ... and M_m are said to be *indirectly imported* modules of M. A module without import clause is called a *primitive module*. Actually a specification forms a directed graph. The modules represent the nodes, and the import clauses, which describe the dependency relationships between the modules, represent the arcs of the graph.

In Chapter 2 the notions of abstract data type and termlanguage were defined for presentations. When we deal with modules, these definitions have to be slightly modified. The *abstract data types* defined by a specification are the abstract data types defined by the presentation obtained by grouping the sorts, operations, declarations and axioms of the modules of the specification. Analogously, the *termlanguage* defined by a specification is defined as the termlanguage defined by the presentation obtained by grouping the sorts, operations, declarations and axioms of the modules of the specification.

The specification of Stack is shown in Fig. 3/1. The modules Bool and Nat are primitive modules, directly imported by the module Stack. Although the specification of Fig. 3/1 is equivalent to that of Fig. 2/14, it is more modular and therefore more readable.

```
module Bool;
  sort Bool;
  operations
    true, false: -> Bool;
end module Bool;

module Nat;
  sort Nat;
  operations
    zero: -> Nat;
    succ: Nat -> Nat;
end module Nat;

module Stack;
  import all from Bool, Nat;
  sort Stack;
  operations
    newstack: -> Stack;
    push: Stack * Nat -> Stack;
    isnewstack: Stack -> Bool;
    pop: Stack -> Stack;
    top: Stack -> Nat;
  declare s: Stack;   n: Nat;
  axioms
    isnewstack( newstack ) == true;
    isnewstack( push( s, n ) ) == false;
    pop( newstack ) == newstack;
    pop( push( s, n ) ) == s;
    top( newstack ) == zero;
    top( push( s, n ) ) == n;
end module Stack;
```

Fig. 3/1

Modularity provides us with a means to specify an abstract data type in a stepwise way. Roughly speaking, in a first step a module is designed containing only the sort and the primitive (i.e. basic) operations. In the next steps modules defining more sophisticated operations are added.

Let us specify sets of natural numbers, see Fig. 3/2. We need the operation emptyset, which represents the empty set, and the operation insert, which puts a natural number into a set. They are defined in the module PrimitiveSet. The axioms state that the order of insertions and the number of duplicates are irrelevant. More sophisticated operations may be the union, the intersection and the operation isin, which indicates whether a natural number belongs to a set. They are specified in module ExtendedSet. ExtendedSet imports from Bool, Nat, ExtendedNat and PrimitiveSet.

```
module ExtendedNat;
  import all from Bool, Nat;
  operation
    equal: Nat * Nat -> Bool;
  declare n, n₁, n₂: Nat;
  axioms
    equal( zero, zero ) == true;
    equal( zero, succ( n ) ) == false;
    equal( succ( n ), zero ) == false;
    equal( succ( n₁ ), succ( n₂ ) ) == equal( n₁, n₂ );
end module ExtendedNat;

module PrimitiveSet;
  import all from Nat;
  sort Set;
  operations
    emptyset: -> Set;
    insert: Nat * Set -> Set;
  declare s: Set;   n, n₁, n₂: Nat;
  axioms
    insert( n₁, insert( n₂, s ) ) == insert( n₂, insert( n₁, s ) );
    insert( n, insert( n, s ) ) == insert( n, s );
end module PrimitiveSet;

module ExtendedSet;
  import all from Bool, Nat, ExtendedNat, PrimitiveSet;
  operations
    isin: Nat * Set -> Bool;
    union, intersection: Set * Set -> Set;
    if: Bool * Set * Set -> Set;
  declare n, n₁, n₂: Nat;   s, s₁, s₂: Set;
  axioms
    isin( n, emptyset ) == false;
    isin( n₁, insert( n₂, s ) ) ==
      if( equal( n₁, n₂ ),
        -- then -- true,
        -- else -- isin( n₁, s ) );
```

```
      union( s, emptyset ) == s;
      union( s₁, insert( n₁, s₂ ) ) == insert( n₁, union( s₁, s₂ ) );
      intersection( s, emptyset ) == emptyset;
      intersection( s₁, insert( n, s₂ ) ) ==
        if( isin( n, s₁ ),
           -- then -- insert( n, intersection( s₁, s₂ ) ),
           -- else -- intersection( s₁, s₂ ) );
      if( true, s₁, s₂ ) == s₁;
      if( false, s₁, s₂ ) == s₂;
   end module ExtendedSet;
```

Fig. 3/2

Convention: If no module name is explicitly given, the convention is that the module name is identical to the first sort name defined within the module. The module Nat of Fig. 3/1 is then equivalent to that of Fig. 3/3.

```
module;
  sort Nat;
  operations
    zero: -> Nat;
    succ: Nat -> Nat;
end module;
```

Fig. 3/3

3.1.2 Import and Export Clauses

The *import clauses* as defined so far will be further refined as in Modula-2 [Wirth82]. Except when the keywords **all** or **all except** are used, the import clause must explicitly list not only the directly imported modules but also the sorts and operations imported from these modules. If a module M imports all sorts and operations that are exported by a module M_i to it, the import clause of M may contain

all from M_i

Analogously, the import clause may contain

all except ... from M_i;

Also export clauses are considered. The *export clause* of a module lists the sorts and operations that are defined within the module and that can be used outside the module. Optionally, the export list may contain the names of the module(s) receiving the export. Clearly, hidden sorts and hidden operations will not be exported in order to disable their use outside the module in which they are defined (information hiding). If all sorts and operations defined within a module are exported, the enumeration list may be replaced by the keyword **all**. One can also use the keywords **all except** followed by the list of sorts and operations that are not exported.

Import and export clauses provide an extra protection for the designer as well as for the user of modules. This protection results in specifications of higher quality and reliability.

A module with import and/or export clauses has the following syntactic form:

```
<module> =
  "module" [ <module name> ] ";"
    [ <import clause> ]
    [ <export clause> ]
    [ <sorts part> ]
    [ <operations part> ]
    [ <declarations part> ]
    [ <axioms part> ]
  "end" "module" [ <module name> ] ";"

<import clause> =
  "import" ( <item name list> "from" <module name list> ";" )+

<export clause> =
  "export" ( <item name list> [ "to" <module name list> ] ";" )+

<item name list> =
    <item name> ( "," <item name> )*
  | "all" [ "except" <item name> ( "," <item name> )* ]

<item name> = <sort name> | <operation name>

<module name list> = <module name> ( "," <module name> )*

<sorts part> =
  ( "sort" | "sorts" ) ( <sort name > ";" )+
```

In Fig. 3/4 the specification of Fig. 3/1 is extended with import and export clauses.

```
module Bool;
  export Bool, true, false;
  sort Bool;
  operations
    true, false: -> Bool;
end module Bool;

module Nat;
  export Nat, zero, succ;
  sort Nat;
  operations
    zero: -> Nat;
    succ: Nat -> Nat;
end module Nat;

module Stack;
  import Bool, true, false from Bool;
    Nat, zero from Nat;
  export all;
  sort Stack;
  operations
    newstack: -> Stack;
    push: Stack * Nat -> Stack;
    isnewstack: Stack -> Bool;
    pop: Stack -> Stack;
    top: Stack -> Nat;
  declare s: Stack;   n: Nat;
  axioms
    isnewstack( newstack ) == true;        -- 1 --
    isnewstack( push( s, n ) ) == false;   -- 2 --
    pop( newstack ) == newstack;           -- 3 --
    pop( push( s, n ) ) == s;              -- 4 --
    top( newstack ) == zero;               -- 5 --
    top( push( s, n ) ) == n;              -- 6 --
end module Stack;
```

Fig. 3/4

3.1.3 *Export of the Import*

A module can not only export the sorts and operations defined within the module itself, but it can also export sorts and operations imported from elsewhere by the module. If an imported sort or operation is exported again, it must be mentioned explicitly in the export clause together with the module it is imported from. An example is given in Fig. 3/5.

```
module ExtendedStack;
  import Nat, zero, succ from Nat;
    Stack, newstack, push, pop, top, isnewstack from Stack;
  export length from ExtendedStack;
    Stack, newstack, push, pop, top, isnewstack from Stack;
  operation
    length: Stack -> Nat;
  declare s: Stack;   n: Nat;
  axioms
    length( newstack ) == zero;
    length( push( s, n ) ) == succ( length( s ) );
end module ExtendedStack;

module X;
  import all from ExtendedStack;
  ... newstack ...
  ... length ...
end module X;
```

Fig. 3/5

3.2 Hierarchical Specifications

In general, a specification forms a directed graph. As mentioned in Section 3.1.1, the modules represent the nodes, and the dependency relationships represent the arcs of the graph. The dependency relationships are described by the import clauses of the modules involved in the graph. A special case is the *hierarchical specification* where the directed graph is acyclic. An example of a hierarchical specification was given in Fig. 3/4. If a module A is directly or indirectly imported by a module B, module B must not be directly or indirectly imported by A in a hierarchical specification. In Section 3.5 non-hierarchical specifications will be studied.

Making hierarchical specifications is a useful design method because the amount of complexity the human mind has to cope with at any level, is considerably less than that of the whole specification. A reader as well as a designer can focus on the primitive modules first. Next, the modules that directly import these ones can be studied and built, and so on. So we need not understand the specification as a whole at once, but we can gain insight in a stepwise way. Such a design is called bottom-up.

Hierarchical Constraints

To maximize the profits of hierarchical specifications during the bottom-up design, each new level of the hierarchy must preserve the structure of the algebra defined by the previous levels. Therefore, two *hierarchical constraints* are introduced. Given a hierarchy H of modules meeting the hierarchical constraints. A new module M, importing from one or more modules of the hierarchy H, can be added to that given hierarchy H without violating the hierarchical constraints if the structure of the algebra defined by H is preserved:

1. Any two objects that were defined as different in the initial algebra of the given hierarchy H, must not become equal after addition of the new module M. This constraint is called *no confusion*. It says that if two arbitrary variable-free terms belonging to the termlanguage of the given hierarchy H cannot be proved to be equal by equational reasoning in H, then it must not be possible to prove them to be equal by equational reasoning after addition of M.

2. A set of objects defined in the initial algebra of the given hierarchy H, must not be extended with new objects after addition of the new module M. This constraint is called *no junk*. It says that if an arbitrary variable-free term t belongs to the termlanguage of the extended hierarchy, and if the sort of t was defined in H, then another variable-free term t' that belongs to the termlanguage of H must exist such that t' can be proved equal to t by equational reasoning in the extended hierarchy.

A set of primitive modules form a hierarchy that always meets the hierarchical constraints.

Example of the Stacks

In the stack example of Fig. 3/4 the dependency graph is hierarchical and the hierarchical constraints are met since the structure of the algebra defined by the hierarchy is preserved when the module Stack is added:

1. The first two axioms are of sort Bool. To prove that true and false do not become equal, it must be proved that newstack and push(s, n) are unequal for each possible assignment. This proof is straightforward. The last two axioms are of sort Nat. Analogously, two natural numbers that are different in module Nat, do not become equal.

2. We will use the property that with axioms 3 and 4 every occurrence of pop in a variable-free term can be eliminated. The only operation that could define a new object belonging to the set Bool is the operation isnewstack. But using the first 2 axioms and the property mentioned, it is easy to see that the result of isnewstack always can be reduced to true or false. Analogously, no new object belonging to the set Nat has been defined.

The first hierarchical constraint would have been violated (confusion) if, e.g., the axiom:

push(newstack, zero) == newstack;

was added because using this and the first 2 axioms it can be proved that:

true == false;

The second hierarchical constraint would have been violated (junk) if, e.g., the first axiom was forgotten, because then

isnewstack(newstack)

would denote a new boolean object.

3.3 Notational Extensions

3.3.1 Ifthenelse Construct

In Fig. 3/6 a queue of natural numbers is specified. A queue is a first-in first-out list. The operation newq creates an empty queue, addq adds a natural number to the given queue, isnewq tests whether a queue is empty, the operation deleteq removes the least recently inserted natural number, frontq returns the least recently inserted natural number, and appendq concatenates two queues into a single one. To avoid error treatment at this stage, which is discussed in Chapter 7, the operation deleteq applied to an empty queue returns the empty queue, and the operation frontq applied to an empty queue returns zero.

```
module Queue;
  import Bool, true, false from Bool;
    Nat from Nat;
  export all;
  sort Queue;
```

```
operations
  newq: -> Queue;
  addq: Queue * Nat -> Queue;
  isnewq: Queue -> Bool;
  deleteq: Queue -> Queue;
  frontq: Queue -> Nat;
  appendq: Queue * Queue -> Queue;
declare q, q₁, q₂: Queue;   n: Nat;
axioms
  isnewq( newq ) == true;
  isnewq( addq( q, n ) ) == false;
  deleteq( newq ) == newq;
  deleteq( addq( q, n ) ) ==
    if isnewq( q )
      then newq
      else addq( deleteq( q ), n )
    end if;
  frontq( newq ) == zero;
  frontq( addq( q, n) ) ==
    if isnewq( q )
      then n
      else frontq ( q )
    end if;
  appendq( q, newq ) == q;
  appendq( q₁, addq( q₂, n ) ) ==
    addq( appendq( q₁, q₂ ), n );
end module Queue;
```

Fig. 3/6

In Fig. 3/6 the *ifthenelse construct*, which the reader is undoubtedly familiar with, is introduced. An ifthenelse construct has the following syntactic form:

```
<ifthenelse construct> =
  "if" <boolean expression>
    "then" <expression>
    "else" <expression>
  "end" "if"
```

The ifthenelse construct is not a new concept, it is only an overloaded language-defined operation in mixfix notation. It is equivalent to a family of user-defined operations ifSort, one for each sort Sort, using the traditional prefix notation. This is done for the example of Fig. 3/6 resulting in the less readable specification of Fig. 3/7.

```
module Queue;
  import Bool, true, false from Bool;
    Nat, zero from Nat;
  export all;
  sort Queue;
  operations
    newq: -> Queue;
    addq: Queue * Nat -> Queue;
    isnewq: Queue -> Bool;
    deleteq: Queue -> Queue;
    frontq: Queue -> Nat;
    appendq: Queue * Queue -> Queue;
    ifNat: Bool * Nat * Nat -> Nat;
    ifQueue: Bool * Queue * Queue -> Queue;
  declare q, q₁, q₂: Queue;  n, n₁, n₂: Nat;
  axioms
    isnewq( newq ) == true;
    isnewq( addq( q, n ) ) == false;
    deleteq( newq ) == newq;
    deleteq( addq( q, n ) ) ==
      ifQueue( isnewq( q ), newq, addq( deleteq( q ), n) );
    frontq( newq ) == zero;
    frontq( addq( q, n) ) ==
      ifNat( isnewq( q ), n, frontq( q ) );
    appendq( q, newq ) == q;
    appendq( q₁, addq( q₂, n ) ) ==
      addq( append( q₁, q₂ ), n );
    ifNat( true, n₁, n₂ ) == n₁;
    ifNat( false, n₁, n₂ ) == n₂;
    ifQueue( true, q₁, q₂ ) == q₁;
    ifQueue( false, q₁, q₂ ) == q₂;
end module Queue;
```

Fig. 3/7

3.3.2 Mixfix Notations

The mixfix notation used for the ifthenelse construct can also be used for user-defined operations as long as the notation remains unambiguous. Prefix, infix and postfix notations are particular cases of mixfix notations.

In Fig. 3/8 a specification for the abstract data type of the boolean values is given, using its classical mixfix notation. The underscore '_' is a place holder (indicating the places of the arguments). Parentheses avoid ambiguous notations.

```
module Bool;
  export all;
  sort Bool;
```

```
operations
  true, false: -> Bool;
  not _: Bool -> Bool;
  _ and _: Bool * Bool -> Bool;
  _ or _: Bool * Bool -> Bool;
  _ => _: Bool * Bool -> Bool;
  _ <= _: Bool * Bool -> Bool;
  _ <=> _: Bool * Bool -> Bool;
declare b, b₁, b₂, b₃: Bool;
axioms
  b and b == b;    b or b == b;
  b₁ and b₂ == b₂ and b₁;    b₁ or b₂ == b₂ or b₁;
  b₁ and ( b₁ or b₂ ) == b₁;    b₁ or ( b₁ and b₂ ) == b₁;
  b and true == b;    b or false == b;
  b and not b == false;    b or not b == true;
  not true == false;    not not b == b;
  ( b₁ and b₂ ) and b₃ == b₁ and ( b₂ and b₃ );
  ( b₁ or b₂ ) or b₃ == b₁ or ( b₂ or b₃ );
  b₁ and ( b₂ or b₃ ) == ( b₁ and b₂ ) or ( b₁ and b₃ );
  b₁ or ( b₂ and b₃ ) == ( b₁ or b₂ ) and ( b₁ or b₃ );
  b₁ => b₂ == if b₁ then b₂ else true end if;
  b₁ <= b₂ == b₂ => b₁;
  b₁ <=> b₂ == (b₁ => b₂) and (b₁ <= b₂);
end module Bool;
```

Fig. 3/8

In Fig. 3/9 the specification of the unbounded array of boolean values
with natural numbers as indices is given. The mixfix notation _ [_ / _]
is used for the assign operation. If no place holders are given for a
nonnullary operation, the operation will be used in the classical prefix
notation with parentheses and commas, e.g., the operation read. We
assume that the module Nat contains an equality operation that has the
classical infix notation with equality sign:

_ = _: Nat * Nat -> Bool;

```
module Array;
  import Bool, true, false, not _ from Bool;
    Nat, _ = _ from Nat;
  export all;
  sort Array;
  operations
    empty: -> Array;
      -- This is the empty array.

    _[ _ / _ ]: Array * Bool * Nat -> Array;
      -- This operation assigns a boolean value to a given array
```

```
          -- with a given natural number as index.
      isdefault: Array * Nat -> Bool;
          -- This operation checks whether the given index (natural number) of
          -- the given array has still its initial default value true.
      read: Array * Nat -> Bool;
          -- This operation returns the boolean value of the index indicated
          -- by the natural number in the given array.
  declare ar: Array;   n, n₁, n₂: Nat;   b, b₁, b₂: Bool;
  axioms
    not ( n₁ = n₂ ) ⇒ ar [ b₁ / n₁ ][ b₂ / n₂ ] == ar [ b₂ / n₂ ][ b₁ / n₁ ];
          -- The order of assignments is irrelevant as long as the indices are not equal.
          -- Conditional axioms are discussed in Section 3.3.3.
    ar [ b₁ / n ][ b₂ / n ] == ar [ b₂ / n ];
          -- For a given index, only the last assignment is relevant.
    isdefault( empty, n ) == true;
    isdefault( ar [ b / n₁ ], n₂ ) ==
      if n₁ = n₂
        then false
        else isdefault( ar, n₂ )
      end if;
    read( empty, n ) == true;   -- Arrays are initialized with true.
    read( ar [ b / n₁ ], n₂ ) ==
      if n₁ = n₂
        then b
        else read( ar, n₂ )
      end if;
  end module Array;
```

Fig. 3/9

3.3.3 *Conditional Axioms*

In Fig. 3/9 a *conditional axiom* was used. This is not a new concept since a conditional axiom of the form

```
    <boolean expression> ⇒ <expression 1> == <expression 2>;
```

can easily be transformed into an unconditional axiom

```
    <expression 1> ==
      if <boolean expression>
        then <expression 2>
        else <expression 1>
      end if;
```

3.3.4 Case Constructs

Using *case constructs*, the number of axioms can sometimes be considerably reduced. A case construct has the following syntactic form:

```
<case construct> =
  "case" <case index> "of"
    ( <case arm> )+
    [ "otherwise" ":" <expression> ";" ]
  "end" "case"

<case index> = <expression>

<case arm> = <choice> ":" <expression> ";"

<choice> = <expression>
```

The case index and the choices of the different case arms of a case construct must be of the same sort. An example of case constructs is given in Fig. 3/10, also the use of **otherwise** is illustrated. The meaning of case constructs is straightforward.

```
module Stack;
  import Bool, true, false from Bool;
    Nat, zero from Nat;
  export all;
  sort Stack;
  operations
    newstack: -> Stack;
    push: Stack * Nat -> Stack;
    isnewstack: Stack -> Bool;
    pop: Stack -> Stack;
    top: Stack -> Nat;
  declare s, s₁: Stack;   n: Nat;
  axioms
    isnewstack( s ) ==
      case s of
        newstack: true;
        otherwise: false;
      end case;
    pop( s ) ==
      case s of
        newstack: newstack;
        push( s₁, n): s₁;
      end case;
    top( s ) ==
      case s of
        newstack: zero;
        push( s₁, n ): n;
```

```
          end case;
      end module Stack;
```

Fig. 3/10

3.3.5 *Let Constructs*

The readability can be enhanced by introducing a *let construct*, which has the form:

```
<let construct> =
  "let"
    <let arm>
    "in"
      <let expression>
  "end" "let"

<let arm> = <variable> "==" <expression> ";"

<let expression> = <expression>
```

with the variable and the expression of the let arm being of the same sort. The sort of the let expression is the sort of the let construct. The meaning of the let construct is the same as that of the expression obtained by replacing in the given let expression all free occurrences of the variable of the let arm by the expression of the let arm.

Also a multiple let construct is possible:

```
<let construct> =
  "let"
    ( <let arm> )+
    "in"
      <let expression>
  "end" "let"

<let arm> = <variable> "==" <expression> ";"

<let expression> = <expression>
```

A multiple let construct has the same meaning as the nesting of the corresponding single let constructs. For instance, Fig. 3/11 is equivalent to Fig. 3/12.

```
let x₁ == <expression 1>;
   x₂ == <expression 2>;
   ...
   xₙ == <expression n>;
in
   <let expression>
end let
```

Fig. 3/11

```
let x₁ == <expression 1>;
  in
    let x₂ == <expression 2>;
      in
        ...
          let xₙ == <expression n>;
            in
              <let expression>
            end let
          ...
      end let
end let
```

Fig. 3/12

An example of the use of a let construct is given in the term of Fig. 3/13, which has the same meaning as the term of Fig. 3/14.

```
declare n₁, n₂: Nat;   s, s₁: Stack;
   ...
   let n₁ == top( s );
      n₂ == top( pop( s ) );
      s₁ == pop( pop( s ) );
   in
      push( push( s₁, n₁ ), n₂ )
   end let
   ...
```

Fig. 3/13

```
declare s: Stack;
  ...
  push( push( pop( pop( s ) ) ), top( s ) ), top( pop( s ) ) )
  ...
```

Fig. 3/14

3.3.6 *Qualified Names and Renaming*

To avoid name conflicts, a sort or an operation name can be qualified by its module name. An example is given in Fig. 3/15.

```
module;
  import z from X;
    t, u, z from Y;
  ... X.z ...
  ... Y.z ...
end module;
```

Fig. 3/15

If a sort or an operation is imported from another module, it can be given a more appropriate name. A *rename clause* has the following syntactic form:

```
<rename clause> = "rename"
  <item name> "as" ( "identifier" | <pattern> ) ( ","
  <item name> "as" ( "identifier" | <pattern> ) )*

<item name> = <sort name> | <operation name>

<sort name> = "identifier" | "qualified identifier"

<operation name> = "identifier" | "qualified identifier" | <pattern>

<pattern> = ( <token> | "_" )+
```

An example is given in Fig. 3/16.

```
module;
  import Bool, true, false, _ and _ from Bool
    rename
      true as waar,
      false as onwaar,
      _ and _ as _ en _;
  ...
end module;
```

Fig. 3/16

3.4 Parameterized Specifications

In the previous sections we studied the stacks of natural numbers. We may specify stacks of booleans, stacks of natural numbers, and even stacks of stacks of natural numbers. It is rather tedious to repeat a stack definition for each new stack with a different sort of stack elements. Indeed, all those definitions hardly depend on the sort of the elements.

For this reason we introduce the notion of *scheme*. Intuitively speaking, a scheme is a meta-language function that at every call (*instantiation*) with the appropriate number of abstract data types (*actual modules*) using a parameter morphism (*parameter binding mechanism*), results in new abstract data types. A scheme has the following syntactic form:

    <scheme> =
      "scheme" <scheme name> ["[" (<requirement>)+ "]"] ";"
      (<module>)+
      "end" "scheme" [<scheme name>] ";"

After the scheme name follow the *requirements* (if any) enclosed in square brackets. These requirements are said to be *claimed* by the scheme. Requirements can be seen as *formal modules* of the scheme, with which actual modules will be bound when an instantiation of the scheme is made. A requirement states that sorts and/or operations in the actual modules of an instantiation must satisfy some syntactic and semantic properties. This is in contrast with Ada [Ada83] where only a syntactic interface for generic packages can be required. A requirement has a syntax analogous to that of a module.

```
<requirement> =
  "requirement" [ <requirement name> ] ";"
    [ <import clause> ]
    [ <export clause> ]
    [ <sorts part> ]
    [ <operations part> ]
    [ <declarations part> ]
    [ <axioms part> ]
  "end" "requirement" [ <requirement name> ] ";"
```

As an example, a scheme for a stack is given in Fig. 3/17. In this simple example the claimed requirement is a syntactic interface only, i.e. the requirement does not contain any axiom. More complex examples will be given later.

```
scheme StackScheme [
   requirement Item;
     export all;
     sort Item;
     operation
       error: -> Item;
   end requirement Item;
  ];

  module Stack;
    import Bool, true, false from Bool;
      all from Item;
    export all;
    sort Stack;
    operations
      newstack: -> Stack;
      push: Stack * Item -> Stack;
      isnewstack: Stack -> Bool;
      pop: Stack -> Stack;
      top: Stack -> Item;
    declare s: Stack;   it: Item;
    axioms
      isnewstack( newstack ) == true;
      isnewstack( push( s, it ) ) == false;
      pop( newstack ) == newstack;
      pop( push( s, it ) ) == s;
      top( newstack ) == error;
      top( push( s, it ) ) == it;
  end module Stack;
end scheme StackScheme;
```

Fig. 3/17

An *instantiation* has the following syntax:

```
<instantiation> =
  "instantiate" <scheme name> [ <rename clause> ] ";"
    ( "with" <requirement name> "as" <module name> [ ( ","
        <item name> "as" <item name> )* ] ";"
    )*
  "end" "instantiate" [ <scheme name> ] ";"

<item name> = <sort name> | <operation name>
```

After the keyword **with** a claimed requirement (formal module) is
bound with a module (actual module). First, the name of the claimed
requirement is bound with the name of the module. Afterwards, the
(formal) sorts and operations of the claimed requirement are bound with
the (actual) sorts and operations of the module. In Fig. 3/18 StackScheme
is instantiated.

```
instantiate StackScheme;
  with Item as Nat,
    Item as Nat,
    error as zero;
end instantiate StackScheme;
```

Fig. 3/18

For this instantiation the requirement Item is bound with the module
Nat in the following way: the formal parameter Item is bound with the
actual sort Nat and the formal parameter error is bound with the actual
operation zero. The instantiation of Fig. 3/18 is equivalent to Fig. 3/19.

```
module Stack;
  import Bool, true, false from Bool;
    Nat, zero from Nat;
  export all;
  sort Stack;
  operations
    newstack: -> Stack;
    push: Stack * Nat -> Stack;
    isnewstack: Stack -> Bool;
    pop: Stack -> Stack;
    top: Stack -> Nat;
  declare s: Stack;   it: Nat;
  axioms
```

```
      isnewstack( newstack ) == true;
      isnewstack( push( s, it ) ) == false;
      pop( newstack ) == newstack;
      pop( push( s, it ) ) == s;
      top( newstack ) == zero;
      top( push( s, it ) ) == it;
   end module Stack;
```

Fig. 3/19

In Fig. 3/20 a scheme for an array is given. Two requirements are claimed, one for the indices and one for the attributes of the array. The requirement Index serves not only as a syntactic but also as a semantic interface, i.e. the requirement contains axioms. The required semantic properties of the equality operation are reflexivity, symmetry and transitivity.

```
scheme ArrayScheme [
    requirement Attribute;
      export all;
      sort Attribute;
      operation
        error: -> Attribute;
    end requirement Attribute;

    requirement Index;
      import Bool, true, _ and _ from Bool;
      export all;
      sort Index;
      operation
        _ = _: Index * Index -> Bool;
      declare i, i₁, i₂, i₃: Index;
      axioms
        i = i == true;
        i₁ = i₂ == i₂ = i₁;
        ( i₁ = i₂ ) and ( i₂ = i₃ ) ⇒ ( i₁ = i₃ )  == true;
    end requirement Index;
  ];

  module Array;
    import Bool, true, false, not _ from Bool;
      all from Attribute, Index;
    export all;
    sort Array;
    operations
      empty: -> Array;
      _ [ _ / _ ]: Array * Attribute * Index -> Array;
      isundefined: Array * Index -> Bool;
      read: Array * Index -> Attribute;
    declare ar: Array;  i, i₁, i₂: Index;  at, at₁, at₂: Attribute;
```

```
    axioms
      not ( i₁ = i₂ ) ⇒ ar [ at₁ / i₁ ][ at₂ / i₂ ] == ar [ at₂ / i₂ ][ at₁ / i₁ ];
      ar [ at₁ / i ][ at₂ / i ] == ar [ at₂ / i ];
      isundefined( empty, i ) == true;
      isundefined( ar [ at / i₁ ], i₂ ) ==
        if i₁ = i₂
          then false
          else isundefined( ar, i₂ )
        end if;
      read( empty, i ) == error;
      read( ar [ at / i₁ ], i₂ ) ==
        if i₁ = i₂
          then at
          else read( ar, i₂ )
        end if;
  end module Array;
end scheme ArrayScheme;
```

Fig. 3/20

In Fig. 3/21 an instantiation of ArrayScheme is given. We assume that a module Iden of identifiers, containing the identifier undefined, and a module Bool have been specified. The requirement Index is bound with the module Nat, the requirement Attribute is bound with the module Iden. The instantiation makes sense since the requirements are met, i.e. the syntactic interfaces are met and the axioms of the requirement Index are satisfied by the actual parameters. Indeed, the reflexivity, symmetry and transitivity of the operation $\_ = \_$: Nat * Nat -> Bool can be proved using equational reasoning and induction.

```
module Nat;
  import Bool, true, false from Bool;
  export all;
  sort Nat;
  operations
    zero: -> Nat;
    succ: Nat -> Nat;
    _=_: Nat * Nat -> Bool;
  declare n, n₁, n₂: Nat;
  axioms
    zero = zero == true;
    zero = succ( n ) == false;
    succ( n ) = zero == false;
    succ( n₁ ) = succ( n₂ ) == n₁ = n₂;
end module Nat;

instantiate ArrayScheme;
  with Index as Nat,
    Index as Nat,
```

```
  _ = _ as _ = _;
with Attribute as Iden,
   Attribute as Iden,
   error as undefined;
end instantiate ArrayScheme;
```

Fig. 3/21

Import Restrictions

Anywhere outside a scheme one must not import from the modules of the
scheme nor from the requirements claimed by the scheme. Also, claimed
requirements of a scheme must not import from the modules of the
scheme.

Before explaining the parameter passing mechanism in more detail, we
will define parameter morphisms.

3.4.1 Parameter Morphisms

A *parameter morphism* m from the claimed requirements $R_1, R_2, ..., R_r$ of a
scheme S to modules $M_1, M_2, ..., M_r$ consists of two families of mappings
$\{ m_{1_s}, m_{2_s}, ..., m_{r_s} \}$ and $\{ m_{1_o}, m_{2_o}, ..., m_{r_o} \}$, with m_{x_s} being a mapping
from all sorts defined in R_x to sorts defined in or imported by M_x, and
with m_{x_o} being a mapping from all operation names defined in R_x to the
operation names defined in or imported by M_x, such that

A.   the rank of the operations is preserved:

    a.   for each nullary operation s_i defined in a requirement R_x as
$s_i: -> S_{i_j}$, we have $m_{x_o}(s_i): -> m_s(S_{i_j})$ with $m_s(S_{i_j})$ defined
as

        • if S_{i_j} was defined in a requirement R_y, then $m_s(S_{i_j}) = m_{y_s}(S_{i_j})$

        • otherwise $m_s(S_{i_j}) = S_{i_j}$

    b.   for each nonnullary operation s_i defined in a requirement R_x as
$s_i: S_{i_1} * S_{i_2} * ... * S_{i_k} -> S_{i_j}$, we have $m_{x_o}(s_i): m_s(S_{i_1}) *
m_s(S_{i_2}) * ... * m_s(S_{i_k}) -> m_s(S_{i_j})$ with m_s as defined above

B.   the axioms are preserved: for each axiom $T_1 == T_2$ in a requirement
R_x the axiom $m(T_1) == m(T_2)$ is satisfied by module M_x, with
$m(T)$ recursively defined as:

a. for each nullary operation $s_i: \; -> S_{i_j}$ we have $m(\; s_i \;) = m_o(\; s_i \;)$ with $m_o(\; s_i \;)$ defined as

- if s_i was defined in a requirement R_y, then $m_o(\; s_i \;) = m_{y_o}(\; s_i \;)$

- otherwise $m_o(\; s_i \;) = s_i$

b. for each nonnullary operation $s_i: \; S_{i_1} * S_{i_2} * ... * S_{i_k} -> S_{i_j}$ we have $m(\; s_i(\; T_1, \; T_2, \; ..., \; T_k \;) \;) = m_o(\; s_i \;)(\; m(\; T_1 \;), \; m(\; T_2 \;), \; ..., \; m(\; T_k \;) \;)$

c. for each variable x of sort S_i we have $m(\; x \;) = x'$ with x' being of sort $m_s(\; S_i \;)$

Notice that each claimed requirement corresponds to one module only. Parameter morphisms are defined in such a way that the modularity of the requirements is preserved.

3.4.2 Instantiations

Standard Parameter Passing

We now come to the problem of parameter passing. The problem of parameterized parameter passing, whereby the actual parameters are sorts and/or operation names defined in the modules or the claimed requirements of a scheme, will be treated in Section 3.4.7.

Instantiation Constraint

The parameter binding mechanism, which allows us to replace all occurrences of the formal parameters of a scheme (i.e. the sorts and operation names defined in the claimed requirements of the scheme) by their corresponding actual parameters (i.e. the sorts and operation names listed after the keywords as in an instantiation), must be a parameter morphism. This is called the *instantiation constraint*. For instance, in Fig. 3/21, the binding of the requirements Index and Attribute to respectively the modules Nat and Iden, forms a parameter morphism. This morphism consists of { { (Index, Nat) }, { (Attribute, Iden) } } and { { (_ = _, _ = _) }, { (error, undefined) } }. It preserves the rank of the operations

_ = _: Index * Index -> Bool;

error: -> Attribute;

since

    _ = _: Nat * Nat -> Bool;
    undefined: -> Iden;

The axioms are preserved as well since

    declare i', i_1', i_2', i_3': Nat;
    axioms
      i' = i' == true;
      i_1' = i_2' == i_2' = i_1';
      (i_1' = i_2') and (i_2' = i_3') $\Rightarrow$ (i_1' = i_3') == true;

can be proved using equational reasoning and induction.

Equivalent Specification

The result of an *instantiation* is defined in terms of *equivalent modules*. Given a scheme S containing modules SM_i and given an instantiation of the scheme S, the instantiation is equivalent to the modules SM_i' obtained as follows. Each module SM_i' is derived from SM_i by replacing the "all ..." and "all except ..." parts in the import and export clauses by explicit lists and consecutively replacing all occurrences of formal parameters by the actual parameters as indicated by the parameter morphism.

From now on, a *specification* may contain modules, schemes and instantiations. If all instantiations of a specification are replaced by their equivalent modules and the schemes are eliminated, we obtain its *equivalent specification*. The *abstract data types* defined by a specification are the abstract data types defined by its equivalent specification.

As an illustration, consider the example of the Array in Fig. 3/21. The instantiation of Fig. 3/21 is equivalent to the specification of Fig. 3/22.

```
module Array;
  import Bool, true, false, not _ from Bool;
    Nat, _ = _ from Nat;
    Iden, undefined from Iden;
  export all;
  sort Array;
  operations
    empty: -> Array;
```

```
    _[ _ / _ ]: Array * Iden * Nat -> Array;
    isundefined: Array * Nat -> Bool;
    read: Array * Nat -> Iden;
  declare ar: Array;   i, i₁, i₂: Nat;   at, at₁, at₂: Iden;
  axioms
    not ( i₁ = i₂ ) ⇏ ar [ at₁ / i₁ ] [ at₂ / i₂ ] == ar [ at₂ / i₂ ] [ at₁ / i₁ ];
    ar [ at₁ / i ] [ at₂ / i ] == ar [ at₂ / i ];
    isundefined( empty, i ) == true;
    isundefined( ar [ at / i₁ ], i₂ ) ==
      if i₁ = i₂
        then false
        else isundefined( ar, i₂ )
      end if;
    read( empty, i ) == undefined;
    read( ar [ at / i₁ ], i₂ ) ==
      if i₁ = i₂
        then at
        else read( ar, i₂ )
      end if;
  end module Array;
```

Fig. 3/22

If sorts or operations defined in an instantiation are needed elsewhere outside the instantiation, they must be imported from the equivalent modules. Assume, e.g., the operation isundefined that is defined by the instantiation of Fig. 3/21, is needed in a module, then the operation isundefined must be imported from the equivalent module Array that was shown in Fig. 3/22.

Modules can be interpreted as special cases of schemes: a module is a scheme that has no claimed requirements (thus no formal parameters) and that is immediately instantiated.

It is important to notice that instantiating schemes is quite different in nature from importing sorts or operations. If schemes are instantiated, new abstract data types are defined. But if sorts and operations are imported, existing abstract data types are used (shared).

3.4.3 Requirements and Induction

It is important to notice that induction (see Section 2.17) must not be used to derive new axioms for sorts defined in requirements. Intuitively speaking, these sorts are in fact formal parameters that will not necessarily be bound by the parameter mechanism with a termalgebra of their (formal) operations.

Take sort Attribute of the requirement Attribute, see Fig. 3/20; we could prove by induction that

declare at_1, at_2: Attribute;
axiom
    $at_1 == at_2$; $-- 0 --$

Indeed, we have no induction conclusion and only one induction base

axiom
    error == error; $-- 1 --$

which can be derived by means of the reflexivity rule of equational reasoning. It is clear that such reasoning by induction does not make any sense.

3.4.4 Remarks on Hierarchical Constraints

A specification is *hierarchical* if and only if its equivalent specification is hierarchical. For instance, the specification of Fig. 3/21 is hierarchical because the equivalent specification, which was given in Fig. 3/22, is hierarchical. An example of a specification which is not hierarchical is shown in Fig. 3/23, where StackScheme is instantiated with Item as Array, and ArrayScheme is instantiated with Attribute as Stack.

```
instantiate StackScheme;
  with Item as Array,
    Item as Array,
    error as empty;
  end instantiate StackScheme;

instantiate ArrayScheme;
  with Index as Nat,
    Index as Nat,
    _ = _ as _ = _;
  with Attribute as Stack,
    Attribute as Stack,
    error as newstack;
  end instantiate;
```

Fig. 3/23

Our specification language allows non-hierarchical specifications to be built. Although non-hierarchical specifications can be very useful, we must keep in mind that we cannot benefit from the additional safety obtained by verifying hierarchical constraints.

A hierarchical specification (containing modules, schemes and instantiations) is said to meet the *hierarchical constraints* if its equivalent specification meets the hierarchical constraints (see Section 3.2) and if no scheme may cause violations of the hierarchical constraints for any possible instantiation.

We now give three rules of thumb for detecting schemes that may violate the hierarchical constraints for some of their instantiations. In this way, a number of pathological cases may be detected before any instantiation has come into existence.

1
☞ Consider the requirements of a scheme as modules. Then, the requirements must meet the first hierarchical constraint (no confusion).

Consider the specification of Fig. 3/24.

```
scheme S [
    requirement R;
      import all from Bool;
      ...
      sort X;
      operations
        x: -> X;
        f: X -> Bool;
        ...
      axioms
        f( x ) == true;
        f( x ) == false;
        ...
    end requirement R;
  ];
  ...
end scheme S;
```

Fig. 3/24

If the requirement R is considered as a module, the first hierarchical constraint (no confusion) is violated since we can prove by equational reasoning that

axiom
    true == false;

Although the terms true and false cannot be proved to be equal by equational reasoning in module Bool, they can after the addition of the requirement R considered as a module. Clearly, requirement R can never be bound by a parameter morphism with an actual module that meets the hierarchical constraints.

Notice that in the formulation of this rule of thumb only the first hierarchical constraint is mentioned, not the second one. Indeed, if we consider the requirement R of Fig. 3/25 as a module, the second hierarchical constraint is not met because, e.g. f(zero) cannot be reduced to true or false. However, the hierarchical constraints will not be violated at instantiation.

```
scheme S [
    requirement R;
      import Bool from Bool;   Nat from Nat;
      operation
        f: Nat -> Bool;
    end requirement R;
  ];
  ...
end scheme X;
```

Fig. 3/25

2
☞ Consider the requirements of a scheme as modules. Then, the modules defined in the scheme must meet the hierarchical constraints.

If we consider in Fig. 3/26 the requirement R as a module, the terms f and g cannot be proved to be equal by equational reasoning, but after the addition of module M they can. Therefore, the first hierarchical constraint (no confusion) is violated.

Indeed, if we instantiate scheme S of Fig. 3/26 by binding the requirement R with the module Bool, sort X with Bool, f with true and g with false, the equivalent module would violate the first hierarchical constraint.

```
scheme S [
    requirement R;
      export all;
      sort X;
```

```
        operations
          f: -> X;
          g: -> X;
       end requirement R;
     ];

     module M;
        import X, f, g from R;
        . . .
        axiom
          f == g;
        . . .
     end module M;
  end scheme S;
```

Fig. 3/26

Another example is shown in Fig. 3/27. If we consider the requirement R as a module, module M violates the second hierarchical constraint (no junk), since a new object, denoted by the nullary operation c, of sort X is defined and it cannot be proved to be equal to a or b.

```
scheme S [
    requirement R;
      export all;
      sort X;
      operations
        a, b: -> X;
    end requirement R;
  ];

  module M;
    import all from R;
    export all;
    operation
      c: -> X;
  end module M;
end scheme S;
```

Fig. 3/27

[3]

☞ Select one of the requirements of a scheme, we call it R. Try to add axioms to the requirement R in such a way that R considered as a module does not violate the first hierarchical constraint (no confusion). Then the other requirements (of the scheme) considered as modules and the modules of the scheme must not violate the first hierarchical constraint with respect to R. This process must be repeated for every requirement.

As an illustration of this rule of thumb, consider the scheme S in Fig. 3/28. If we add the axiom

axiom
    a == b;

to requirement R, requirement R considered as a module does not violate the first hierarchical constraint. However, module M does not meet the first hierarchical constraint any more after the addition.

```
scheme S [
    requirement R;
      export all;
      sort X;
      operations
        a, b: -> X;
      end requirement R;
    ];

    module M;
      . . .
      operation
        f: X -> Bool;
      . . .
      axioms
        f( a ) == true;
        f( b ) == false;
      . . .
    end module M;
end scheme S;
```

Fig. 3/28

Indeed, if we bind the formal sort X with Nat and both a and b with zero, the module equivalent to this instantiation would violate the first hierarchical constraint.

In general, verifying the hierarchical constraints is a very hard job. In Chapter 4 a subset of specifications will be considered for which they can be verified easily.

3.4.5 Renaming and Qualified Names

If a scheme is instantiated more than once, name conflicts may occur. Therefore, it is possible to rename for an instantiation the modules, sorts and operations defined in or claimed by the scheme. The renaming mechanism is analogous to the renaming in import clauses. In Fig. 3/29 the instantiation of Fig. 3/18 is extended with a renaming clause.

```
instantiate StackScheme
   rename
      Stack as Numbertable,
      newstack as inittable,
      push as entertable,
      isnewstack as isinittable,
      pop as leavetable,
      top as retrievetable;
   with Item as Nat,
      Item as Nat,
      error as zero;
end instantiate StackScheme;
```

Fig. 3/29

The equivalent module is given in Fig. 3/30. Notice that both the module name Stack and the sort name Stack have been renamed to Numbertable.

```
module Numbertable;
   import Nat, zero from Nat;
      Bool, true, false from Bool;
   export Numbertable, inittable, entertable, leavetable, retrievetable, isinittable;
   sort Numbertable;
   operations
      inittable: -> Numbertable;
      entertable: Numbertable * Nat -> Numbertable;
      leavetable: Numbertable -> Numbertable;
      retrievetable: Numbertable -> Nat;
      isinittable: Numbertable -> Bool;
   declare s: Numbertable;   it: Nat;
   axioms
      isinittable( inittable ) == true;
      isinittable( entertable( s, it ) ) == false;
      leavetable( inittable ) == inittable;
      leavetable( entertable( s, it ) ) == s;
      retrievetable( inittable ) == zero;
      retrievetable( entertable( s, it ) ) == it;
```

```
end module Numbertable;
```

Fig. 3/30

Renaming makes it possible to define, e.g., a stack of stacks of natural numbers, see Fig. 3/31.

```
instantiate StackScheme
  rename
    Stack as StackNat,
    newstack as newstackNat,
    push as pushNat,
    isnewstack as isnewstackNat,
    pop as popNat,
    top as topNat;
  with Item as Nat,
    Item as Nat,
    error as zero;
end instantiate StackScheme;

instantiate StackScheme
  rename
    Stack as StackStackNat,
    newstack as newstackStackNat,
    push as pushStackNat,
    isnewstack as isnewstackStackNat,
    pop as popStackNat,
    top as topStackNat;
  with Item as StackNat,
    Item as StackNat,
    error as newstackNat;
end instantiate StackScheme;
```

Fig. 3/31

In general, a rename clause has the following syntax:

```
<rename clause> = "rename"
  ( <item name> | <element name> ) "as" ( "identifier" | <pattern> )
  ( ","
  ( <item name> | <element name> ) "as" ( "identifier" | <pattern> )
  )*

<item name> = <sort name> | <operation name>

<element name> =
  <module name> | <scheme name> | <requirement name>
```

In the example of Fig. 3/32 sorts and operation names are qualified with the module (or requirement) name they are imported from in order to avoid name conflicts.

```
module Victim;
   import Iden from Iden;
     Nat from Nat;
     ...
   export all;
   ...
   operations
     name, street, village: ->Iden;
     number, zip: -> Nat;
     ...
end module Victim;

module Criminal;
   import Iden from Iden;
     Nat from Nat;
     ...
   export all;
   ...
   operations
     name, street, village: ->Iden;
     number, zip: -> Nat;
     ...
end module Criminal;

module Crime;
   import all from Victim, Criminal;
   ... Victim.name ...
   ... Criminal.name ...
end module Crime;
```

Fig. 3/32

3.4.6 *Partial Instantiations*

Consider a scheme S with requirements R_{x_1}, ..., R_{x_p}, $R_{x_{p+1}}$, ..., R_{x_r}. If none of the requirements $R_{x_{p+1}}$, ..., R_{x_r} is directly nor indirectly imported by the requirements R_{x_1}, ..., R_{x_p}, a *partial instantiation* is possible. A partial instantiation is an instantiation in which the formal parameters of the requirements R_{x_1}, ..., R_{x_p} only, are replaced by the actual parameters as explained by the partial parameter morphism. A partial parameter morphism is a parameter morphism from part of the requirements of a scheme, preserving the rank of the operations and preserving the axioms. The result of a partial instantiation is a new scheme. Therefore, a partial instantiation is only allowed on places where schemes are allowed. Partial instantiations are very useful in software design, since they enable the construction of new schemes from existing ones.

The ArrayScheme of Fig. 3/20 is partially instantiated in Fig. 3/33 by binding the requirement Index to the module Nat.

```
instantiate ArrayScheme rename ArrayScheme as NatArrayScheme;
   with Index as Nat,
     Index as Nat,
     _ = _ as _ = _;
   end instantiate;
```

Fig. 3/33

The resulting scheme is equivalent to Fig. 3/34.

```
scheme NatArrayScheme [
   requirement Attribute;
     export all;
     sort Attribute;
     operation
       error: -> Attribute;
   end requirement Attribute;
];

module Array;
   import Bool, true, false, not _ from Bool;
     all from Attribute;   Nat, _ = _ from Nat;
   export all;
   sort Array;
   operations
     empty: -> Array;
     _ [ _ / _ ]: Array * Attribute * Nat -> Array;
     isundefined: Array * Nat -> Bool;
     read: Array * Nat -> Attribute;
   declare ar: Array;   i, i₁, i₂: Nat;   at, at₁, at₂: Attribute;
   axioms
```

$not (i_1 = i_2) \Rightarrow ar [at_1 / i_1][at_2 / i_2] == ar [at_2 / i_2][at_1 / i_1];$
$ar [at_1 / i][at_2 / i] == ar [at_2 / i];$
$isundefined(empty, i) == true;$
$isundefined(ar [at / i_1], i_2) ==$
$\quad if \ i_1 = i_2$

```
           then false
           else isundefined( ar, i₂ )
        end if;
     read( empty, i ) == error;
     read( ar [ at / i₁ ], i₂ ) ==
        if i₁ = i₂
           then at
           else read( ar, i₂ )
        end if;
  end module Array;
end scheme NatArrayScheme;
```

Fig. 3/34

3.4.7 *Parameterized Parameter Passing*

This section treats the problem of *parameterized parameter passing*, with the actual parameters being sorts and/or operation names defined in the modules or the claimed requirements of a scheme.

We defined a parameter morphism as two families of mappings from the claimed requirements R_1, R_2, ..., R_r of a scheme S to modules M_1, M_2, ..., M_r. If a scheme S is instantiated within another scheme S', each requirement R_y' of S' may be used as a module M_x for the parameter morphism in the instantiation of S.

As an example we want to insert the scheme ArrayScheme (with Index and Attribute as requirements), which was defined in Fig. 3/20, into the scheme StackScheme (with Item as requirement), which was defined in Fig. 3/17, resulting in the new scheme StackArrayScheme (with Index and Attribute as requirements). Of course, the meaning of the resulting scheme depends on the parameter passing mechanism between the two schemes. The skeletons of the schemes StackScheme and ArrayScheme and the resulting scheme StackArrayScheme are given below.

```
scheme StackScheme [
   requirement Item;
     export all;
     sort Item;
     operation
       error: -> Item;
   end requirement Item;
];

module Stack;
   ...  -- see Fig. 3/17
end module Stack;
```

```
end scheme StackScheme;


scheme ArrayScheme [
    requirement Attribute;
      export all;
      sort Attribute;
      operation
        error: -> Attribute;
      end requirement Attribute;

    requirement Index;
      import Bool, true, _ and _ from Bool;
      export all;
      sort Index;
      operation
        _ = _: Index * Index -> Bool;
      declare i, i₁, i₂, i₃: Index;
      axioms
        i = i  ==  true;
        i₁ = i₂  ==  i₂ = i₁;
        ( i₁ = i₂ ) and ( i₂ = i₃ ) ⇒ ( i₁ = i₃ )  ==  true;
      end requirement Index;
    ];

  module Array;
    ...  -- see Fig. 3/22
  end module;
end scheme ArrayScheme;


scheme StackArrayScheme [
    requirement Attribute;
      export all;
      sort Attribute;
      operation
        error: -> Attribute;
      end requirement Attribute;

    requirement Index;
      import Bool, true, _ and _ from Bool;
      export all;
      sort Index;
      operation
        _ = _: Index * Index -> Bool;
      declare i, i₁, i₂, i₃: Index;
      axioms
        i = i  ==  true;
        i₁ = i₂  ==  i₂ = i₁;
        ( i₁ = i₂ ) and ( i₂ = i₃ ) ⇒ ( i₁ = i₃ )  ==  true;
      end requirement Index;
    ];

  instantiate ArrayScheme;
    with Index as Index,
      Index as Index,
      _ = _ as _ = _;
```

```
        with Attribute as Attribute,
          Attribute as Attribute,
          error as error;
        end instantiate ArrayScheme;

      instantiate StackScheme;
        with Item as Array,
          Item as Array,
          error as empty;
        end instantiate StackScheme;
      end scheme StackArrayScheme;
```

Fig. 3/35

Notice that the morphism of the instantiation of ArrayScheme maps the requirements Index and Attribute of ArrayScheme to the requirements Index and Attribute of StackArrayScheme.

The equivalent scheme of StackArrayScheme is given in Fig. 3/36.

```
scheme StackArrayScheme [
    requirement Attribute;
      export all;
      sort Attribute;
      operation
        error: -> Attribute;
      end requirement Attribute;

    requirement Index;
      import Bool, true, _ and _ from Bool;
      export all;
      sort Index;
      operation
        _ = _: Index * Index -> Bool;
      declare i, i₁, i₂, i₃: Index;
      axioms
        i = i == true;
        i₁ = i₂ == i₂ = i₁;
        ( i₁ = i₂ ) and ( i₂ = i₃ ) ⇒ ( i₁ = i₃ )  ==  true;
      end requirement Index;
    ];

    module Array;
      import Bool, true, false, not _ from Bool;
        all from Attribute, Index;
      export all;
      sort Array;
      operations
        empty: -> Array;
        _[ _ / _ ]: Array * Attribute * Index -> Array;
        isundefined: Array * Index -> Bool;
        read: Array * Index -> Attribute;
```

```
    declare ar: Array;   i, i₁, i₂: Index;   at: Attribute;
    axioms
      not ( i₁ = i₂ ) ⇒ ar [ at₁ / i₁ ] [ at₂ / i₂ ] == ar [ at₂ / i₂ ] [ at₁ / i₁ ];
      ar [ at₁ / i ] [ at₂ / i ] == ar [ at₂ / i ];
      isundefined( empty, i ) == true;
      isundefined( ar [ at / i₁ ], i₂ ) ==
        if i₁ = i₂
          then false
          else isundefined( ar, i₂ )
        end if;
      read( empty, i ) == error;
      read( ar [ at / i₁ ], i₂ ) ==
        if i₁ = i₂
          then at
          else read( ar, i₂ )
        end if;
  end module Array;

  module Stack;
    import Array, empty from Array;
      Bool, true, false from Bool;
    export all;
    sort Stack;
    operations
      newstack: -> Stack;
      push: Stack * Array -> Stack;
      isnewstack: Stack -> Bool;
      pop: Stack -> Stack;
      top: Stack -> Array;
    declare s: Stack;   a: Array;
    axioms
      isnewstack( newstack ) == true;
      isnewstack( push( s, a ) ) == false;
      pop( newstack ) == newstack;
      pop( push( s, a ) ) == s;
      top( newstack ) == empty;
      top( push( s, a ) ) == a;
  end module Stack;
end scheme StackArrayScheme;
```

Fig. 3/36

StackArrayScheme has been instantiated in Fig. 3/37.

```
instantiate StackArrayScheme;
  with Index as Nat,
    Index as Nat,
    _ = _ as _ = _;
  with Attribute as Iden,
    Attribute as Iden,
    error as undefined;
```

> end instantiate StackArrayScheme;

Fig. 3/37

Instead of combining the two schemes into a new scheme and then instantiating it, we can also first instantiate ArrayScheme and then instantiate StackScheme with its result. This has been done in Fig. 3/38.

```
instantiate ArrayScheme;
  with Index as Nat,
    Index as Nat,
    _ = _ as _ = _;
  with Attribute as Iden,
    Attribute as Iden,
    error as undefined;
end instantiate ArrayScheme;

instantiate StackScheme;
  with Item as Array,
    Item as Array,
    error as empty;
end instantiate StackScheme;
```

Fig. 3/38

Both approaches yield the same results. Although the composition of schemes is a parameterized composition (because it depends on the parameter morphisms), it makes sense to speak of a composition. Actually the composition of schemes behaves like the usual composition of functions where we have associativity, i.e. $f \circ (g \circ h) = (f \circ g) \circ h$, and compatibility with evaluation, i.e. $(f \circ g) (x) = f(g(x))$ [Ehrig84, Ehrig85].

3.4.8 Parameterizing Requirements

Analogous to the parameterization of a group of modules, a group of requirements can be parameterized in exactly the same way. An example is shown in Fig. 3/39.

```
scheme SomeOperationRequirementScheme [
  requirement Item;
    export all;
    sort X;
```

```
      end requirement Item;
    ];
    requirement SomeOperation;
      import X from Item;
    export error;
    operation
      error: -> X;
    end requirement SomeOperation;
end scheme SomeOperationRequirementScheme;

scheme Y [
    requirement Objects;
      export Things;
      sort Things;
    end requirement Objects;

    instantiate SomeOperationRequirementScheme;
      with Item as Objects,
        X as Things;
    end instantiate;
    ];
    . . .
end scheme Y;
```

Fig. 3/39

In the given example the scheme SomeOperationRequirementScheme has been parameterized by the requirement Item. In scheme Y the scheme SomeOperationRequirementScheme is instantiated with requirement Objects. The result of the instantiation is a requirement SomeOperation where a nullary operation is requested. In Fig. 3/40 an equivalent specification is given.

```
scheme Y [
    requirement Objects;
      export Things;
      sort Things;
    end requirement Objects;

    requirement SomeOperation;
      import Things from Objects;
    export error;
    operation
      error: -> Things;
    end requirement SomeOperation;
    ];
    . . .
end scheme Y;
```

Fig. 3/40

Scheme SomeOperationRequirementScheme of Fig. 3/39 may also be instantiated as is shown in Fig. 3/41, where the requirement Item is bound with a module.

```
scheme Z [
    instantiate SomeOperationRequirementScheme;
      with Item as Nat,
        X as Nat;
    end instantiate;
  ];
  . . .
end scheme Z;
```

Fig. 3/41

Fig. 3/41 is equivalent to Fig. 3/42.

```
scheme Z [
    requirement SomeOperation;
      import Nat from Nat;
      export error;
      operation
        error: -> Nat;
    end requirement SomeOperation;
  ];
  . . .
end scheme Z;
```

Fig. 3/42

Using schemes of requirements, Fig. 3/35 can be rewritten as in Fig. 3/43.

```
scheme ItemRequirementScheme;
  requirement Item;
    export all;
    sort Item;
    operation
      error: -> Item;
  end requirement Item;
end scheme ItemRequirementScheme;


scheme StackScheme [ instantiate ItemRequirementScheme; end instantiate; ];
```

```
   module Stack;
      ...  -- see Fig. 3/17
   end module Stack;
end scheme StackScheme;


scheme AttributeRequirementScheme;
   requirement Attribute;
      export all;
      sort Attribute;
      operation
         error: -> Attribute;
   end requirement Attribute;
end scheme AttributeRequirementScheme;


scheme IndexRequirementScheme;
   requirement Index;
      import Bool, true, _ and _ from Bool;
      export all;
      sort Index;
      operation
         _ = _: Index * Index -> Bool;
      declare i, i₁, i₂, i₃: Index;
      axioms
         i = i  ==  true;
         i₁ = i₂  ==  i₂ = i₁;
         ( i₁ = i₂ ) and ( i₂ = i₃ ) ⇒ ( i₁ = i₃ )  ==  true;
   end requirement Index;
end scheme IndexRequirementScheme;


scheme ArrayScheme [
      instantiate AttributeRequirementScheme; end instantiate;
      instantiate IndexRequirementScheme ; end instantiate; ]
   ];
   module Array;
      ...  -- see Fig. 3/22
   end module;
end scheme ArrayScheme;


scheme StackArrayScheme [
      instantiate AttributeRequirementScheme; end instantiate;
      instantiate IndexRequirementScheme; end instantiate; ];
   ];

   instantiate ArrayScheme;
      with Index as Index,
         Index as Index,
         _ = _ as _ = _;
      with Attribute as Attribute,
         Attribute as Attribute,
         error as error;
   end instantiate ArrayScheme;
```

```
instantiate StackScheme;
  with Item as Array,
    Item as Array,
      error as empty;
end instantiate StackScheme;
end scheme StackArrayScheme;
```

Fig. 3/43

In this section we have shown that the idea of parameterization as it has been applied to groups of modules can be applied to groups of requirements as well, resulting in a very orthogonal language definition. Even a mixed group of modules and requirements can be parameterized. In Section 4.10 we will discuss where such a mixed group of requirements and modules does make sense.

3.5 Clusters

As mentioned in Section 3.1.1, a specification forms a directed graph. Making this graph acyclic is not always possible because of mutual recursivities between the abstract data types. Collecting the modules of the specification into one big module would reduce the readability. An example of recursivity can be found in the algebraic specification of Karel The Robot [Lewi85b]. A selected part is given in Fig. 3/44. The module Commands defines the different commands of the robot, which are executed in a certain environment. The module Environment makes use of, among others, a library of newly defined commands. In module Library a library is defined as a mapping from identifiers to commands. The import of the modules Commands, Environment and Library is recursively defined.

```
module Position;
  import ...;
  export  Pos, forward to Commands; ...
  sort Pos;
  operations
    makePosition: ... -> Pos;
    forward: Pos -> Pos;
    ...
end module Position;

module Library;
  import Com from Commands;
```

```
      Iden from Identifiers;
    export Lib to Environment, Commands;
    sort Lib;
    operations
      newlib: -> Lib;
      addlib: Lib * Iden * Com -> Lib;
      ...
  end module Library;

  module Environment;
    import Lib from Library; ...
    export Env, makeEnv to Commands; ...
    sort Env;
    operations
      makeEnv: ... * Lib * ... -> Env;
      ...
  end module Environment;

  module Commands;
    import Env, makeEnv from Environment;
      Pos, forward from Position;
      Lib from Library; ...
    export Com to Library; ...
    sort Com;
    operations
      move, turnleft: -> Com;
      ...
      C: Com * Env -> Env;
    declare pos: Pos;   lib: Lib;
    axioms
      C( move, makeEnv( pos, ..., lib, ... ) ) ==
        ... makeEnv( forward( pos ), ..., lib, ... ) ...;
  end module Commands;
```

Fig. 3/44

The recursive dependencies between the modules Commands, Environment and Library are inherent in the specified problem. The cyclic graph of modules can be transformed into a hierarchy of modules by grouping the mutually recursive modules into one supermodule, called *cluster*. A cluster is a simple packing of individual modules involved in a loop in a directed graph. A cluster has the following syntax:

```
<cluster> =
  "cluster" [ <cluster name> ] ";"
    ( <module> | <instantiation> | <requirement> )+
  "end" "cluster" [ <cluster name> ] ";"
```

An example of a cluster is shown in Fig. 3/45.

```
module Position;
  import ...;
  export  Pos, forward to Commands; ...
  sort Pos;
  operations
    makePosition: ... -> Pos;
    forward: Pos -> Pos;
    ...
end module Position;

cluster Robot;

  module Library;
    import Com from Commands;
      Iden from Identifiers;
    export Lib to Environment, Commands;
    sort Lib;
    operations
      newlib: -> Lib;
      addlib: Lib * Iden * Com -> Lib;
      ...
  end module Library;

  module Environment;
    import Lib from Library; ...
    export Env, makeEnv to Commands; ...
    sort Env;
    operations
      makeEnv: ... * Lib * ... -> Env;
      ...
  end module Environment;

  module Commands;
    import Env, makeEnv from Environment;
      Pos, forward from Position;
      Lib from Library; ...
    export Com to Library; ...
    sort Com;
    operations
      move, turnleft: -> Com;
      ...
      C: Com * Env -> Env;
    declare pos: Pos;   lib: Lib;
    axioms
      C( move, makeEnv( pos, ..., lib, ... ) ) ==
        ... makeEnv( forward( pos ), ..., lib, ... ) ...;
  end module Commands;

end cluster Robot;
```

Fig. 3/45

3.6 Bibliographic Notes

Modularity and Hierarchical Specifications

Since the early beginning of algebraic specifications, most abstract data types described in literature have been of a hierarchical nature. In [Goguen78] a classification of techniques is given.

- An abstract data type that does not use other abstract data types and is defined without axioms, is called a *fundamental type*.

- If a new module that imposes further axioms on an already existing abstract data type is added, the resulting type is called the *quotient* of the old one. E.g., set can be defined as a quotient of bag. Notice that this violates our first hierarchical constraint.

- If abstract data types are enriched with new operations meeting our hierarchical constraints, but no new sorts are defined, it is called an *enrichment*.

- If both new operations and new sorts meeting our hierarchical constraints are defined, it is called an *extension*.

- A new type can also be defined as n-tuples of existing abstract data types. This is called *tupling of types*.

Using the terminology of [Goguen78], if the hierarchical constraints are met, the existing abstract data types are said to be *protected*.

If a hierarchy meets our first hierarchical constraint, it is called *consistent* in [Ehrig85], whereas a hierarchy that meets our second hierarchical constraint is called *complete*. Generally, the problem of whether the hierarchical constraints are met is undecidable [Ehrig85].

[Futatsugi85] calls a module *protecting* if it meets our hierarchical constraints, it is called *extending* if it meets our first hierarchical constraint, and it is called *using* otherwise.

In [Nakajima80] an algebraic specification language, called iota, is proposed. In iota a program consists of a tree-like hierarchy of modular components. Our modules and schemes correspond to their *type modules* and *procedure modules*, our requirements correspond to their *sype modules*.

In [Bergstra85] a graphical notation for hierarchies of modules and schemes, called *structured diagrams*, is proposed. Each module (scheme) is represented by a rectangular box. The name of each module (scheme) is shown at the bottom of its box. All modules imported by a module (scheme) X are represented by structure diagrams inside the box representing X. All requirements of a scheme are represented by ellipses carrying their names. For instance, the structure diagram of the scheme Stack of Fig. 3/17 is given in Fig. 3/46.

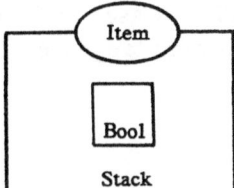

Fig. 3/46

An instantiation is represented by lines joining the requirements of the scheme to the modules in which the corresponding actual parameters are defined. For instance, the module StackNat of Fig. 3/18 is defined by binding the requirement Item to the module Nat. This is shown in Fig. 3/47.

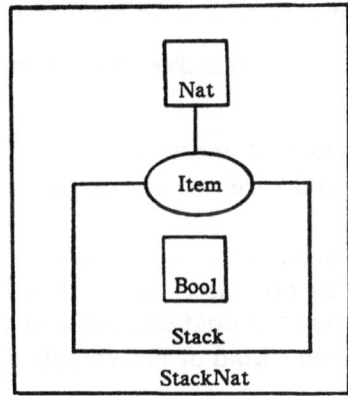

Fig. 3/47

Our import and export clauses were based on the import clauses of Modula-2 [Wirth82].

The need for a cluster structure has appeared in [Lewi85b]. The recursive nature of sorts and operations makes the use of a hierarchy of modules impossible there.

Notational Extensions

In most articles ifthenelse constructs are used as built-in operations. Conditional axioms are used in [Laut83] and in OBJ [Goguen84c, Futatsugi85]. The mixfix notation was first introduced for algebraic specifications in the iota language [Nakajima80] and the OBJ language [Goguen82, Goguen84c, Futatsugi85]. Case and let constructs are frequently used in functional programming languages.

Parameterized Specifications

Although the first publications on algebraic specifications already used parameterized specifications, theoretical studies originally did not treat generics [Goguen78, Guttag78a]. The first fundamental contributions to the theory of parameterized specifications were [Ehrig78, Thatcher78, Burstall80]. A standard work is [Ehrig85], where the semantics of a parameterized specification are defined as a *free functor*, which is a fundamental concept in *category theory* [Hilton74, Goldblatt79]. In [Ehrig84, Ehrig85] it is proved that

- the actual parameters are protected if parameter morphisms are used

- the composition of schemes is associative and compatible with evaluation.

In [Ganzinger81] it is also shown that most of the results concerning parameter passing treated with initial algebras can be transmitted in the framework of final algebras.

Our ideas about (parameter) morphisms, standard parameter passing and parameterized parameter passing are based on [Ehrig84]. Notice that we did not modify the mathematical foundations defined in Chapter 2. Actually, we treat parameterization as a kind of macro-substitution.

ACT ONE

ACT ONE (*A*lgebraic *S*pecification *T*echniques for *C*orrect and *T*rusty *S*oftware *S*ystems) is an algebraic specification language developed at the Technical University in Berlin by Hartmut Ehrig and Bernd Mahr [Ehrig85]. An example is given in Fig. 3/48.

In ACT ONE the concept of *combination* is useful to combine specifications or to add sorts or operations to a given specification such that a hierarchy is built. It is analogous to our import clause mechanism of Section 3.1.1. In Fig. 3/49 the specifications of nat and bool are extended with the specification of the stack.

```
def nat is
  sorts nat
  opns
    0: -> nat
    SUCC: nat -> nat
    ADD: nat nat -> nat
  eqns of sort nat
    for all n, m in nat:
    ADD( n, 0 ) = n
    ADD( n, SUCC( m ) ) = SUCC( ADD( n, m ) )
end of def
```

Fig. 3/48

```
def stack is nat and bool
  sorts stack
  opns
    EMPTY: -> stack
    PUSH: stack nat -> stack
    ISEMPTY: stack -> bool
    TOP: stack -> nat
    POP: stack -> stack
  eqns of sort bool
    ISEMPTY( EMPTY ) = TRUE
    ...
end def
```

Fig. 3/49

In ACT ONE a scheme is called a *parameterized specification* and an instantiation is called an *actualization*. An example of a parameterized specification is shown in Fig. 3/50.

```
def parstack is
  formal sorts data
  formal opns error: -> data
  sorts stack
  opns
    EMPTY: -> parstack
    ...
end of def
```

Fig. 3/50

OBJ

In the specification language OBJ2 [Goguen84c, Futatsugi85] an analogous parameterization mechanism is provided. Requirements are called *theories* and morphisms are called *views*. If no ambiguity rises, default views are possible by only indicating to which module a theory is mapped. Also *parameterized theories* may be used. Parameterizing a theory is in fact claiming another requirement and importing from this requirement. OBJ2 differs from our algebraic specification language in that in OBJ2 only one module can be parameterized, whereas our schemes may contain several modules.

The OBJ family of algebraic specification languages has been developed by the group of Goguen. It was originally based on the specification language Clear [Burstall77]. The oldest member of this family is OBJ0, later called OBJT [Goguen79]. OBJ1 was a significant improvement by including associative-commutative rewriting [Goguen83]. The main characteristic of OBJ2 is the concept of *subsorts*. At the moment, OBJ3 is being developed [Goguen87c]. OBJ2 has also an object-oriented version, called FOOPS [Goguen86]. A combination of equational logic of OBJ with the Horn clause logic of Prolog resulted in Eqlog [Goguen 84d].

A very typical feature of OBJ2 is the concept of *subsorts* [Futatsugi85, Goguen85, Goguen87b]. One sort of data is often contained in another, e.g., the natural numbers are contained in the integers. Then the sort Nat is a subsort of Int, written as Nat < Int. Moreover, an operation may restrict to subsorts of its rank and still be "the same" operation [Futatsugi85]. For example, the addition operation _ + _: Nat Nat -> Nat is a restriction of _ + _: Int Int -> Int.

The following specification introduces the sort Int of integers with the subsort Nat of natural numbers. Furthermore, the non-zero natural numbers are a subsort of the natural numbers and a subsort of the non-zero integers which in turn are a subsort of the integers, see Fig. 3/51.

```
obj INT is
   sorts NzNat Nat NzInt Int .
   subsorts NzNat < Nat < Int .
   subsorts NzNat < NzInt < Int .
   op 0 : -> Nat .
   op s_ : Nat -> NzNat .
   op -_ : Nat -> Int .
   op -_ : NzNat -> NzInt .
   op _+_ : Int Int -> Int [assoc comm id: 0]
   op _*_ : Int Int -> Int [assoc comm]
   vars U V : Nat .
   var X : Int .
   vars A B : NzNat .
   eq : - 0 = 0 .
```

```
eq : X + 0 = X .
eq : (s U) + (s V) = s s (U + V) .
eq : (- s U) + (s V) = (- U) + V .
eq : (- s U) + (- s V) = - s s (U + V) .
eq : X * 0 = 0 .
eq : X * s V = X * V + X .
eq : X * - s V = - (X * V + X) .
jbo
```

Fig. 3/51

An object (abbreviated obj) is a module containing executable code [Futatsugi85]. This object is called INT. The nullary operation 0 denotes a natural number. The result of the successor operation s_ is a non-zero natural number. The unary operation -_ returns a (non-zero) integer if its argument is a (non-zero) natural number. Finally, the addition and multiplication operations are declared. The attribute *assoc* indicates that an operation is associative, and *id: 0* indicates that it has 0 as an identity. After the keywords *var* and *vars* variables are declared. Axioms are given after the keywords *eq*.

Although the logic of subsorts can be reduced to standard equational logic (i.e. based on many-sorted initial algebras) using coercing functions [Goguen85, Futatsugi85], a new mathematical foundation, called *order-sorted algebra approach*, is proposed in [Goguen85, Futatsugi85, Goguen87b].

4. Constructive Specifications

"Abstraction and specification must be the linchpins
of any effective approach to programming."
Barbara Liskov and John Guttag

Roughly speaking, constructive specifications are specifications that can always be directly implemented, enabling rapid prototyping. An important benefit from making constructive specifications is that it enables software designers and customers to get user feedback and hands-on experience with the system before the implementation gets started. In this way, design errors due to misunderstandings between designers and customers, as well as lack of understanding of service mechanisms can be detected and corrected at an early stage in the software life cycle. With constructive specifications, the boundaries between specification and implementation are not very sharp. Both may be considered as programs, but the former is of a higher level of abstraction (i.e. less implementation details) than the latter. So, making constructive specifications is comparable to writing programs. As for programming, not only insight but also discipline and style are necessary. Here, the style consists of dividing the operations into two groups, one for data abstractions (constructors) and one for procedural abstraction (non-constructor operations). The constructors provide us with a system of canonical forms. The axioms are considered as a left-to-right term rewriting system that reduces terms containing non-constructor operation names to terms built up of constructor names only. By introducing constraints of uniqueness and completeness, which can be checked mechanically, the chance of writing erroneous specifications can be reduced considerably. In this way, software correctness can be enhanced up to a large extent.

Constructive specifications have the advantage over non-constructive ones that they always give rise to rapid prototyping. However, non-constructive specifications often are of a higher level of abstraction than their constructive versions and, therefore, are more appropriate for system documentation purposes. It is our personal conviction that in a first step one has to try to construct a specification without considering any constructivity constraint. If we obtain a specification that is non-constructive, we build a constructive version of it in a second step. Some of the axioms found in the first step are then added to the constructive specification as provable theorems, representing valuable documentation of the system properties. As already mentioned, non-constructive specifications do not always form a left-to-right term rewriting system. However, they are very valuable in the early stages of the software life cycle when we only have some ideas about operation properties but are yet unable to describe them constructively. We must keep in mind that we probably aim at an implementation where we must eventually give algorithms. So eventually non-constructive specifications have to be replaced step by step by constructive ones.

Furthermore, constructor axioms are considered. A limited use of constructor axioms gives rise to semi-constructive specifications. Although constructor axioms cannot always be considered as pure left-to-right term rewriting rules, semi-constructive specifications can be directly implemented, enabling rapid prototyping.

One of the advantages of formal specification languages over traditional programming languages is that semantic properties (in the form of theorems) can be required from the actual parameters when parameterized specifications are used. In this chapter a three-step method to build such semantic interfaces is presented. The method is illustrated by means of an abstract data type defining geometric functions.

4.1 Simple Example

In this section we introduce the notions of constructors, non-constructor operations and constructivity by means of a simple example. The exact definitions will be given in Section 4.2.

Consider the specification of stacks in Fig. 4/1. It differs from the specification given in Fig. 3/17 in that the operations of module Stack are divided into two groups: constructors and non-constructor operations. In Fig. 4/1 the constructors are newstack and push whereas the non-constructor operations are isnewstack, pop and top. With the constructors we can generate all the objects of the abstract data type Stack and each object of the abstract data type can be denoted by just one constant term built up of newstack and push only. Non-constructor operations describe the functional behaviour of the objects of the abstract data type Stack. They are defined in terms of the constructors.

```
scheme StackScheme [
    requirement Item;
        export all to Stack;
        sort Item;
```

```
        operation
          error: -> Item;
      end requirement Item;
    ];

  module Stack;
    import Bool, true, false from Bool;   Item, error from Item;
    export all;
    sort Stack;
    constructors
      newstack: -> Stack;
      push: Stack * Item -> Stack;
    operations
      isnewstack: Stack -> Bool;
      pop: Stack -> Stack;
      top: Stack -> Item;
    declare s: Stack;   it: Item;
    operation axioms
      isnewstack( newstack ) == true;
      isnewstack( push( s, it ) ) == false;
      pop( newstack ) == newstack;
      pop( push( s, it ) ) == s;
      top( newstack ) == error;
      top( push( s, it ) ) == it;
  end module Stack;
end scheme StackScheme;
```

Fig. 4/1

The operation axioms of Stack can be seen as rules of a left-to-right term rewriting system that reduces variable-free terms containing non-constructor operation names to canonical forms built up of constructor names only. As an example, if StackScheme is instantiated by binding the requirement Item with a module defining natural numbers, the term

pop(push(pop(push(push(newstack, 5), 7)), 9))

can be reduced to

push(newstack, 5)

which is a canonical form. Notice that from now on we write, e.g., 5 instead of succ(succ(succ(succ(succ(zero))))).
Another example is the term

isnewstack(pop(push(pop(push(newstack, 5)), 7)))

which is reduced to

true

By using the operation axioms as left-to-right term rewriting rules, each non-constructor operation applied to the appropriate arguments can be symbolically executed yielding the answer in a canonical form. As we will see in Section 4.2, in order to use specifications as left-to-right term rewriting systems, the specification has to meet a number of constraints, called constructivity constraints. Constructive specifications are important for rapid prototyping.

Notice that from now on we use the term *operation axiom(s)* and the keyword **operation axiom(s)**, in order to distinguish this kind of axioms from constructor axioms, which will be defined in Section 4.6.

4.2 Constructive Specifications

We recall that in our terminology a specification consists of modules, instantiations and schemes (schemes consist of requirements, modules and instantiations), whereas an equivalent specification only consists of modules, see Section 3.4.2.

Constructor and Non-Constructor Operations

The operations are divided into two groups: *constructors* and *non-constructor operations*. Constructors are operations that are chosen so that every congruence class of the initial algebra contains a constant term built up of constructor names only. The constructors provide us with a system of canonical forms. Distinguishing between constructors and non-constructor operations is in fact distinguishing between *data abstraction* and *procedural abstraction*. Intuitively speaking, constructors are operations that generate objects of the abstract data type whereas non-constructor operations, called *operations* for short, rather describe the functional behaviour of the objects.

Constructiveness Constraints

A specification is said to meet the *constructiveness constraints* if for each module of the specification the following conditions hold:

1. The left-hand side of each axiom starts with a non-constructor operation name that is defined in the same module, and all proper subterms of the left-hand side are built up of variables and constructor names only. Furthermore, the choices of case arms are built up of variables and constructor names only.

2. A variable occurs at most once at the left-hand side of an axiom or in the choice of a case arm.

3. Only variables that are used at the left-hand side of an axiom, may be used at the right-hand side of the axiom. There are two exceptions: the variable introduced by a let construct may also be used in its let expression, and the variables introduced by the choice of a case arm may also be used in the corresponding expression.

4. Conditional axioms (see Section 3.3.3) are not allowed. But ifthenelse constructs are available as explained in Section 3.3.1.

5. All constructors of a sort must be defined in the module defining the sort.

These constraints can easily be checked in a mechanical way [Goovaerts84, Van Puymbroeck84].

Uniqueness and Completeness Constraints

Consider a specification within which a non-constructor operation is defined. The specification is said to meet the *uniqueness and completeness constraints with respect to that non-constructor operation*, if the left-hand sides of the axioms for the non-constructor operation cover its domain exactly once.

A specification is said to meet the *uniqueness and completeness constraints with respect to a case construct*, if the choices of the case arms of the case construct cover its domain exactly once.

A specification is said to meet the *uniqueness and completeness constraints*, if the specification (e.g., Fig. 4/1) meets these constraints with respect to each non-constructor operation and to each case construct. Also the uniqueness and completeness property can easily be checked in a mechanical way [Van Puymbroeck84].

Terminating Specifications

A specification (consisting of modules, schemes and instantiations) is *terminating* if the equivalent specification is terminating and if no scheme may be responsible for producing non-terminating specifications for any possible correct instantiation. An equivalent specification is *terminating* if no variable-free term can be reduced infinitely using the axioms as left-to-right term rewriting rules.

We now give a rule of thumb for detecting schemes that may be responsible for producing non-terminating specifications for some of their instantiations.

☞ Given a scheme consisting of requirements and modules. We apply the definition of termination to these modules, considering each variable of a sort defined in one of the requirements as a constructor name of that sort.

In general, the termination of the reduction process cannot be checked mechanically, unless if, e.g., only structural recursion [Boyer79, Bevers85, Bevers87] is used. The specification of Fig. 4/1 uses no recursion at all, and it is easy to check that the reduction process always terminates.

Constructive Specifications

A specification is *constructive* if the constructiveness, uniqueness and completeness constraints are met and if it is terminating. This property is called *constructivity*.

Notice that every congruence class of the initial algebra of a constructive specification contains just one constant term built up of constructor names only. A very interesting property is that the hierarchical constraints in constructive specifications are automatically met.

4.3 Theorems

Axioms of a non-constructive specification can be considered as *theorems* for the corresponding constructive specification. Strictly speaking, theorems in modules are redundant information with respect to the axioms, but they play an important role in the documentation to better understand specifications and to gain confidence that the specifications express what we have in mind. Theorems can be proved using equational reasoning and induction, see Chapter 2.

In Fig. 3/8 a non-constructive specification for the abstract data type of boolean values was given. In Fig. 4/2 we give a constructive specification of this data type. The remaining axioms of Fig. 3/8 are added as theorems.

```
module Bool
  export all;
  sort Bool;
  constructors
    true, false: -> Bool;
  operations
    not _: Bool -> Bool;
    _ and _: Bool * Bool -> Bool;
    _ or _: Bool * Bool -> Bool;
    _ => _: Bool * Bool -> Bool;
    _ <= _: Bool * Bool -> Bool;
    _ <=> _: Bool * Bool -> Bool;
  declare b, b₁, b₂, b₃: Bool;
  operation axioms
    not true == false;    not false == true;
    b and true == b;      b and false == false;
    b or true == true;    b or false == b;
    true => b == b;       false => b == true;
    b <= true == b;       b <= false == true;
    true <=> b == b;      false <=> b == not b;
  theorems
    b and b == b;    b or b == b;
    b₁ and b₂ == b₂ and b₁;    b₁ or b₂ == b₂ or b₁;
    b₁ and ( b₁ or b₂ ) == b₁;    b₁ or ( b₁ and b₂ ) == b₁;
    b and not b == false;   b or not b == true;
    not not b == b;
    ( b₁ and b₂ ) and b₃ == b₁ and ( b₂ and b₃ );
    ( b₁ or b₂ ) or b₃ == b₁ or ( b₂ or b₃ );
    b₁ and ( b₂ or b₃ ) == ( b₁ and b₂ ) or ( b₁ and b₃ );
    b₁ or ( b₂ and b₃ ) == ( b₁ or b₂ ) and ( b₁ or b₃ );
    b₁ => b₂ == if b₁ then b₂ else true end if;
    b₁ <= b₂ == b₂ => b₁;
    b₁ <=> b₂ == (b₁ => b₂) and (b₁ <= b₂);
  end module Bool;
```

Fig. 4/2

In our example of Fig. 4/2, the choice of constructors is straightforward. The operation axioms, however, can be constructed in many different ways. In the given specification the constructiveness, uniqueness and completeness constraints are met. This can be checked mechanically. Because the specification of Fig. 4/2 is also terminating, it is constructive.

Notice that the axioms of a requirement (e.g., Fig. 3/20) are not involved in the left-to-right term rewriting process. They only represent some conditions that must be met by the actual parameters to meet the instantiation constraints. They are in fact theorems, see Fig. 4/3. In these cases, instead of the keyword **axiom(s)**, we will write the keyword **theorem(s)** to indicate that the axioms are not taken into account for the constructiveness, uniqueness and completeness constraints and for the termination. Notice also that a requirement must not define formal constructors but only formal operations. The formal operations can be bound with actual constructors as well as with actual operations.

```
scheme ArrayScheme [
   requirement Attribute;
     export all;
     sort Attribute;
     operation
       error: -> Attribute;
   end requirement Attribute;

   requirement Index;
     import Bool, true, _ and _ from Bool;
     export all;
     sort Index;
     operation
       _ = _: Index * Index -> Bool;
     declare i, i1, i2, i3: Index;
     theorems
       i = i == true;
       i1 = i2 == i2 = i1;
       i1 = i2 and i2 = i3 => i1 = i3  ==  true;
   end requirement Index;
   ];

   module Array;
     import Bool, true, false, not _ from Bool;
       all from Attribute, Index;
     export all;
     sort Array;
     constructors
       empty: -> Array;
       _ [ _ / _ ]: Array * Attribute * Index -> Array;
     operations
       isundefined: Array * Index -> Bool;
       read: Array * Index -> Attribute;
     ...
   end module Array;
end scheme ArrayScheme;
```

Fig. 4/3

4.4 Equality Operation

The equalities of the congruence relations defined by the axioms can be simulated by user-defined equality operations. This is illustrated in Fig. 4/4 for the natural numbers.

```
module Nat;
  import Bool, true, false, _ and _ from Bool;
  export all;
  sort Nat;
  constructors
    zero: -> Nat;
    succ: Nat -> Nat;
  operation
    _ = _: Nat * Nat -> Bool;
  declare n, n_1, n_2, n_3: Nat;
  operation axioms
    zero = succ( n ) == false;
    zero = zero == true;
    succ( n ) = zero == false;
    succ( n_1 ) = succ( n_2 ) == n_1 = n_2;
  theorems
    n = n == true;  -- reflexivity
    n_1 = n_2 == n_2 = n_1;  -- symmetry
    ( n_1 = n_2 ) and ( n_2 = n_3 ) => n_1 = n_3 == true;  -- transitivity
end module Nat;
```

Fig. 4/4

It is important to notice the difference between some user-defined equality operation and the equality of the congruence relation of the initial algebra. In Fig. 4/5 an abstract data type containing an equality operation is specified in such a way that the objects denoted by a and b are different (i.e. they do not belong to the same congruence class) although the equality operation _ = _ indicates them as equal.

```
. . .
sort X;
constructors
  a: -> X;
  b: -> X;
```

```
operation
   _ = _: X * X -> Bool;
declare x₁, x₂: X;
operation axiom
   x₁ = x₂ == true;
   . . .
```

Fig. 4/5

4.5 Example

In Fig. 4/6 a generic specification is given for the data type List.
Comments are added to explain the meaning of the constructors and
operations in an informal way.

```
scheme ListScheme [
    requirement Item;
      import Bool, true, _ and _ from Bool;
      export all;
      sort Item;
      operations
        undefined: -> Item;
        _ = _: Item * Item -> Bool;
      declare it, it₁, it₂, it₃: Item;
      theorems
        it = it  ==  true;  -- reflexivity
        it₁ = it₂  ==  it₂ = it₁;  -- symmetry
        ( it₁ = it₂ ) and ( it₂ = it₃ ) ⇒ it₁ = it₃  ==  true;  -- transitivity
      end requirement Item;
    ];

    module List;
      import all from Bool, Item;
      export all;
      sort List;
      constructors
        nil: -> List;  -- denotes the empty List
        _ | _: Item * List -> List;  -- adds Item to List
      operations
        head: List -> Item;  -- returns the first Item of List
        tail: List -> List;  -- returns all but the first Item of List
        _ & _: List * List -> List; -- appends the first List to the second List
        delete: Item * List -> List; -- deletes the last occurrence of Item (if any) in List
        remove: List * List -> List; -- deletes in the second List the last occurrence of
          -- each Item which is enumerated in the first List
        _ isin _: Item * List -> Bool;  -- indicates whether Item is a member of List
        _ partof _: List * List -> Bool; -- indicates whether each item of the first List
```

```
               -- has at least the same number of occurrences in the second List
         permutation: List * List -> Bool;   -- indicates whether the two given Lists
               -- are permutations
      declare it, it₁, it₂: Item;   list, list₁, list₂: List;
      operation axioms
        head( nil ) == undefined;
        head( it | nil ) == it;
        head( it₂ | it₁ | list ) == head( it₁ | list );
        tail( nil ) == nil;
        tail( it | nil ) == nil;
        tail( it₂ | it₁ | list ) == it₂ | tail( it₁ | list );
        nil & list == list;
        ( it | list₁ ) & list₂ == it | ( list₁ & list₂ );
        delete( it, nil ) == nil;
        delete( it₁, it₂ | list ) ==
          if it₁ = it₂
            then list
            else it₂ | delete( it₁, list )
          end if;
        remove( nil, list ) == list;
        remove( it | list₁, list₂ ) == remove( list₁, delete( it, list₂ ) );
        it isin nil == false;
        it₁ isin it₂ | list ==
          if it₁ = it₂
            then true
            else it₁ isin list
          end if;
        nil partof list == true;
        it₁ | list₁ partof list₂ ==
          if it₁ isin list₂
            then list₁ partof delete( it₁, list₂ )
            else false
          end if;
        permutation( list₁, list₂ ) == ( list₁ partof list₂ ) and (list₂ partof list₁ );
    end module List;
  end scheme ListScheme;
```

Fig. 4/6

4.6 Constructor Axioms

The need for constructor axioms can best be explained through a simple
example. Consider the abstract data type Set that contains an empty set ∅,
the operation { _ } to create a singleton, the operations insert and delete to
put an item into or delete it from the set respectively, the operations _ ∪
_ and _ ∩ _ to take the union and the intersection of two sets
respectively, and the operation isin to test whether an item belongs to a set.
The operations part is shown in Fig. 4/7.

```
operations
  Ø: -> Set;
  { _ }: Item -> Set;
  insert, delete: Item * Set -> Set;
  _ ∪ _: Set * Set -> Set;
  _ ∩ _: Set * Set -> Set;
  isin: Item * Set -> Bool;
```

Fig. 4/7

In the next step we have to choose the constructors. Many solutions are possible. Mathematicians usually choose Ø, { _ } and _ ∪ _ as constructors. Programmers like to use Ø and insert. Still other combinations are possible. The complete scheme SetScheme is shown in Fig. 4/8, in which Ø and insert are chosen as constructors. The non-constructor operations are delete, { _ }, _ ∪ _, _ ∩ _ and isin. They are defined by describing their effect on terms built up of constructor names and variables only.

```
scheme ItemRequirementScheme;
  requirement Item;
    import Bool, true, _ and _ from Bool;
    export all;
    sort Item;
    operation
      _ = _: Item * Item -> Bool;
    declare it, it₁, it₂, it₃: Item;
    theorems
      it = it  ==  true;
      it₁ = it₂  ==  it₂ = it₁;
      ( it₁ = it₂ ) and ( it₂ = it₃ ) ⇒ it₁ = it₃  ==  true;
  end requirement Item;
end scheme ItemRequirementScheme;

scheme SetScheme [ instantiate ItemRequirementScheme; end instantiate; ];
  module Set;
    import Bool, true, false from Bool;
      all from Item;
    export all;
    sort Set;
    constructors
      Ø: -> Set;
      insert: Item * Set -> Set;
    operations
      delete: Item * Set -> Set;
      { _ }: Item -> Set;
```

```
     _ ∪ _: Set * Set -> Set;
     _ ∩ _: Set * Set -> Set;
    isin: Item * Set -> Bool;
  declare s, s₁, s₂: Set;   it, it₁, it₂: Item;
  operation axioms
    delete( it, ∅ ) == ∅;
    delete( it₁, insert( it₂, s ) ) ==
      if it₁ = it₂
        then delete( it₁, s )
        else insert( it₂, delete( it₁, s ) )
      end if;
    { it } == insert( it, ∅ );
    s ∪ ∅ == s;
    s₁ ∪ insert( it, s₂ ) == insert( it, s₁ ∪ s₂ );
    s ∩ ∅ == ∅;
    s₁ ∩ insert( it, s₂ ) ==
      if isin( it, s₁ )
        then insert( it, s₁ ∩ s₂ )
        else s₁ ∩ s₂
      end if;
    isin( it, ∅ ) == false;
    isin( it₁, insert( it₂, s ) ) ==
      if it₁ = it₂
        then true
        else isin( it₁, s )
      end if;
  end module Set;
end scheme SetScheme;
```

Fig. 4/8

Although this specification seems to define the abstract data type Set, it does not meet the following two important properties:

- the order of the insertions is irrelevant:

$$\text{insert}(it_1, \text{insert}(it_2, s)) == \text{insert}(it_2, \text{insert}(it_1, s));$$

- an inserted item may be added more than once without changing the set:

$$\text{insert}(it, \text{insert}(it, s)) == \text{insert}(it, s);$$

We have an analogous problem if other operations are chosen as constructors, e.g., ∅, { _ } and _ ∪ _, see Fig. 4/9.

```
scheme SetScheme [ instantiate ItemRequirementScheme; end instantiate; ];
  module Set;
    import Bool, true, false, _ or _ from Bool;
```

```
    all from Item;
  export all;
  sort Set;
  constructors
    Ø: -> Set;
    { _ }: Item -> Set;
    _ ∪ _: Set * Set -> Set;
  operations
    insert: Item * Set -> Set;
    delete: Item * Set -> Set;
    _ ∩ _: Set * Set -> Set;
    isin: Item * Set -> Bool;
  declare s, s₁, s₂: Set;   it, it₁, it₂: Item;
  operation axioms
    insert( it, s ) == { it } ∪ s;
    delete( it, Ø ) == Ø;
    delete( it₁, { it₂ } ) ==
      if it₁ = it₂
      then Ø
        else { it₂ }
      end if;
    delete( it, s₁ ∪ s₂ ) == delete( it, s₁ ) ∪ delete( it, s₂ )
    s ∩ Ø == Ø;
    s ∩ { it } ==
      if isin( it, s )
        then { it }
        else Ø
      end if;
    s ∩ ( s₁ ∪ s₂ ) == ( s ∩ s₁ ) ∪ ( s ∩ s₂ );
    isin( it, Ø ) == false;
    isin( it₁, { it₂ } ) ==
      if it₁ = it₂
        then true
        else false
      end if;
    isin( it, s₁ ∪ s₂ ) == isin( it, s₁ ) or isin( it, s₂ );
  end module Set;
end scheme SetScheme;
```

Fig. 4/9

This specification does not meet the following important properties:

- Ø is the neutral element of the union function:

  $$\varnothing \cup s == s; \quad s \cup \varnothing == s;$$

- the commutativity of the union function:

  $$s_1 \cup s_2 == s_2 \cup s_1;$$

- the associativity of the union function:

$$s_1 \cup (s_2 \cup s_3) == (s_1 \cup s_2) \cup s_3;$$

- and the idempotence of the union function:

$$s \cup s == s;$$

The properties given above are examples of constructor axioms. They cannot be derived as theorems from the specification. Notice that the use of such constructor axioms as left-to-right term rewriting rules would cause a termination problem.

A *constructor axiom* of a module is an axiom whose left- and right-hand side (but its condition if any) only consist of variables and constructor names defined in this module and that has a left- (and right-) hand side the sort of which is also defined in this module.

4.7 Semi-Constructive Specifications

Specifications containing constructor axioms do not meet the constructiveness constraints and thus, strictly speaking, are not constructive. This means that in general we cannot use such specifications as a left-to-right term rewriting system for rapid prototyping purposes. By imposing constraints on constructor axioms, rapid prototyping becomes still possible. These constraints are called semi-constructivity constraints and the specifications meeting these constraints are called semi-constructive.

A specification is said to be *semi-constructive* if the following *semi-constructivity constraints* hold:

- If the constructor axioms were deleted from the specification, the specification would become constructive.

- Starting from an arbitrary term built up of variables and constructor names of the specification, it is impossible to derive an infinite number of literally different terms using the constructor axioms as left-to-right term rewriting rules.

- The specification is ground confluent. A specification (consisting of modules, schemes and instantiations) is *ground confluent* if the equivalent specification is ground confluent and if no scheme may be responsible for producing specifications that are not ground confluent for any possible correct instantiation.

An equivalent specification is *ground confluent* if the following condition holds: If s, t_1 and t_2 are terms built up of constructor names only, such that both t_1 and t_2 are derived from s using the constructor axioms as left-to-right term rewriting rules, then there exists a term u built up of constructor names only such that u can be derived from t_1 as well as t_2 using the constructor axioms as left-to-right term rewriting rules. This property, called *ground confluence* [Huet80], is graphically represented in Fig. 4/10.

Fig. 4/10

We now give a rule of thumb for detecting schemes that may be responsible for producing specifications that are not ground confluent for some of their instantiations.

☞ Given a scheme consisting of requirements and modules. We apply the definition of ground confluency to these modules, considering each variable of a sort defined in one of the requirements as a constructor name of that sort.

By introducing semi-constructive specifications, a limited form of local non-constructivity is allowed. For each module, this non-constructivity (if any) is usually localized in a small number of constructor axioms. In general, the semi-constructivity constraints cannot be checked mechanically. In Fig. 4/11 the semi-constructive specification for sets is based on Fig. 4/8.

```
scheme SetScheme [ instantiate ItemRequirementScheme; end instantiate; ];
  module Set;
    import Bool, true, false from Bool;
      all from Item;
    export all;
    sort Set;
```

```
    constructors
      Ø: -> Set;
      insert: Item * Set -> Set;
    operations
      delete: Item * Set -> Set;
      { _ }: Item -> Set;
      _ ∪ _: Set * Set -> Set;
      _ ∩ _: Set * Set -> Set;
      isin: Item * Set -> Bool;
    declare s, s₁, s₂: Set;   it, it₁, it₂: Item;
    constructor axioms
      insert( it₁, insert( it₂, s ) ) == insert( it₂, insert( it₁, s ) );
      insert( it, insert( it, s ) ) == insert( it, s );
    operation axioms
      delete( it, Ø ) == Ø;
      delete( it₁, insert( it₂, s ) ) ==
        if it₁ = it₂
          then delete( it₁, s )
          else insert( it₂, delete( it₁, s ) )
        end if;
      { it } == insert( it, Ø );
      s ∪ Ø == s;
      s₁ ∪ insert( it, s₂ ) == insert( it, s₁ ∪ s₂ );
      s ∩ Ø == Ø;
      s₁ ∩ insert( it, s₂ ) ==
        if isin( it, s₁ )
          then insert( it, s₁ ∩ s₂ )
          else s₁ ∩ s₂
        end if;
      isin( it, Ø ) == false;
      isin( it₁, insert( it₂, s ) ) ==
        if it₁ = it₂
          then true
          else isin( it₁, s )
        end if;
  end module Set;
end scheme SetScheme;
```

Fig. 4/11

To enable direct execution of semi-constructive specifications, the non-termination of the reduction process must be intercepted. A possible solution is one based on the *run with memory* option used in the OBJ1 and OBJT systems [Goguen82, Futatsugi85, Goguen87c]. Constructor axioms are only applied if no operation axiom can be applied. Intermediate terms built up of constructor names only are remembered, and a constructor axiom is prevented from being applied if it produces a term that has already come up. The disadvantage of this method is a loss of efficiency in time and/or space of the reductor system.

Another example of a semi-constructive specification is the array, see Fig. 4/12.

```
scheme ArrayScheme [
    instantiate AttributeRequirementScheme; end instantiate;
    instantiate IndexRequirementScheme; end instantiate;
    -- see Fig. 3/43
  ];

  module Array;
    import Bool, true, false, not _ from Bool;
      all from Attribute, Index;
    export all;
    sort Array;
    constructors
      empty: -> Array;
      _[ _ / _ ]: Array * Attribute * Index -> Array;
    operations
      isundefined: Array * Index -> Bool;
      read: Array * Index -> Attribute;
    declare ar: Array;  i, i₁, i₂: Index;   at, at₁, at₂: Attribute;
    constructor axioms
      not ( i₁ = i₂ ) ⟹ ar [ at₁ / i₁ ][ at₂ / i₂ ] == ar [ at₂ / i₂ ][ at₁ / i₁ ];
      ar [ at₁ / i ][ at₂ / i ] == ar [ at₂ / i ];
    operation axioms
      isundefined( empty, i ) == true;
      isundefined( ar [ at / i₁ ], i₂ ) ==
        if i₁ = i₂
          then false
          else isundefined( ar, i₂ )
        end if;
      read( empty, i ) == error;
      read( ar [ at / i₁ ], i₂ ) ==
        if i₁ = i₂
          then at
          else read( ar, i₂ )
        end if;
  end module Array;
end scheme ArrayScheme;
```

Fig. 4/12

The specification of Fig. 4/13 is not semi-constructive because starting from, e.g., the term zero, it is possible to derive an infinite number of literally different terms using the constructor axioms as left-to-right term rewriting rules. Indeed, we obtain zero, succ(pre(zero)), succ(pre(succ(pre(zero)))), ... The specification can be made semi-constructive by interchanging the left- and right-hand side in each constructor axiom.

```
module Integer;
  export all;
  sort Integer;
  constructors
    zero: -> Integer;
    succ: Integer -> Integer;
    pre: Integer -> Integer;
  operations
    . . .
  declare i: Integer;
  constructor axioms
    i == succ( pre( i ) );
    i == pre( succ( i ) );
  operation axioms
    . . .
end module Integer;
```

Fig. 4/13

An example of a specification that is not semi-constructive is given in Fig. 4/14 [Mallgren82]. If the sets of variable-free terms of sort Value and of sort Point are both not empty (let us assume there is a term v of sort Value and a term p of sort Point that are both built up of constructor names only), then the specification of Fig. 4/14 is not ground confluent and thus not semi-constructive. Indeed, the term

compose(compose(scale(v), translate(p)), scale(v))

can be reduced to

compose(scale(v), compose(translate(p), scale(v)))

using the first constructor axiom. But it can also be reduced to

compose(translate(v . p), scale(v * v))

using the fourth, the first and the second constructor axiom respectively. There exists no term that can be derived from the two results using the constructor axioms as left-to-right term rewriting rules.

```
module GeomF;
  import Value, _ * _ from Value;  Point, _ + _, _ . _ from Point;
  export all;
  sort GeomF;
```

```
    constructors
      scale: Value -> GeomF;
      translate: Point -> GeomF;
      compose: GeomF * GeomF -> GeomF;
    operations
      ...
    declare gf₁, gf₂, gf₃: GeomF;  v₁, v₂: Value;  p₁, p₂: Point;
    constructor axioms
      compose( compose( gf₁, gf₂ ), gf₃ ) == compose( gf₁, compose( gf₂, gf₃ ) );
      compose( scale( v₁ ), scale( v₂ ) ) == scale( v₁ * v₂ );
      compose( translate( p₁ ), translate( p₂ ) ) == translate( p₁ + p₂ );
      compose( scale( v₁ ), translate( p₁ ) ) == compose( translate( v₁ . p₁ ), scale( v₁ ) );
    operation axioms
      ...
  end module GeomF;
```

Fig. 4/14

The first semi-constructivity constraint states that, if the constructor axioms are deleted, the specification must be constructive and thus meet the uniqueness and completeness constraints. If constructor axioms were taken into account in the definitions of the uniqueness and completeness constraints, these constraints could not be checked mechanically. Notice also that the constructor axioms in a semi-constructive specification contain redundant information with respect to the operation axioms. As an example, consider the ArrayScheme of Fig. 4/12 which we instantiate by binding the indices as well as the attributes with the natural numbers, the term

isundefined(empty [1 / 2][2 / 3], 2)

can be reduced in two different ways: the second operation axiom can be applied two times consecutively or the first constructor axiom can be applied and then the second operation axiom can be applied. Both give false as result.

4.8 Inconsistency

If constructor axioms are added to a constructive specification, we must be very careful not to violate the first hierarchical constraint, otherwise we may obtain an *inconsistent* specification. Assume that the specification of Fig. 4/11 contains the operation last as defined in Fig. 4/15.

The specification is inconsistent because the term last(insert(it₁, insert(it₂, ∅))) where it₁ and it₂ are different items, may be reduced to

```
operation
  last: Set -> Item;
declare it: Item;   s: Set;
operation axioms
  last( insert( it, s ) ) == it;
  ...
```

Fig. 4/15

it_1 as well as it_2 depending on whether the constructor axiom is applied before the operation axiom of Fig. 4/15.

In the next section a method for constructing requirements will be discussed that results in consistent parameterized specifications.

4.9 On Constructing Requirements

One of the main advantages of formal specification languages over traditional programming languages is the ability to provide not only syntactic but also semantic interfaces between the various parts of a system. Consider, e.g., generic packages in Ada [Ada83]; only syntactic information (including types) can be required from the parameters. With formal specifications also semantic properties (in the form of theorems) can be required from the parameters.

In literature, however, most examples illustrating the parameterization of formal specifications contain rather trivial interfaces. The interfaces usually state that sorts and operations must be given. Semantic properties are seldom required except for reflexivity, symmetry and transitivity of the equality operations. This section describes a general method for building semantic interfaces in parameterized formal specifications. Moreover, the method is illustrated by means of an example dealing with a non-trivial semantic interface.

The abstract data type GeomF, defining geometric functions, is specified by the module GeomF in Fig. 4/16. A parameterized version of GeomF will be given in Fig. 4/19. The abstract data type GeomF was used by Mallgren [Mallgren82] for the description of graphical languages. Examples of geometric functions are translations and scalings. Furthermore, the composition of two geometric functions yields a new geometric function. To limit the length of the example, we restrict ourselves to translations and compositions. We assume that a module Point has been predefined with a sort Point, an origin and two operations _ + _ and _ - _ .

The module GeomF defines the sort GeomF of geometric functions. It has two constructors: translate and compose. The definition of the operation identity is straightforward. The operation inverse returns the inverse of a geometrical function. The ultimate goal is to apply the geometric functions to points, therefore an operation transform is defined. The meaning of the theorems is obvious.

We decided to define compose as a constructor and not as an operation, as in [Mallgren82], where not only translations but also scalings are defined. Then, a composition of a translation and a scaling is, in general, neither a translation nor a scaling. In our example, compose is defined as a constructor for reasons of extendibility of our example with scalings.

```
module GeomF;
  import Point, origin, _ + _, _ - _ from Point;
  export all;
  sort GeomF;
  constructors
    translate : Point -> GeomF;
    compose : GeomF * GeomF -> GeomF;
  operations
    identity : -> GeomF;
    inverse : GeomF -> GeomF;
    transform : GeomF * Point -> Point;
  declare p, p1, p2: Point;   gf, gf1, gf2, gf3: GeomF;
  constructor axioms
    compose( translate( p1 ), translate( p2 ) ) == translate( p1 + p2 );        -- c1
    compose( compose( gf1, gf2 ), gf3 ) == compose( gf1, compose( gf2, gf3 ) );  -- c2
  operation axioms
    identity == translate( origin );                                            -- o1
    inverse( translate( p ) ) == translate( origin - p );                       -- o2
    inverse( compose( gf1, gf2 ) ) == compose( inverse( gf2 ), inverse( gf1 ) ); -- o3
    transform( translate( p1 ), p2 ) == p1 + p2;                                -- o4
    transform( compose( gf1, gf2 ), p ) == transform( gf1, transform( gf2, p ) ); -- o5
  theorems
    transform( identity, p ) == p;                                             -- t1
    compose( identity, gf ) == gf;                                             -- t2
    compose( gf, identity ) == gf;                                             -- t3
    inverse( inverse( gf ) ) == gf;                                            -- t4
    compose( gf, inverse( gf ) ) == identity;                                  -- t5
    compose( inverse( gf ), gf ) == identity;                                  -- t6
end module GeomF;
```

Fig. 4/16

Points in [Mallgren82] are two-dimensional Cartesian coordinates. In practice, points may also be n-dimensional Cartesian coordinates or polar coordinates. Therefore, parameterization of the module GeomF would enhance its reusability. The syntactic part of the needed requirement, say requirement Point, can be derived from the import clause of Fig. 4/16, resulting in Fig. 4/17.

```
requirement Point;
  export all;
  sort Point;
  operations
    origin : - > Point;
    _+_ : Point * Point -> Point;
    _-_ : Point * Point -> Point;
  theorems
    . . .  -- semantic properties
end requirement Point;
```

Fig. 4/17

Stating the claimed semantic properties, i.e. constructing the theorems of the requirement, is a non-trivial job. We will propose a three-step method for constructing theorems of requirements. In a first step, theorems are deduced by proving the consistency of the operation axioms of the parameterized modules with respect to the constructor axioms. Proving the ground confluence property of the scheme, in particular of the constructor axioms of the parameterized modules, yields a second group of theorems of requirements. In a third step, theorems of requirements are derived from the theorems of the parameterized modules of the scheme. Consequently, the obtained theorems of the requirements guarantee that the constructor axioms and the operation axioms of the parameterized modules are ground confluent and consistent respectively, and that the theorems of the parameterized modules are always valid.

Theorems Deduced from the Consistency Property

By proving the consistency of the operation axioms of the parameterized module with respect to its constructor axioms (see Section 4.8), a first group of theorems for the requirement Point may be derived. Applying the operation inverse to the left-hand side of each constructor axiom must yield the same result as applying it to the corresponding right-hand side. The same must be true for the operation transform.

1. Operation inverse and constructor axiom c1:

a) inverse(compose(translate(p_1), translate(p_2)))
    == compose(inverse(translate(p_2),
       inverse(translate(p_1))))   -- see o3
    == compose(translate(origin - p_2), translate(origin - p_1))   -- see o2
    == translate((origin - p_2) + (origin - p_1))   -- see c1
b) inverse(translate($p_1 + p_2$))
    == translate(origin - ($p_1 + p_2$))   -- see o2
☞ (origin - p_2) + (origin - p_1) == origin - ($p_1 + p_2$);

2. Operation inverse and constructor axiom c2:

a) inverse(compose(compose(gf_1, gf_2), gf_3))
    == compose(inverse(gf_3), inverse(compose(gf_1, gf_2)))   -- see o3
    == compose(inverse(gf_3),
       compose(inverse(gf_2), inverse(gf_1)))   -- see o3
b) inverse(compose(gf_1, compose(gf_2, gf_3)))
    == compose(inverse(compose(gf_2, gf_3)), inverse(gf_1))   -- see o3
    == compose(compose(inverse(gf_3),
       inverse(gf_2)), inverse(gf_1))   -- see o3
    == compose(inverse(gf_3),
       compose(inverse(gf_2), inverse(gf_1)))   -- see c2
Both deductions yield the same result.

3. Operation transform and constructor axiom c1:

a) transform(compose(translate(p_1), translate(p_2)), p)
    == transform(translate(p_1),
       transform(translate(p_2), p))   -- see o5
    == transform(translate(p_1), ($p_2 + p$))   -- see o4
    == $p_1 + (p_2 + p)$ -- see o4
b) transform(translate($p_1 + p_2$), p)
    == ($p_1 + p_2$) + p   -- see o4
☞ $p_1 + (p_2 + p) == (p_1 + p_2) + p$;

4. Operation transform and the constructor axiom c2:

a) transform(compose(compose(gf_1, gf_2), gf_3), p)
    == transform(compose(gf_1, gf_2), transform(gf_3, p))   -- see o5
    == transform(gf_1, transform(gf_2, transform(gf_3, p)))   -- see o5
b) transform(compose(gf_1, compose(gf_2, gf_3)), p)

$==$ transform(gf_1, transform(compose(gf_2, gf_3), p))   -- see o5
$==$ transform(gf_1, transform(gf_2, transform(gf_3 ,p)))   -- see o5
Both deductions yield the same result.

Theorems Deduced from the Ground Confluence Property

Proving the ground confluence property of the scheme, in particular of the constructor axioms of the parameterized modules (see Section 4.7), yields a second group of theorems of requirements.

The minimal overlapping term between the left-hand sides of the constructor axioms c1 and c2 is:

compose(compose(translate(p_1), translate(p_2)), gf)

Assume that every geometric function of Fig. 4/16 can be written as a translation. Then, we can replace the variable gf in the minimal overlapping term by the term translate(p_3).

compose(compose(translate(p_1), translate(p_2)), translate(p_3))

The rule of thumb of Section 4.7 says that if we consider p_1, p_2 and p_3 as constructor names of sort Point, the above term (built up of constructor names only) must be reduced to the same result via both constructor axioms.

compose(compose(translate(p_1),
  translate(p_2)), translate(p_3)) $==$
a) compose(translate(p_1 + p_2), translate(p_3))   -- see c1
  $==$ translate((p_1 + p_2) + p_3)   -- see c1
b) compose(translate(p_1),
    compose(translate(p_2), translate(p_3)))   -- see c2
  $==$ compose(translate(p_1), translate(p_2 + p_3))   -- see c1
  $==$ translate(p_1 + (p_2 + p_3))   -- see c1
☞ p_1 + (p_2 + p_3) $==$ (p_1 + p_2) + p_3;

In order to assert this suffices to prove the ground confluence of the scheme, we still have to prove that every geometric function of Fig. 4/16 can be written as a translation. If we denote this property as istranslation(

gf), it can be proved according to the following induction scheme

$$
\boxed{
\begin{array}{ll}
 & \text{istranslation(translate(p))} \\
\text{istranslation(gf}_1 \text{) and} & \\
\quad \text{istranslation(gf}_2 \text{) =>} & \text{istranslation(compose(gf}_1, \text{gf}_2 \text{))}
\end{array}
}
$$

induction base:
  istranslation(translate(p))
  == true   -- see definition of istranslation
induction hypotheses:
  istranslation(gf$_1$) == true;
   or gf$_1$ may be written as translate(p$_1$)
  istranslation(gf$_2$) == true;
   or gf$_2$ may be written as translate(p$_2$)
induction conclusion:
  istranslation(compose(gf$_1$, gf$_2$))
  == istranslation(compose(translate(p$_1$) , translate(p$_2$)))
                                       -- see ind. hyp.
  == istranslation(translate(p$_1$ + p$_2$))   -- see c1
  == true   -- see definition of istranslation

Theorems Deduced from the Theorems of the Scheme

In a last step, theorems of requirements are derived from the theorems of the parameterized modules. We derive sufficient and necessary theorems for the requirement Point so that the theorems of module GeomF are valid.

In order to prove

  transform(identity, p) == p;   -- t1

  transform(identity, p)
   == transform(translate(origin), p)   -- see o1
   == origin + p   -- see o4
  ☞ origin + p == p;

In order to prove

  compose(identity, gf) == gf;   -- t2

we use induction over the variable gf according to the following induction scheme where theorem 2 is denoted as t2(gf)

$$\boxed{\begin{array}{ll} & t2(\ translate(\ p\ )\ ) \\ t2(\ gf_1\ ) => & t2(\ compose(\ gf_1,\ gf_2\ )\ ) \end{array}}$$

induction base:
  compose(identity, translate(p))
  == compose(translate(origin), translate(p))   -- see o1
  == translate(origin + p)   -- see c1
  ☞ origin + p == p;
induction hypothesis:
  compose(identity, gf_1) == gf_1;
induction conclusion:
  compose(identity, compose(gf_1, gf_2))
  == compose(compose(identity, gf_1), gf_2)   -- see c2
  == compose(gf_1, gf_2)   -- see ind. hyp.

For the example of Fig. 4/16 a simpler proof of theorem 2 can be given based on the property that every geometric function can be written as a translation. We have given a proof that can easily be generalized if scalings [Mallgren82] or rotations [Huyghe87] are introduced.

In order to prove

  compose(gf, identity) == gf;   --t3

we use induction over the variable gf according to the following induction scheme where theorem 3 is denoted as t3(gf)

$$\boxed{\begin{array}{ll} & t3(\ translate(\ p\ )\ ) \\ t3(\ gf_2\ ) => & t3(\ compose(\ gf_1,\ gf_2\ )\ ) \end{array}}$$

induction base:
  compose(translate(p), identity)
  == compose(translate(p), translate(origin))   -- see o1
  == translate(p + origin)   -- see c1
  ☞ p + origin == p;
induction hypothesis:
  compose(gf_2, identity) == gf_2;
induction conclusion:
  compose(compose(gf_1, gf_2), identity)

$==$ compose(gf_1, compose(gf_2, identity)) $--$ see c2
$==$ compose(gf_1, gf_2) $--$ see ind. hyp.

In order to prove

  inverse(inverse(gf)) $==$ gf; $--$ t4

we use induction over the variable gf according to the following induction
scheme where theorem 4 is denoted as t4(gf)

	t4(translate(p))
t4(gf_1) and t4(gf_2) $=>$	t4(compose(gf_1, gf_2))

  induction base:
   inverse(inverse(translate(p)))
   $==$ inverse(translate(origin $-$ p)) $--$ see o2
   $==$ translate(origin $-$ (origin $-$ p)) $--$ see o2
   ☞ origin $-$ (origin $-$ p) $==$ p;
  induction hypotheses:
   inverse(inverse(gf_1)) $==$ gf_1;
   inverse(inverse(gf_2)) $==$ gf_2;
  induction conclusion:
   inverse(inverse(compose(gf_1, gf_2)))
   $==$ inverse(compose(inverse(gf_2), inverse(gf_1))) $--$ see o3
   $==$ compose(inverse(inverse(gf_1)), inverse(inverse(gf_2)))
                                                                                  $--$ see o3
   $==$ compose(gf_1, gf_2) $--$ see ind. hyp.

In order to prove

  compose(gf, inverse(gf)) $==$ identity; $--$ t5

we use induction over the variable gf according to an induction scheme
similar to that of theorem 4.

  induction base:
   compose(translate(p), inverse(translate(p)))
   $==$ compose(translate(p), translate(origin $-$ p)) $--$ see o2
   $==$ translate(p $+$ (origin $-$ p)) $--$ see c1
   ☞ p $+$ (origin $-$ p) $==$ origin;
  induction hypotheses:
   compose(gf_1, inverse(gf_1)) $==$ identity;

compose(gf_2, inverse(gf_2)) == identity;

induction conclusion:

compose(compose(gf_1, gf_2), inverse(compose(gf_1, gf_2)))

== compose(compose(gf_1, gf_2),

compose(inverse(gf_2), inverse(gf_1)))   -- see o3

== compose(compose(compose(gf_1, gf_2), inverse(gf_2)),

inverse(gf_1))   -- see c2

== compose(compose(gf_1, compose(gf_2, inverse(gf_2))),

inverse(gf_1))   -- see c2

== compose(compose(gf_1, identity), inverse(gf_1))   -- see ind. hyp.

== compose(gf_1, inverse(gf_1))   -- see t3

== identity   -- see ind. hyp.

In order to prove

compose(inverse(gf), gf) == identity;   -- t6

we use induction over the variable gf according to an induction scheme
similar to that of theorem 4.

induction base:

compose(inverse(translate(p)), translate(p))

== compose(translate(origin - p), translate(p))   -- see o2

== translate((origin - p) + p)   -- see c1

☞ (origin - p) + p == origin;

induction hypotheses:

compose(inverse(gf_1), gf_1) == identity;

compose(inverse(gf_2), gf_2) == identity;

induction conclusion:

compose(inverse(compose(gf_1, gf_2)), compose(gf_1, gf_2))

== compose(compose(inverse(gf_2), inverse(gf_1)),

compose(gf_1, gf_2))   -- see o3

== compose(inverse(gf_2),

compose(inverse(gf_1), compose(gf_1, gf_2)))   -- see c2

== compose(inverse(gf_2),

compose(compose(inverse(gf_1), gf_1), gf_2))   -- see c2

== compose(inverse(gf_2), compose(identity, gf_2))   -- see ind. hyp.

== compose(inverse(gf_2), gf_2)   -- see t2

== identity   -- see ind. hyp.

The theorems deduced above are grouped in a requirement called Point,
shown in Fig. 4/18. The first theorem expresses the associativity of the

addition. The next two theorems state that origin denotes the identity of the addition. Then, two theorems dictate that every point has an inverse element with respect to the addition. The last two theorems are redundant since they can be derived by equational reasoning from the previous ones. Mathematicians would say that sort Point with the operation _ + _ must form a group.

```
requirement Point;
  export all;
  sort Point;
  operations
    origin: -> Point;
    _ + _: Point * Point -> Point;
    _ - _: Point * Point -> Point;
  declare p, p₁, p₂, p₃ : Point;
  theorems
    p₁ + ( p₂ + p₃ ) == ( p₁ + p₂ ) + p₃;
    origin + p == p;
    p + origin == p;
    p + ( origin - p) == origin;.
    ( origin - p) + p == origin;
    origin - ( origin - p ) == p;
    ( origin - p₂ ) + ( origin - p₁ ) == origin - ( p₁ + p₂ );
  end requirement Point;
```

Fig. 4/18

In Fig. 4/19 the obtained scheme is shown.

```
scheme GeomFScheme [
  requirement Point;
    import all from domain;
    export all;
    sort Point;
    operations
      origin: -> Point;
      _ + _: Point * Point -> Point;
      _ - _: Point * Point -> Point;
    declare p, p₁, p₂, p₃ : Point;
    theorems
      p₁ + ( p₂ + p₃ ) == ( p₁ + p₂ ) + p₃;
      origin + p == p;
      p + origin == p;
      p + ( origin - p) == origin;.
      ( origin - p) + p == origin;
```

```
        end requirement Point;
    ];
    module GeomF;
      import all from Point;
      export all;
      sort GeomF;
      constructors
        translate: Point -> GeomF;
        compose: GeomF * GeomF -> GeomF;
      operations
        transform: GeomF * Point -> Point;
        inverse: GeomF -> GeomF;
        identity: -> GeomF;
      declare p, p_1, p_2: Point;   gf, gf_1, gf_2, gf_3: GeomF;
      constructor axioms
        compose( translate( p_1 ), translate( p_2 ) ) ==
          translate( p_1 + p_2 );
        compose( compose( gf_1, gf_2 ), gf_3 ) ==
          compose( gf_1, compose( gf_2, gf_3 ) );
      operation axioms
        identity == translate( origin );
        inverse( translate( p ) ) == translate( origin - p );
        inverse( compose( gf_1, gf_2 ) ) == compose( inverse( gf_2 ), inverse( gf_1 ) );
        transform( translate( p_1 ), p_2 ) == p_1 + p_2;
        transform( compose( gf_1, gf_2 ), p ) == transform( gf_1, transform( gf_2, p ) );
      theorems
        transform( identity, p ) == p;
        compose( identity, gf ) == gf;
        compose( gf, identity ) == gf;
        inverse( inverse( gf ) ) == gf;
        compose( gf, inverse( gf ) ) == identity;
        compose( inverse( gf ), gf ) == identity;
    end module GeomF;
  end scheme GeomFScheme;
```

Fig. 4/19

In this section we have presented a three–step method to build semantic interfaces of parameterized specifications. The method is based on proving the consistency and the ground confluence of the parameterized modules and on the validation of their theorems. Consequently, this consistency, ground confluence and validity are guaranteed.

The three–step method has been illustrated by means of the example of geometric functions. The resulting interface nicely expresses that the sort Point with its addition must form a group. The axioms and theorems of the non-parameterized module we started from (see Fig. 4/16), were taken from a subset of Mallgren's specification of geometric functions [Mallgren82]. Mallgren did not treat parameterization in his specification. It was nice to see that neither the axioms nor the theorems had to be modified to obtain the resulting interface by means of our three–step method. The same method can be applied to Mallgren's complete specification. Therefore, the original specification (see Fig. 4/14) has to be made ground confluent by adding the appropriate constructor axioms. The resulting semantic interface will state that the points and the scalar values (used for scaling) must form a field.

Our three-step method requires specifications to be ground confluent and consistent, thus restricting the class of specifications that can be treated. Another point is that deriving semantic interfaces by means of our three-step method can be a tedious job. To make such a process feasible, powerful theorem provers are a necessity.

4.10 Claiming Modules

In Chapter 3 the definition of a requirement was given. Many examples illustrating the notion of requirement can be found in Chapters 3 and 4. The notion of requirement has been defined in such a way that the abstract data type defined by an actual module need not be an initial algebra of the requirement. The abstract data type of the actual module may have less, the same or more objects with respect to the initial algebra of the requirement. Consider Fig. 4/20.

```
scheme XScheme [
    requirement ListNat;
     import Nat from Nat;
     export all;
     sort L
     operations
       new: -> L;
        add: Nat * L -> L;
     end requirement ListNat;
    ];

    module X;
     . . .
    end module X;
   end scheme XScheme;
```

Fig. 4/20

It is not allowed to define within the module X a new operation as in Fig. 4/21.

```
module X;
  ...
  operation
    first: L -> Nat;
  declare n, n₁, n₂: Nat;   l: L;
  operation axioms
    first( new ) == zero;
    first( add( n, new ) ) == n;
    first( add( n₁, add( n₂, l ) ) ) == first( add( n₂, l ) );
  ...
end module X;
```

Fig. 4/21

Nor is it allowed to use a case construct with a case index of sort L. The reason for this is that the uniqueness and completeness constraints cannot be guaranteed to be met for all possible instantiations. The module X in Fig. 4/21 is safe only if we could guarantee the existence of a bijection between the objects of sort L and the objects of the sort defined by any possible actual module that may be bound with the requirement ListNat.

Therefore, a more restricted kind of requirements is introduced by allowing a scheme to claim not only requirements but also modules. If a module is claimed by a scheme, the following conditions must be met by any (partial) instantiation that binds the claimed module with an actual module.

1. Every formal sort defined in the claimed module must be bound with a sort defined by or imported in the actual module.

2. Every formal constructor defined in the claimed module must be bound with a constructor or an operation that is defined by or imported in the actual module, such that the rank of the constructor is preserved.
    Every formal non-constructor operation defined in the claimed module must be bound with a constructor or an operation that is defined by or imported in the actual module, such that the rank of the operation is preserved.

3. The formal constructor axioms, operation axioms and theorems of the claimed module must be preserved by the actual data types.

4. For every formal sort s_f of the claimed module that is bound with an actual sort s_a, a (data) bijection must exist between the (formal) objects of sort s_f belonging to the initial algebra of the claimed

module and the objects of sort s_a of the abstract data type defined by the actual module.

The first three conditions can be considered as a restricted version of the conditions in the definition of parameter morphism for claimed requirements, see Section 3.4.1. The extra fourth condition is the essential difference between claiming a module and claiming a requirement.

An example of claiming a module is given in Fig. 4/22. Mod3 is the formal module whereas ThreeThings is the actual module.

```
scheme XScheme [
    module Mod3;
      export all;
      sort Mod3;
      constructors
        zero: -> Mod3;
        succ: Mod3 -> Mod3;
      constructor axiom
        succ( succ( succ( zero ) ) ) == zero;
    end module Mod3;
  ];

  module X;
    import all from Mod3
    . . .
    operation
      f: Mod3 -> ...;
    . . .
    declare m: Mod3; ...
    operation axioms
      f( zero ) == ...;
      f( succ( m ) ) == ...;
    . . .
  end module X;
end scheme XScheme;


module ThreeThings;
  export all;
  sort ThreeThings;
  constructors
    one, two, three: -> ThreeThings;
  operation
    next: ThreeThings -> ThreeThings;
  operation axioms
    next( one ) == two;
    next( two ) == three;
    next( three ) == one;
end module ThreeThings;

instantiate XScheme;
```

```
  with Mod3 as ThreeThings,
    zero as one,
    succ as next;
end instantiate;
```

Fig. 4/22

Notice the (data) bijection between the objects of the initial algebra of the claimed module Mod3 and the actual objects of sort ThreeThings:

$$
\begin{array}{ccc}
\text{zero} & \leftrightarrow & \text{one} \\
\text{succ(zero)} & \leftrightarrow & \text{two} \\
\text{succ(succ(zero))} & \leftrightarrow & \text{three}
\end{array}
$$

Both modules and requirements can be claimed by a scheme. Instead of writing claimed modules or requirements, an instantiation may be given that is equivalent to one or more modules and/or requirements. An example is given in Fig. 4/23. Between the square brackets an instantiation is given which is equivalent to a module List. This module List is claimed by the scheme FerryProblem.

```
scheme FerryProblem [
    requirement Object;
      import Bool, true, _ and _ from Bool;
      export all;
      sort Object;
      operations
        error: -> Object;
        _ = _: Object * Object -> Bool;
      declare ob, ob₁, ob₂, ob₃: Object;
      theorems
        ob = ob == true;
        ob₁ = ob₂ == ob₂ = ob₁;
        ( ob₁ = ob₂ ) and ( ob₂ = ob₃ ) ⇒ ob₁ = ob₃  ==  true;
    end requirement Object;

    instantiate ListScheme;   -- see Fig. 4/6
      with Item as Object,
        Item as Object,
        undefined as error,
        _ = _ as _ = _;
    end instantiate ListScheme;

    requirement Constraints;
      import all from List;
      ...
    end requirement Constraints;
    ];
    ...
```

end scheme FerryProblem;

4.11 The Cartesian Product of Sorts

An advanced feature is the possibility to define a new sort as the Cartesian product of other sorts. A *Cartesian product*

sort $S == S_1 * S_2 * ... * S_c$;

stands for the definition of sort S

sort S;

with one constructor

constructor
  ($\_$, $\_$, ..., $\_$): $S_1 * S_2 * ... * S_c$ -> S;

and a selector and an update operation for each of the sorts S_1, S_2, ... and S_c:

operations
  s_1Of $\_$: S -> S_1;
  s_2Of $\_$: S -> S_2;
  . . .
  s_cOf $\_$: S -> S_c;
  $\_$[$\_$ / s_1]: S * S_1 -> S;
  $\_$[$\_$ / s_2]: S * S_2 -> S;
  . . .
  $\_$[$\_$ / s_c]: S * S_c -> S;
declare x_1, y_1: S_1; x_2, y_2: S_2; ...., x_c, y_c: S_c;
operation axioms
  s_1Of (x_1, x_2, ..., x_c) == x_1;
  s_2Of (x_1, x_2, ..., x_c) == x_2;
  . . .
  s_cOf (x_1, x_2, ..., x_c) == x_c;
  (x_1, x_2, ..., x_c) [y_1 / s_1] == (y_1, x_2, ..., x_c);

$$(x_1, x_2, ..., x_c) [y_2 / s_2] == (x_1, y_2, ..., x_c);$$
$$\cdots$$
$$(x_1, x_2, ..., x_c) [y_c / s_c] == (x_1, x_2, ..., y_c);$$

Each time a Cartesian product is formed, a new sort with appropriate constructor, selector and update operations is defined. An example is shown in Fig. 4/24.

---

sort PABX == PhonePool * BookingOffice * WakeUpService * MeetingPool;

Fig. 4/24

This definition stands for the sort, constructor, selector and update operations of Fig. 4/25.

```
sort PABX;
constructor
   ( _, _, _, _ ): PhonePool * BookingOffice * WakeUpService * MeetingPool -> PABX;
operations
   phonePoolOf _: PABX -> PhonePool;
   bookingOfficeOf _: PABX -> BookingOffice;
   wakeUpServiceOf _: PABX -> WakeUpService;
   meetingPoolOf _: PABX -> MeetingPool;
   _ [ _ / phonePool ]: PABX * PhonePool -> PABX;
   _ [ _ / bookingOffice ]: PABX * BookingOffice -> PABX;
   _ [ _ / wakeUpService ]: PABX * WakeUpService -> PABX;
   _ [ _ / meetingPool ]: PABX * MeetingPool -> PABX;
declare pabx: PABX;  pl: PhonePool;  be: BookingOffice;  we: WakeUpService;
   ml: MeetingPool;
operation axioms
   phonePoolOf ( pl, be, we, ml ) == pl;
   bookingOfficeOf ( pl, be, we, ml ) == be;
   wakeUpServiceOf ( pl, be, we, ml ) == we;
   meetingPoolOf ( pl, be, we, ml ) == ml;
   pabx [ pl / phonePool ] == ( pl, bookingOfficeOf pabx, wakeUpServiceOf pabx,
      meetingPoolOf pabx );
   pabx [ be / bookingOffice ] == ( phonePoolOf pabx, be, wakeUpServiceOf pabx,
      meetingPoolOf pabx );
   pabx [ we / wakeUpService ] == ( phonePoolOf pabx, bookingOfficeOf pabx, we,
      meetingPoolOf pabx );
   pabx [ ml / meetingPool ] == ( phonePoolOf pabx, bookingOfficeOf pabx,
      wakeUpServiceOf pabx, ml );
```

Fig. 4/25

4.12 Constructivity and Abstraction

The main characteristic of the specification language proposed in this
chapter is that the specifications are (semi-)constructive. In the sequel, by
non-constructive specifications we mean specifications that are neither
constructive nor semi-constructive. Constructivity is a very important
property since it enables rapid prototyping. In this way, a software
system can be tested before it is implemented. The drawback of
constructivity is a possible loss of abstraction. Indeed, if a non-
constructive specification is found, it often has a higher level of abstraction
than the constructive version.

This will be illustrated by the example of a very simple robot system.
The world of the robot is a large flat plane. Criss-crossing this world are
horizontal streets and vertical avenues at regular one block intervals. A
corner is located wherever a street and an avenue intersect. The robot can
be placed on any corner, facing one of the four compass orientations. The
instruction start places the robot in its initial position. When the robot
executes the instruction move, he moves forward one block and continues
to face the same direction. When the robot executes the instruction turn,
he turns 90 degrees to the left. A non-constructive specification is shown
in Fig. 4/26.

```
sort Position;
operations
  start: -> Position;
  move: Position -> Position;
  turn: Position -> Position;
declare pos: Position;
axioms
  turn( turn( turn( turn( pos ) ) ) ) == pos;
  turn( move( turn( move( turn( move( turn( move( pos ) ) ) ) ) ) ) ) == pos;
  turn( turn( move( turn( turn( move( pos ) ) ) ) ) ) == pos;
```

Fig. 4/26

The first axiom states that if the robot executes the instruction turn four
times, its place and direction are the original ones. The second axiom states
that if the robot executes four times the instruction sequence move and
turn (i.e. goes around a block), its place and direction are the original ones.
The last axiom indicates that if the robot moves forwards, turns 180
degrees, moves forwards and turns 180 degrees, its place and direction are
again the original ones.

A semi-constructive specification may be as shown in Fig. 4/27.

```
module Street;
  export Street, startStreet, nextStreet, prevStreet;
  sort Street;
  constructors
    startStreet: -> Street;
    nextStreet: Street -> Street;
    prevStreet: Street -> Street;
  declare s: Street;
  constructor axioms
    prevStreet( nextStreet( ( s ) ) == s;
    nextStreet( prevStreet( ( s ) ) == s;
end module Street;

module Avenue;
  export Avenue, startAvenue, nextAvenue, prevAvenue;
  sort Avenue;
  constructors
    startAvenue: -> Avenue;
    nextAvenue: Avenue -> Avenue;
    prevAvenue: Avenue -> Avenue;
  declare a: Avenue;
  constructor axioms
    prevAvenue( nextAvenue( a ) ) == a;
    nextAvenue( prevAvenue( a ) ) == a;
end module Avenue;

module Robot;
  import Orientation, north, east, south, west, turnleft from Orientation; -- see Fig. 2/16
    Street, startStreet, nextStreet, prevStreet from Street;
    Avenue, startAvenue, nextAvenue, prevAvenue from Avenue;
  export start, move, turn;
  sort Position == Street * Avenue * Orientation;
  operations
    start: -> Position;
    move: Position -> Position;
    turn: Position -> Position;
  declare s: Street;  a: Avenue;  o: Orientation;  pos: Position;
  operation axioms
    start == ( startStreet, startAvenue, east );
    move( ( s, a, north ) ) == ( nextStreet( s ), a, north );
    move( ( s, a, east ) ) == ( s, nextAvenue( a ), east );
    move( ( s, a, south ) ) == ( prevStreet( s ), a, south );
    move( ( s, a, west ) ) == ( s, prevAvenue( a ), west );
    turn( ( s, a, o ) ) == ( s, a, turnleft( o ) );
  theorems
    turn( turn( turn( turn( pos ) ) ) ) == pos;
    turn( move( turn( move( turn( move( turn( move( pos ) ) ) ) ) ) ) ) == pos;
    turn( turn( move( turn( turn( move( pos ) ) ) ) ) ) == pos;
end module Robot;
```

Fig. 4/27

This semi-constructive specification is longer and less abstract than the non-constructive one. The former may be considered as an implementation of the latter. The advantage of the semi-constructive specification is that rapid prototyping is possible. Furthermore, rigorous reasoning is easier. As an example, for the non-constructive specification it is very hard to prove that

theorem
  turn(turn(turn(move(turn(move(pos))))))) ==
    move(turn(turn(turn(move(turn(pos)))))));

(though it can be done using equational reasoning). For the constructive specification, however, the above theorem can easily be proved using the axioms as left-to-right term rewriting rules, if we replace the variable pos successively by (s, a, north), (s, a, east), (s, a, south) and (s, a, west). If the robot system and its world are extended with walls, beepers and a library of instructions, the semi-constructive version is most appropriate [Lewi85b]. The price that must be paid is a lower level of abstraction.

4.13 Bibliographic Notes

Although in the early days of algebraic specifications no explicit distinction between constructors and non-constructor operations was made, the pioneers of algebraic specifications intuitively did, e.g., [Guttag78a, Goguen78]. It demonstrates that it is quite natural to distinguish between data and procedural abstraction. Making this distinction explicit results in more readable and reliable specifications [Mallgren82, Goovaerts84, Van Puymbroeck84].

Constructors are called *generators* in [Goovaerts84, Van Puymbroeck84] and *basic generators* in [Mallgren82]. No explicit distinction between data and procedural abstraction is made neither in OBJ [Futatsugi85] nor in ACT ONE [Ehrig85].

The uniqueness and completeness constraints were taken from [Goovaerts84, Van Puymbroeck84], where the completeness constraint is called *exhaustiveness constraint*. In [Van Puymbroeck84] an algorithm can be found to check the uniqueness and completeness constraints in a mechanical way.

The addition of axioms of non-constructive specifications as theorems to a constructive specification was done by [Mallgren82] also.

Semi-Constructive Specifications

A more severe property than ground confluence is *confluence* [Huet80, Lescanne85]. The conditions for confluence are as follows: if s, t_1 and t_2 are terms built up of variables and constructor names, such that both t_1 and t_2 are derived from s using the constructor axioms as left-to-right term rewriting rules, then there exists a term u built up of variables and constructor names such that u can be derived from t_1 as well as t_2 using the constructor axioms as left-to-right term rewriting rules.

Confluence as well as ground confluence, and thus semi-constructivity, are in general undecidable [Huet80, Gobel87].

The confluence property is equivalent to the *Church-Rosser* property. The Church-Rosser property states that, for all terms s and t, s and t can be proved equal by equational reasoning if and only if there exists a term u such that both s and t can be reduced to u using the axioms as left-to-right term rewriting rules [Huet80, Coleman85].

One can get around the problems with constructor axioms in many ways. A first solution consists of not using constructor axioms; both Fig. 4/8 and Fig. 4/9 are then considered as specifications for sets.

Another solution is to use hidden operations for some of the constructors. By using the hidden operation hinsert, the module Set of Fig. 4/8 is redefined in Fig. 4/28.

```
scheme SetScheme [
    requirement Item;
      import Bool, true, _ and _, not _ from Bool;
      export all;
      sort Item;
      operations
          _ = _: Item * Item -> Bool;
          _ < _: Item * Item -> Bool;
      declare it, it₁, it₂, it₃: Item;
      theorems
        it = it == true;
        it₁ = it₂ == it₂ = it₁;
        ( it₁ = it₂ ) and ( it₂ = it₃ ) ⇒ it₁ = it₃   == true;
        it₁ = it₂ ⇒ it₁ < it₂ == false;
        not ( it₁ = it₂ ) ⇒ it₁ < it₂ == not( it₂ < it₁ );
        ( it₁ < it₂ ) and ( it₂ < it₃ ) ⇒ it₁ < it₃   == true;
    end requirement Item;
  ];

  module Set;
    import Bool, true, false from Bool;
      all from Item;
      export all except hinsert;
```

```
    sort Set;
    constructors
      Ø: -> Set;
      hinsert: Item * Set -> Set;
    operations
      insert: Item * Set -> Set;
      delete: Item * Set -> Set;
      { _ }: Item -> Set;
      _ ∪ _: Set * Set -> Set;
      _ ∩ _: Set * Set -> Set;
      isin: Item * Set -> Bool;
    declare s, s₁, s₂: Set;   it, it₁, it₂: Item;
    operation axioms
      insert( it, Ø ) == hinsert( it, Ø );
      insert( it₁, hinsert( it₂, s ) ) ==
        if it₁ < it₂
          then hinsert( it₁, hinsert( it₂, s ) )
          else
            if it₁ = it₂
              then hinsert( it₂, s )
              else hinsert( it₂, insert( it₁, s ) )
            end if
        end if;
      delete( it, Ø ) == Ø;
      delete( it₁, hinsert( it₂, s ) ) ==
        if it₁ = it₂
          then s
          else
            if it₁ < it₂
              then hinsert( it₂, s )
              else hinsert( it₂, delete( it₁, s ) )
            end if
        end if;
      { it } == hinsert( it, Ø );
      s ∪ Ø == s;
      s₁ ∪ hinsert( it, s₂ ) == insert( it, s₁ ∪ s₂ );
      s ∩ Ø == Ø;
      s₁ ∩ hinsert( it, s₂ ) ==
        if isin( it, s₁ )
          then insert( it, s₁ ∩ s₂ )
          else s₁ ∩ s₂
        end if;
      isin( it, Ø ) == false;
      isin( it₁, hinsert( it₂, s ) ) ==
        if it₁ = it₂
          then true
          else
            if it₁ < it₂
              then false
              else isin( it₁, s )
            end if
        end if;
  end module Set;
end scheme SetScheme;
```

Fig. 4/28

We believe that this solution is too implementation–oriented.

In OBJ2 [Futatsugi85] attributes are added to the operations instead of writing constructor axioms. In OBJ2 attributes are only provided for expressing associativity, commutativity, identity elements and idempotence, see Fig. 3/51.

Termination

Termination of a term rewriting system is in general undecidable [Huet78]. However good methods that can prove termination in most of the cases, do exist. A straightforward method is suggested in [Dershowitz85]:

> A term rewriting system is terminating if there exists a *well-founded ordering* > (i.e. without any infinite descending sequence of terms) that is *compatible with rewriting* (i.e. for all terms s and t: if s rewrites to t then s > t).

However this method is not very practical because to be sure of termination, one has to check all rewrites, which usually form an infinite set.

Partial orderings >, with the property that if s > t, then also f(... s ...) > f(... t ...) (the *replacement property*) are called *monotonic*. The following method, due to Manna and Ness [Manna70], eliminates the need for considering all rewrites s → t and is often used to prove termination:

> A term rewriting system is terminating if there exists a monotonic well-founded ordering > such that l > r, for each rewrite rule l -> r and for any substitution of terms for the variables of the rule.

Monotonic well-founded orderings that are used to prove termination are, e.g., the Knuth-Bendix ordering [Knuth70, Martin87] and orderings based on polynomial interpretations of the operation symbols [Manna70, Cherifa86].

In [Dershowitz79] the important notion of *simplification ordering* has been introduced. A monotonic partial ordering > is a simplification ordering if it possesses the *subterm property*, i.e. if for all terms t: f(... t ...) > t. Dershowitz proved that any simplification ordering is a monotonic well-founded ordering for rewriting.

A lot of research has been done in constructing simplification orderings. Most of them are based on a partial ordering of the operation symbols, called a *precedence*. Examples of so called *precedence orderings* are the *Path of Subterms Orderings* (PSO) [Plaisted78], the *Recursive Path Ordering* (RPO) [Dershowitz82] and its extension *with Status* (RPOS) [Kamin80], the *Recursive Decomposition Ordering* (RDO) [Jouannaud82] and its extension *with Status* (RDOS) [Lescanne84], and the *path ordering of Kapur, Narendran and Sivakumar* (KNS) [Kapur85]. All these orderings are *closed under substitution,* i.e. if s > t then s' > t', with s' and t' being the result of applying the substitution σ to s and t respectively, for all terms s and t and for all substitutions σ. The relations between these orderings have been examined in [Rusinowitch85] and can be summarized in the following diagram (where each arrow means: is included in):

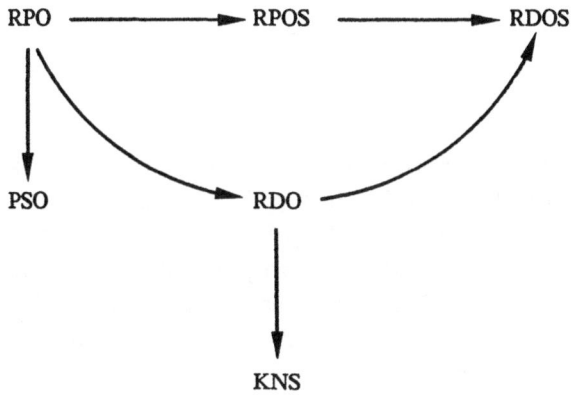

Fig. 4/29

A general and thorough survey of termination and orderings is given in [Dershowitz85].

In [Bevers87] we describe a generalization of RPOS, the *Extended Recursive Path Ordering with Status* (ERPOS). ERPOS contains a number of parameters to be chosen, such as the precedence and orderings $<_{ss}$ on sequences of terms. It has been proved that if these orderings $<_{ss}$ meet certain conditions, ERPOS is a simplification ordering and closed under substitution. In the same paper a special tailored ordering for term rewriting systems with constructors has been defined (*the constructive ordering* $<_c$) by choosing appropriate orderings for $<_{ss}$. It has been proved that RPOS is included in this ordering, but that $<_c$ is neither included in RDOS nor in KNS.

5. A Case Study: the Ferry Problem

"An ounce of application is worth a ton of abstraction."
Booker's law

In most articles on algebraic specifications trivial examples like stacks, queues and sets are used [Goguen78, Guttag78]. As an unbounded stack does not exist in reality, it seems cooked up by the algebraicists because it suits their approach so well. Actually, examples like stacks, queues and sets are useful to illustrate the basic principles of algebraic specifications to those who want to have a first impression. As for programming in the small versus programming in the large, techniques and notations for designing small specifications do not necessarily apply to large ones. In Chapters 5 and 6, we deal with examples of a degree of complexity which is representative for large specifications. It is our intention to show that algebraic specifications, as described in the previous chapters, are appropriate not only for small examples but also for non-trivial case studies.

In this chapter, the algebraic specification for the ferry problem is discussed. The specification is characterized by its high degree of parameterization. It is an example illustrating how a solution for a particular problem can be generalized to a solution for a class of similar problems, by using the technique of *abstraction by parameterization*. Originally, we started from the well-known riddle of the farmer, the wolf, the goat and the cabbage wanting to cross a river. This example is frequently used in the field of logic programming, see, e.g., [Kowalski82]. Through adequate parameterization the riddle was generalized to a whole family of similar problems, called the ferry problem. Thus we can see the riddle of the farmer, the wolf, the goat and the cabbage as a particular instantiation, just like the riddle of the missionaries and the cannibals. At the end of this chapter, a specification of a search strategy for the ferry problem based on backtracking can be found. The idea here is that a problem solution may be described by several specifications each of a different level of abstraction. A design module may serve as specification for one person, but as implementation for another.

5.1 Informal Description of the Ferry Problem

The Farmer, the Wolf, the Goat and the Cabbage

A typical riddle in the field of artificial intelligence is the problem of the
farmer, the wolf, the goat and the cabbage crossing a river. A farmer, a
wolf, a goat and a cabbage want to cross a river for which they dispose of
one small boat. The farmer can cross the river but he can only carry one
passenger at the most. When the farmer is absent, the wolf may eat the
goat and the goat may eat the cabbage. So the problem of how to cross the
river safely arises.

The Missionaries and the Cannibals

Another famous riddle is that of the missionaries and cannibals. Three
missionaries and three cannibals are at one bank of a river. Only a two-
seater rowboat is at their disposal. Both the missionaries and cannibals can
row. Usually the cannibals are friendly, but as soon as they are in the
majority they become dangerous to the missionaries. How can they cross
the river safely?

This riddle can easily be generalized by allowing an arbitrary number
of missionaries and cannibals. Of course, there must be at least as many
missionaries as cannibals. A variant is obtained by introducing the
restriction that only the missionaries can row.

The Ferry Problem

The ferry problem is obtained by generalizing the two previous problems
to a more general problem using the technique of abstraction. The problem
is how to transport a number of objects (human beings, animals or things)
by means of a ferry between two banks of a river. The bank the ferry is
located at originally, is called thisBank. The other bank is called
yonderBank. Several constraints must be met and using the ferry is the
only way to cross the river.

The *initial situation* is defined by listing the objects which are originally
at thisBank, and by listing the objects which are originally at yonderBank.
The former list of objects is called initThisBankList, the latter one is called
initYonderBankList.

The *target situations* are defined by listing objects which must eventually be at thisBank, and by listing objects which must eventually be at yonderBank. The former list of objects is called targetThisBankList, the latter one is called targetYonderBankList. Furthermore, targetFerryDestination determines the target destination of the ferry. Possible destinations are: thisBank, if the ferry must eventually be back at thisBank, yonderBank, if the ferry must eventually be at yonderBank, and thisOrYonderBank, if the destination of the ferry is irrelevant.

A *restriction* is that the ferry must be operational whenever it crosses the river. It will be indicated by the boolean function operational. Moreover the combinations of objects on the ferry, on thisBank as well as on yonderBank must always be stable. They will respectively be indicated by the boolean functions stableFerry, stableThisBank and stableYonderBank.

A *solution* is defined as a sequence of crossings starting from the initial situation and ending in a target situation, such that in each intermediate situation the combinations of objects on the ferry, on thisBank and on yonderBank are stable, and such that during each crossing the ferry is operational.

5.2 Formal Specification of the Ferry Problem

A formal specification of the ferry problem is given in Fig. 5/1. This is a high-level specification of a solution (the *what*) without giving an implementation (algorithm) to find this solution (the *how*). The specification of an implementation using backtracking will be given in Section 5.5.

Notice that the scheme FerryProblem claims a requirement Object, a module that is equivalent to an instantiation of ListScheme (see Section 4.10) and a requirement Constraints. ListScheme is instantiated by binding its (formal) requirement Item to Object. Since Object is itself a requirement of the scheme FerryProblem, it will be bound to an actual module when FerryProblem is instantiated. In this way, the requirement Item will be bound to that actual module. The requirement Constraints is an example of a requirement in which semantic properties are involved.

```
module FerryDestination;
  import Bool, true, false from Bool;
  export all;
  sort FerryDestination;
```

```
    constructors
       thisBank, yonderBank, thisOrYonderBank: -> FerryDestination;
    operation
       _ = _: FerryDestination * FerryDestination -> Bool;
    operation axioms
       thisBank = thisBank == true;   yonderBank = yonderBank == true;
       thisOrYonderBank = thisOrYonderBank == true;
       thisBank = yonderBank == false;   thisBank = thisOrYonderBank == false;
       yonderBank = thisBank == false;   yonderBank = thisOrYonderBank == false;
       thisOrYonderBank = thisBank == false;   thisOrYonderBank = yonderBank == false;
end module FerryDestination;


scheme FerryProblem [
    requirement Object;
       import Bool, true, _ and _ from Bool,
       export all;
       sort Object;
       operations
          errObject: -> Object;   -- needed for the instantiation of ListScheme
          _ = _: Object * Object -> Bool;
       declare ob, ob₁, ob₂, ob₃: Object;
       theorems
          ob = ob == true;
          ob₁ = ob₂ == ob₂ = ob₁;
          ( ob₁ = ob₂ ) and ( ob₂ = ob₃ ) ⇒ ob₁ = ob₃ == true;
       end requirement Object;

    instantiate ListScheme rename List as ListOfObjects;
       with Item as Object,
          Item as Object,
          undefined as errObject,
          _ = _ as _ = _;
    end instantiate ListScheme;

    requirement Constraints;
       import all from Bool, FerryDestination, ListOfObjects;
       export all;
       operations
          initThisBankList, initYonderBankList: -> ListOfObjects;   -- initial situation
          targetThisBankList, targetYonderBankList: -> ListOfObjects;
             -- target situations
          targetFerryDestination: -> FerryDestination;
          operational, stableFerry, stableThisBank, stableYonderBank:
             ListOfObjects -> Bool;   -- restrictions
       declare obj₁, obj₂: Object;  list₁, list₂, list₃: ListOfObjects; .
       theorems
          ( targetThisBankList & targetYonderBankList ) partof
          ( initThisBankList & initYonderBankList )  ==  true;  -- feasibility
          -- the result of the operations operational, stableFerry, stableThisBank and
          -- stableYonderBank must be independent from the order of the objects
          -- of the given list
          operational( list₃ & ( obj₂ | list₂ ) & ( obj₁ | list₁ ) ) ==
             operational( list₃ & ( obj₁ | list₂ ) & ( obj₂ | list₁ ) );
          stableFerry( list₃ & ( obj₂ | list₂ ) & ( obj₁ | list₁ ) ) ==
             stableFerry( list₃ & ( obj₁ | list₂ ) & ( obj₂ | list₁ ) );
          stableThisBank( list₃ & ( obj₂ | list₂ ) & ( obj₁ | list₁ ) ) ==
```

```
                  stableThisBank( list₃ & ( obj₁ | list₂ ) & ( obj₂ | list₁ ) );
               stableYonderBank( list₃ & ( obj₂ | list₂ ) & ( obj₁ | list₁ ) ) ==
                  stableYonderBank( list₃ & ( obj₁ | list₂ ) & ( obj₂ | list₁ ) );
           end requirement Constraints;
   ];

   module IsSolution;
      import all from Bool, FerryDestination, ListOfObjects, Constraints;
      export all;
      sort CrossSequence;
      constructors
         initial: -> CrossSequence;   -- denotes the initial situation
         cross: ListOfObjects * CrossSequence -> CrossSequence;
            -- after the given CrossSequence the ferry crosses the river with ListOfObjects
            -- aboard
      operations
         isSolution: CrossSequence -> Bool;   -- indicates whether the CrossSequence is
            -- a solution of the ferry problem
         apt: CrossSequence -> Bool;   -- indicates whether the CrossSequence does not
            -- violate the restrictions
         sameBankList, otherBankList: CrossSequence -> ListOfObjects;
            -- returns the ListOfObjects on the bank the ferry has arrived after
            -- CrossSequence, and on the other bank respectively
         thisBankList, yonderBankList: CrossSequence -> ListOfObjects;
            -- returns the ListOfObjects on thisBank and yonderBank respectively
            -- after CrossSequence
         ferryOver: CrossSequence -> Bool;   -- indicates whether the ferry is at
            -- yonderBank
      declare seq, seq₀: CrossSequence;  list: ListOfObjects;
      operation axioms
         isSolution( seq ) == apt( seq ) and ( targetThisBankList partof thisBankList( seq ) )
            and (targetYonderBankList partof yonderBankList( seq ) ) and
            if ferryOver( seq )
               then not ( targetFerryDestination = thisBank )
               else not ( targetFerryDestination = yonderBank )
            end if;
         apt( seq ) == stableThisBank( thisBankList( seq ) ) and
            stableYonderBank( yonderBankList( seq ) ) and
            case seq of
               initial: true;
               cross( list, seq₀ ): ( list partof sameBankList( seq₀ ) ) and operational( list )
                  and stableFerry( list ) and apt( seq₀ );
            end case;
         sameBankList( initial ) == initThisBankList;
         sameBankList( cross( list, seq ) ) == list & otherBankList( seq );
         otherBankList( initial ) == initYonderBankList;
         otherBankList( cross( list, seq ) ) == remove( list, sameBankList( seq ) );
         thisBankList( seq ) ==
            if ferryOver( seq )
               then otherBankList( seq )
               else sameBankList( seq )
            end if;
         yonderBankList( seq ) ==
            if ferryOver( seq )
               then sameBankList( seq )
               else otherBankList( seq )
            end if;
```

```
        ferryOver( initial ) == false;
        ferryOver( cross( list, seq ) ) == not ferryOver( seq );
    end module IsSolution;
end scheme FerryProblem;
```

Fig. 5/1

Refutation of a Common Misconception

Programmers are often puzzled by the remarkable high degree of recursion of algebraic specifications. The ferry problem contains several such instances. One example is the operation apt which takes a sequence of crossings as its single argument and returns a boolean value. Students often raise the question why this function should be recursive: *"After all, when executing the crossings, any unstable intermediate state would result in something being eaten. That could never be a solution as it would be detected in an earlier stage."*

The refutation obviously lies in the fact that nothing gets executed; there simply do not exist any 'earlier stages' as there is *no* inherent time concept. The operation apt is defined on *objects* of sort CrossSequence. Thanks to the mathematical foundation of algebraic specifications (see Chapter 2), the second operation axiom of Fig. 5/1 defines for *which* sequences of crossings the operation apt yields true or false. *How* an apt sequence is obtained or *how* the operation apt may be implemented is irrelevant at this level of abstraction.

It is true that rapid prototyping based on the direct implementation of Fig. 5/1 is inefficient, but that has no influence on the mathematical definition of the abstract data types. Later, when implementing a search strategy, one obviously may (and should) use the fact that any sequence so far constructed is apt in order to avoid extraneous checks, but this pertains to the implementation effort and obviously not to the high level specification.

5.3 The Farmer, the Wolf, the Goat and the Cabbage

The riddle of the farmer, the wolf, the goat and the cabbage is a special case (instantiation) of the ferry problem, see Fig. 5/2.

```
module FarmerWolfGoatCabbage;
  import Bool, true, false from Bool;
  export all;
  sort Thing;
  constructors
    farmer, wolf, goat, cabbage: -> Thing;
  operation
    _ = _: Thing * Thing -> Bool;
  operation axioms
    farmer = farmer == true;   wolf = wolf == true;
    goat = goat == true;   cabbage = cabbage == true;
    farmer = wolf == false;   farmer = goat == false;   farmer = cabbage == false;
    wolf = farmer == false;   wolf = goat == false;   wolf = cabbage == false;
    goat = farmer == false;   goat = wolf == false;   goat = cabbage == false;
    cabbage = farmer == false;   cabbage = wolf == false;   cabbage = goat == false;
end module FarmerWolfGoatCabbage;

instantiate ListScheme rename List as ListOfThings;   -- see Fig. 4/6
  with Item as FarmerWolfGoatCabbage;
    Item as Thing,
    undefined as farmer,   -- arbitrary
    _ = _ as _ = _;
end instantiate ListScheme;

module Conditions;
  import all from Bool, FerryDestination, FarmerWolfGoatCabbage, ListOfThings;
  export all;
  operations
    initThisBankList, initYonderBankList: -> ListOfThings;   -- initial situation
    targetThisBankList, targetYonderBankList: -> ListOfThings;   -- target situations
    targetFerryDestination: -> FerryDestination;
    loadable: ListOfThings -> Bool;   -- the ferry can only ship a limited quantity of
      -- freight
    capable: ListOfThings -> Bool;   -- not every Thing is capable of steering the ferry
    navigable: ListOfThings -> Bool;   -- the ferry is navigable if its freight is
      -- loadable and capable
    stable: ListOfThings -> Bool;
  declare th, th_1, th_2, th_3: Thing;   list: ListOfThings;
  operation axioms
    initThisBankList == cabbage | goat | wolf | farmer | nil;
    initYonderBankList == nil;
    targetThisBankList == nil;
    targetYonderBankList == cabbage | goat | wolf | farmer | nil;
    targetFerryDestination == yonderBank;
    loadable( nil ) == true;
    loadable( th | nil ) == true;
    loadable( th_2 | th_1 | nil ) == true;
    loadable( th_3 | th_2 | th_1 | list ) == false;
    capable( list ) == farmer isin list;
    navigable( list ) == loadable( list ) and capable( list );
    stable( list ) == ( farmer isin list ) or ( not ( goat isin list and cabbage isin list ) and
      not ( goat isin list and wolf isin list ) );
end module Conditions;

instantiate FerryProblem;
  with Object as FarmerWolfGoatCabbage,
```

```
        Object as Thing, errObject as farmer -- arbitrary --,
        _ = _ as _ = _;
    with ListOfObjects as ListOfThings;
    with Constraints as Conditions,
        initThisBankList as initThisBankList, initYonderBankList as initYonderBankList,
        targetThisBankList as targetThisBankList,
        targetYonderBankList as targetYonderBankList,
        targetFerryDestination as targetFerryDestination,
        operational as navigable, stableFerry as stable,
        stableThisBank as stable, stableYonderBank as stable;
    end instantiate FerryProblem;
```

Fig. 5/2

5.4 The Missionaries and the Cannibals

The generalized riddle of the missionaries and cannibals as described in Section 5.1 will be specified as an instantiation of the ferry problem, see Fig. 5/3.

```
    module Person;
      import Bool, true, false from Bool;
      export all;
      sort Person;
      constructors
        missionary, cannibal: -> Person;
      operation
        _ = _: Person * Person -> Bool;
      operation axioms
        missionary = missionary == true;   cannibal = cannibal == true;
        missionary = cannibal == false;   cannibal = missionary == false;
    end module Person;

    instantiate ListScheme rename List as ListOfPersons;
      with Item as Person,
        Item as Person,
        undefined as missionary,   -- arbitrary
        _ = _ as _ = _;
    end instantiate ListScheme;

    scheme RiddleMissionariesAndCannibals [
        requirement Numbers;
          import all from Bool, Nat;
          export all;
          operations
            numberOfMissionaries, numberOfCannibals: -> Nat;
          theorem
```

```
              numberOfCannibals ⩽ numberOfMissionaries == true;
          end requirement Numbers;
    ];

    module Conditions;
      import all from Bool, Nat, FerryDestination, Person, ListOfPersons, Numbers;
      export all;
      operations
        initThisBankList, initYonderBankList: -> ListOfPersons;  -- initial situation
        targetThisBankList, targetYonderBankList: -> ListOfPersons;  -- target situations
        targetFerryDestination: -> FerryDestination;
        loadable, capable, navigable, stable: ListOfPersons -> Bool;  -- restrictions
        create: Nat * Person -> ListOfPersons;  -- creates a ListOfPersons built up
          -- of Nat occurrences of Person
        noMajorityOfCannibals: ListOfPersons -> Bool;  -- indicates whether
          -- there are at least as many missionaries as cannibals
      declare pers, pers₁, pers₂, pers₃: Person;  list: ListOfPersons;  n: Nat;
      operation axioms
        initThisBankList == create( numberOfMissionaries, missionary ) &
          create( numberOfCannibals, cannibal );
        initYonderBankList == nil;
        targetThisBankList == nil;
        targetYonderBankList == create( numberOfMissionaries, missionary ) &
          create( numberOfCannibals, cannibal );
        targetFerryDestination == yonderBank;
        loadable( nil ) == true;
        loadable( pers | nil ) == true;
        loadable( pers₂ | pers₁ | nil ) == true;
        loadable( pers₃ | pers₂ | pers₁ | list ) == false;
        capable( list ) == not permutation( list, nil );
        navigable( list ) == loadable( list ) and capable( list );
        stable( list ) ==
          if missionary isin list
            then noMajorityOfCannibals( list )
            else true
          end if;
        create( zero, pers ) == nil;
        create( succ( n ), pers ) == pers | create( n, pers );
        noMajorityOfCannibals( list ) ==
          if cannibal isin list
            then
              if missionary isin list
                then noMajorityOfCannibals( remove( missionary | cannibal | nil, list ) )
                else false
              end if
            else true
          end if;
    end module Conditions;

    instantiate FerryProblem;
      with Object as Person,
        Object as Person, errObject as missionary  -- arbitrary --,
        _ = _ as _ = _;
      with ListOfObjects as ListOfPersons;
      with Constraints as Conditions,
        initThisBankList as initThisBankList, initYonderBankList as initYonderBankList,
        targetThisBankList as targetThisBankList,
```

```
        targetYonderBankList as targetYonderBankList,
        targetFerryDestination as targetFerryDestination,
        operational as navigable, stableFerry as stable,
        stableThisBank as stable, stableYonderBank as stable;
    end instantiate FerryProblem;
end scheme RiddleMissionariesAndCannibals;
```

Fig. 5/3

The variant in which only the missionaries can row, can be obtained by modifying the specification of the operation capable in the following way:

capable(list) == missionary isin list;

As an example the scheme given above, is instantiated with three missionaries and three cannibals, see Fig. 5/4.

```
instantiate RiddleMissionariesAndCannibals;
  with Number as Nat,
    numberOfMissionaries as 3,
    numberOfCannibals as 3;
end instantiate RiddleMissionariesAndCannibals;
```

Fig. 5/4

5.5 Specification of a Search Strategy

In Fig. 5/5 an implementation of the ferry problem is specified by means of a search strategy based on backtracking. The modules of Fig. 5/5 have to be added to the scheme FerryProblem of Fig. 5/1.

```
-- Auxiliary structure List of ListOfObjects
instantiate ListScheme
  rename
    List as ListOfListsOfObjects,
    nil as nilL,
    _ | _ as _ lL _,
    head as headL,
    tail as tailL,
    _ & _ as _ &L _,
```

```
      delete as deleteL,
      remove as removeL,
      _ isin _ as _ isinL _,
      _ partof _ as _ partofL _,
      permutation as permutationL;
   with Item as ListOfObjects,
      Item as ListOfObjects,
      undefined as nil,
      _ = _ as permutation;
end instantiate ListScheme;

module ListSubLists;
   import all from Object, ListOfObjects, ListOfListsOfObjects;
   export all;
   operations
      listSubLists: ListOfObjects -> ListOfListsOfObjects;
         -- lists all ListOfObjects that are partof the given ListOfObjects
      addL: Object * ListOfListsOfObjects -> ListOfListsOfObjects;
         -- adds Object to every member of ListOfListsOfObjects
   declare obj: Object;  list: ListOfObjects;  listL: ListOfListsOfObjects;
   operation axioms
      listSubLists( nil ) == nil lL nilL;
      listSubLists( obj l list ) == addL( obj, listSubLists( list ) ) &L listSubLists( list );
      addL( obj, nilL ) == nilL;
      addL( obj, list lL listL ) == ( obj l list ) lL addL( obj, listL );
end module ListSubLists;

module Backtrack;
   import all from Bool, IsSolution, ListOfObjects, ListOfListsOfObjects, ListSubLists;
   export all;
   sort ExtendedCrossSequence;   -- simulates an extension of the sort CrossSequence
      -- with the exception unsolvable
   constructors
      unsolvable: -> ExtendedCrossSequence;
      solvedThru: CrossSequence -> ExtendedCrossSequence;
   operations
      solution: -> ExtendedCrossSequence;   -- returns a solution to the ferry problem
      generate: CrossSequence -> ExtendedCrossSequence;   -- generates a solution,
         -- if any, starting with CrossSequence
      try: CrossSequence * ListOfListsOfObjects -> ExtendedCrossSequence;
         -- tries to generate a solution starting from CrossSequence by crossing the river
         -- with a member of ListOfListsOfObjects aboard
      circular: CrossSequence -> Bool;   -- indicates whether the CrossSequence has
         -- passed through two identical situations
      occurred: ListOfObjects * CrossSequence -> Bool;   -- indicates whether the
         -- situation with ListOfObjects on the bank the ferry now is located,
         -- has occurred before
      isunsolvable: ExtendedCrossSequence -> Bool;
   declare seq: CrossSequence;   list, list_1, list_2, list_3: ListOfObjects;
      listL: ListOfListsOfObjects;
   operation axioms
      solution == generate( initial );
      generate( seq ) ==
         if isSolution( seq )
            then solvedThru( seq )
            else
               if apt( seq ) and not circular( seq )
```

```
                then try( seq, listSubLists( sameBankList( seq ) ) )
                else unsolvable
            end if
        end if;
    try( seq, nilL ) == unsolvable;
    try( seq, list IL listL ) ==
        if isunsolvable( generate( cross( list, seq ) ) )
            then try( seq, listL )
            else generate( cross( list, seq ) )
        end if;
    circular( initial ) == false;
    circular( cross( list, seq ) ) == occurred( sameBankList( cross( list, seq ) ),
        cross( list, seq ) ) or circular( seq );
    occurred( list, initial ) == false;
    occurred( list₁, cross( list₂, initial ) ) == false;
    occurred( list₁, cross( list₂, cross( list₃, seq ) ) ) ==
        permutation( list₁, sameBankList( seq ) ) or occurred( list₁, seq );
    isunsolvable( unsolvable ) == true;
    isunsolvable( solvedThru( seq ) ) == false;
end module Backtrack;
```

Fig. 5/5

5.6 Conclusion

The ferry problem was a nice example of a parameterized specification. Building parameterized specifications requires considerably more time, but this additional effort is justified by the obtained reusability of the specifications. A distinction was made between the specification of a solution (the *what*), in Section 5.2, and the specification of the implementation (the *how*), in Section 5.5. If a mathematician ever finds an analytic formula to obtain a solution of the ferry problem, we will only have to replace Section 5.5, and not Section 5.2.

In [Warren74, Warren76] a planning problem, called Warplan, is given. Warplan can be considered as an even more general problem than the Ferry Problem. The main difference is that no requirements for the data of Warplan are given. The coherence of the data is the responsibility of the user [Kluzniak85]. Furthermore, instantiating Warplan requires substantially more work than instantiating the Ferry Problem.

6. A Case Study: the Mini-PABX

"Alexander Graham Bell is alive and well in New York,
and still waiting for a dial tone."
/usr/games/fortune

One of the most interesting case studies we made is the formal specification of a substantial part of a call handling system, the *ITT 5400 BCS* (Business Communication System) [Bell85b]. The ITT 5400 BCS is a modern Private Automatic Branch Exchange (PABX for short), which has been developed and produced by Bell Telephone Mfg. Co. Geel (Belgium) in the context of ITT's Office 2000 concept. Because voice communication accounts for some 80% of all office communications [Bell85a], the ITT 5400 BCS is supplied with a wide range of features. These features considerably improve the flow of information, provide more ease of operation and save time and costs. The range of features for voice communications includes extension features (i.e. features for the ordinary users), operator features and system features.

In [Goovaers86] a first attempt was made to describe several extension features of the ITT 5400 BCS in a formal way. The whole PABX was designed as a single monolithic data structure. This design decision resulted in a specification with poor modularity, readability and extendibility. Poor extendibility means that the number of telephone states grew out of control very rapidly when new features were added. This phenomenon is called *state explosion* in [Jacobs86].

Having learned from this experiment J. De Man (Bell Telephone Mfg. Co. Antwerp) suggested to use a more object-oriented approach, inspired by state transition models [Sunshine82] used for the specifications of protocols. In [Vergauwen87] we have developed such an object-oriented design method and we have used it for the specification of the ITT 5400 BCS. The resulting specification is highly modular and adaptable and therefore more readable. The so-called state explosion has been mastered in an elegant way. In the specification abstraction is made from any hardware aspect of the PABX, in contrast with [Biebow85] where a component of a telephone system, in particular a 'switching module', is specified.

Because of the length of this industrial case study, we have extracted a *mini-PABX* from the PABX. This mini-PABX provides only the two-party voice calls and the enquiry feature of the ITT 5400 BCS.

6.1 Object–Oriented Design Method

In this section the design method of the PABX is explained. We call this method *object-oriented* in the sense that the various logical *objects* are identified and specified. Each (logical) object is always in a definite *state*. Furthermore, the objects may communicate with each other by sending *messages*. When an object receives a message, the state of the object may be changed and the object in turn may send messages to other objects. This will be explained and illustrated later on.

Within the world of our mini-PABX, we can distinguish two sorts of logical objects: the telephonic apparatuses, abbreviated phones, and the users of the mini-PABX. The former are part of the mini-PABX whereas the latter are not. We are not interested in the state of the users but only in the messages they send to the phones. The word message must be interpreted in its broadest sense. Examples of messages sent by users are:

- a message for terminating a call:

  onHook: -> UserMessage;

- a message for calling someone:

  dialCode: Code -> UserMessage;

- a message for enquiring:

  button: -> UserMessage;

Phones cannot send messages to users. We assume that the users can inspect the states of their phones. Phones are characterized by a state. An example is shown in Fig. 6/1, where phone A is in state C(dialTone).

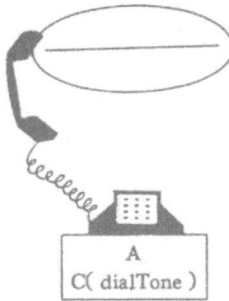

Fig. 6/1

Not only users may send messages to phones, phones may also send messages to each other.

Assume that the user of phone A sends the message U(dialCode(phoneCode(B))) to phone A, i.e. the user of phone A dials the number of phone B. When phone A receives this message, two actions will happen:

- The state of phone A will be changed to C(callWaiting(B)).

- Phone A will send the message C(callRequest(A)) to phone B. In general, an object may send several messages to several objects.

This is graphically shown in Fig. 6/2. Notice that a graphical representation of a phone contains its name and its state, messages are represented by labelled full arrows, and when the state of a phone is changed, it is represented with the old as well as with the new state connected by a dotted arrow. Furthermore, the actions (of changing states and sending messages) are chronologically numbered.

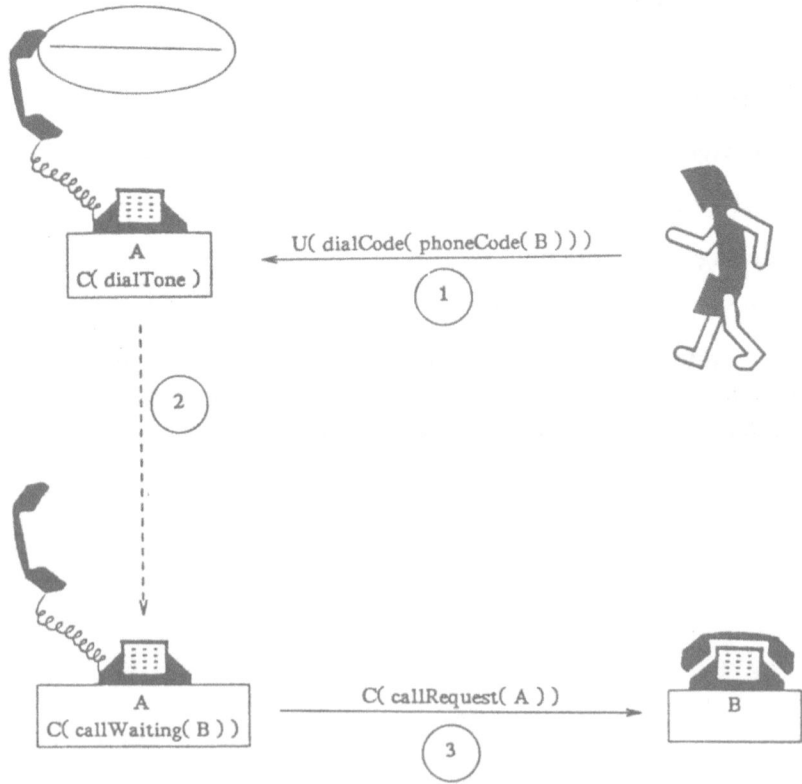

Fig. 6/2

In a similar way, the state of phone B may be changed when it receives the message from phone A and phone B may send messages to other objects.

How the state of a phone is changed when it receives a phone message, is specified with the operation next, see Fig. 6/3. The sort Phone consists of the Cartesian product of sort PhoneIdentity with several sorts indicating the state of a phone. The sort PhoneMessage consists of the messages that can be send to a phone (examples of phone messages are the message C(callRequest(A)) and the user messages given above).

```
   ...
   sort Phone == PhoneIdentity * ... ;
   ...
   sort PhoneMessage;
   ...
   operation
     next: PhoneMessage * Phone -> Phone;
   ...
```

Fig. 6/3

Which phone messages are send to which phones when a phone receives a phone message is specified by the operation out, see Fig. 6/4. The sort ListOfMessages is a list of message pairs. A message pair is a phone message together with its destination.

```
   ...
   sort MessagePair;
   constructor
     send _ toPhone _: PhoneMessage * PhoneIdentity -> MessagePair;
   ...

instantiate ListScheme rename List as ListOfMessages; -- see Fig. 4/6
   with ...,
     Item as MessagePair;
end instantiate ListOfScheme;

   ...
   operation
     out: PhoneMessage * Phone -> ListOfMessages;
   ...
```

Fig. 6/4

6.2 Modularity

Because of the complexity of our case study, modularity is a necessary condition for obtaining a readable and extendible specification. The specification of the mini-PABX contains a two-level structure of modularity. The first level is related to the partitioning into modules as it was done in the examples of the previous chapters. The second level of modularity is related to the stepwise extension of the mini-PABX. We start with the base case: a two-party voice call. In a second step, the enquiry feature is added. Finally, the user actions are studied. With each new feature corresponds a new step. In the specification of the ITT 5400 BCS [Vergauwen87], we used thirteen steps. Notice that the user actions are treated in a separate step since user actions may be related to various features. For instance, going on-hook may terminate a two-party voice call as well as an enquiry call.

This modularity based on the various features is reflected in the use of the object-oriented mechanism as well. In the previous section we explained that the messages that can be sent to a phone are defined by sort PhoneMessage. Instead of defining sort PhoneMessage by directly enumerating the various messages that can be received by a phone, we define it as a union of a number of sorts corresponding to the messages introduced for the various features, see Fig. 6/5. Sort CallMessage specifies the messages concerning the two-party voice calls. Sort UserMessage specifies the messages that can be sent by the users. Each time a new feature is introduced, a new module defining the specific messages sent to phones will be specified and the module PhoneMessages will be adapted so that sort PhoneMessage contains the new messages as well. The great advantage of this method is that the other modules defining messages of the previous features remain unchanged.

```
module CallMessages;
   . . .
   sort CallMessage;
   constructors
     callRequest: PhoneIdentity -> CallMessage;
   . . .
end module CallMessages;

module UserMessages;
   . . .
   sort UserMessage;
   constructors
     dialCode: Code -> UserMessage;
   . . .
```

```
    end module UserMessages;

    ...

  module PhoneMessages;
    ...
    sort PhoneMessage;
    constructors
      C: CallMessage -> PhoneMessage;
      U: UserMessage -> PhoneMessage;
    ...
  end module PhoneMessages;
```

Fig. 6/5

Analogously, the operation next of Fig. 6/3 is defined as the union of a number of operations corresponding to the messages of the various features, see Fig. 6/6.

```
  module NextCallPhone;
    ...
    operation
      next: CallMessage * Phone -> Phone;
    ...
  end module NextCallPhone;

  module NextUserPhone;
    ...
    operation
      next: UserMessage * Phone -> Phone;
    ...
  end module NextUserPhone;

  ...

  module NextPhone;
    ...
    operation
      next: PhoneMessage * Phone -> Phone;
    declare callmsg: CallMessage;  usermsg: UserMessage;  ph: Phone;
    operation axioms
      next( C( callmsg ), ph ) == NextCallPhone.next( callmsg, ph );
      next( U( usermsg ), ph ) == NextUserPhone.next( usermsg, ph );
    ...
  end module NextPhone;
```

Fig. 6/6

Analogously, the operation out of Fig. 6/4 is defined as the union of a number of operations corresponding with the messages of the various features, see Fig. 6/7.

```
module OutCallListOfMessages;
  . . .
  operation
    out: CallMessage * Phone -> ListOfMessages;
  . . .
end module OutCallListOfMessages;

module OutUserListOfMessages;
  . . .
  operation
    out: UserMessage * Phone -> ListOfMessages;
  . . .
end module OutUserListOfMessages;

. . .

module OutPhone;
  . . .
  operation
    out: PhoneMessage * Phone -> ListOfMessages;
    declare callmsg: CallMessage;   usermsg: UserMessage;   ph: Phone;
  operation axioms
    out( C( callmsg ), ph ) == OutCallListOfMessages.out( callmsg, ph );
    out( U( usermsg ), ph ) == OutUserListOfMessages.out( usermsg, ph );
    . . .
end module OutPhone;
```

Fig. 6/7

6.3 The Abstract Data Type Phone

Our mini-PABX has only one sort of logical objects, i.e. the sort Phone. Every phone has an identity. This identity may be a five-digit number, a room identification, the name of the subscriber, a colour, ... The concrete definition of the identity is not relevant for the specification of our mini-PABX. Therefore, the specification of the mini-PABX will be parameterized with the requirement PhoneIdentity, where a sort PhoneIdentity, an object errPhoneIdentity for error handling and a classical equality operation are required, see Fig. 6/8.

```
requirement PhoneIdentity;
  import Bool, true, _ and _ from Bool;
  export all;
  sort PhoneIdentity;
  operations
    errPhoneIdentity: -> PhoneIdentity;
    _ = _: PhoneIdentity * PhoneIdentity -> Bool;
  declare i, i₁, i₂, i₃: PhoneIdentity;
  theorems
    i = i == true;
    i₁ = i₂ == i₂ = i₁;
    (i₁ = i₂) and (i₂ = i₃) ⇒ (i₁ = i₃) == true;
end requirement PhoneIdentity;
```

Fig. 6/8

Besides an identity, a phone has also a phonestate. The modularity obtained by stepwise extending the mini-PABX is reflected in the definition of the sort Phone in two ways. Firstly, the sort phone is a Cartesian product of sort Identity and sort PhoneState. Each time a new feature is introduced, the Cartesian product may be extended with new characteristics (e.g., PhoneMode when the enquiry feature is introduced, see Section 6.9). Secondly, sort PhoneState is a union of sorts corresponding with the states (if any) introduced for the various features.

The skeleton for the definition of the abstract data type phone is given in Fig. 6/9.

```
module CallStates;
  ...
  sort CallState;
  constructors
    dialTone: -> CallState;
    callWaiting: PhoneIdentity -> CallState;
  ...
end module CallStates;

module PhoneStates;
  ...
  sort PhoneState;
  constructors
    C: CallState -> PhoneState;  -- Notice that this constructor C is
       -- distinct from the C of module PhoneMessages (overloading).
  ...
end module PhoneStates;

...

module Phone;
```

```
      . . .
   sort Phone == PhoneIdentity * PhoneState * PhoneMode * ...
      . . .
end module Phone;
```

Fig. 6/9

6.4 Error Handling

A designer may build a specification so that certain situations cannot occur. For example, in Section 6.8 a phone will receive the message C(callAccepted) only if it is in the state C(callWaiting(_)). Because of the completeness constraints, the operations next and out must also be defined for a phone in another state receiving this message. Instead of writing an arbitrary term, we will write error. Error may be interpreted as an overloaded nullary operation that is propagated by the other operations.

Because of physical limitations of the classical telephonic apparatuses, certain combinations of user actions are impossible. E.g., it is impossible to hang up twice without picking up the receiver. We will abstract from these physical limitations of phones. Indeed, we may imagine apparatuses where going on-hook is performed by operating a button. With such phones, hanging up twice without going off-hook is simply done by pushing the (on-hook) button twice.

Erroneous actions performed by users are treated in the same object-oriented and modular way as the not-erroneous actions. E.g., in Section 6.8 dialling a wrong number is discussed.

6.5 The Abstract Data Type Mini-PABX

It is obvious that our mini-PABX will contain several phones. Therefore, sort PhonePool is defined in Fig. 6/10 by instantiating scheme ObjectPoolScheme. ObjectPoolScheme defines a pool of objects (second requirement of the scheme) where each object has an identity (first requirement of the scheme). The constructor emptyObjectPool creates an empty pool, whereas the constructor addObject adds the given object to the given pool. The information about an object may be overridden by means of the operation update. The operation select selects the object with the given identity in the given pool. The operation isIn checks whether the given pool contains an object with the given identity.

```
scheme ObjectPoolScheme [
    requirement Identity;
      import Bool, true, _ and _ from Bool;
      export all;
      sort Identity;
      operation
        _ = _: Identity * Identity -> Bool;
      declare i, i₁, i₂, i₃: Identity;
      theorems
        i = i == true;
        i₁ = i₂ == i₂ = i₁;
        (i₁ = i₂) and (i₂ = i₃) ⟹ (i₁ = i₃) == true;
    end requirement Identity;

    requirement Object;
      import Identity from Identity;
      export all;
      sort Object;
      operations
        errObject: -> Object;
        identityOf _: Object -> Identity;
    end requirement Object;
];

module ObjectPool;
    import Object, errObject, identityOf_ from Object;
      Bool, true, false, not from Bool;  Identity, _ = _ from Identity;
    export ObjectPool, emptyObjectPool, addObject, update, select, isIn, remove;
    sort ObjectPool;
    constructors
        emptyObjectPool: -> ObjectPool;
        addObject: ObjectPool * Object -> ObjectPool;
    operations
        update: ObjectPool * Object -> ObjectPool;
        select: ObjectPool * Identity -> Object;
        remove: ObjectPool * Identity -> ObjectPool;
        isIn: ObjectPool * Identity -> Bool;
    declare obj, obj₁, obj₂: Object;  id: Identity;  pl: ObjectPool;
    constructor axioms
      not (identityOf obj₁ = identityOf obj₂) ⟹
        addObject( addObject( pl, obj₁ ), obj₂ ) ==
        addObject( addObject( pl, obj₂ ), obj₁ );
      (identityOf obj₁ = identityOf obj₂) ⟹
        addObject( addObject( pl, obj₁), obj₂ ) ) ==
        addObject( pl, obj₂ );
    operation axioms
      update( emptyObjectPool, obj ) == error;
      update( addObject( pl, obj₁ ), obj₂ ) ==
        if identityOf obj₁ = identityOf obj₂
          then addObject( pl, obj₂ )
            else addObject( update( pl, obj₂ ), obj₁ )
          end if;
      select( emptyObjectPool, id ) == errObject;
      select(addObject( pl, obj ), id ) ==
```

```
            if identityOf obj = id
               then obj
               else select( pl, id )
            end if;
         remove( emptyObjectPool, id ) == error;
         remove( addObject( pl, obj ), id ) ==
            if identityOf obj = id
               then pl
               else addObject( remove( pl, id ), obj )
            end if;
         isIn( emptyObjectPool, id ) == false;
         isIn( addObject( pl, obj ), id ) ==
            if identityOf obj = id
               then true
               else isIn( pl, id )
            end if;
      end module ObjectPool;
   end scheme ObjectPoolScheme;

   instantiate ObjectPoolScheme
      rename ObjectPool as PhonePool, emptyObjectPool as emptyPhonePool,
         addObject as addPhone;
      with Object as Phone,
         Object as Phone,
         errObject as errPhone,
         identityOf _ as phoneIdentityOf _;
      with Identity as PhoneIdentity,
         Identity as PhoneIdentity,
         _ = _ as _ = _;
   end instantiate ObjectPoolScheme;
```

Fig. 6/10

In [Vergauwen87] the sort PABX is defined as

```
sort PABX == PhonePool * BookingOffice * WakeUpService * MeetingPool;
```

Fig. 6/11

Sorts BookingOffice, WakeUpService and MeetingPool are respectively
related to the booking feature, the wake up feature and the conference
feature. This reflects the modularity obtained by stepwise extending the
mini-PABX. Each time a new feature is added, the Cartesian product may
be extended. In our mini-PABX we will only need sort PhonePool, see Fig.
6/12.

```
module MiniPABX;
  import PhonePool from PhonePool;
  export all;
  sort MiniPABX == PhonePool;
end module MiniPABX;
```

Fig. 6/12

6.6 The Scheduling of the Messages

Assume that a user sends a message to his phone (e.g., he hangs up, i.e. he sends the user message onHook). As explained in Section 6.1, his phone may be changed of state and his phone may send messages to other phones. These phones in turn may be changed of states and send messages to other phones, and so on. The state of the mini-PABX is stable when the whole chain of receiving and sending has been finished. This transformation of the mini-PABX activated by a single message can be described in a formal way by means of the operation transform. The expression transform(msg, oldMiniPABX) denotes the new stable state of the mini-PABX, obtained after sending the message msg to the mini-PABX that was in state oldMiniPABX.

The operation transform is specified in module MessageScheduler, see Fig. 6/13, using the hidden operation hiddenTransform. The operation hiddenTransform has a list of messages and a mini-PABX as arguments and returns a transformed, stable mini-PABX, obtained by sending the given and activated messages one by one to the mini-PABX.

```
module MessageScheduler;
  import all from MiniPABX;  all from PhonePool;
    PhoneIdentity from PhoneIdentity;  Phone from Phone;
    next from NextPhone;  out from OutPhone;  all from ListOfMessages;
    all from MessagePairs;  PhoneMessage from PhoneMessages;
  export transform;
  operations
    transform: MessagePair * MiniPABX -> MiniPABX;
    hiddenTransform: ListOfMessages * MiniPABX -> MiniPABX;
  declare pabx, newpabx: MiniPABX;  msg: MessagePair;
    listofmsg, outmsg: ListOfMessages;  phmsg: PhoneMessage;
    ph, newph: Phone;  phid: PhoneIdentity;  phpool: PhonePool;
  operation axioms
    transform( msg, pabx ) == hiddenTransform( msg I nil, pabx );
    hiddenTransform( nil, pabx ) == pabx;
    hiddenTransform( send phmsg toPhone phid I listofmsg, pabx) ==
```

```
        let  phpool == phonePoolOf pabx;
          ph == select( phpool, phid );
          newph == NextPhone.next( phmsg, ph );
          newpabx == update( pabx, newph );
          outmsg == OutPhone.out( phmsg, ph );
        in
          hiddenTransform( outmsg & listofmsg, newpabx )
        end let;
    end module MessageScheduler;
```

Fig. 6/13

6.7 Skeleton of the Mini-PABX

In Fig. 6/14 the concepts and structures discussed in the previous sections
are combined into the skeleton of the mini-PABX.

scheme MiniPABX [

> **for every sort Object of logical objects of the mini-PABX
> that requires an identity:**

>> a data module requiring a sort ObjectIdentity

```
            requirement PhoneIdentity;
              ... -- see Fig. 6/8
            end requirement PhoneIdentity;
    ];
```

> **for every sort Object of logical objects of the mini-PABX,
> the following modules are defined:**

>> a data module defining the sort Object

```
            module Phone;
              ... -- see Fig. 6/9
            end module Phone;
```

>> a data module defining the sort ObjectMessage

```
            module PhoneMessages;
              ... -- see Fig. 6/5
            end module PhoneMessages;
```

>> a functional module defining the operation next

```
                    module NextPhone;
                    ...  -- see Fig. 6/6
                    end module NextPhone;
```

> a functional module defining the operation out

```
                    module OutPhone;
                    ...  -- see Fig. 6/7
                    end module OutPhone;
```

> the mini-PABX and the MessageScheduler

> a data module defining the sort MiniPABX

```
                    module MiniPABX;
                    ...  -- see Fig. 6/12
                    end module MiniPABX;
```

> data modules defining the sorts MessagePair and ListOfMessages

```
                    module MessagePairs;
                    ...  -- see Fig. 6/4
                    end module MessagePairs;

                    module ListOfMessages;
                    ...  -- see Fig. 6/4
                    end module ListOfMessages;
```

> a functional module defining the operation transform

```
                    module MessageScheduler;
                    ...  -- see Fig. 6/13
                    end module MessageScheduler;
```

```
end scheme miniPABX;
```

Fig. 6/14

6.8 A Two-Party Voice Call

A *two-party voice call* [Steegmans84] is the simplest call type which a user
may make to and receive from another party, without intervention of a
third party. A user may go off-hook and dial the number of the wanted
party. If the called phone is busy, he receives the busy tone. If the called
phone is free, he receives the ring tone and the called phone starts ringing.
When the called party goes off-hook, the two-party voice call has been
realized. The call is terminated as soon as one of both goes on-hook.

6.8.1 The Module Phone

In Fig. 6/15 the module Phone is defined as explained in Section 6.3. We remember that sort PhoneState is a union of sort CallState with other sorts that will be added when new features of the mini-PABX are defined.

```
module CallStates;
  import PhoneIdentity from PhoneIdentity;
  export all;
  sort CallState;
  constructors
    idle: -> CallState;
    ringing: PhoneIdentity -> CallState;
    dialTone: -> CallState;
    callWaiting: PhoneIdentity -> CallState;
    busyTone: PhoneIdentity -> CallState;
    ringTone: PhoneIdentity -> CallState;
    errorTone: -> CallState;
    connected: PhoneIdentity -> CallState;
    terminating: -> CallState;
end module CallStates;

module PhoneStates;
  import CallState from CallStates;
  export all;
  sort PhoneState;
  constructor
    C: CallState -> PhoneState;
end module PhoneStates;

module Phone;
  import PhoneIdentity, errPhoneIdentity from PhoneIdentity;
    PhoneState, C from PhoneStates;   idle from CallStates;
  export all except (_, _), _[ _ / phoneIdentity ];
  sort Phone == PhoneIdentity * PhoneState
    rename phoneIdentityOf _ as identityOf _;
  operations
    newPhone: PhoneIdentity -> Phone;
    errPhone: -> Phone;
  declare id: PhoneIdentity;
  operation axioms
    newPhone( id ) == ( id, C( idle ) );
    errPhone == ( errPhoneIdentity, C( idle ) );
end module Phone;
```

Fig. 6/15

6.8.2 *The Module PhoneMessages*

A *call connection* from phone A to phone B has been established if and only if:

- phoneStateOf phone(A) == C(ringTone(B));
- phoneStateOf phone(B) == C(ringing(A));

A *talk connection* between phone A and phone B has been established if and only if:

- phoneStateOf phone(A) == C(connected(B));
- phoneStateOf phone(B) == C(connected(A));

The messages that will be introduced for specifying two-party voice calls can be partitioned into four classes:

- messages for establishing a call connection,
- messages for terminating a call connection,
- messages for transforming a call connection into a talk connection,
- messages for terminating a talk connection.

If phone A wants to realize a two-party voice call to phone B, it must establish a call connection first, which can be transformed into a talk connection.

Establishing a Call Connection

For establishing a call connection from phone A to phone B, phone A sends the message C(callRequest(A)) to phone B. If phone B accepts this request, it answers with the message C(callAccepted). If phone B does not accept, e.g., because it is busy, it sends the message C(callRefused) to phone A. These two scenarios are graphically illustrated in Fig. 6/16 and 6/17.

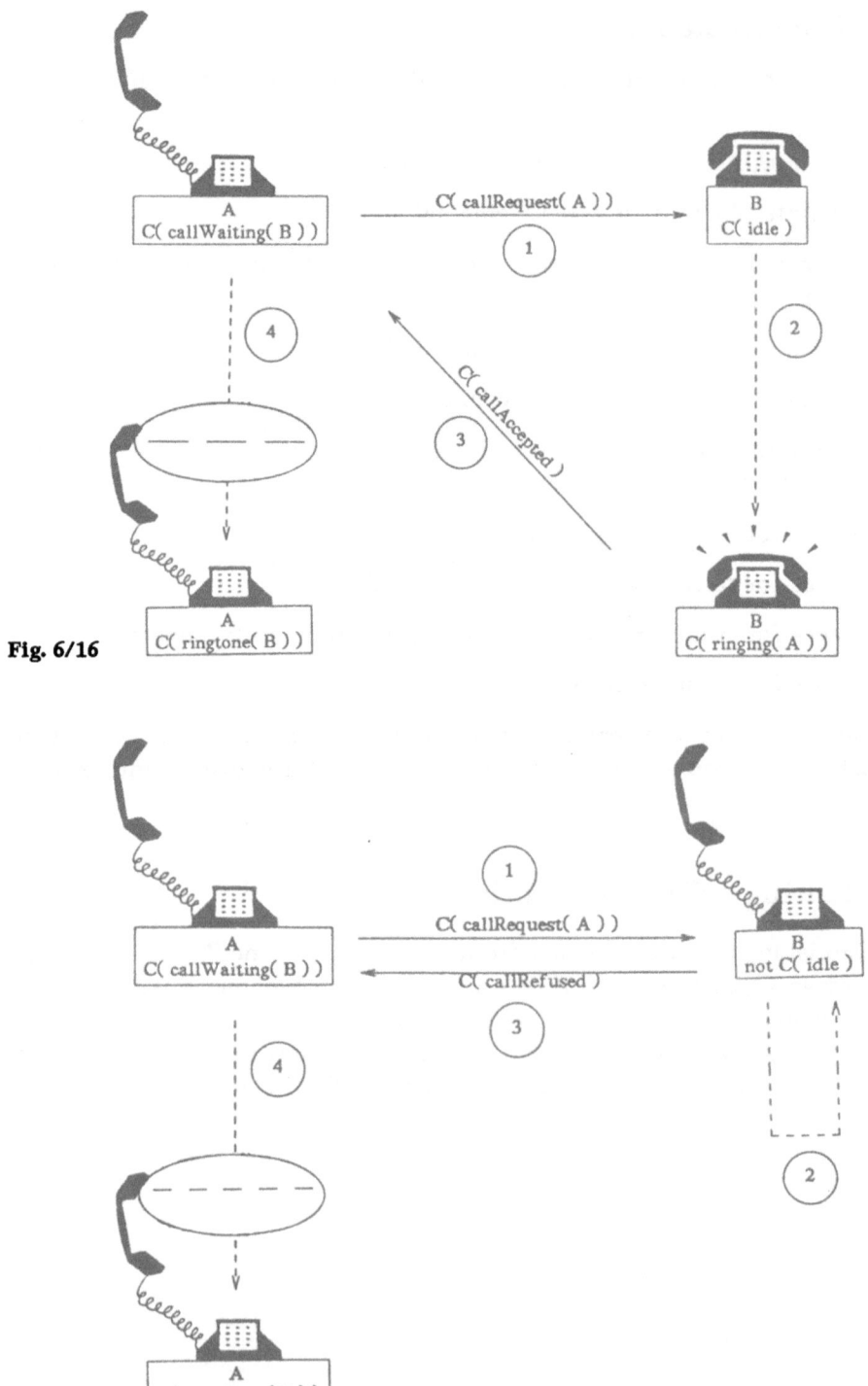

Fig. 6/16

Fig. 6/17

The reader may wonder what happens when the user of phone A dials a wrong nummer, i.e. phone A sends the message C(callRequest(A)) to a phone that is not in the phone pool. According to the specification of the operation select in Fig. 6/10, the message C(callRequest(A)) will be sent to the phone errPhone. When errPhone receives this message, it will send back the message C(callErroneous) to phone A. This object-oriented error handling is graphically shown in Fig. 6/18.

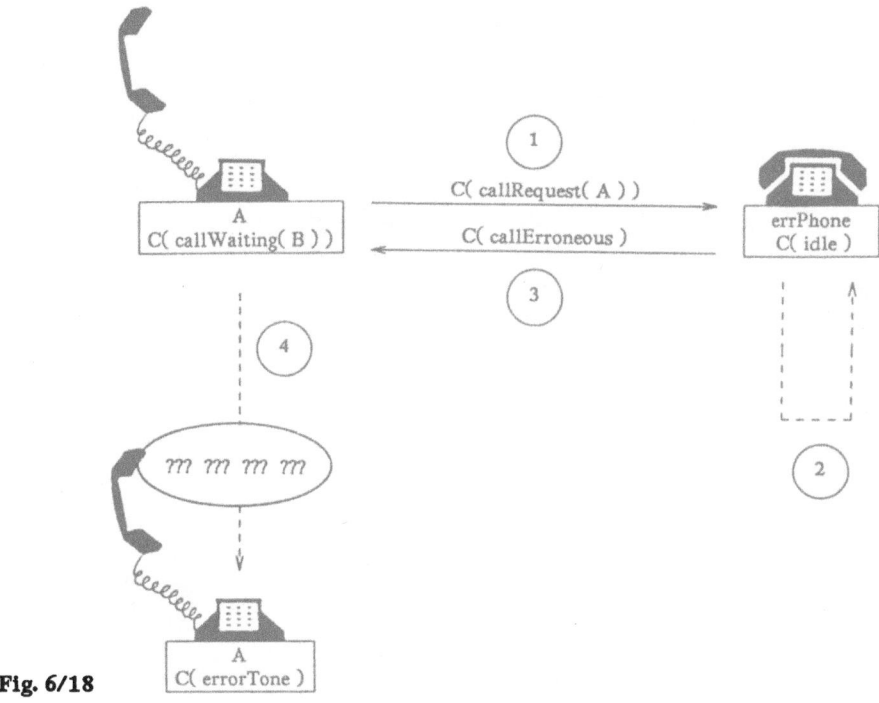

Fig. 6/18

Terminating a Call Connection

A call connection from phone A to phone B can only be terminated by phone A by sending the message C(ringingTermination) to phone B. This is shown in Fig. 6/19.

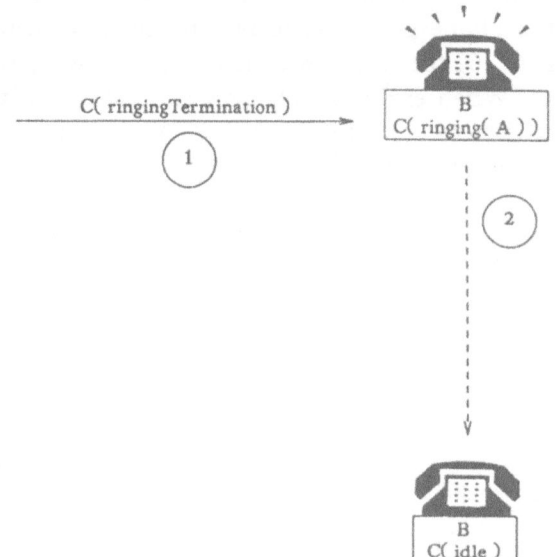

Fig. 6/19

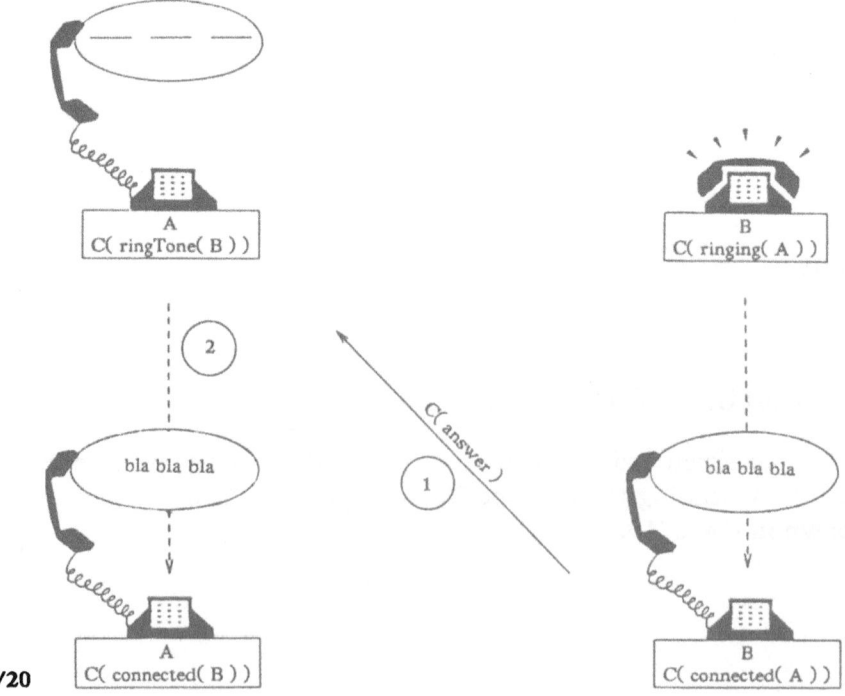

Fig. 6/20

Transforming a Call Connection into a Talk Connection

Only the called phone B can transform the call connection into a talk connection. This can be done by sending the message C(answer) to the calling phone A, see Fig. 6/20.

Terminating a Talk Connection

Both parties of a talk connection may terminate the talk connection by sending the message C(callTermination) to the other phone, see Fig. 6/21.

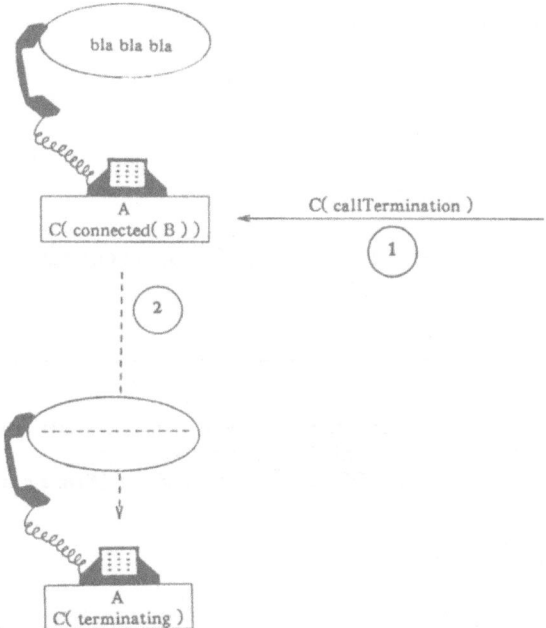

Fig. 6/21

All these messages are formally specified in the module CallMessages, see Fig. 6/22. The sort PhoneMessage is the union of sort CallMessage with other sorts that will be added when new features of the mini-PABX are defined, see Section 6.2.

```
module CallMessages;
  import PhoneIdentity from PhoneIdentity;
  export all;
  sort CallMessage;
  constructors
    callRequest: PhoneIdentity -> CallMessage;
```

```
    callAccepted: -> CallMessage;
    callRefused: -> CallMessage;
    callErroneous: -> CallMessage;
    ringingTermination: -> CallMessage;
    answer: -> CallMessage;
    callTermination: -> CallMessage;
  end module CallMessages;

  module PhoneMessages;
    import CallMessage from CallMessages;
    export all;
    sort PhoneMessage;
    constructor
      C: CallMessage -> PhoneMessage;
  end module PhoneMessages;
```

Fig. 6/22

6.8.3 The Module NextPhone

The operation next is defined in Fig. 6/23, according to the method
discussed in Sections 6.1 and 6.2.

```
  module NextCallPhone;
    import PhoneIdentity, errPhoneIdentity from PhoneIdentity;  all from CallMessages;
      C from PhoneStates;  all except dialTone from CallStates;
      Phone, identityOf _, phoneStateOf _, _[ _ / phoneState ] from Phone;
    export next to NextPhone;
    operation
      next: CallMessage * Phone -> Phone;
    declare id: PhoneIdentity;  ph: Phone;
    operation axioms
      next( callRequest( id ), ph ) ==
        if identityOf ph = errPhoneIdentity
          then ph
          else
            case phoneStateOf ph of
              C( idle ): ph [ C( ringing( id ) ) / phoneState ];
              otherwise: ph;
            end case
        end if;

      next( callAccepted, ph ) ==
        case phoneStateOf ph of
          C( callWaiting( id ) ): ph [ C( ringTone( id ) ) / phoneState ];
          otherwise: error;
        end case;

      next( callRefused, ph ) ==
        case phoneStateOf ph of
```

```
              C( callWaiting( id ) ): ph [ C( busyTone( id ) ) / phoneState ];
              otherwise: error;
           end case;

        next( ringingTermination, ph ) ==
           case phoneStateOf ph of
              C( ringing( id ) ): ph [ C( idle ) / phoneState ];
              otherwise: error;
           end case;

        next( answer, ph ) ==
           case phoneStateOf ph of
              C( ringTone( id ) ): ph [ C( connected( id ) ) / phoneState ];
              otherwise: error;
           end case;

        next( callTermination, ph ) ==
           case phoneStateOf ph of
              C( connected( id ) ): ph [ C( terminating ) / phoneState ];
              otherwise: error;
           end case;

        next( callErroneous, ph ) ==
           ph [ C( errorTone ) / phoneState ];
     end module NextCallPhone;

     module NextPhone;
        import all from PhoneMessages;   Phone from Phone;
           CallMessage from CallMessages;   next from NextCallPhone;
        export next;
        operation
           next: PhoneMessage * Phone -> Phone;
        declare callmsg: CallMessage;   ph: Phone;
        operation axiom
           next( C( callmsg ), ph ) == NextCallPhone.next( callmsg, ph );
     end module NextPhone;
```

Fig. 6/23

6.8.4 The Module OutPhone

Analogously, the operation out is given in Fig. 6/24.

```
     module OutCallListOfMessages;
        import PhoneIdentity, errPhoneIdentity from PhoneIdentity;   C from PhoneMessages;
           ListOfMessages, nil, _ | _ from ListOfMessages;   idle from CallStates;
           Phone, identityOf _, phoneStateOf _ from Phone;   C from PhoneStates;
           all from CallMessages;   send _ toPhone _ from MessagePairs;
        export out to OutPhone;
        operation
           out: CallMessage * Phone -> ListOfMessages;
```

```
    declare id: PhoneIdentity;   ph: Phone;
    operation axioms
      out( callRequest( id ), ph ) ==
        if identityOf ph = errPhoneIdentity
          then send C( callErroneous ) toPhone id | nil
          else
            case phoneStateOf ph of
              C( idle ): send C( callAccepted ) toPhone id | nil;
              otherwise: send C( callRefused ) toPhone id | nil;
            end case
          end if;

      out( callAccepted, ph ) == nil;

      out( callRefused, ph ) == nil;

      out( ringingTermination, ph ) == nil;

      out( answer, ph ) == nil;

      out( callTermination, ph ) == nil;

      out( callErroneous, ph ) == nil;
    end module OutCallListOfMessages;

    module OutPhone;
      import all from PhoneMessages;   Phone from Phone;
        CallMessage from CallMessages;   out from OutCallListOfMessages;
        ListOfMessages from ListOfMessages;
      export out;
      operation
        out: PhoneMessage * Phone -> ListOfMessages;
        declare callmsg: CallMessage;   ph: Phone;
      operation axiom
        out(C(callmsg), ph) == OutCallListOfMessages.out(callmsg, ph);
    end module OutPhone;
```

Fig. 6/24

6.9 Enquiry Call

A user engaged in any call (e.g., a two-party voice call) may initiate an enquiry call to a third party, set up a conversation with this third party and then return to his previous party.

To do so, the following actions must be taken. One of the two parties involved in the original call, say the first party, operates the recall button, dial tone is returned to this party. The first party can dial now the third party's number. According to the state of the third party, ring tone or busy tone is returned. If the phone of the third party is free, it starts ringing. When the third party goes off-hook, an *enquiry call* [Steegmans85] has been realized, communication between the first and third party is possible. During the whole enquiry call, the second party cannot communicate with the first party any more, the second party is held in a kind of waiting state. The first party in conversation with the third party returns to the second party operating the recall button. Then, the enquiry call to the third party is terminated.

In [Steegmans85, Vergauwen87] a third party cannot make an enquiry to a further party during the enquiry call. Here, we will abandon this restriction, resulting in a more general definition of the enquiry call.

6.9.1 The Module Phone

Up to now, a phone could be involved in one connection at most. This connection could be a call or talk connection. A phone involved in one connection at most is said to be in a normal mode. Introducing enquiry calls means that a phone may be involved in two connections: the *underlying connection* and the *enquiry connection*. The enquiry connection may be a call or talk connection. The underlying connection may only be a *blocked connection* (this will be defined later). The enquiry connection, which is the active connection, will still be described by means of the sort PhoneState, which is a component of the sort Phone. We introduce a new sort, called PhoneMode, to describe the underlying connection, see Fig. 6/25.

```
module PhoneModes;
  import PhoneIdentity from PhoneIdentity;
  export all;
  sort PhoneMode;
  constructors
    normal: -> PhoneMode;
    enquiry: PhoneIdentity -> PhoneMode;
    enquiryNil: -> PhoneMode;
end module PhoneModes;
```

Fig. 6/25

The mode normal indicates that the phone has not initiated an enquiry call (but it may, e.g., have been called by a phone in enquiry mode). A phone B has mode enquiry(A) as soon as it has operated the recall button

to initiate an enquiry call during a call connection with phone A. If phone
A hangs up during the enquiry call, however, the mode of phone B becomes
enquiryNil. In Fig. 6/26 the sort PhoneMode is added to sort Phone.

```
module Phone;
  import PhoneIdentity, errPhoneIdentity from PhoneIdentity;
    PhoneState, C from PhoneStates;
    PhoneMode, normal from PhoneModes;  idle from Callstates;
  export all except ( _, _, _ ) , _ [ _ / phoneIdentity ];
  sort Phone == PhoneIdentity * PhoneState * PhoneMode
    rename phoneIdentityOf _ as identityOf _;
  operations
    newPhone: PhoneIdentity -> Phone;
    errPhone: -> Phone;
  declare id: PhoneIdentity;
  operation axiom
    newPhone( id ) == ( id, C( idle ), normal );
    errPhone == ( errPhoneIdentity, C( idle ), normal );
end module Phone;
```

Fig. 6/26

For introducing the enquiry feature, only one new phone state is
needed. If phone A has a talk connection with phone B and B initiates an
enquiry call, phone A comes into the enquiry state heldBy(B), see Fig.
6/27.

```
module EnquiryStates;
  import PhoneIdentity from PhoneIdentity;
  export all;
  sort EnquiryState;
  constructor
    heldBy: PhoneIdentity -> EnquiryState;
end module EnquiryStates;

module PhoneStates;
  import CallState from CallStates;
    EnquiryState from EnquiryStates;
  export all;
  sort PhoneState;
  constructors
    C: CallState -> PhoneState;
    E: EnquiryState -> PhoneState;
end module PhoneStates;
```

Fig. 6/27

6.9.2 *The Module PhoneMessages*

A *blocked connection* from phone B to phone A has been established if and only if:

- phoneModeOf phone(B) == enquiry(A);
- phoneStateOf phone(A) == E(heldBy(B));

The messages that will be introduced for specifying enquiry calls can be partitioned into three classes:

- messages for transforming a talk connection into a blocked connection,
- messages for terminating a blocked connection,
- messages for transforming a blocked connection into a talk connection.

Transforming Talk Connection into Blocked Connection

A talk connection from phone A to phone B can only be transformed into a blocked connection if the party initiating the transformation, say B, is in mode normal. Phone B, which comes in mode enquiry(A), establishes the transformation by sending the message E(onHold) to phone A. Then, phone A comes in phone state heldBy(B), see Fig. 6/28.

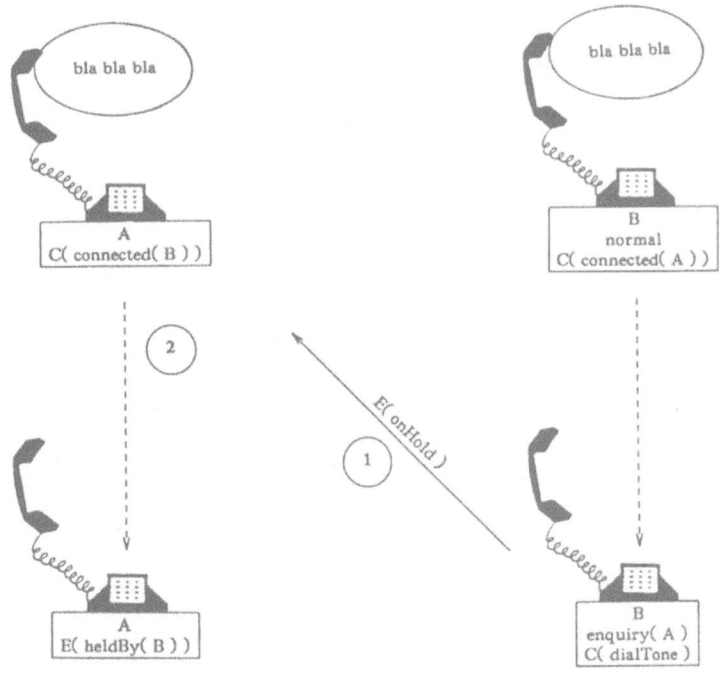

Fig. 6/28

Terminating a Blocked Connection

Both parties of a blocked connection may terminate the connection by sending the message E(onHoldTermination(X)) to the other party, with X standing for the identity of the phone terminating the blocked connection. This is graphically illustrated in Fig. 6/29 and 6/30.

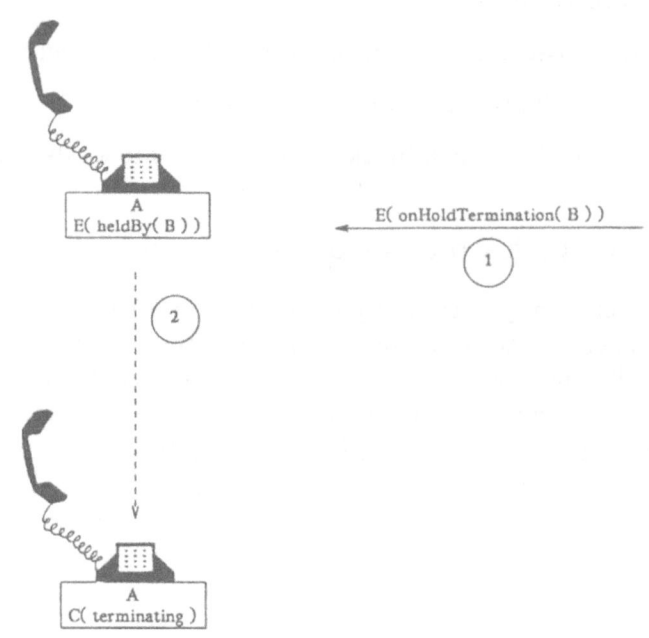

Fig. 6/29

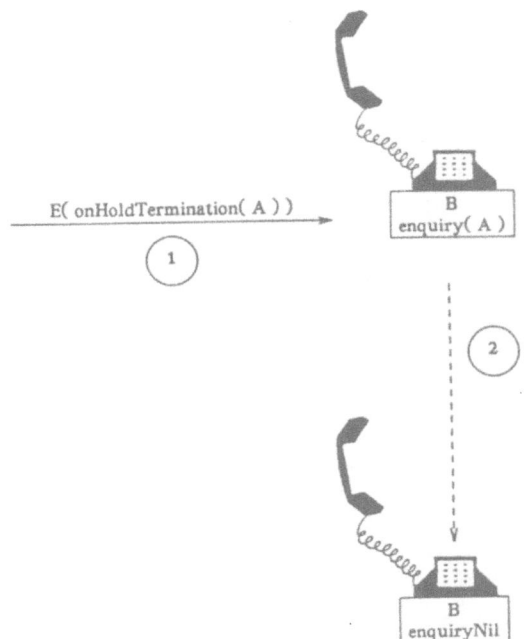

Fig. 6/30

Transforming Blocked Connection into Talk Connection

Only the phone that initiated the blocked connection may transform it back into a talk connection by sending the message E(onHoldResolved) to its previous partner, see Fig. 6/31.

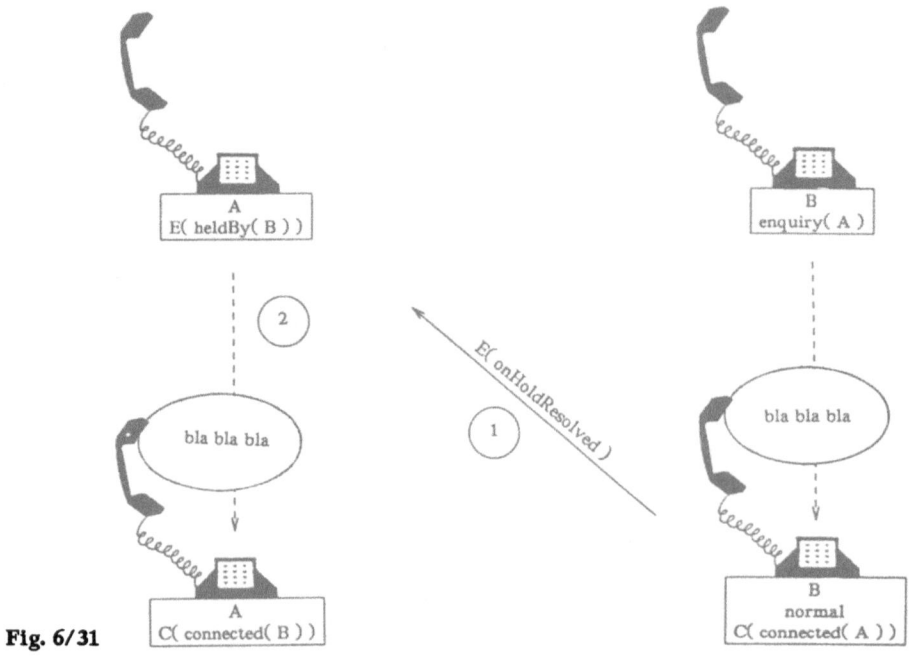

Fig. 6/31

All these messages are formally specified in the module EnquiryMessages, see Fig. 6/32. The sort PhoneMessage is the union of sort CallMessage and EnquiryMessage.

```
module EnquiryMessages;
  import PhoneIdentity from PhoneIdentity;
  export all;
  sort EnquiryMessage;
  constructors
    onHold: -> EnquiryMessage;
    onHoldTermination: PhoneIdentity -> EnquiryMessage;
    onHoldResolved: -> EnquiryMessage;
end module EnquiryMessages;

module PhoneMessages;
  import CallMessage from CallMessages;
    EnquiryMessage from EnquiryMessages;
  export all;
  sort PhoneMessage;
  constructors
    C: CallMessage -> PhoneMessage;
    E: EnquiryMessage -> PhoneMessage;
end module PhoneMessages;
```

Fig. 6/32

6.9.3 *The Module NextPhone*

As explained in Section 6.2, the operation next of module NextPhone is
defined as the union of a number of operations corresponding to the
messages of the various features. The operation next corresponding to the
call messages was given in Fig. 6/23. In Fig. 6/33 the operation next
corresponding to the enquiry messages is given.

```
module NextEnquiryPhone;
  import PhoneIdentity from PhoneIdentity;  all from PhoneModes;
    all from EnquiryMessages;  connected, terminating from CallStates;
    Phone, phoneStateOf _, phoneModeOf _, _[ _/ phoneState ],
    _[ _/ phoneMode ] from Phone;  C, E from PhoneStates;
  export next to NextPhone;
  operation
    next: EnquiryMessage * Phone -> Phone;
    declare mode: PhoneMode;  ph: Phone;  id, id₁: PhoneIdentity;
  operation axioms
    next( onHold, ph ) ==
      case phoneStateOf ph of
        C( connected( id ) ): ph [ E( heldBy( id ) ) / phoneState ];
        otherwise: error;
      end case;

    next( onHoldTermination( id ), ph ) ==
        enquiry( id ): ph [ enquiryNil / phoneMode ];
        otherwise:
          case phoneStateOf ph of
            E( heldBy( id ) ): ph [ C(terminating) / phoneState ]
            otherwise: error;
          end case;
      end case;

    next( onHoldResolved, ph ) ==
      case phoneStateOf ph of
        E( heldBy( id ) ): ph [ C( connected( id ) ) / phoneState ];
        otherwise: error;
      end case;
end module NextEnquiryPhone;

module NextPhone;
  import all from PhoneMessages;  Phone from Phone;
    CallMessage from CallMessages;  next from NextCallPhone1;
    EnquiryMessage from EnquiryMessages;  next from NextEnquiryPhone;
  export next;
  operation
    next: PhoneMessage * Phone -> Phone;
  declare callmsg: CallMessage;  enquirymsg: EnquiryMessage;  ph: Phone;
  operation axioms
    next( C( callmsg ), ph ) == NextCallPhone.next( callmsg, ph );
    next( E( enquirymsg ), ph ) == NextEnquiryPhone.next( enquirymsg, ph );
```

```
end module NextPhone;
```

Fig. 6/33

6.9.4 The Module OutPhone

Analogously, the operation out is given in Fig. 6/34.

```
module OutEnquiryListOfMessages;
  import all from EnquiryMessages;
    PhoneIdentity from PhoneIdentity;
    Phone from Phone;
    nil, ListOfMessages from ListOfMessages;
  export out to OutPhone;
  operation
    out: EnquiryMessage * Phone -> ListOfMessages;
  declare enquirymsg: EnquiryMessage;   ph: Phone;
  operation axioms
    out( enquirymsg, ph) == nil;
end module OutEnquiryListOfMessages;

module OutPhone;
  import all from PhoneMessages;   Phone from Phone;
    CallMessage from CallMessages;   out from OutCallListOfMessages;
    EnquiryMessage from EnquiryMessages;   out from OutEnquiryListOfMessages;
    ListOfMessages from ListOfMessages;
  export out;
  operation
    out: PhoneMessage * Phone -> ListOfMessages;
  declare callmsg: CallMessage;   enquirymsg: EnquiryMessage;   ph: Phone;
  operation axioms
    out(C(callmsg), ph) == OutCallListOfMessages.out(callmsg, ph);
    out(E(enquirymsg), ph) == OutEnquiryListOfMessages.out(enquirymsg, ph);
end module OutPhone;
```

Fig. 6/34

6.10 User Actions

In the previous sections the two–party voice call and the enquiry feature
were described. In [Vergauwen87] a lot of other features can be found. It
is important to notice that so far only the interaction between the objects

of the mini-PABX (usually phones) were discussed but not the interaction between the users and their phones. The reason is that a user action may be related to various features. For instance, going on-hook may terminate a two-party voice call as well as an enquiry call. Therefore, the user actions are treated here, in a separate section. The module Phone, as defined in the previous section, remains unchanged. The modules PhoneMessages, NextPhone and OutPhone are extended in the same systematic way as was done in the previous sections. User messages are defined as a new kind of phone messages for indicating the interactions from the users to their phones. Phones cannot send messages to users. We assume that the users can inspect the states of their phones.

6.10.1 The Module PhoneMessages

In order to enable communication from the user to his phone, a phone is provided with a number of communication parts. The physical appearances of these parts are irrelevant. Every use of a communication part is abstracted by means of a user message. We distinguish the following user messages:

- offHook: -> UserMessage;

  This message corresponds to picking up a receiver.

- onHook: -> UserMessage;

  This message corresponds to hanging up (replacing the receiver).

- dialCode(_): Code -> UserMessage;

  This message corresponds to dialling a code. The codes are described in module Codes, see Fig. 6/35. In our mini-PABX we only have phoneCode with a phone identity as parameter. This corresponds to dialling a number.

```
module Codes;
  import PhoneIdentity from PhoneIdentity;
  export all;
  sort Code;
  constructors
    phoneCode: PhoneIdentity -> Code;
end module Codes;
```

Fig. 6/35

• button: -> UserMessage;

This message corresponds to operating the recall button.

All these messages are formally specified in Fig. 6/36. The sort PhoneMessage is the union of sort CallMessage, EnquiryMessage and UserMessage.

```
module UserMessages;
  import PhoneIdentity from PhoneIdentity;   Code from Codes;
  export all;
  sort UserMessage;
  constructors
    onHook: -> UserMessage;
    offHook: -> UserMessage;
    dialCode: Code -> UserMessage;
    button: -> UserMessage;
end module UserMessages;

module PhoneMessages;
  import CallMessage from CallMessages;   UserMessage from UserMessages;
    EnquiryMessage from EnquiryMessages;
  export all;
  sort PhoneMessage;
  constructors
    C: CallMessage -> PhoneMessage;
    E: EnquiryMessage -> PhoneMessage;
    U: UserMessage -> PhoneMessage;
end module PhoneMessages;
```

Fig. 6/36

6.10.2 *The Module NextPhone*

The operation next is defined as the union of a number of operations corresponding to the messages of the various features. The operations next corresponding to the call messages and the enquiry messages were given in Fig. 6/23 and 6/33 respectively. In Fig. 6/37 the operation next corresponding to the user messages is given.

```
module NextUserPhone;
  import PhoneIdentity from PhoneIdentity;  all from Phone;  all from Codes;
    all from UserMessages;  all except PhoneMode from PhoneModes;
    C from PhoneStates;  all except CallState from CallStates;
  export next to NextPhone;
  operation
```

```
      next: UserMessage * Phone -> Phone;
    declare id, id₁: PhoneIdentity;   ph: Phone;   code: Code;
    operation axioms
      next( onHook, ph ) ==
        case phoneModeOf ph of
          normal:
            case phoneStateOf ph of
              C( idle ), C( ringing( id₁ ) ): ph;
              otherwise: ph [ C( idle·) / phoneState ];
            end case;
          enquiryNil, enquiry( id): ph [ C( idle ) / phoneState ] [ normal / phoneMode ];
        end case;

      next( offHook, ph ) ==
        case phoneStateOf ph of
          C( idle ): ph [ C( dialTone ) / phoneState ];
          C( ringing( id₁ ) ): ph [ C( connected( id₁ ) ) / phoneState ];
          otherwise: ph;
        end case;

      next( dialCode( code ), ph ) ==
        case phoneStateOf ph of
          C( dialTone ):
            case code of
              phoneCode( id₁ ): ph [ C( callWaiting( id₁ ) ) / phoneState ];
            end case;
          otherwise: ph;
        end case;

      next( button, ph ) ==
        case phoneModeOf ph of
          normal:
            case phoneStateOf ph of
              C( connected( id₁ ) ):
                ph [ C( dialTone ) / phoneState ] [ enquiry( id₁ ) / phoneMode ];
              otherwise: ph;
            end case;
          enquiryNil: ph [ C( terminating ) / phoneState ] [ normal / phoneMode ];
          enquiry( id ): ph [ C( connected( id ) ) / phoneState ] [ normal / phoneMode ];
    end module NextUserPhone;

module NextPhone;
  import all from PhoneMessages;   Phone from Phone;
    CallMessage from CallMessages;   next from NextCallPhone;
    EnquiryMessage from EnquiryMessages;   next from NextEnquiryPhone;
    UserMessage from UserMessages;   next from NextUserPhone;
  export next;
  operation
    next: PhoneMessage * Phone -> Phone;
  declare callmsg: CallMessage;   enquirymsg: EnquiryMessage;
    usermsg: UserMessage;   ph: Phone;
  operation axioms
    next( C( callmsg ), ph ) == NextCallPhone.next( callmsg, ph );
    next( E( enquirymsg ), ph ) == NextEnquiryPhone.next( enquirymsg, ph );
    next( U( usermsg ), ph ) == NextUserPhone.next( usermsg, ph );
  end module NextPhone;
```

Fig. 6/37

6.10.3 The Module OutPhone

Analogously, the operation out is given in Fig. 6/38.

```
module OutUserListOfMessages;
  import PhoneIdentity from PhoneIdentity;   all from ListOfMessages;
    all except PhoneMode from PhoneModes;   C, E from PhoneStates;
    callTermination, answer, ringingTermination, callRequest from CallMessages;
    onHold, onHoldTermination, onHoldResolved from EnquiryMessages;
    C, E from PhoneMessages;   send _ toPhone _ from MessagePairs;
    Phone, identityOf _, phoneStateOf _, phoneModeOf _ from Phone;
    connected, ringTone, dialTone, ringing from CallStates;
    all from Codes;   all from UserMessages;
  export out to OutPhone;
  operation
    out: UserMessage * Phone -> ListOfMessages;
  declare id, id₁: PhoneIdentity;   code: Code;   ph: Phone;
  operation axioms

  out( onHook, ph ) ==
    case phoneModeOf ph of
      normal, enquiryNil:
        case phoneStateOf ph of
          C( connected( id₁ ) ):
            send C( callTermination ) toPhone id₁ | nil;
          C( ringTone( id₁ ) ):
            send C( ringingTermination ) toPhone id₁ | nil;
          E( heldBy( id ) ):
            send E( onHoldTermination( identityOf ph ) toPhone id | nil;
          otherwise: nil;
        end case;
      enquiry( id ):
        case phoneStateOf ph of
          C( connected( id₁ ) ):
            send E( onHoldTermination( identityOf ph ) toPhone id
            | send C( callTermination ) toPhone id₁ | nil;
          C( ringTone( id₁ ) ):
            send E( onHoldTermination( identityOf ph ) toPhone id
            | send C( ringingTermination ) toPhone id₁ | nil;
          E( heldBy( id₁ ) ):
            send E( onHoldTermination( identityOf ph ) toPhone id
            | send E( onHoldTermination( identityOf ph ) toPhone id₁ | nil;
          otherwise:
            send E( onHoldTermination( identityOf ph ) ) toPhone id | nil;
        end case;
    end case;

  out( offHook, ph ) ==
    case phoneStateOf ph of
      C( ringing( id₁ ) ): send C( answer ) toPhone id₁ | nil;
      otherwise: nil;
    end case;

  out( dialCode( code ), ph ) ==
    case phoneStateOf ph of
```

```
        C( dialTone ):
          case code of
            phoneCode( id1 ):
              send C( callRequest( identityOf ph ) ) toPhone id1 | nil;
          end case;
        otherwise: nil;
      end case;

    out( button, ph ) ==
      case phoneModeOf ph of
        normal:
          case phoneStateOf ph of
            C( connected( id1 ) ):
              send E( onHold ) toPhone id1 | nil;
            otherwise: nil;
          end case;
        enquiryNil:
          case phoneStateOf ph of
            C( connected( id1 ) ):
              send C( callTermination ) toPhone id1 | nil;
            C( ringTone( id1 ) ):
              send C( ringingTermination ) toPhone id1 | nil;
            E( heldBy( id1 ) ):
              send E( onHoldTermination( identityOf ph ) ) toPhone id1 | nil;
            otherwise: nil;
          end case;
        enquiry( id ):
          case phoneStateOf ph of
            C( connected( id1 ) ):
                send E( onHoldResolved ) toPhone id
              | send C( callTermination ) toPhone id1 | nil;
            C( ringTone( id1 ) ):
                send E( onHoldResolved ) toPhone id
              | send C( ringingTermination ) toPhone id1 | nil;
            E( heldBy( id1 ) ):
                send E( onHoldResolved ) toPhone id
              | send E( onHoldTermination( identityOf ph ) ) toPhone id1 | nil;
            otherwise: send E( onHoldResolved ) toPhone id | nil;
          end case;
      end case;
end module OutUserListOfMessages;

module OutPhone;
  import all from PhoneMessages;   Phone from Phone;
    CallMessage from CallMessages;
    out from OutCallListOfMessages;   EnquiryMessage from EnquiryMessages;
    out from OutEnquiryListOfMessages;   UserMessage from UserMessages;
    out from OutUserListOfMessages;   ListOfMessages from ListOfMessages;
  export out;
  operation
    out: PhoneMessage * Phone -> ListOfMessages;
  declare callmsg: CallMessage;   enquirymsg: EnquiryMessage;
    usermsg: UserMessage;   ph: Phone;
  operation axioms
    out( C( callmsg ), ph ) == OutCallListOfMessages.out( callmsg, ph );
    out( E( enquirymsg ), ph ) == OutEnquiryListOfMessages.out( enquirymsg, ph );
    out( U( usermsg ), ph ) == OutUserListOfMessages.out( usermsg, ph );
```

end module OutPhone;

Fig. 6/38

6.11 Conclusion

The original informal descriptions of the features of the PABX [Steegmans84, Steegmans85] often were ambiguous and incomplete [Jacobs86]. Because the various features were described independently, it was impossible to overlook the interactions between them. Therefore, designers, implementors, sales representatives and customers may interpret the features in a different way. Detailed questions about the features (the *what*) can only be answered as soon as they have been implemented either by looking at the assembler code (the *how*) or by executing the code.

As a remedy for this we have proposed a formal specification. It is our experience that a formal specification is very useful as a standard (norm). Detailed questions can be answered in a precise and unambiguous way thanks to the mathematical foundations of the formal specification. We do not assert that informal specifications are worthless. Formal and informal specifications must be considered complementary. Therefore, each feature was always described informally first, making use of many graphical representations. The informal specification was used as documentation for the formal specification, which is, by definition, the standard. Furthermore, we found out that by making a formal specification we were forced to probe the matter to the very bottom and to specify it in a very precise and complete way.

In [Vergauwen87] a lot of other features can be found that were added in the same way. We mention camping and intrusion, transfer, the pick-up feature, the booking feature, a wake-up service, two kinds of conference calls and time-outs. Thanks to the modularity, the object-oriented design method and adapted data structures, the complexity of the PABX can be mastered. Another important software engineering principle is abstraction. Only the characteristics of the features were specified, not irrelevant information (e.g., a user need not know the ITT 5400 BCS is based on a 16-bit micro-processor).

Using only constructive specifications enables rapid prototyping. Tests and experiments can be done by designers and customers and the specification can be tuned until the desired behaviour is obtained. In our department an environment for algebraic specifications is under development. This environment already consists of a syntax checker, a type controller, a checker for the uniqueness and completeness constraints, an import–export checker, a checker for the constructiveness constraints, and a reductor.

In the future we hope to build a theorem prover. Indeed, thanks to the mathematical foundations rigorous reasoning becomes possible. Rapid prototyping and theorem proving must be seen as complementary methods for better understanding specifications and for gaining confidence that they express what we have in mind. If we define the appropriate equality operations, interesting theorems about the mini-PABX in a stable situation are, e.g.,

- **declare** M: MiniPABX;   phoneA, phoneB: Phone;
  A, B: phoneIdentity;
  theorem
    let
      phoneA == select(phonePoolOf MiniPABX, A);
      phoneB == select(phonePoolOf MiniPABX, B);
    in
        phoneStateOf phoneA = C(connected(B)) <=>
          phoneStateOf phoneB = C(connected(A))
    end let == true;

- **declare** M: MiniPABX;   phoneA, phoneB: Phone;
  A, B: phoneIdentity;
  theorem
    let
      phoneA == select(phonePoolOf MiniPABX, A);
      phoneB == select(phonePoolOf MiniPABX, B);
    in
        phoneStateOf phoneA = C(ringtone(B)) <=>
          phoneStateOf phoneB = C(ringing(A))
    end let == true;

- **declare** M: MiniPABX;   phoneA, phoneB: Phone;
  A, B: phoneIdentity;
  theorem
    let
      phoneA == select(phonePoolOf MiniPABX, A);
      phoneB == select(phonePoolOf MiniPABX, B);
    in
        phoneStateOf phoneA = E(heldBy(B)) <=>
          phoneModeOf phoneB = enquiry(A)
    end let == true;

- **declare** M: MiniPABX;   phoneA: Phone;   A, B: phoneIdentity;
  theorem
    let
      phoneA == select(phonePoolOf MiniPABX, A);
      in
        (phoneStateOf phoneA = C(idle)) or
        (phoneStateOf phoneA = C(ringing(B))
        => phoneModeOf phoneA = normal
    end let == true;

- **declare** M: MiniPABX;   phoneA: Phone;   A, B: phoneIdentity;
  theorem
    let
      phoneA == select(phonePoolOf MiniPABX, A);
      in
        (phoneStateOf phoneA = E(heldBy(B))) and
        (phoneModeOf phoneA = enquiry(B))
    end let == false;

- Another family of theorems is obtained by proving that all places in the specification where error is written are not reachable when only transformations by user actions are considered.

We believe that algebraic specifications are very suitable for specifying data structures. However, reducing a PABX to a single monolithic data structure is unrealistic and results in a less readable specification, because the number of states grows out of control very rapidly [Goovaers86, Jacobs86]. Therefore, we use an object-oriented design method. A state is associated with the logical objects. Furthermore, the objects can communicate with each other by sending messages. When an object receives a message, its state can be changed and the object in turn can send messages to other objects. This object-oriented mechanism is not supported by the algebraic specification language. An interesting topic would be to incorporate it in the specification language. Moreover, by allowing messages to be be sent in parallel, concurrency can be introduced in the language.

7. Error Handling

"Errors, like straws, upon the surface flow.
He who would search for pearls must dive below."
John Dryden

A well-defined algebraic specification does not only precisely describe an abstract data type in its normal situations, but also in its abnormal (exceptional) ones. A trivial example of an abnormal situation for the abstract data type Stack is when an empty stack is popped. A well-defined algebraic specification describes *when* abnormal situations occur and *what* exactly happens in such cases. Error handling is of utmost importance, especially when one deals with constructive specifications used for rapid prototyping. An adequate error handling enhances robustness, i.e. the ability of a software system to function even in abnormal situations.

Error handling must be introduced in algebraic specifications in such a way that the principles of rigorous reasoning remain valid. In principle, algebraic specification languages based on many-sorted initial algebras are powerful enough to specify any required error handling. However, most of them do not provide any direct support for a rigorous and readable treatment of exceptions. In literature on algebraic specifications the activities on error handling can be divided into two classes. There are the activities to extend the mathematical framework so that it incorporates error handling. Other activities treat error handling within an existing mathematical framework. Our approach of error handling lies in the second class. On the algebraic specification language, as described in Chapters 3 and 4, we superimpose a notation that supports not only the specification of error handling, but also a *specification method* to deal with error handling. Following this method, algebraic specifications can be built in two steps. In a first step, one only deals with the normal situations, giving rise to an incomplete specification. In a second step, all the abnormal situations are treated. This two-step method increases readability and modularity of specifications.

7.1 The Need for an Error Handling System

By further elaborating the specification of the natural numbers, the need
for a direct support for a rigorous treatment of exceptions will be
illustrated. Let us add the predecessor function to the specification. A
problem arises with the predecessor of zero. Intuitively speaking, we like
to add an unsafe object to the set of natural numbers without disturbing
anything else. This is done in Fig. 7/1, where the unsafe object is called
errNat.

```
module Nat;
  export all;
  sort Nat;
  constructors
    zero: -> Nat;
    succ: Nat -> Nat;
    errNat: -> Nat;
  operations
    pre: Nat -> Nat;
    add: Nat * Nat -> Nat;
    mult: Nat * Nat -> Nat;
  declare n, n1, n2: Nat;
  operation axioms
    pre( zero ) == errNat;
    pre( succ( n ) ) == n;
    add( zero, n ) == n;
    add( succ( n1 ), n2 ) == succ( add( n1, n2 ) );
    mult( zero, n ) == zero;
    mult( succ( n1 ), n2 ) == add( n2, mult( n1, n2 ) );
end module Nat;
```

Fig. 7/1

By defining the new constructor errNat, the completeness constraints
are not met. Indeed, what is, e.g., pre(errNat)? We can simply add the
constructor axiom and the operation axioms that are given in Fig. 7/2.

```
constructor axiom
  succ( errNat ) == errNat;
```

```
operation axioms
  pre( errNat ) == errNat;
  add( errNat, n ) == errNat;
  mult( errNat, n ) == errNat;
```

Fig. 7/2

Unfortunately, in the resulting specification not all terms containing an unsafe subterm are reduced to errNat (which is what we have in mind). This is shown by the following equalities derived from previous axioms:

$$\text{mult}(\text{zero, pre(zero)}) = \text{mult}(\text{zero, errNat}) = \text{zero}$$

Adding new operation axioms

```
operation axioms
  mult( n, errNat ) == errNat;
  add( n, errNat ) == errNat;
```

Fig. 7/3

to introduce strict error propagation, violates the uniqueness constraints. E.g., the term mult(zero, errNat) can be reduced to zero as well as to errNat. The difficulties arise because the axioms of Fig. 7/1 are only intended for normal situations, whereas the axioms of Fig. 7/2 and 7/3 are only applicable in erroneous situations.

The problem can be solved by distinguishing explicitly between two kinds of natural numbers using a boolean function safeNat, which is called the *safety function* of the natural numbers. Firstly, we have *safe objects:* natural numbers such that safeNat results in true. Secondly, we have *unsafe objects:* natural numbers such that safeNat results in false. In Fig. 7/4 a specification for the natural numbers is given using this safety function safeNat in a systematic way.

```
module Nat;
  import Bool, true, false, not _, _ and _ from Bool;
  export all;
  sort Nat;
  constructors
    zero: -> Nat;
    succ: Nat -> Nat;
```

```
    errNat: -> Nat;
  operations
    safeNat: Nat -> Bool;
    pre: Nat -> Nat;
    add: Nat * Nat -> Nat;
    mult: Nat * Nat -> Nat;
  declare n, n₁, n₂: Nat;
  constructor axiom
    not safeNat( n ) ⇛ n == errNat;
  operation axioms
    safeNat( zero ) == true;
    safeNat( succ( n ) ) == safeNat( n );
    safeNat( errNat ) == false;
    pre( zero ) == errNat;
    pre( succ( n ) ) ==
      if safeNat( succ( n ) )
        then n
        else errNat
      end if;
    pre( errNat ) == errNat;
    add( zero, n ) ==
      if safeNat( n )
        then n
        else errNat
      end if;
    add( succ( n₁ ), n₂ ) ==
      if safeNat( succ( n₁ ) ) and safeNat( n₂ )
        then succ( add( n₁, n₂ ) )
        else errNat
      end if;
    add( errNat, n ) == errNat;
    mult( zero, n ) ==
      if safeNat( n )
        then zero
        else errNat
      end if;
    mult( succ( n₁ ), n₂ ) ==
      if safeNat( succ( n₁ ) ) and safeNat( n₂ )
        then add( n₂, mult( n₁, n₂ ) )
        else errNat
      end if;
    mult( errNat, n ) == errNat;
  end module Nat;
```

Fig. 7/4

Notice that all natural numbers are safe objects except errNat, which is an unsafe object. An optimized version of the module Nat is given in Fig. 7/5.

Although we specified the intended abstract data type, we are not satisfied with the specification as it is rather cumbersome. The complexity will increase for larger specifications, resulting in unreadable specifications. A good error handling mechanism must reduce this complexity, and the key information on error handling must be visible at first sight.

```
module Nat;
  import all from Bool;
  export all;
  sort Nat;
  constructors
    zero: -> Nat;
    succ: Nat -> Nat;
    errNat: -> Nat;
  operations
    safeNat: Nat -> Bool;
    pre: Nat -> Nat;
    add: Nat * Nat -> Nat;
    mult: Nat * Nat -> Nat;
  declare n, n1, n2: Nat;
  constructor axiom
    succ( errNat ) == errNat;
  operation axioms
    safeNat( zero ) == true;
    safeNat( succ( n ) ) == safeNat( n );
    safeNat( errNat ) == false;
    pre( zero ) == errNat;
    pre( succ( n ) ) == n;
    pre( errNat ) == errNat;
    add( zero, n ) == n;
    add( succ( n1 ), n2 ) == succ( add( n1, n2 ) );
    add( errNat, n ) == errNat;
    mult( zero, n ) ==
      if safeNat( n )
        then zero
        else errNat
      end if;
    mult( succ( n1 ), n2 ) == add( n2, mult( n1, n2 ) );
    mult( errNat, n ) == errNat;
end module Nat;
```

Fig. 7/5

We will introduce a shorthand notation to construct safety functions and to indicate which axioms are applicable. The notation is a trade-off between readability and the class of error situations it can handle. Also a two-step method for designing specifications will be provided, which enhances modularity. In a first step the specification is given with error detection only, in a second step error handling is added.

7.2 Safety Functions

A boolean function that divides a set of objects into *safe* objects and *unsafe* objects is called the *safety function* of the sort. For example, the function safeNat in Fig. 7/4 is the safety function of sort Nat.

In Fig. 7/6 the safety function safeNat is defined by the syntactic constructs that we introduce on the constructors. Every constructor has to be marked either by $$ or ??. A constructor marked by ?? always denotes an unsafe object (i.e. the safety function returns false). A constructor marked by $$ denotes a safe object (i.e. the safety function returns true) if and only if all the requested arguments of the constructor are safe objects. A constructor argument is requested to be safe if the corresponding sort in the rank declaration of the constructor is preceded by a *propagation marker* $.

```
module Nat;
  import all from Bool;
  export all;
  sort Nat;
  constructors
    zero: -> Nat $$;
    succ: $ Nat -> Nat $$;
    errNat: -> Nat ??;
  operations
    pre: Nat -> Nat;
    add: Nat * Nat -> Nat;
    mult: Nat * Nat -> Nat;
  -- ... see Fig. 7/4 --
end module Nat;
```

Fig. 7/6

Here, the markers indicate the following: 1) the constructor zero denotes a safe object; 2) a term succ(n) denotes a safe object if and only if n denotes a safe object; 3) errNat denotes an unsafe object. This definition of safeNat is equivalent to the one given in Fig. 7/4. The definition of the safety function can be derived mechanically from the shorthand notation.

Generally speaking, in order to have consistent specifications, applying the appropriate safety function to the left-hand side of a constructor axiom must always yield the same result as applying this safety function to the right-hand side of the constructor axiom.

7.3 Safety and Unsafety Markers

Safety markers and *unsafety markers* indicate in which situations axioms can be applied. There are two safety markers, namely $ and $$, and three unsafety markers, !, ? and ??. An axiom may contain more than one marker. In that case all corresponding conditions must be met. Markers may occur in both left-hand and right-hand sides of axioms.

- If a term in an axiom is preceded by $, the axiom is only applicable if the term denotes a safe object. Assume that an axiom

    ... $ t ... == ...;

    contains a term t of sort S_i preceded by $, the axiom is equivalent to

    safeS_i(t) $\Rightarrow$ ... t ... == ...;

- If a term in an axiom is preceded by !, the axiom is only applicable if the term denotes an unsafe object. Assume that an axiom

    ... ! t ... == ...;

    contains a term t of sort S_i preceded by !, the axiom is equivalent to

    not safeS_i(t) $\Rightarrow$ ... t ... == ...;

- If just k terms in an axiom are preceded by ?, the axiom is only applicable if at least one of these terms denotes an unsafe object. Assume that an axiom

    ... ? t_1 ... ? t_2 ... == ... ? t_k ...;

    contains just k terms preceded by ?, respectively of sort S_{i_1}, S_{i_2}, ... S_{i_k}, the axiom is equivalent to

    not (safeS_{i_1}(t_1) and safeS_{i_2}(t_2) and ... and safeS_{i_k}(t_k)) $\Rightarrow$
    ... t_1 ... t_2 ... == ... t_k ...;

- If a constructor or operation in an axiom is preceded by $$, the axiom is only applicable if all the arguments of the constructor or operation denote a safe object. Assume that an axiom

... \$\$ f(t_1, t_2, ..., t_k) ... == ...;

contains a constructor or operation f declared as f: S_{i_1} * S_{i_2} * ... * S_{i_k} -> S_j, the axiom is equivalent to

safeS$_{i_1}$(t_1) and safeS$_{i_2}$(t_2) and ... and safeS$_{i_k}$(t_k) $\Rightarrow$
    ... f(t_1, t_2, ..., t_k) ... == ...;

- If a constructor or operation in an axiom is preceded by ??, the axiom is only applicable if at least one of the arguments of the constructor or operation denotes an unsafe object. Assume that an axiom

    ... ?? f(t_1, t_2, ..., t_k) ... == ...;

contains a constructor or operation f declared as f: S_{i_1} * S_{i_2} * ... * S_{i_k} -> S_j, the axiom is equivalent to

not(safeS$_{i_1}$(t_1) and safeS$_{i_2}$(t_2) and ... and safeS$_{i_k}$(t_k)) $\Rightarrow$
    ... f(t_1, t_2, ..., t_k) ... == ...;

To avoid syntactical overloading each term may be preceded by at most one marker. It is still allowed to use the safety functions explicitly. The meaning of the markers is summarized in Fig. 7/7.

Marker	The situation in which the axiom may be applied
\$	all indicated terms denote safe objects
!	all indicated terms denote unsafe objects
?	at least one term preceded by ? denotes an unsafe object
\$\$	all arguments of the indicated nonnullary operation are safe objects
??	at least one argument of the indicated nonnullary operation is an unsafe object

Fig. 7/7

Notice that placing a marker \$ or ! before the left-hand side of an operation axiom does not make any sense. Indeed, the marker indicates that the operation axiom may only be applied to an expression that can be reduced to a term denoting a safe object, respectively unsafe object. But in order to reduce, the operation axiom must be applied. Analogously, placing a marker ? before the left-hand side of an operation axiom does not make any sense.

Example

In Fig. 7/8 safety and unsafety markers are used to specify the natural numbers.

```
module Nat;
  export all;
  sort Nat;
  constructors
    zero: -> Nat $$;
    succ: $ Nat -> Nat $$;
    errNat: -> Nat ??;
  operations
    pre: Nat -> Nat;
    add: Nat * Nat -> Nat;
    mult: Nat * Nat -> Nat;
  declare n, n₁, n₂: Nat;
  constructor axiom
  ! n == errNat;
  operation axioms
  $$ pre( zero ) == errNat;                        -- 1 --
  $$ pre( succ( n ) ) == n;                        -- 2 --
  $$ add( zero, n ) == n;                          -- 3 --
  $$ add( succ( n₁ ), n₂ ) == succ( add( n₁, n₂ ) );   -- 4 --
  $$ mult( zero, n ) == zero;                      -- 5 --
  $$ mult( succ( n₁ ), n₂ ) == add( n₂, mult( n₁, n₂ ) );  -- 6 --

  ?? pre( n ) == errNat;                           -- 7 --
  ?? add( n₁, n₂ ) == errNat;                      -- 8 --
  ?? mult( n₁, n₂ ) == errNat;                     -- 9 --
end module Nat;
```

Fig. 7/8

It is important to notice that no new concepts are introduced. We only used a new syntactic notation. Operation axiom 6 is equivalent to

safeNat(succ(n_1)) and safeNat(n_2) $\Rightarrow$
   mult(succ(n_1), n_2) == add(n_2, mult(n_1, n_2));

Operation axiom 9 is equivalent to

not(safeNat(n_1) and safeNat(n_2)) $\Rightarrow$
   mult(n_1, n_2) == errNat;

The constructor axiom of Fig. 7/8 is equivalent to

not safeNat(n) $\Rightarrow$ n == errNat;

The specification of Fig. 7/8 is equivalent to that of Fig. 7/4. But the specification of Fig. 7/8 is more concise, reflecting clearly the error handling information.

7.4 Method of Error Specification

An important feature of the proposed error handling mechanism is the possibility to construct specifications in two steps. In a first step, incomplete specifications are built with error detection only. Roughly speaking, such a specification describes the operations for safe operands only. The specification is irrelevant when the operands are unsafe. In a second step, error handling is superimposed. This method is illustrated by the well-known example of the stack.

First Step

In the first step, the completeness constraints are only met with respect to the safe objects, see Fig. 7/9.

```
module Stack;
   import Bool, true, false from Bool;
     Nat, errNat from Nat;
   export all;
   sort Stack;
   constructors
     newstack: -> Stack $$;
     push: $ Stack * Nat -> Stack $$;
     errStack: -> Stack ??;
   operations
     pop: Stack -> Stack;
     top: Stack -> Nat;
     isnewstack: Stack -> Bool;
   declare s: Stack;   n: Nat;
   operation axioms
   $$ pop( newstack) == errStack;
   $$ pop( push( s, n ) ) == s;
   $$ top( newstack ) == errNat;
   $$ top( push( s, n ) ) == n;
   $$ isnewstack( newstack ) == true;
```

```
$$ isnewstack( push( s, n ) ) == false;
end module Stack;
```

Fig. 7/9

Notice that pushing an unsafe natural number on a safe stack results in a safe stack because only the first argument of the constructor push is requested to be safe. The safety function safeStack of Fig. 7/9 is given explicitly in Fig. 7/10.

```
declare s: Stack;   n: Nat;
operation axioms
  safeStack( newstack ) == true;
  safeStack( push( s, n ) ) == safeStack( s );
  safeStack( errStack ) == false;
```

Fig. 7/10

Although the specification given in Fig. 7/9 is incomplete (the operations are only specified for safe operands), rapid prototyping is already possible. Two different approaches are possible when an error occurs. Firstly, one can always map the result of an operation with unsafe arguments onto an unsafe object errSort of the sort of the operation. Secondly, we can consider a large set of unsafe objects that provide a trace to the place where the error occurred, e.g.:

   top(pop(errStack))

Second Step

In a second step, information concerning error handling is added. In Fig. 7/11 the specification of Fig. 7/9 is extended with error information in such a way that errors are propagated, except for the error recovery operation recover that returns its argument if this argument is a safe stack, and newstack otherwise.

```
module Stack;
  import Bool, true, false, errBool from Bool;
```

```
     Nat, errNat from Nat;
  export all;
  sort Stack;
  constructors
    newstack: -> Stack $$;
    push: $ Stack * Nat -> Stack $$;
    errStack: -> Stack ??;
  operations
    pop: Stack -> Stack;
    top: Stack -> Nat;
    isnewstack: Stack -> Bool;
    recover: Stack -> Stack;
  declare s: Stack;   n: Nat;
  constructor axiom
   ! s == errStack;
  operation axioms
  $$ pop( newstack) == errStack;                    -- 1 --
  $$ pop( push( s, n ) ) == s;                       -- 2 --
  $$ top( newstack ) == errNat;                      -- 3 --
  $$ top( push( s, n ) ) == n;                       -- 4 --
  $$ isnewstack( newstack ) == true;                 -- 5 --
  $$ isnewstack( push( s, n ) ) == false;            -- 6 --
  $$ recover( s ) == s;                              -- 7 --

  ?? pop( s ) == errStack;                           -- 8 --
  ?? top( s ) == errNat;                             -- 9 --
  ?? isnewstack( s ) == errBool;                     -- 10 --
  ?? recover( s ) == newstack;                       -- 11 --
  end module Stack;
```

Fig. 7/11

Remember that the constructor axiom of Fig. 7/11 is equivalent to

$$\text{not safeStack(s) } \Rightarrow s == errStack;$$

It states that all unsafe stacks are equal to errStack.
Operation axiom 1 is equivalent to

$$\text{safeStack(newstack) } \Rightarrow pop(newstack) == errStack;$$

the condition of which is always true, and therefore $$ may be omitted.
Operation axiom 2 is equivalent to

$$\text{safeStack(push(s, n)) } \Rightarrow pop(push(s, n)) == s;$$

Operation axiom 8 is equivalent to

$$\text{not safeStack(s) } \Rightarrow pop(s) == errStack;$$

Operation axioms 1, 2 and 8 together are equivalent to the following unconditional operation axiom.

```
pop( s ) ==
  if safeStack( s )
    then
      case s of
        newstack: errStack;
        push( s₁, n ): s₁;
        otherwise -- unreachable -- errStack;
      end case
    else errStack
  end if;
```

Notice that these transformations can be done in a mechanical way.

7.5 Safety Conditions

Although we can already specify many interesting abstract data types, the mechanism developed so far is not powerful enough to describe more complex data types, e.g., bounded types. Therefore the markers $$ and ?? of the constructors part, will be extended to safety conditions. Safety conditions together with propagation markers will indicate whether a constructor denotes a safe or an unsafe object.

To illustrate the need for safety conditions, consider the example of a bounded stack, e.g., a stack that contains at most 100 elements. The constructor push cannot be marked by $$ or ?? because push(boundedstack, n) may give a safe or an unsafe object, depending on the length of the stack. If the stack is safe and contains, e.g., 61 elements, then the constructor push gives a safe object. But if the stack is safe and contains 100 elements, an unsafe stack is obtained because an overflow occurs. So the constructor push gives a safe object if and only if its first argument is a safe object and the following boolean term, called safety condition, is satisfied:

$$length(boundedstack) \leqslant 99$$

A *safety condition* is a boolean term that is associated with a constructor. A constructor denotes a safe object if the requested arguments are safe objects and the safety condition of the constructor is true. But if one of its requested arguments is unsafe or the safety condition yields either false or an exceptional object, the constructor denotes an unsafe object. The safety condition is written between dollar signs following the declaration of the constructor. Each variable used in a safety condition, is associated with an argument of the constructor (at most one variable may be associated with every argument).

In the safety condition of the constructor push given in Fig. 7/12, the variable boundedstack is associated with the first argument of push. To make an automatic association possible between the variables of a safety condition and the arguments of the constructor, each variable has the same name as the sort of the associated argument (but starting with a lower case letter). If two or more arguments of a constructor have the same sort, the variable names are distinguished by a number that indicates the argument associated with it. The safety condition $ true $ may be abbreviated $$, the safety condition $ false $ may be abbreviated ??.

In Fig. 7/12 the specification of a bounded stack without error handling is given. The stack size is limited to 100. The operation _ $\leqslant$ _ is assumed to be defined in the module Nat.

```
module BoundedStack;
   import Bool, true, false from Bool;
      Nat, zero, succ, _ ≤ _, errNat from Nat;
   export all;
   sort BoundedStack;
   constructors
      newstack: -> BoundedStack $$;
      push: $ BoundedStack * Nat -> BoundedStack  $ length( boundedstack ) ≤ 99 $;
      errBoundedStack: -> BoundedStack ??;
   operations
      length: BoundedStack -> Nat;
      pop: BoundedStack -> BoundedStack;
      top: BoundedStack -> Nat;
      isnewstack: BoundedStack -> Bool;
      recover: BoundedStack -> BoundedStack;
   declare b: BoundedStack;   n: Nat;
   operation axioms
   $$ length( newstack ) == zero;
   $$ length( push( b, n ) ) == succ( length( b ) ) ;
   $$ pop( newstack) == errBoundedStack;
   $$ pop( push( b, n ) ) == b;
   $$ top( newstack ) == errNat;
   $$ top( push( b, n ) ) == n;
   $$ isnewstack( newstack ) == true;
   $$ isnewstack( push( b, n ) ) == false;
   $$ recover( b ) == b;
```

```
end module BoundedStack;
```

Fig. 7/12

Notice that a safety condition can be interpreted as a precondition on the constructor.

In Fig. 7/13 the safety function safeBoundedStack is given, which can automatically be derived from the propagation marker and the safety conditions of Fig. 7/12.

```
operation
  safeBoundedStack: BoundedStack -> Bool;
declare b: BoundedStack;   n: Nat;
operation axioms
  safeBoundedStack( newstack ) == true;
  safeBoundedStack( push( b, n ) ) ==
    if length( b ) ≤ 99
      then safeBoundedStack( b )
      else false
    end if;
  safeBoundedStack( errBoundedStack ) == false;
```

Fig. 7/13

In Fig. 7/14 the specification of a bounded stack with error handling is given.

```
module BoundedStack;
  import Bool, true, false, errBool from Bool;
    Nat, zero, succ, _ ≤ _, errNat from Nat;
  export all;
  sort BoundedStack;
  constructors
    newstack: -> BoundedStack $$;
    push: $ BoundedStack * Nat -> BoundedStack $ length( boundedstack ) ≤ 99 $;
    errBoundedStack: -> BoundedStack ??;
  operations
    length: BoundedStack -> Nat;
    pop: BoundedStack -> BoundedStack;
    top: BoundedStack -> Nat;
    isnewstack: BoundedStack -> Bool;
    recover: BoundedStack -> BoundedStack;
  declare b: BoundedStack;   n: Nat;
```

```
constructor axiom
! b == errBoundedStack;
operation axioms
$$ length( newstack ) == zero;
$$ length( push( b, n ) ) == succ( length( b ) ) ;
$$ pop( newstack) == errBoundedStack;
$$ pop( push( b, n ) ) == b;
$$ top( newstack ) == errNat;
$$ top( push( b, n ) ) == n;
$$ isnewstack( newstack ) == true;
$$ isnewstack( push( b, n ) ) == false;
$$ recover( b ) == b;

?? length( b ) == errNat;
?? pop( b ) == errBoundedStack;
?? top( b ) == errNat;
?? isnewstack( b ) == errBool;
?? recover( b ) == newstack;
end module BoundedStack;
```

Fig. 7/14

Notice the mutual recursive definitions of the operation length and the safety function safeBoundedStack.

Remember that if b stands for a (safe) bounded stack of length 100,

$$length(push(b, zero))$$

is equal to errNat and not to 101 because push(b, zero) is not safe and, as a consequence, the second operation axiom must not be applied.

A more refined error handling for the bounded stack is obtained by distinguishing between two unsafe objects: underflow and overflow. The resulting specification is given in Fig. 7/15.

```
module BoundedStack;
  import Bool, true, false, errBool from Bool;
    Nat, zero, succ, _ ≤ _, errNat from Nat;
  export all;
  sort BoundedStack;
  constructors
    newstack: -> BoundedStack $$;
    push: $ BoundedStack * Nat -> BoundedStack $ length( boundedstack ) ≤ 99 $;
    underflow: -> BoundedStack ??;
    overflow: -> BoundedStack ??;
  operations
    length: BoundedStack -> Nat;
    pop: BoundedStack -> BoundedStack;
    top: BoundedStack -> Nat;
```

```
    isnewstack: BoundedStack -> Bool;
    recover: BoundedStack -> BoundedStack;
  declare b: BoundedStack;   n: Nat;
  constructor axioms
   ! push( $ b, n ) == overflow;
     push( ! b, n ) == b;
  operation axioms
  $$ length( newstack ) == zero;
  $$ length( push( b, n ) ) == succ( length( b ) );
  $$ pop( newstack) == underflow;
  $$ pop( push( b, n ) ) == b;
  $$ top( newstack ) == errNat;
  $$ top( push( b, n ) ) == n;
  $$ isnewstack( newstack ) == true;
  $$ isnewstack( push( b, n ) ) == false;
  $$ recover( b ) == b;

  ?? length( b ) == errNat;
  ?? pop( b ) == b;
  ?? top( b ) == errNat;
  ?? isnewstack( b ) == errBool;
  ?? recover( b ) == newstack;
  end module BoundedStack;
```

Fig. 7/15

The first constructor axiom of Fig. 7/15 states that when a safe stack
becomes unsafe after pushing a natural number onto it, then an overflow
occurs. The second constructor axiom of Fig. 7/15 indicates that if a stack
is unsafe, pushing a natural number has no effect (i.e. an underflow
remains an underflow and an overflow remains an overflow). The
constructor axioms of Fig. 7/15 are equivalent to

```
 constructor axioms
   safeBoundedStack( b ) and not safeBoundedStack( push( b, n ) ) ⇒
     push( b, n ) == overflow;
   not safeBoundedStack( b ) ⇒ push( b, n ) == b;
```

Fig. 7/16

The information whether a stack is safe or unsafe, cannot be found in the
constructor axioms. This information is localized in the safety functions.
The safety function safeBoundedStack is equivalent to

```
operation
  safeBoundedStack: BoundedStack -> Bool;
declare b: BoundedStack;  n: Nat;
operation axioms
  safeBoundedStack( newstack ) == true;
  safeBoundedStack( push( b, n ) ) ==
    if length( b ) ≤ 99
      then safeBoundedStack( b )
      else false
    end if;
  safeBoundedStack( underflow ) == false;
  safeBoundedStack( overflow ) == false;
```

Fig. 7/17

Remember that if b is unsafe, length(b) yields errNat, see Fig. 7/15. In that case, length(b) ≤ 99 will yield errBool, see Fig. 7/25. Because of the definition of the ifthenelse operation, see Fig. 7/26, the right-hand side of the second operation axiom in Fig. 7/17 will then yield false.

The Parameterized Bounded Array

Another interesting example is the specification of a bounded array, i.e. an array with indices lying between a given lower and upper bound. Assigning to a bounded array with an index not lying between these bounds yields an unsafe bounded array. In Fig. 7/18 a parameterized specification with error detection only is given.

```
scheme BoundedArrayScheme [
    requirement Attribute;
      export all;
      sort Attribute;
      operation
        initial: -> Attribute;
    end requirement Attribute;

    requirement OrderedIndex;
      import Bool, true, _ and _, _ or _ from Bool;
      export all;
      sort Index;
      operations
        _ = _: Index * Index -> Bool;
        _ ≤ _: Index * Index -> Bool;
      declare i, i₁, i₂, i₃: Index;
      theorems
        ( $i = $i ) == true;
```

```
                    ( $i₁ = $i₂ ) == ( $i₂ = $i₁ );
                    ( $i₁ = $i₂ ) and ( $i₂ = $i₃ ) ⇒ ( $i₁ = $i₃ ) == true;
                    ( $i₁ ⩽ $i₂ ) or ( $i₂ ⩽ $i₁ ) == true;
                    ( $i₁ ⩽ $i₂ ) and ( $i₂ ⩽ $i₁ ) ⇒ ( $i₁ = $i₂ ) == true;
                    ( $i₁ = $i₂ ) ⇒ ( $i₁ ⩽ $i₂ ) == true;
                    ( $i₁ ⩽ $i₂ ) and ( $i₂ ⩽ $i₃ ) ⇒ ( $i₁ ⩽ $i₃ ) == true;
                end requirement OrderedIndex;
        };

        module BoundedArray;
          import not _, _ and _ from Bool;
            all from Attribute, OrderedIndex;
          export all;
          sort BoundedArray;
          constructors
            empty: $ Index * $ Index -> BoundedArray $$;
            _[ _ / _ ]: $ BoundedArray * Attribute * $ Index -> BoundedArray
              $ ( lwb( boundedArray ) ⩽ index ) and ( index ⩽ upb( boundedArray ) ) $;
          operations
            lwb, upb: BoundedArray -> Index;
            read: BoundedArray * Index -> Attribute;
          declare ba: BoundedArray;  at, at₁, at₂: Attribute;  i, i₁, i₂, i₃: Index;
          constructor axioms
            not( i₁ = i₂ ) ⇒
              $ ( ba [ at₁ / i₁ ][ at₂ / i₂ ]) ==
              $ ( ba [ at₂ / i₂ ][ at₁ / i₁ ]);
            i₁ = i₂ ⇒ $ ( ba [ at₁ / i₁ ][ at₂ / i₂ ]) == $ ( ba [ at₂ / i₂ ]);
          operation axioms
          $$ lwb( empty( i₁, i₂ ) ) == i₁;
          $$ upb( empty( i₁, i₂ ) ) == i₂;
          $$ lwb( ba [ at / i ]) == lwb( ba );
          $$ upb( ba [ at / i ]) == upb( ba );
          $$ read( empty( i₁, i₂ ), i₃ ) == initial;
          $$ read( ba [ at / i₁ ], i₂ ) ==
              if i₁ = i₂
                then at
                else read( ba, i₂ )
              end if;
          end module BoundedArray;
        end scheme BoundedArrayScheme;
```

Fig. 7/18

Notice that requirement OrderedIndex implicitly requires a safety function
safeIndex by using safety markers. The safety function safeBoundedArray
of module BoundedArray is equivalent to the one of Fig. 7/19.

```
operation
  safeBoundedArray: BoundedArray -> Bool;
declare ba: BoundedArray;  i, i₁, i₂: Index;  at: Attribute;
```

```
operation axioms
  safeBoundedArray( empty( i₁, i₂ ) ) == safeIndex( i₁ ) and safeIndex( i₂ );
  safeBoundedArray( ba [ at / i ] ) ==
    if ( lwb( ba ) ⩽ i ) and ( i ⩽ upb( ba ) )
      then safeBoundedArray( ba ) and safeIndex( i )
      else false
    end if;
```

Fig. 7/19

Error handling is added in Fig. 7/18 resulting in Fig. 7/20.

```
scheme BoundedArrayScheme [
  requirement Attribute;
    export all;
    sort Attribute;
    operation
      initial, errAttribute: -> Attribute;
    end requirement Attribute;

  requirement OrderedIndex;
    import Bool, true, errBool, _ and _, _ or _ from Bool;
    export all;
    sort Index;
    operations
      _ = _: Index * Index -> Bool;
      _ ⩽ _: Index * Index -> Bool;
    declare i, i₁, i₂, i₃: Index;
    theorems
      ( $i = $i ) == true;
      ( $i₁ = $i₂ ) == ( $i₂ = $i₁ );
      ( $i₁ = $i₂ ) and ( $i₂ = $i₃ ) ⇒ ( $i₁ = $i₃ ) == true;
      ( $i₁ ⩽ $i₂ ) or ( $i₂ ⩽ $i₁ ) == true;
      ( $i₁ ⩽ $i₂ ) and ( $i₂ ⩽ $i₁ ) ⇒ ( $i₁ = $i₂ ) == true;
      ( $i₁ = $i₂ ) ⇒ ( $i₁ ⩽ $i₂ ) == true;
      ( $i₁ ⩽ $i₂ ) and ( $i₂ ⩽ $i₃ ) ⇒ ( $i₁ ⩽ $i₃ ) == true;
      ?i₁ ⩽ ?i₂ == errBool;
    end requirement OrderedIndex;
  ];

  module BoundedArray;
    import not _, _ and _ from Bool;
      all from Attribute, OrderedIndex;
    export all;
    sort BoundedArray;
    constructors
      empty: $ Index * $ Index -> BoundedArray $$;
      _[ _ / _ ]: $ BoundedArray * Attribute * $ Index -> BoundedArray
        $ ( lwb( boundedArray ) ⩽ index ) and ( index ⩽ upb( boundedArray ) ) $;
    operations
      lwb, upb: BoundedArray -> Index;
      read: BoundedArray * Index -> Attribute;
```

```
declare ba: BoundedArray;  at, at₁, at₂: Attribute;  i, i₁, i₂, i₃: Index;
constructor axioms
   not( i₁ = i₂ ) ⇒
     $( ba [ at₁ / i₁ ][ at₂ / i₂ ]) ==
     $( ba [ at₂ / i₂ ][ at₁ / i₁ ]);
   i₁ = i₂ ⇒ $( ba [ at₁ / i₁ ][ at₂ / i₂ ]) == $( ba [ at₂ / i₂ ]);
operation axioms
   lwb( empty( i₁, i₂ )) == i₁;
   upb( empty( i₁, i₂ )) == i₂;
   lwb( ba [ at / i ]) == lwb( ba );
   upb( ba [ at / i ]) == upb( ba );
  '$$ read( empty( i₁, i₂ ), i₃ ) == initial;
  $$ read( ba [ at / i₁ ], i₂ ) ==
      if i₁ = i₂
        then at
        else read( ba, i₂ )
      end if;
  ?? read( ba, i ) == errAttribute;
 end module BoundedArray;
end scheme BoundedArrayScheme;
```

Fig. 7/20

Another possibility is that we require that, after an object has been assigned with a wrong index, all objects that are later assigned with a correct index must be readable. If BoundedArrayScheme is instantiated by taking as attributes the boolean values and as indices the natural numbers, it must, e.g., be possible to read the element with index 3 of the array

$$\text{empty}(1, 3) [\text{true} / 1] [\text{true} / 12] [\text{true} / 3]$$

In Fig. 7/21 the required error handling is obtained by modifying the safety function: the first argument of the assign constructor is not requested to be safe. The constructor empty returns a safe bounded array if and only if its lower and upper bound are safe indices. The assign constructor returns an unsafe bounded array if and only if the index of the last assigned element is an unsafe index or this index is not lying between the given bounds.

```
scheme BoundedArrayScheme [
  -- ... see Fig. 7/20 --

  constructors
    empty: $ Index * $ Index -> BoundedArray $$;
    assign: BoundedArray * Attribute * $ Index -> BoundedArray
      $( lwb( boundedArray ) ≤ index ) and ( index ≤ upb( boundedArray ) ) $;

  -- ... see Fig. 7/20 --
```

end scheme BoundedArrayScheme;

Fig. 7/21

The safety function safeBoundedArray is equivalent to the one of Fig. 7/22.

```
operation
  safeBoundedArray: BoundedArray -> Bool;
declare ba: BoundedArray;   i, i₁, i₂: Index;   at: Attribute;
operation axioms
  safeBoundedArray( empty( i₁, i₂ ) ) == safeIndex( i₁ ) and safeIndex( i₂ );
  safeBoundedArray( ba [ at / i ] ) ==
    if ( lwb( ba ) ≤ i ) and ( i ≤ upb( ba ) )
      then safeIndex( i )
      else false
    end if;
```

Fig. 7/22

If BoundedArrayScheme of Fig. 7/21 is instantiated by taking as attributes the boolean values and as indices the natural numbers, we prefer the bounded array

empty(errNat, 5) [true / 2]

to be unsafe. This bounded array is unsafe thanks to the theorem

$?i_1 \leq ?i_2$ == errBool;

in the requirement OrderedIndex. Indeed, the safety condition applied to the given bounded array does not result in true. errNat ≤ 2 results in errBool. The boolean operation and propagates the error object. When the if-argument of an ifthenelse construct is not equal to true, the ifthenelse construct is equivalent to its else-argument, which is false. As a consequence, the safety condition applied to the given bounded array yields false.

The Peekstack

A semi-constructive specification of the peekstack, which was discussed in Section 2.18, is given in Fig. 7/23 using our error handling notation.

```
scheme PeekstackScheme [
    requirement Item;
      export all;
      sort Item;
      operation
        error: -> Item;
    end requirement Item;
  ];

  module Peekstack;
    import true, false from Bool;   Item, error from Item;
    export all except shove;
    sort Peekstack;
    constructors
      newstack: -> Peekstack $$;
      push: $ Peekstack * Item -> Peekstack
        $ case peekstack of
            shove( s, it ): false;
            otherwise: true;
          end case $;
      shove: $ Peekstack * Item -> Peekstack $$;   -- hidden operation --
      err: -> Peekstack ??;
    operations
      pop: Peekstack -> Peekstack;
      read: Peekstack -> Item;
      return: Peekstack -> Peekstack;
      down: Peekstack -> Peekstack;
    declare s: Peekstack;   it: Item;
    constructor axiom
      ? s == err;
    operation axioms
    $$ pop( newstack ) == err;
    $$ pop( push( s, it ) ) == s;
    $$ pop( shove( s, it ) ) == err;
    $$ read( newstack ) == error;
    $$ read( push( s, it ) ) == it;
    $$ read( shove( s, it ) ) == read( s );
    $$ return( newstack ) == newstack;
    $$ return( push( s, it ) ) == push( s, it );
    $$ return( shove( s, it ) ) == push( return( s ), it );
    $$ down( newstack ) == err;
    $$ down( push( s, it ) ) == shove( s, it );
    $$ down( shove( s, it ) ) == shove( down( s ), it );

    ?? pop( s ) == err;
    ?? read( s ) == error;
    ?? return( s ) == err;
    ?? down( s ) == err;
  end module Peekstack;
end scheme PeekstackScheme;
```

Fig. 7/23

7.6 Miscellanies

The Boolean Abstract Data Type

In the previous sections the boolean abstract data type Bool was assumed
to be defined in the usual way. All boolean operations (but the ifthenelse
construct, see below) propagate errors. The only boolean error object is
denoted by errBool. The predefined module Bool is equivalent to Fig. 7/24.

```
module Bool
  export all;
  sort Bool;
  constructors
    true, false: -> Bool $$;
    errBool: -> Bool ??;
  operations
    not _: Bool -> Bool;
    _ and _: Bool * Bool -> Bool;
    _ or _: Bool * Bool -> Bool;
    _ => _: Bool * Bool -> Bool;
    _ <= _: Bool * Bool -> Bool;
    _ <=> _: Bool * Bool -> Bool;
    _ = _: Bool * Bool -> Bool;
  declare b, b_1, b_2, b_3: Bool;
  operation axioms
    not true == false;        not false == true;
    $b and true == $b;        $b and false == false;
    $b or true == true;       $b or false == $b;
    true => $b == $b;         false => $b == true;
    $b <= true == $b;         $b <= false == true;
    true <=> $b == $b;        false <=> $b == not $b;

    not errBool == errBool;       ?b_1 and ?b_2 == errBool;
    ?b_1 or ?b_2 == errBool;      ?b_1 => ?b_2 == errBool;
    ?b_1 <= ?b_2 == errBool;      ?b_1 <=> ?b_2 == errBool;

    b = b == true;
    true = false == false;        true = errBool == false;
    false = true == false;        false = errBool == false;
    errBool = true == false;      errBool = false == false;

  theorems
    b and b == b;        b or b == b;
    b_1 and b_2 == b_2 and b_1;      b_1 or b_2 == b_2 or b_1;
    b_1 and ( b_1 or $b_2 ) == b_1;       b_1 or ( b_1 and $b_2 ) == b_1;
    $b and not $b == false;       $b or not $b == true;
    not not $b == $b;
    ( b_1 and b_2 ) and b_3 == b_1 and ( b_2 and b_3 );
    ( b_1 or b_2 ) or b_3 == b_1 or ( b_2 or b_3 );
    b_1 and ( b_2 or b_3 ) == ( b_1 and b_2 ) or ( b_1 and b_3 );
    b_1 or ( b_2 and b_3 ) == ( b_1 or b_2 ) and ( b_1 or b_3 );
```

```
$b₁ => $b₂  ==  if $b₁ then $b₂ else true end if;
b₁ <= b₂  ==  b₂ => b₁;
b₁ <=> b₂  ==  (b₁ => b₂) and (b₁ <= b₂);
b₁ = b₂ == b₂ = b₁;
(b₁ = b₂) and (b₂ = b₃) ⇒ (b₁ = b₃);
end module Bool;
```

Fig. 7/24

The Abstract Data Type of the Natural Numbers

In Fig. 7/25 a specification with error handling is given for the natural
numbers including equality and inequality operations.

```
module Nat;
   import Bool, true, false, errBool, _ or _ from Bool;
   export all;
   sort Nat;
   constructors
      zero: -> Nat $$;
      succ: $ Nat -> Nat $$;
      errNat: -> Nat ??;
   operations
      pre: Nat -> Nat;
      add: Nat * Nat -> Nat;
      mult: Nat * Nat -> Nat;
      _ = _: Nat * Nat -> Bool;
      _ < _: Nat * Nat -> Bool;
      _ ≤ _: Nat * Nat -> Bool;
   declare n, n₁, n₂: Nat;
   constructor axiom
   ! n == errNat;
   operation axioms
   $$ pre( zero ) == errNat;
   $$ pre( succ( n ) ) == n;
   $$ add( zero, n ) == n;
   $$ add( succ( n₁ ), n₂ ) == succ( add( n₁, n₂ ) );
   $$ mult( zero, n ) == zero;
   $$ mult( succ( n₁ ), n₂ ) == add( n₂, mult( n₁, n₂ ) );
   $$ ( zero = zero ) == true;
   $$ ( succ( n ) = zero ) == false;
   $$ ( zero = succ( n ) ) == false;
   $$ ( succ( n₁ ) = succ( n₂ ) ) == n₁ = n₂;
   $$ ( n < zero ) == false;
   $$ ( zero < succ( n ) ) == true;
   $$ ( succ( n₁ ) < succ( n₂ ) ) == n₁ < n₂;
   $$ ( succ( n₁ ) ≤ succ( n₂ ) ) == ( n₁ < n₂ ) or ( n₁ = n₂ );

   ?? pre( n ) == errNat;
```

```
    ?? add( n₁, n₂ ) == errNat;
    ?? mult( n₁, n₂ ) == errNat;
     $ n₁ = ! n₂ == false;
     ! n₁ = $ n₂ == false;
     ! n₁ = ! n₂ == true;
    ?? ( n₁ < n₂ ) == errBool;
    ?? ( n₁ ≤ n₂ ) == errBool;
  end module Nat;
```

Fig. 7/25

Ifthenelse Construct

The ifthenelse construct is an example of a recovery operation. For each sort X the language-defined ifthenelse construct is equivalent to

```
operation
  if _ then _ else _ end if: Bool * X * X -> X;
declare b: Bool;  x₁, x₂: X;
operation axioms
  if true then x₁ else x₂ end if == x₁;
  if false then x₁ else x₂ end if == x₂;
  if !b then x₁ else x₂ end if == x₂;
```

Fig. 7/26

Therefore, the expression

```
 if n = 0
   then x₁
   else x₁ / n
 end if
```

where the variable n stands for a natural number and $\_ / \_$ is the division of natural numbers, results in x_1 when n is bound with 0. Remember that the order of evaluation has not been defined.

Markers and Case Constructs

If a safety or an unsafety marker is used in the choice of a case arm in an axiom, this marker is only related to the choice of the case arm and not to the whole axiom. E.g.,

```
declare b, b₁: Stack;   n: Nat;
operation axiom
  f( b, n ) = ...
    case push( b, n ) of
      $ b₁: ...
      ! b₁: ...
    end case ... ;
```

Fig. 7/27

does not mean that b_1, i.e. push(b, n), must be safe as well as unsafe, which is in conflict. It means that if b_1 is safe, the first case arm must be taken, otherwise b_1 is unsafe and the second case arm must be taken.

Cartesian Products of Sorts

If Cartesian products of sorts (see Section 4.11) are used, a composed object is safe if and only if all its elementary objects are safe. Assume, e.g., that a sort Corner is defined as the Cartesian product of the sorts Street and Avenue:

```
sort Corner == Street * Avenue;
```

Fig. 7/28

then it stands for

```
sort Corner;
constructor
  ( _, _): $ Street * $ Avenue -> Corner $$;
```

```
operations
  streetOf _: Corner -> Street;
  avenueOf _: Corner -> Avenue;
  _[ _/ street ]: Corner * Street -> Corner;
  _[ _/ avenue ]: Corner * Avenue -> Corner;
  -- safeCorner: Corner -> Bool;
declare s: Street;  a: Avenue;  c: Corner;
operation axioms
  streetOf ( s, a ) == s;
  avenueOf ( s, a ) == a;
  c [ s / street ] == ( s, avenueOf c );
  c [ a / avenue ] == ( streetOf c, a );
  -- safeCorner( ( s, a ) ) == safeStreet( s ) and safeAvenue( a );
```

Fig. 7/29

Uniqueness and Completeness Constraints

The attentive reader may have noticed that the uniqueness and completeness constraints are not always met. E.g., in Fig. 7/14, operation axioms of the form

```
$$ length( errStack ) == ...;
$$ pop( errStack ) == ...;
$$ top( errStack ) == ...;
$$ isnewstack( errStack ) == ...;
```

have been omitted because they would never be applied. We assumed that the checker of the uniqueness and completeness constraints is intelligent enough to handle such situations.

Shorthand Notation and Import Clauses

Sorts, constructors and operations that are not explicitly written down in a module or a requirement, need not be mentioned in the import clause of the module or the requirement. E.g., the sort Bool and the constructors true and false were not mentioned in the import clause of module BoundedArray of Fig. 7/18, although they were used in the equivalent specification of the safety function in Fig. 7/19.

Parameterized Specifications with Error Handling

Up to now, the parameterization concept and error handling have been
defined independently in order to obtain a language with orthogonal
features. The relation between them is that when an operation safeX is
explicitly required in a requirement, the operation safeX must be explicitly
bound with the safety function of the sort that is bound with X. For
instance, if the requirement

```
requirement Item;
  import Bool from Bool;
  export all;
  sort Item;
  operation
    safeItem: Item -> Bool;
end requirement Item;
```

Fig. 7/30

is required, the operation safeItem must be bound with the safety function
of the sort that is bound with Item. If the operation safeX is implicitly
required, e.g., by using safety markers as in requirement OrderedIndex of
Fig. 7/20, it will implicitly be bound with the safety function of the sort
that is bound with X. It is obvious that in both cases a safety function
must have been defined for the sort that is bound with X.

7.7 Bibliographic Notes

[Guttag78] treats neither error propagation nor error recovery. In that
article, as soon as an error is detected, UNDEFINED is returned. For
example,

TOP(Stack) -> item $\cup$ { UNDEFINED }

. . .

TOP(NEWSTACK) = UNDEFINED

If UNDEFINED is a value, what is its sort? Or is TOP a partial function?
Guttag gives no precise meaning of UNDEFINED (he kept the meaning
undefined). We believe that a kind of incomplete specification is intended,

analogous to the first step of our error specification method. Eventually, one must indicate what the operations do to UNDEFINED, otherwise the benefit from working with algebras is lost [Goguen78].

[Goguen78] defines an *error* object and an *OK function* for each sort. Axioms are replaced by *conditional error axioms*. These are axioms in which terms are checked to be OK. This method is hardly supported by their algebraic specification language, leading to a large amount of axioms for definitions of OK functions and for error and OK propagation. Error recovery is not provided. The method we proposed can be viewed as an improved extension of this technique. The safety function corresponds to the OK function introduced in [Goguen78].

In OBJ2 [Goguen84, Futatsugi85, Goguen85] *subsorts* are defined, see Section 3.6. Although this concept can be defined within the framework of many-sorted initial algebras using implicit coercion and retraction functions between the sorts [Futatsugi85], a new mathematical foundation, called *Order-Sorted Algebra*, is used in [Goguen85, Goguen87b]. For example, the sort NeStack of non-empty stacks is defined as a subsort of the sort Stack. The operations top and pop are defined for non-empty stacks only. If, e.g., the operation top is applied to a stack, the stack is implicitly retracted (inverse coercion) to a non-empty stack. This is a kind of run-time type checking. If an error occurs, the rest of the term is further reduced. In the example of the non-empty stacks the result is then, e.g., pop(retract(newstack)). These objects are in fact unsafe objects. No error recovery is provided although *error handlers* are suggested [Futatsugi85, Goguen87c], but at the moment they have not yet been published.

Another problem is that the mechanism of subsorts is not powerful enough for, e.g., bounded stacks. Therefore, *sort constraints*, which are related to our safety conditions, are introduced [Goguen84, Goguen85].

A new mathematical foundation is developed by Gogolla [Gogolla84a]. The sets of many-sorted algebras are heterogeneous: they are divided into *ok* and *error objects*, corresponding with safe and unsafe objects respectively. The functions are divided into two classes: *o.k.* and *unsafe* functions. Only unsafe functions may introduce errors when applied to ok objects. This guarantees that whenever an expression consisting of ok functions only is applied to ok arguments, it will result in an ok object. Another important characteristic is that two different types of variables are introduced for the same sort. Variables to which only ok objects may be bound, and variables to which both ok and error objects may be bound. The drawback is that functions can only be marked as o.k. or unsafe, this is not powerful enough for more complex data types, e.g., bounded stacks.

In the algebraic specification language PLUSS [Bidoit85b] the notions of *multi-target operators* and *multi-target algebras* are introduced. The basic idea is to split safe and unsafe objects into different sets. But this method is not adequate enough for bounded types. In [Bernot86] a new mathematical foundation is proposed, called *exception algebras*. Labels may be associated with terms. This label information may be used in the axioms. This formalism is powerful, but it is also very complex. The formalism leaves the classical framework of many-sorted initial algebras.

8. Abstract Implementations

> "Everything should be built top-down,
> except the first time."
> */usr/games/fortune*

Working with *abstract implementations*, sometimes called *data refinements*, is a powerful method to design and implement algebraic specifications. It enables top-down design, top-down verification and also top-down testing. As an introduction to abstract implementations first an intuitive discussion of the general principles of the method is given. These principles are then illustrated by a simple example. A detailed treatment of abstract implementations will be worked out in the subsequent sections.

When working with abstract implementations, the software life cycle does not consist of a single design and a single implementation phase (as shown in Fig. 1/1), but it has several design-implementation levels forming a pyramid-like structure, where the implementation at one level is considered as the design-specification at the lower level. The lower the level, the lower the degree of abstraction, i.e. the number of implementation details increases. An example of such a pyramid-like structure, called *design-implementation structure* in the sequel, is given in Fig. 8/1. This example will be thoroughly discussed further on. One of the main reasons why the idea of abstract implementations is so important is that each level can be tested through rapid prototyping and verified using equational reasoning (see Section 2.13) and induction (see Section 2.17), before the lower levels need be constructed. Therefore, working with abstract implementations improves correctness, extendibility, reusability, modularity and continuity of software systems. By combining the technique of abstract implementations with the technique of parameterization, a high degree of reusability can be obtained. It will be illustrated by two examples: the stack and the symbol table.

Given an abstract data type A consisting of a set of objects and a number of functions. As a *first step*, the abstract data type A will be algebraically specified by a module A defining among others the sort A. In the sequel, specifications will be (semi-)constructive (see Chapter 4). So, in the module A a distinction is made between constructors and operations. Clearly, A may import from other modules. The module A together with all its imported (directly and indirectly) modules constitute the highest level of the design-implementation structure. Due to rapid prototyping based on direct implementation (see Chapter 4), the modules at this level can be directly executed and tested so that experiments with the software system are possible at an early stage of its development.

As an example, consider the highest level of the design-implementation structure for the symbol table in Fig. 8/1. The module Symboltable defines the sort Symboltable by means of a number of constructors and operations. The module Symboltable imports from the modules Identifier, Attribute and Bool. The specification details of the module Symboltable will be given in Section 8.5.

In a *second step*, the module A is implemented by assigning a specific meaning to the objects (constructors in A) and functions (operations in A) of the abstract data type A. The implementation of module A is itself a module, called *implementation module* and denoted ↓A. The implementation module ↓A is defined in terms of the sort, constructors and operations of another module B. Clearly, ↓A may still import from other modules. The implementation module ↓A and all its imported modules constitute the second level of the design-implementation structure. As with the first level of the structure, the modules of the second level can be directly executed and tested by rapid prototyping based on direct implementation. By using the implementation module ↓A as implementation for module A instead of using the direct implementation of module A, direct execution at the first level will be more efficient.

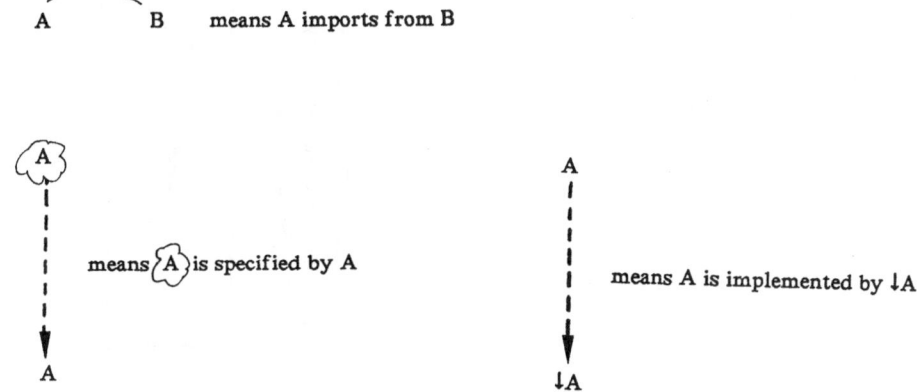

Fig. 8/1 (continued)

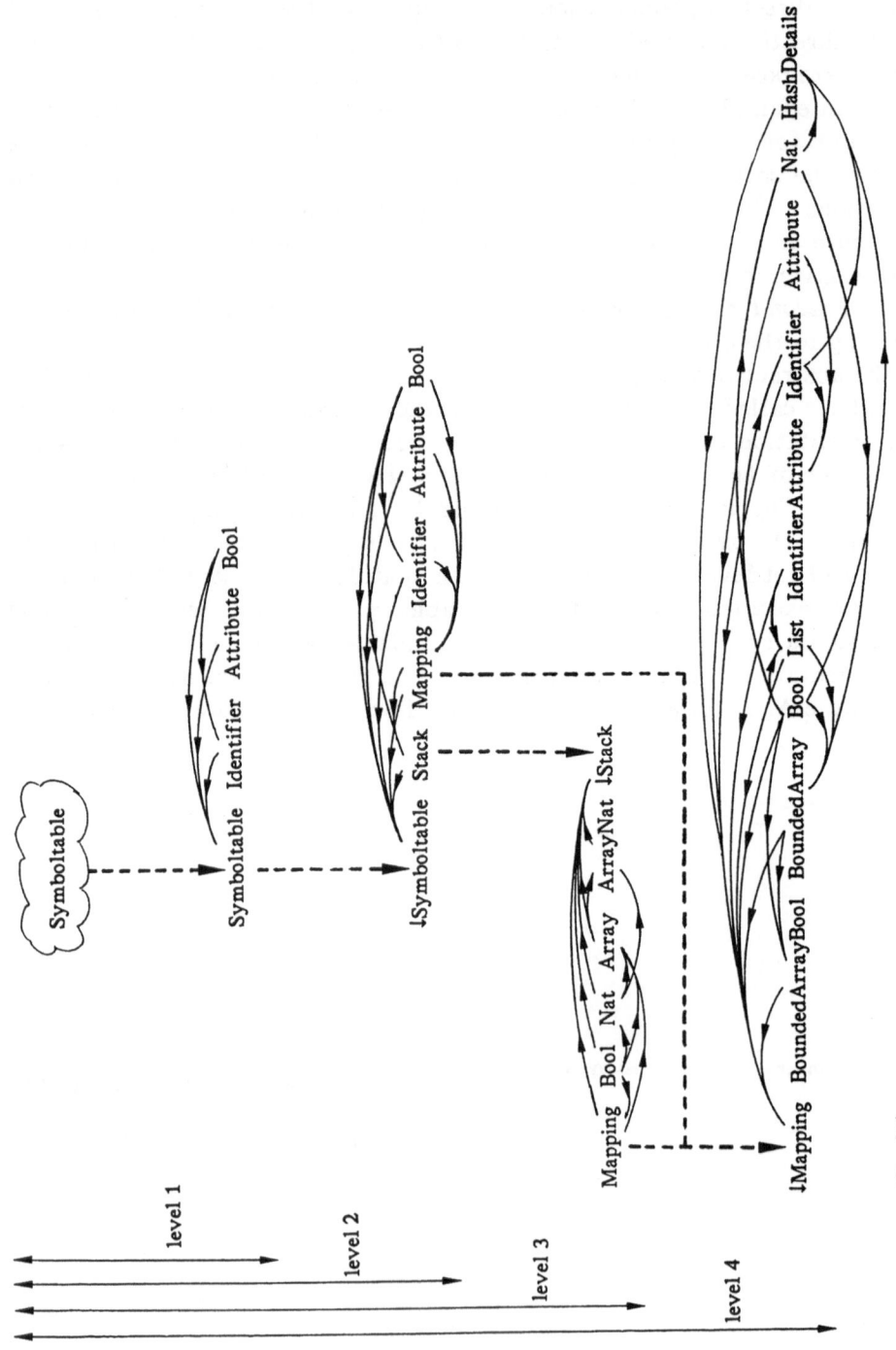

Fig. 8.1

During the second step, one can also verify that the implementation ↓A meets its specification A. Correctness of implementation will be further explained in Section 8.3. An important aspect of the technique of abstract implementations is that rapid prototyping and verification at level 2 is based on the specifications of the imported modules of ↓A, but not on their implementations.

In our example shown in Fig. 8/1, the symbol table is implemented as a stack of mappings from identifiers onto attributes. The programs implementing the symbol table have the form of axioms. These programs constitute the implementation module ↓Symboltable, which is defined in terms of the sort, constructors and operations imported from module Stack. ↓Symboltable also imports from the modules Mapping, Identifier, Attribute and Bool. All these modules constitute level 2 of the design-implementation structure of the symbol table.

In a *next step*, one of the modules for which no implementation module is provided, can be implemented in turn as explained in step 2. It yields the implementation module ↓C and a number of modules imported by ↓C. Hereafter, all modules for which no implementation modules are yet provided constitute a next level. This process of implementation refinement goes on until one obtains a level of modules that has a direct implementation that meets the claimed efficiency requirement. Consider again the symbol table as shown in Fig. 8/1. The stack is implemented by an ArrayNat object. Each ArrayNat object consists of an array of mappings and a natural number referring to the first free array entry. The programs implementing the module Stack constitute the implementation module ↓Stack. The implementation module ↓Stack imports from modules ArrayNat, Array, Mapping, Nat and Bool. Level 3 of the design-implementation structure consists of the modules ↓Symboltable, ↓Stack, Mapping, ArrayNat, Array, Nat, Identifier, Attribute and Bool. Direct execution at level 3 is already much more efficient than at level 2. Level 4 can be obtained by providing an implementation for, e.g., Mapping. This implementation of Mapping can be constructed independently from the implementation of Stack. At level 4, Mapping is implemented by a module in which an efficient hashcoding technique is used for the retrieval of information. All specification details of the four-level structure of the Symboltable, as shown in Fig. 8/1, will be given in Section 8.5.

8.1 Example of the Stacks

In this section the method of abstract implementations is introduced by means of a simple example: the stack of natural numbers. As a first approximation, error handling, error recovery and parameterization are not considered. They will be discussed in Sections 8.4 and 8.5. Precise definitions of the concepts of abstract implementations will be given in Section 8.2. The design-implementation structure is shown in Fig. 8/2.

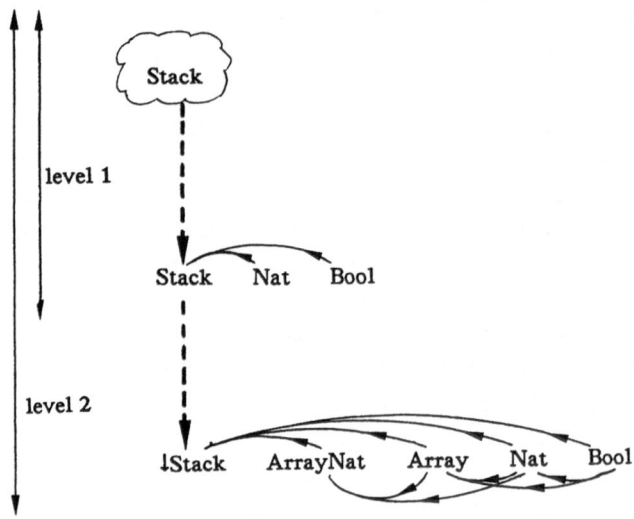

Fig. 8/2

At level 1, we have the module Stack specifying the abstract data type Stack. Stack imports from the modules Nat and Bool. At level 2, the module Stack is implemented yielding the implementation module ↓Stack, which is defined in terms of the module ArrayNat, defining pairs of arrays and natural numbers. The implementation module ↓Stack imports from the modules ArrayNat, Array, Nat and Bool.

The Module Stack

```
module Stack;
  import Bool, true, false from Bool;
```

```
        Nat, zero from Nat rename Nat as Item, zero as errItem;
    export all;
    sort Stack;
    constructors
        newstack: -> Stack;
        push: Stack * Item -> Stack;
    operations
        pop: Stack -> Stack;
        top: Stack -> Item;
        replace: Stack * Item -> Stack;
        isnewstack: Stack -> Bool;
    declare s: Stack;  it, it₁, it₂: Item;
    operation axioms
        pop( newstack ) == newstack;
        pop( push( s, it ) ) == s;
        top( newstack ) == errItem;
        top( push( s, it ) ) == it;
        replace( newstack, it ) == newstack;
        replace( push( s, it₁ ), it₂ ) == push( s, it₂ );
        isnewstack( newstack ) == true;
        isnewstack( push( s, it ) ) == false;
    end module Stack;
```

Fig. 8/3

The Module ↓Stack

```
module ↓Stack;
    import ArrayNat, ( _ , _ ), arrayOf _, natOf _ from ArrayNat;
        Array, empty, _ [ _ / _ ], read from Array;  Bool from Bool;
        Nat, zero, succ, pre, _ = _ , _ < _ from Nat
            rename Nat as Item, zero as 0, zero as errItem, succ as _ + 1, pre as _ - 1;
    operations
        ↓newstack: -> ArrayNat;
        ↓push: ArrayNat * Item -> ArrayNat;
        ↓pop: ArrayNat -> ArrayNat;
        ↓top: ArrayNat -> Item;
        ↓replace: ArrayNat * Item -> ArrayNat;
        ↓isnewstack: ArrayNat -> Bool;
    declare an: ArrayNat;   it: Item;
    operation axioms
        ↓newstack == ( empty, 0 );
        ↓push( an, it ) == ( arrayOf an [ it / natOf an ], natOf an + 1 );
        ↓pop( an ) ==
            if natOf an = 0
                then an
                else ( arrayOf an, natOf an - 1 )
            end if;
        ↓top( an ) ==
            if natOf an = 0
```

```
            then errItem
            else read( arrayOf an, natOf an - 1 )
          end if;
       ↓replace( an, it ) ==
          if natOf an = 0
            then an
            else ( arrayOf an [ it / natOf an - 1 ], natOf an )
          end if;
       ↓isnewstack( an ) == natOf an = 0;
    end module ↓Stack;
```

Fig. 8/4

The Module ArrayNat

```
module ArrayNat;
  import Array from Array;   Nat from Nat;
  export all;
  sort ArrayNat == Array * Nat;
  -- As explained in Section 4.11, the Cartesian product stands for:
  --    sort ArrayNat;
  --    constructor
  --      ( _ , _ ): Array * Nat -> ArrayNat;
  --    operations
  --      arrayOf _: ArrayNat -> Array;
  --      natOf _: ArrayNat -> Nat;
  --      _[ _ / array ]: ArrayNat * Array -> ArrayNat;
  --      _[ _ / nat ]: ArrayNat * Nat -> ArrayNat;
  --    declare a: Array;   n: Nat;   an: ArrayNat;
  --    operation axioms
  --      arrayOf ( a, n ) == a;
  --      natOf ( a, n ) == n;
  --      an [ a / array ] == ( a, natOf an );
  --      an [ n / nat ] == ( arrayOf an, n );
end module ArrayNat;
```

Fig. 8/5

The Module Array

```
module Array;
  import Bool, true, false from Bool;   Nat, zero, _ = _ from Nat
```

```
      rename Nat as Index, Nat as Attribute, zero as initial;
   export all;
   sort Array;
   constructors
     empty: - > Array;
     _[ _ / _ ]: Array * Attribute * Index -> Array;
   operations
     read: Array * Index -> Attribute;
     isundefined: Array * Index -> Bool;
   declare a: Array;   i, i₁, i₂: Index;   at, at₁, at₂: Attribute;
   constructor axioms
     not ( i₁ = i₂ ) ⇏ ( ar [ at₁ / i₁ ][ at₂ / i₂ ]) == ( ar [ at₂ / i₂ ][ at₁ / i₁ ]);
     ( ar [ at₁ / i ][ at₂ / i ]) == ( ar [ at₂ / i ]);
   operation axioms
     isundefined( empty, i ) == true;
     isundefined( a [ at / i₁ ], i₂ ) ==
       if i₁ = i₂ then false else isundefined( a, i₂ ) end if;
     read( empty, i ) == initial;
     read( a [ at / i₁ ], i₂ ) ==
       if i₁ = i₂ then at else read( a, i₂ ) end if;
   end module Array;
```

Fig. 8/6

Notice that the facility of renaming sorts, constructors and operations that are imported from other modules enhances readability. As an example, sort Nat is imported by the modules Stack and Array, but renamed differently. Stack and Array have different views on the module Nat. The module Stack uses natural numbers as items (Item), whereas Array uses natural numbers as indices (Index) and attributes (Attribute). These views are made explicit by the renaming facilities. In Section 8.4 where the example is worked out with schemes, the elements Item, Index and Attribute will play the role of formal parameters.

At the lowest level, the stack objects are implemented by means of pairs of arrays and natural numbers, see implementation module ↓Stack in Fig. 8/4. Such a natural number represents the array index (relative address), indicating the first free entry in the array. Indices start from 0. As an example, consider the term

pop(push(push(push(newstack, 10), 20), 30))

This term denotes an object of sort Stack. This object is implemented (as defined by the implementation module ↓Stack) as a pair (ar, i). The array ar contains 10 at index 0, 20 at index 1 and 30 at index 2. The value of i is 2.

The implementation module ↓Stack, see Fig. 8/4, defines two kinds of operations: the operations implementing the data part (constructors newstack and push) of the module Stack and the operations implementing the procedure part (operations pop, top, replace and isnewstack) of the module Stack. The former operations are called *data representation operations*. The latter operations are called *procedure implementation operations*. The data representation operations of ↓Stack are ↓newstack and ↓push. The procedure implementation operations of ↓Stack are ↓pop, ↓top, ↓replace and ↓isnewstack. Both data representation and procedure implementation operations are defined in terms of elements of the modules ArrayNat, Array, Nat and Bool.

The construction of ↓Stack implies two mappings. A mapping m_{data} that maps the constructors of module Stack onto data representation operations of ↓Stack, and a mapping m_{proc} that maps the operations of module Stack onto procedure implementation operations of ↓Stack. The implementation of Stack by means of ArrayNat yields the construction of the implementation module ↓Stack, together with the representation function ρ^T, the implementation invariant I, the abstraction function @ and the equivalence function _ ~ _. These concepts will be thoroughly discussed in the next section.

8.2 Concepts of Abstract Implementations

In this section we take a closer look at the elements of an implementation of module A by module B. An *implementation of module* A *by module* B consists of six elements:

1. the *data representation part* of the implementation module ↓A (see Section 8.2.1),

2. the *procedure implementation part* of the implementation module ↓A (see Section 8.2.2),

3. a *representation function* ρ^T (see Section 8.2.3),

4. an *implementation invariant* I (see Section 8.2.4),

5. an *abstraction function* @ (see Section 8.2.5) and

6. an *equivalence function* _ ~ _ (see Section 8.2.6).

Constraints

At this stage, error handling and parameterization are not taken into account. They will be treated in Sections 8.4 and 8.5.

In the sequel, modules A and B will meet the following constraints:

- The modules A and B belong to a hierarchical specification that meets the hierarchical constraints (see Section 3.2). This constraint excludes pathological cases due to junk and confusion.

- The hierarchical specification to which modules A and B belong is semi-constructive (see Section 4.7). This constraint is quite natural since we deal with implementation and rapid prototyping aspects of algebraic specifications.

- Module A defines just one sort, called sort A. Module B defines a sort B. The situation where module A does not define a new sort, can be considered as a special case, see Section 8.2.7. The constraint of defining at most one sort in a module simplifies the definitions related to abstract implementations to a great extent. This constraint is not very limiting in practice. The treatment of abstract implementations can be rephrased in terms of modules defining more than one sort. Such a treatment is not included in the book.

Convention: The operation $\_ = \_$ denotes the equality function defined by the axioms. So, we have

$x_1 == x_2$;

if and only if

$x_1 = x_2 ==$ true;

A-Constructors and A-Operations

Before discussing the concepts of abstract implementations, we first introduce the definitions of A-constructor and A-operation.

s_i is an *A-constructor* if

- s_i is a constructor and
- s_i is defined in module A.

The fact that an A-constructor always is of sort A follows from the constraint that A is the only sort defined in module A and from the (semi-)constructiveness constraints.

s_i is an *A-operation* if

- s_i is an operation,

- s_i is defined in module A and

- the sort of the range of s_i is A or s_i has at least one argument of sort A.

8.2.1 Data Representation Part of ↓A

A first element of an implementation of module A by module B is the *data representation part*. The data representation part of the implementation module ↓A consists of a number of operations of sort B, called *data representation operations*, implementing the A-constructors (data part) of module A. The introduction of a data representation part implies a mapping m_{data} from A-constructors onto data representation operations in ↓A, such that the rank of each A-constructor is preserved as follows:

- for each nullary A-constructor s_i in A, declared as s_i: -> A, we have in ↓A:

    $m_{data}(s_i)$: -> B;

- for each nonnullary A-constructor s_i in A, declared as s_i: S_{i_1} * S_{i_2} ... * S_{i_k} -> A, we have in ↓A:

    $m_{data}(s_i)$: $r(S_{i_1})$ * $r(S_{i_2})$ * ... * $r(S_{i_k})$ -> B;

    with $r(S_h) = B$ if $S_h = A$, and $r(S_h) = S_h$ otherwise.

Usually, the mapping m_{data} is implicit by an appropriate choice of the names of the data representation operations. If the mapping m_{data} is bijective (and mostly it is), every data representation operation will be named after the corresponding A-constructor preceded by the symbol ↓.

Example

Consider the implementation of module Stack by module ArrayNat as described in Fig. 8/4. The Stack-constructors are newstack and push. The data representation part of ↓Stack consists of the data representation operations ↓newstack and ↓push.

```
operations
  ↓newstack: -> ArrayNat;
  ↓push: ArrayNat * Item -> ArrayNat;
declare an: ArrayNat;  it: Item;
operation axioms
  ↓newstack == ( empty, 0 );
```

$\downarrow$push(an, it) == (arrayOf an [it / natOf an], natOf an + 1);

Fig. 8/7

The mapping m_{data} = { (newstack, $\downarrow$newstack), (push, $\downarrow$push) } is implicit, due to the appropriate name choice.

8.2.2 Procedure Implementation Part of $\downarrow$A

A second element of an implementation of module A by module B is the *procedure implementation part*. The procedure implementation part of the implementation module $\downarrow$A consists of a number of operations, called *procedure implementation operations*, implementing the A-operations (procedure part) of module A. The introduction of a procedure implementation part implies a mapping m_{proc} from A-operations onto procedure implementation operations in $\downarrow$A such that the rank for each A-operation is preserved as follows:

- For each A-operation s_i, declared as $s_i: S_{i_1} * S_{i_2} * ... * S_{i_k} \rightarrow S_j$, we have in $\downarrow$A:

$$m_{proc}(s_i): r(S_{i_1}) * r(S_{i_2}) * ... * r(S_{i_k}) \rightarrow r(S_j);$$

   with $r(S_h) = B$ if $S_h = A$, and $r(S_h) = S_h$ otherwise.

As with m_{data}, the mapping m_{proc} will usually be implicit, due to an appropriate name choice. As with m_{data}, the symbol $\downarrow$ will be used for this purpose.

Example

Consider the implementation of module Stack by module ArrayNat as described in Fig. 8/4. The Stack-operations are pop, top, replace and isnewstack. The procedure implementation part of Stack consists of the procedure implementation operations $\downarrow$pop, $\downarrow$top, $\downarrow$replace and $\downarrow$isnewstack.

```
operations
  ↓pop: ArrayNat -> ArrayNat;
  ↓top: ArrayNat -> Item;
  ↓replace: ArrayNat * Item -> ArrayNat;
  ↓isnewstack: ArrayNat -> Bool;
declare an: ArrayNat;  it: Item;
```

```
operation axioms
  ↓pop( an ) ==
    if natOf an = 0
      then an
      else ( arrayOf an, natOf an - 1 )
    end if;
  ↓top( an ) ==
    if natOf an = 0
      then errItem
      else read( arrayOf an, natOf an - 1 )
    end if;
  ↓replace( an, it ) ==
    if natOf an = 0
      then an
      else ( arrayOf an [ it / natOf an - 1 ], natOf an )
    end if;
  ↓isnewstack( an ) == natOf an = 0;
```

Fig. 8/8

The mapping m_{proc} = { (pop, ↓pop), (top, ↓top), (isnewstack, ↓isnewstack), (replace, ↓replace) }.

Implementation Operations

In the sequel, both data representation operations and procedure implementation operations will be called *implementation operations*. In our example, the implementation operations of the implementation module ↓Stack are ↓newstack, ↓push, ↓pop, ↓top, ↓replace and ↓isnewstack.

8.2.3 *Representation Function*

A third element of an implementation of module A by module B is the *representation function*. Roughly speaking, the representation function maps from abstract onto concrete. An important remark to start with is that the representation function is a function from a subset of variable-free terms to variable-free terms and not from objects to objects. The reason for this is simple. In general, an abstract object may have more than one concrete object as its representation. The representation function will be denoted ρ^T, where the superscript T indicates that the function is defined on terms and not on objects. The domain of ρ^T is a subset of variable-free terms, called A–terms.

A-Terms

Before discussing the concept of representation function, we first introduce the definition of A-term. Given an implementation of module A by module B. A term $s_i(t_1, t_2, ..., t_n)$ is an *A-term* (with $n \geqslant 0$) if

- $s_i(t_1, t_2, ..., t_n)$ is a variable-free term,

- s_i is either an A-constructor or an A-operation and

- for each t_j $(1 \leqslant j \leqslant n)$: t_j is of sort A implies that t_j is an A-term.

Conventions:

- The set of variable-free terms is denoted T.

- The set of variable-free terms of sort A is denoted T_A.

- The set of A-terms is denoted T^A.

- The set of A-terms of sort A is denoted T_A^A.

The definition of A-term is such that, in particular, the following three classes of variable-free terms are excluded:

- $s_i(t_1, t_2, ..., t_n)$ is a variable-free term and s_i is not defined in A.

- $s_i(t_1, t_2, ..., t_n)$ is a variable-free term, s_i is an operation defined in A, s_i is not of sort A and for each t_i $(1 \leqslant i \leqslant n)$ t_i is not of sort A.

- $s_i(t_1, t_2, ..., t_n)$ is a variable-free term, s_i is an operation or a constructor defined in A and there exists at least one t_i $(1 \leqslant i \leqslant n)$ of sort A such that t_i is not an A-term.

Example

Consider the module Stack in Fig. 8/3. Examples of Stack-terms are:

```
newstack
pop( push( newstack, 0 ) )
pop( pop( push( push( newstack, 1 ), 2 ) ) )
```

Representation Function

The representation function ρ^T of an implementation of module A by module B is a mapping

$$\rho^T: T^A \rightarrow T;$$

where T^A represents the set of A-terms and T represents the set of variable-free terms. Given an arbitrary A-term $s_i(x_1, x_2, ..., x_k)$, the representation function ρ^T is defined as

$$\rho^T(s_i(x_1, x_2, ..., x_n)) == m'(s_i) (m(x_1), m(x_2), ..., m(x_k));$$

 with

  $m'(s_i) = m_{data}(s_i)$ if s_i is an A-constructor

  $m'(s_i) = m_{proc}(s_i)$ if s_i is an A-operation

  $m(x_h) = \rho^T(x_h)$ if x_h is an A-term of sort A

  $m(x_h) = x_h$ otherwise

If a is an A-term of sort A, b is a variable-free term of sort B and $\rho^T(a)$ = b, the object denoted by b is said to be a *representation* of the object denoted by a. We also say that the term b is a *representation* of the term a.

Example

The representation function of the implementation of module Stack by module ArrayNat (see Fig. 8/3, 8/4 and 8/5) is given in Fig. 8/9.

---

operation
 $\rho^T: T^{Stack} \rightarrow T;$ -- T^{Stack} is the set of Stack-terms
declare
 st: $T^{Stack}_{Stack};$ -- T^{Stack}_{Stack} is the set of Stack-terms of sort Stack
 it: $T_{Item};$ -- T_{Item} is the set of variable-free terms of sort Item
operation axioms
 $\rho^T(newstack) == \downarrow newstack;$
 $\rho^T(push(st, it)) == \downarrow push(\rho^T(st), it);$
 $\rho^T(pop(st)) == \downarrow pop(\rho^T(st));$
 $\rho^T(top(st)) == \downarrow top(\rho^T(st));$
 $\rho^T(replace(st, it)) == \downarrow replace(\rho^T(st), it);$
 $\rho^T(isnewstack(st)) == \downarrow isnewstack(\rho^T(st));$

Fig. 8/9

As an example,

$$\delta.\rho^T(pop(push(newstack, 10))) = \downarrow pop(\downarrow push(\downarrow newstack, 10))$$

where δ stands for the denotation function defined in Chapter 2. When we apply the operation axioms for $\downarrow pop$, $\downarrow push$ and $\downarrow newstack$ (as defined in

Fig. 8/7 and 8/8), we obtain the theorem

$\delta.\rho^T(\ pop(\ push(\ newstack,\ 10\ )\ )\ )\ ) == (\ empty\ [\ 10\ /\ 0\ ],\ 0\ );$

The following variable-free terms of sort Stack define the same (abstract) object:

newstack
pop(push(newstack, 10))
pop(pop(push(push(newstack, 10), 20)))

The representation function ρ^T applied to these terms yields variable-free terms of sort ArrayNat. They are respectively:

(empty, 0)
(empty [10 / 0], 0)
(empty [10 / 0] [20 / 1], 0)

These last three terms denote distinct objects of sort ArrayNat.

Remarks

- Notice the difference between the declaration

    s: Stack;

  in Fig. 8/3 and the declaration

    st: T^{Stack}_{Stack};

  in Fig. 8/9. The variable s ranges over Stack objects, whereas st ranges over Stack terms. Also, the term pop(push(newstack, 10)) in Fig. 8/3 denotes a Stack object, whereas the same term in Fig. 8/9 denotes the variable-free term pop(push(newstack, 10)) itself. Therefore, the following theorem is not valid:

    $\rho^T(\ pop(\ push(\ newstack,\ 10\ )\ )\ ) == \rho^T(\ newstack\ );$

- Consider the abstract implementation of module Stack by module ArrayNat. The reader may notice that due to the definition of A-term the following relation exists:

    $\delta.\rho^T(\ top(\ push(\ newstack,\ it\ )\ )\ )\ ) = \downarrow top(\ \downarrow push(\ \downarrow newstack,\ it\ )\ )$

  for any variable-free term it of sort Nat. This relation holds even if the variable-free term it is, e.g.,

    top(push(push(newstack, 10), 10))

- Consider a specification containing modules A and C, as shown in Fig. 8/10. An implementation of module A by a module B is provided.

```
module A;
   ...
   sort A;
   constructors
   ...
   operations
     f: A -> D;
     h: E -> A;
   ...
end module A;

module C;
   ...
   operation
     g: E -> A;
   ...
end module C;
```

Fig. 8/10

Following the definition of A-term, e is a variable-free term of sort E implies that f(h(e)) is an A-term, but does not imply that f(g(e)) is an A-term. This means that ρ^T(f(g(e))) is not defined. This is quite natural since, although the sort of g(e) is A, no procedure implementation operation ↓g is provided.

8.2.4 Implementation Invariant

A fourth element of an implementation of module A by module B is the *implementation invariant*. The implementation invariant is a boolean function I: B -> Bool. As we will see later (see property 9 in Section 8.6), an implementation invariant I expresses necessary conditions that must be met by any object of sort B for being a representation of some object of sort A. I is often the conjunction of a number of invariants I_1 and I_2 ... and ... I_q with I_i: B -> Bool. The subset of B consisting of only those objects meeting the implementation invariant of an implementation, is called the *domain* of the implementation, denoted Dom. We have the following relation:

$\forall b \in$ B: b $\in$ Dom $\Leftrightarrow$ I(b) == true;

Example

Consider the implementation of module Stack by module ArrayNat as described in Fig. 8/4. An implementation invariant is

---

declare an: ArrayNat;

I(an) ==
   Vn ∈ Nat: if n ⩾ natOf an then true else not isundefined(arrayOf an, n) end if;

Fig. 8/11

The explicit universal quantifier of the variable n can be eliminated using the auxiliary function alldefined:

---

operation
  I: ArrayNat -> Bool;
declare an: ArrayNat;
operation axiom
  I(an) == alldefined(arrayOf an, natOf an);

Fig. 8/12

with alldefined specified below

---

operation
  alldefined: Array * Nat -> Bool;
declare a: Array;   n: Nat;
operation axiom
  alldefined(a, n) ==
    if n = 0
      then true
      else
        if isundefined(a, n - 1)
          then false
          else alldefined(a, n - 1)
        end if
    end if;

Fig. 8/13

The domain of an implementation is called *minimal* if each object of the domain is a representation of some object of sort A:

Dom is minimal $\Leftrightarrow$ $\forall b \in Dom, \exists a \in T_A^A: b == \delta.\rho^T(a)$;

The domain defined by the implementation invariant I given above is not minimal because the object denoted by

(empty [10 / 0] [20 / 2], 1)

is not a representation of an object of sort Stack. The following implementation invariant I′ defines a minimal domain:

```
operations
  I′: ArrayNat -> Bool;
  allpreviousdefined: Array * Array -> Bool;
    -- the recursive auxiliary operation allpreviousdefined yields
    -- true if the following relation holds:
    -- if a value has been assigned to index n in the first array
    -- then a value must have been assigned to each index that is
    -- smaller than n in the second array
declare an: ArrayNat;  a, a₁, a₂: Array;  n: Nat;  it: Item;
operation axioms
  I′( an ) == alldefined( arrayOf an, natOf an ) and
    allpreviousdefined( arrayOf an, arrayOf an );
  allpreviousdefined( empty, a ) == true;
  allpreviousdefined( a₁ [ it / n ], a₂ ) ==
    alldefined( a₂, n ) and allpreviousdefined( a₁, a₂ );
```

Fig. 8/14

Remarks

In general, several choices of a domain are possible. The minimal domain is not always the best choice. In the subsequent sections we will use the domain defined by I and not the minimal domain defined by I′. Clearly, the smaller the domain, the smaller the proofs will be that concern the implementation constraints 4 and 5 in Section 8.3. On the other hand, a non-minimal domain may be easier to be defined or a non-minimal domain may make it easier to prove that all implementation operations are closed (see implementation constraint 1 in Section 8.3). Also, when a multi-step implementation is built, as explained in Section 8.2.7, taking a minimal domain in the first steps, may unnecessarily limit the choice of procedure implementation operations in later steps.

8.2.5 Abstraction Function

A fifth element of an implementation of module A by module B is the abstraction function. An *abstraction function* @: B -> A is a mapping from sort B onto sort A. As we will see in Section 8.3 (implementation constraint 2), any object of sort B being a representation of an object of sort A is mapped by @ onto the latter. Given the domain Dom of the implementation, two abstraction functions $@_1$: B -> A and $@_2$: B -> A will be considered equal if each object of sort B belonging to Dom is mapped onto the same object of A. Although the abstraction function is only relevant for objects of Dom, we prefer to define it as a total function over B instead of working with partial functions.

Example

The abstraction function @ for the implementation of module Stack by module ArrayNat (see Fig. 8/4) is:

```
operation
  @: ArrayNat -> Stack;
declare a: Array;   n: Nat;
operation axiom
  @( ( a, n ) ) ==
    if n = 0
      then newstack
      else push( @( ( a, n - 1 ) ), read( a, n - 1 ) )
    end if;
```

Fig. 8/15

Abstraction Function and Terms

Notice that an abstraction function is different in nature from a representation function. An abstraction function @ is a mapping from objects (of sort B) onto objects (of sort A), whereas the representation function is a mapping from variable-free terms (A-terms) onto variable-free terms.

Because the representation function ρ^T is only defined on terms, we also introduce an abstraction function $@^T$: T_B -> T_A, defined on terms. Clearly, $@^T$ and @ are closely related. From the function @ and the definitions of the operations of sort B, the function $@^T$ can be derived systematically.

Example

Consider the implementation of module Stack by module ArrayNat. The abstraction function $@^T$ is shown in Fig. 8/16.

```
operations
   @ᵀ: T_ArrayNat -> T_Stack;
   δ_Nat: T_Nat -> Nat;
     -- This hidden operation δ_Nat is actually the denotation function δ
     -- of Chapter 2 restricted to terms of sort Nat and used in prefix notation.
declare a: T_Array;  n: T_Nat;  an: T_ArrayNat;  it: T_Item;
operation axioms
   δ_Nat( 0 ) == 0;
   δ_Nat( n + 1 ) == δ_Nat( n ) + 1;
   δ_Nat( n - 1 ) == δ_Nat( n ) - 1;
   δ_Nat( natOf ( a, n ) ) == δ_Nat( n );
   δ_Nat( natOf ↓newstack ) == δ_Nat( natOf ( empty, 0 ) );
   δ_Nat( natOf ↓push( an, it ) ) ==
       δ_Nat( natOf ( arrayOf an [ it / natOf an ], natOf an + 1 ) );
   δ_Nat( natOf ↓pop( an ) ) ==
     if δ_Nat( natOf an ) = 0
        then δ_Nat( natOf an )
        else δ_Nat( natOf ( arrayOf an, natOf an - 1 ) )
     end if;
   δ_Nat( natOf ↓replace( an, it ) ) ==
     if δ_Nat( natOf an ) = 0
        then δ_Nat( natOf an )
        else δ_Nat( natOf ( arrayOf an [ it / natOf an - 1 ], natOf an ) )
     end if;
   ... -- operation axioms must be given for every operation of sort Nat
   @ᵀ( ( a, n ) ) ==
     if δ_Nat( n ) = 0
        then newstack
        else push( @ᵀ( ( a, n - 1 ) ), read( a, n - 1 ) )
     end if;
   @ᵀ( ↓newstack ) == @ᵀ( ( empty, 0 ) );
   @ᵀ( ↓push( an, it ) ) == @ᵀ( ( arrayOf an [ it / natOf an ], natOf an +1 ) );
   @ᵀ( ↓pop( an ) ) ==
     if δ_Nat( natOf an ) = 0
        then @ᵀ( an )
        else @ᵀ( ( arrayOf an, natOf an - 1 ) )
     end if;
   @ᵀ( ↓replace( an, it ) ) ==
     if δ_Nat( natOf an ) = 0
        then @ᵀ( an )
        else @ᵀ( ( arrayOf an [ it / natOf an - 1 ], natOf an ) )
```

end if;	

Fig. 8/16

The use of the hidden operation δ_{Nat} is necessary to define $@^T$ with a finite number of axioms.

Remarks

- The following remark is analogous to the first remark given for the representation function. The expression empty in Fig. 8/6 denotes an Array object, whereas empty in Fig. 8/16 denotes the variable-free term empty itself.

- In general, the relation between $@$ and $@^T$ is expressed as follows:

  $$\delta.\delta.@^T(\ b\ ) = \delta.@(\ b\ )$$

where b stands for any variable free term of sort B. The function δ stands for the denotation function as defined in Chapter 2. Association is from right to left. As an illustration, we have

$$\delta.\delta.@^T(\ \downarrow newstack\ ) = \delta.newstack =$$
$$\delta.@(\ \downarrow newstack\ ) = (\ \delta.@\ )(\delta.\downarrow newstack\ )$$

This property is illustrated in Fig. 8/17.

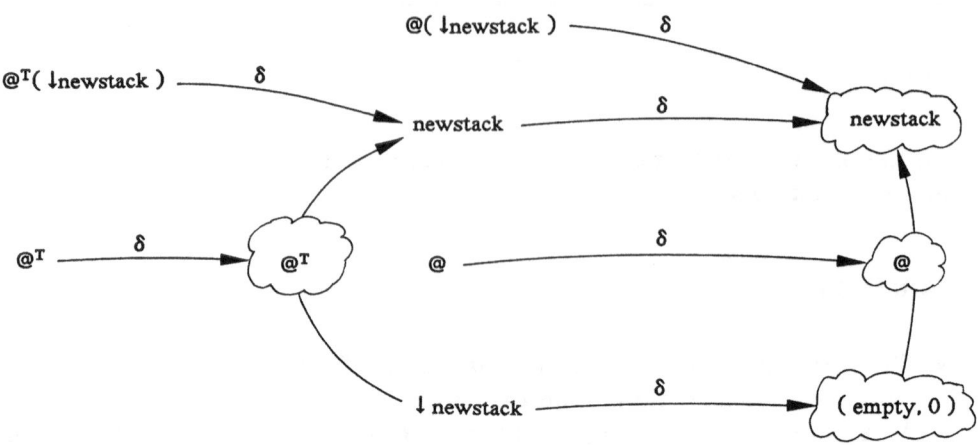

Fig. 8/17

Convention: From now on, we will omit the symbol δ, as it is common practice not to write the denotation function explicitly. For instance,

> **theorem**
> $\delta.@^T(\ b\ ) == \delta.@^T(\ b'\ )$;

where b and b' stand for terms of sort B, will be written as

> **theorem**
> $@^T(\ b\ ) == @^T(\ b'\ )$;

which is by definition of $@^T$ equivalent to

> **theorem**
> $@(\ b\ ) == @(\ b'\ )$;

8.2.6 *Equivalence Relation*

A sixth and last element of an implementation of module A by module B is the *equivalence relation* _ ~ _. As we will see in Section 8.3 (implementation constraint 3), two objects, b_1 and b_2, of sort B being representations of objects of sort A, are equivalent if they are representations of the same object of sort A. The *equivalence function* _ ~ _: B * B -> Bool is a binary boolean function indicating whether its arguments are equivalent. We have:

$b_1 \sim b_2$;

if and only if

$b_1 \sim b_2 ==$ true;

Naturally, the equivalence function must be reflexive, symmetric and transitive:

```
operation
    _ ~ _: B * B -> Bool;
declare b, b₁, b₂, b₃: B;
theorems
    b ~ b == true;
    b₁ ~ b₂ == b₂ ~ b₁;
    b₁ ~ b₂ and b₂ ~ b₃ ⇒ b₁ ~ b₃ == true;
```

Fig. 8/18

Given the domain Dom of the implementation, two equivalence functions $\_ \sim_1 \_: B * B ->$ Bool and $\_ \sim_2 \_: B * B ->$ Bool will be considered equal if and only if each pair of objects of sort B belonging to Dom, is or is not equivalent according to both equivalence functions. Although the equivalence function is only relevant for objects of Dom, we prefer to define it as a total function over B instead of working with partial functions.

Example

An equivalence function for the implementation of module Stack by module ArrayNat (see Fig. 8/4) is:

```
operation
    _ ~ _: ArrayNat * ArrayNat -> Bool;
declare a₁, a₂: Array;   n₁, n₂: Nat;
operation axiom
    ( a₁, n₁ ) ~ ( a₂, n₂ ) ==
        ( n₁ = n₂ ) and
        ( ∀k ∈ Nat: if k < n₁ then read( a₁, k ) = read( a₂, k ) else true end if );
```

Fig. 8/19

The explicit universal quantifier of the variable k can be eliminated by defining the equivalence function recursively.

```
operation axiom
  ( a₁, n₁ ) ~ ( a₂, n₂ ) ==
    if n₁ = n₂
      then
        if n₁ = 0
          then true
          else ( read( a₁, n₁ - 1 ) = read( a₂, n₁ - 1 ) ) and ( ( a₁, n₁ - 1 ) ~ ( a₂, n₂ - 1 ) )
        end if
      else false
    end if;
```

Fig. 8/20

8.2.7 A Multi-Step Implementation Method

The implementation of module A by module B as described in the preceding sections, can be developed in two steps.

In a *first step*, the abstract implementation is constructed from A by considering only the constructors defined in A. In this way, we obtain an implementation module called $\downarrow A_{data}$, which is the data representation part of $\downarrow A$ (the procedure implementation part is empty). We also obtain a representation function ρ^T, an implementation invariant I, an abstraction function @ and an equivalence function _ ~ _.

A benefit from this step by step development of the abstract implementation is that the implementation process for module A can be halted temporarily at this point. Rapid prototyping will then combine the data representation operations defined in $\downarrow A_{data}$ with the operations of module A. Roughly speaking, in such a configuration, only the data part (constructors) of A is implemented, not the procedure part (operations) of A. The data representation, obtained by this step, can be treated by rapid prototyping, before the procedure implementation is considered.

In a *second step*, the procedure implementation operations are written, yielding the module $\downarrow A_{proc}$. This module is constructed by considering constructors as well as operations defined in A. Rapid prototyping at this stage of development uses the module $\downarrow A_{data}$ as well as $\downarrow A_{proc}$.

In general, more steps are possible. Assume that later in the life cycle of the software system, new operations have to be added to module A or to a new module A'. These operations can be implemented in a new module, say A'_{proc}. Rapid prototyping will then use the implementation modules $\downarrow A_{data}$, $\downarrow A_{proc}$ and $\downarrow A'_{proc}$.

As an illustration, consider the implementation of Stack by ArrayNat. In a first step, the module ↓Stack$_{data}$ (data representation part) is constructed by only considering the constructors defined in Stack. Later, for efficiency reasons, an implementation operation may be necessary for the operation pop, yielding the module ↓Stack$_{proc}$. This (partial) procedure implementation part can later be extended with other modules containing other procedure implementation operations.

8.3 Implementation Constraints

This section concerns correctness aspects of abstract implementations. An abstract implementation must meet three classes of constraints:

- A first class contains more general constraints as defined in Chapters 3 and 4. The implementation operations, the implementation invariant, the abstraction function and the equivalence function must not violate the (semi-)constructivity and the hierarchical constraints. Thus, they have to be unique, complete, terminating, consistent, ...

- A second class consists of constraints that are related to definitions of concepts, given in the previous sections. An example of such a constraint is that equivalence relations must be reflexive, symmetric and transitive. Also, the mappings m$_{data}$ and m$_{proc}$ must preserve the ranks of constructors and operations.

- A third class consists of the *implementation constraints*. Implementation constraints guarantee that an implementation meets its specification.

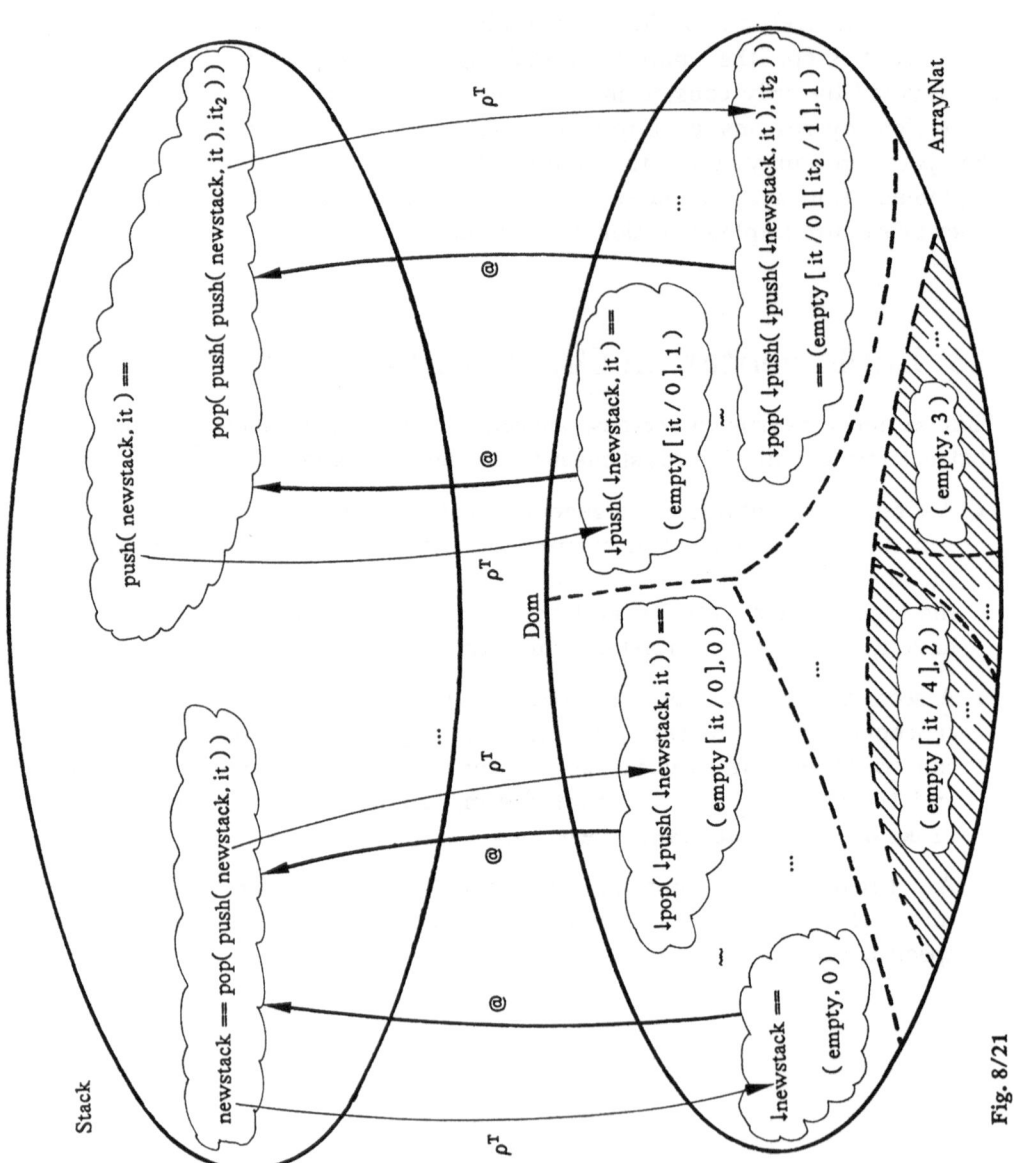

Fig. 8/21

Before we attack the problem of implementation constraints, the following remark is in place here. It is true that in principle algebraic specifications allow the designer to use rigorous (mathematical) reasoning. Clearly, it would be very nice if we could prove that the abstract implementation meets all the constraints mentioned above. This would indeed lead to the development of software of high quality what correctness is concerned (if we make abstraction from the potential errors within the proofs). In practice, however, the situation is far from ideal. Proving that an implementation meets its specification seems to be a tremendous work even for relative small examples, if we do not have powerful theorem provers to our disposal. Unfortunately, such tools are yet beyond today's proving technology. A realistic attitude would be to concentrate on (partial) proofs of the most important constraints of the abstract implementation. In spite of the far from ideal situation concerning correctness proofs, a rigorous formulation of the implementation constraints is of most importance for (formal or informal) reasoning about the correctness of the implementation. In this section, no complete proofs for the examples are given. They can be found in [Monteyne88].

In Fig. 8/21 a graphical representation of the concepts of the abstract implementation of Stack by ArrayNat is shown. The domain is the non-shaded part of ArrayNat. The equivalence relation is defined by indicating the equivalence classes in ArrayNat by a dotted line. The representation function ρ^T: T^{Stack} -> T is represented by a thin arrow. The abstraction function @: ArrayNat -> Stack is represented by a thick arrow. Notice that the object denoted by push(newstack, it) has several distinct objects of ArrayNat as representation. This is the reason why ρ^T is defined on Stack-terms and not on objects.

The *implementation constraints* that must be met by an implementation to be correct are:

1. The implementation operations of sort B must be closed with respect to the implementation invariant I. This is further explained. Let s_i be an A-constructor or an A-operation of sort A whose j_1^{th}, ... and j_n^{th} arguments are its only arguments of sort A. As the rank must be preserved, the j_1^{th}, ... and j_n^{th} arguments and the range of the implementation operation $\downarrow s_i$ are of sort B. The result of the implementation operation $\downarrow s_i$ must meet the implementation invariant I (i.e. the implementation invariant applied to the result yields true) if the j_1^{th}, ... and j_n^{th} arguments meet the implementation invariant:

   I(b_{j_1}) and ... and I(b_{j_n}) => I($\downarrow s_i$(...., b_{j_1}, ..., b_{j_n}, ...)) == true;

Example

declare an: ArrayNat;   it: Item;
theorem
$\quad$ I(an) $\Rightarrow$ I($\downarrow$push(an, it)) == true;

Fig. 8/22

2. The object denoted by an A-term of sort A must be the same as the
    object denoted by the term obtained by consecutively applying the
    representation and the abstraction function to the given term:
    $$@^T(\rho^T(a)) == a;$$

    Convention: If we write
    $$t_1 == t_2 == t_3 == \ldots == t_n$$
    we mean
    $$t_1 == t_2; \quad t_2 == t_3; \quad \ldots \quad t_{n-1} == t_n;$$
    If we write
    $$b \Rightarrow t_1 == t_2 == t_3 == \ldots == t_n$$
    with b a boolean expression, we mean
    $$b \Rightarrow t_1 == t_2; \quad b \Rightarrow t_2 == t_3; \quad \ldots \quad b \Rightarrow t_{n-1} == t_n;$$
    The same notational conventions may be used for the equivalence
    relation $\sim$ or even for a combination of == and $\sim$.

Example

declare it: T_{Item};
theorems
$\quad @^T(\rho^T(\text{pop}(\text{push}(\text{newstack, it})))) ==$
$\quad @^T(\downarrow\text{pop}(\downarrow\text{push}(\downarrow\text{newstack, it}))) ==$
$\quad @^T(\downarrow\text{pop}(\downarrow\text{push}((\text{empty, 0}), \text{it}))) ==$
$\quad @^T(\downarrow\text{pop}((\text{empty} [\text{it} / 0], 1))) ==$
$\quad @^T((\text{empty} [\text{it} / 0], 0)) ==$
$\quad \text{newstack} ==$
$\quad \text{pop}(\text{push}(\text{newstack, it}))$

Fig. 8/23

3. If two A-terms of sort A denote the same object, then their representations must denote equivalent objects of sort B:

$$a_1 = a_2 \Rightarrow \rho^T(a_1) \sim \rho^T(a_2);$$

Example

---

declare it: T_{Item};
theorems
  pop(push(newstack, it)) = newstack $\Rightarrow$
  ρ^T(pop(push(newstack, it))) == $\downarrow$pop($\downarrow$push($\downarrow$newstack, it)) ==
  (empty [it / 0], 0) $\sim$ (empty, 0) == ρ^T(newstack)

Fig. 8/24

4. If two terms of sort B denote equivalent objects of the domain Dom, then their abstractions must denote the same object of sort A:

$$I(b_1) \text{ and } I(b_2) \text{ and } (b_1 \sim b_2) \Rightarrow @(b_1) == @(b_2):$$

Example

---

declare it_1, it_2: Item;
theorems
  $I(($ empty [it_1 / 0][it_2 / 1], 1)) and $I(($ empty [it_1 / 0], 1)) and
  (empty [it_1 / 0][it_2 / 1], 1) $\sim$ (empty [it_1 / 0], 1) $\Rightarrow$
  $@(($ empty [it_1 / 0][it_2 / 1], 1)) ==
  push(newstack, it_1) ==
  $@(($ empty [it_1 / 0], 1))

Fig. 8/25

5. If a term of sort B denotes an object belonging to the domain Dom, then this object must be equivalent to the object denoted by the term obtained by consecutively applying the abstraction and the representation function to the given term:

$$I(b) \Rightarrow \rho^T(@^T(b)) \sim b;$$

Example

declare it_1, it_2: T_{Item};
theorems
  $I(($ empty $[it_1 / 0][it_2 / 1], 1)) \Rightarrow$
    $\rho^T(@^T(($ empty $[it_1 / 0][it_2 / 1], 1)) ==$
    $\rho^T($ push$($ newstack, read$($ empty $[it_1 / 0][it_2 / 1], 1 - 1))) ==$
    $\downarrow$push$(\downarrow$newstack, read$($ empty $[it_1 / 0][it_2 / 1], 1 - 1)) ==$
    $\downarrow$push$(\downarrow$newstack, it_1 $) ==$
    $($ empty $[it_1 / 0], 1) \sim ($ empty $[it_1 / 0][it_2 / 1], 1)$

Fig. 8/26

6. An A-term x not of sort A must denote the same object as the term
obtained by applying the representation function to the given term:
  $x == \rho^T(x)$;

Example

declare it: T_{Item};
theorems
  isnewstack$($ push$($ newstack, it $)) ==$
  false $==$
  $\downarrow$isnewstack$(($ empty $[it / 0], 1)) ==$
  $\downarrow$isnewstack$(\downarrow$push$(($ empty, 0 $)$, it $)) ==$
  $\downarrow$isnewstack$(\downarrow$push$(\downarrow$newstack, it $)) ==$
  $\rho^T($ isnewstack$($ push$($ newstack, it $)))$

Fig. 8/27

7. Let s_i be an A-constructor or an A-operation of sort A whose j_1^{th}, ...
and j_n^{th} arguments are its only arguments of sort A. As the rank
must be preserved, the j_1^{th}, ... and j_n^{th} arguments and the range of the
implementation operation $\downarrow s_i$ are of sort B. If b_{j_1} and b'_{j_1}, ... and b_{j_n}
and b'_{j_n} are pairwise equivalent terms of sort B belonging to the
domain Dom then replacing b_{j_1} by b'_{j_1} as j_1^{th} argument of $\downarrow s_i$, ... and
b_{j_n} by b'_{j_n} as j_n^{th} argument of $\downarrow s_i$ must result in an equivalent object

of B:

$I(\,b_{j_1}\,)$ and $I(\,b'_{j_1}\,)$ and $(\,b_{j_1} \sim b'_{j_1}\,)$ and ...

and $I(\,b_{j_n}\,)$ and $I(\,b'_{j_n}\,)$ and $(\,b_{j_n} \sim b'_{j_n}\,) \Rightarrow$

$\downarrow s_i(\,....,\,b_{j_1},\,....,\,b_{j_n},\,...\,) \sim \downarrow s_i(\,....,\,b'_{j_1},\,....,\,b'_{j_n},\,...\,)$;

Example

```
declare it₁, it₂, it₃: Item;
theorems
  I( ( empty [ it₁ / 0 ][ it₂ / 1 ], 1 ) ) and I( ( empty [ it₁ / 0 ], 1 ) ) and
  ( empty [ it₁ / 0 ][ it₂ / 1 ], 1 ) ~ ( empty [ it₁ / 0 ], 1 ) ⇒
  ↓replace( ( empty [ it₁ / 0 ], 1 ), it₃ ) == ( empty [ it₁ / 0 ][ it₃ / 0 ], 1 ) ==
  ( empty [ it₃ / 0 ], 1 ) ~ ( empty [ it₂ / 1 ][ it₃ / 0 ], 1 ) ==
  ( empty [ it₁ / 0 ][ it₂ / 1 ][ it₃ / 0 ], 1 ) ==
  ↓replace( ( empty [ it₁ / 0 ][ it₂ / 1 ), 1 ), it₃ )
```

Fig. 8/28

8. Let s_i be an A-operation not of sort A whose j_1^{th}, ... and j_n^{th} arguments are its only arguments of sort A. As the rank must be preserved, the j_1^{th}, ... and j_n^{th} arguments of the implementation operation $\downarrow s_i$ are of sort B, whereas the range of $\downarrow s_i$ is of the same sort as the range of s_i. If b_{j_1} and b'_{j_1}, ... and b_{j_n} and b'_{j_n} are pairwise equivalent terms of sort B belonging to the domain Dom then replacing b_{j_1} by b'_{j_1} as j_1^{th} argument of $\downarrow s_i$, ... and b_{j_n} by b'_{j_n} as j_n^{th} argument of $\downarrow s_i$ must result in the same object:

$I(\,b_{j_1}\,)$ and $I(\,b'_{j_1}\,)$ and $(\,b_{j_1} \sim b'_{j_1}\,)$ and

... and $I(\,b_{j_n}\,)$ and $I(\,b'_{j_n}\,)$ and $(\,b_{j_n} \sim b'_{j_n}\,) \Rightarrow$

$\downarrow s_i(\,....,\,b_{j_1},\,....,\,b_{j_n},\,...\,) == \downarrow s_i(\,....,\,b'_{j_1},\,....,\,b'_{j_n},\,...\,)$;

Example

```
declare it₁, it₂: Item;
theorems
  I( ( empty [ it₁ / 0 ][ it₂ / 1 ], 1 ) ) and I( ( empty [ it₁ / 0 ], 1 ) ) and
  ( empty [ it₁ / 0 ][ it₂ / 1 ], 1 ) ~ ( empty [ it₁ / 0 ], 1 ) ⇒
  ↓isnewstack( ( empty [ it₁ / 0 ], 1 ) ) == false ==
```

$$\downarrow isnewstack((\, empty\, [\, it_1\, /\, 0\,][\, it_2\, /\, 1\,],\, 1\,)\,)$$

Fig. 8/29

8.4 Example: Scheme of Stacks

In Section 8.1 the stack was used to introduce the concepts of abstract
implementations. There, the stack was simplified in the sense that stack
items were restricted to natural numbers and error handling was
introduced in a naive way. In this section the stack is further elaborated
so that maximum use is made of parameterization, yielding a specification
with a high degree of reusability. Parameterization is done at six different
places in the specifications. We have the following six schemes:
StackScheme, ↓StackScheme, ArrayScheme, ItemRequirementScheme,
AttributeRequirementScheme and IndexRequirementScheme. Another
important aspect dealt with in this section, is the systematic use of error
handling as described in Chapter 7. A global picture of the abstract
implementation of Stack was shown in Fig. 8/2.

StackScheme

Fig. 8/30 defines stacks by means of a scheme, called StackScheme. The
requirement of StackScheme is Item. This requirement is an instantiation
of another scheme, ItemRequirementScheme. Recall that an instantiation
of a requirement scheme yields a requirement (formal module). The
introduction of requirement schemes enables the designer to localize the
requirement information at one single place in the specification. In the case
of ItemRequirementScheme, instantiations are used in StackScheme (see
Fig. 8/30) and in ↓StackScheme (see Fig. 8/31).
To handle stack underflow, a new constructor errStack is introduced.
Error handling was thoroughly discussed in Chapter 7.

```
scheme ItemRequirementScheme;
  requirement Item;
    export all;
    sort Item;
    operation
      errItem: -> Item;
  end requirement Item;
end scheme ItemRequirementScheme;
```

```
scheme StackScheme [ instantiate ItemRequirementScheme; end instantiate; ];
  module Stack;
    import Bool, true, false, errBool from Bool;
      Item, errItem from Item;
    export all;
    sort Stack;
    constructors
      newstack: -> Stack $$ ;
      push: $ Stack * Item -> Stack $$ ;
      errStack: -> Stack ?? ;
    operations
      pop: Stack -> Stack;
      top: Stack -> Item;
      replace: Stack * Item -> Stack;
      isnewstack: Stack -> Bool;
    declare s: Stack; it, it₁, it₂: Item;
    constructor axiom
    ! s == errStack;
    operation axioms
    $$ pop( newstack ) == errStack;
    $$ pop( push( s, it ) ) == s;
    $$ top( newstack ) == errItem;
    $$ top( push( s, it ) ) == it;
      replace( $ newstack, it ) == errStack;
      replace( $ push( s, it₁ ), it₂ ) == push( s, it₂ );
    $$ isnewstack( newstack ) == true;
    $$ isnewstack( push( s, it ) ) == false;
    ?? pop( s ) == errStack;
    ?? top( s ) == errItem;
      replace( ! s, it ) = errStack;
    ?? isnewstack( s ) == errBool;
  end module Stack;
end scheme StackScheme;
```

Fig. 8/30

↓StackScheme

The implementation of StackScheme by means of the module ArrayNat yields another scheme ↓StackScheme, defined in Fig. 8/31.

As for StackScheme, the requirement of ↓StackScheme is Item, which is an instantiation of the scheme ItemRequirementScheme. The main module of ↓StackScheme is ↓Stack. This module is defined in terms of the modules ArrayNat, Array, Nat and Bool and in terms of the requirement Item. The module Array is local to the scheme ↓StackScheme by means of an instantiation of the scheme ArrayScheme (see Fig. 8/35). Also, ArrayNat is a module that is local to the scheme ↓StackScheme.

The main module ↓Stack of the scheme ↓StackScheme contains the definitions of the data representation operations and the procedure implementation operations of the abstract implementation.

```
scheme ↓StackScheme [ instantiate ItemRequirementScheme; end instantiate; ];
  instantiate ArrayScheme;
    with Index as Nat,
      Index as Nat,
      _ = _ as _ = _;
    with Attribute as Item,
      Attribute as Item,
      initial as errItem,
      errAttribute as errItem;
  end instantiate ArrayScheme;

  module ArrayNat;
    import Array, errArray from Array;
      Nat, errNat from Nat;
    export ArrayNat, ( _, _ ), arrayOf _, natOf _, errArrayNat, safeArrayNat;
    sort ArrayNat = Array * Nat;
    operation
      errArrayNat: -> ArrayNat;
    operation axiom
      errArrayNat == ( errArray, errNat );
  end module ArrayNat;

  module ↓Stack;
    import ArrayNat, ( _, _ ), arrayOf _, natOf _, errArrayNat,
      safeArrayNat from ArrayNat;
    Array, empty, _[ _ / _ ], read from  Array;
    Nat, zero, succ, pre, _ = _, _ < _ from Nat
      rename zero as 0, succ as _ + 1, pre as _ - 1;
    Bool, true, false, errBool from Bool;   Item, errItem from Item;
    operations
      ↓newstack: -> ArrayNat;
      ↓push: ArrayNat * Item -> ArrayNat;
      ↓errStack: -> ArrayNat;
      ↓pop: ArrayNat -> ArrayNat;
      ↓top: ArrayNat -> Item;
      ↓replace: ArrayNat * Item -> ArrayNat;
      ↓isnewstack: ArrayNat -> Bool;
      ↓safeStack: ArrayNat -> Bool;
    declare an: ArrayNat;   it: Item;
    operation axioms
      ↓newstack == ( empty, 0 );
      ↓push( $ an, it ) == (arrayOf an [ it / natOf an ], natOf an + 1);
$$ ↓pop( an ) ==
    if natOf an = 0
      then ↓errStack
      else ( arrayOf an, natOf an - 1 )
    end if;
$$ ↓top( an ) ==
```

```
                if natOf an = 0
                   then errItem
                   else read( arrayOf an, natOf an - 1 )
                end if;
             ↓replace( $ an, it ) ==
                if natOf an = 0
                   then ↓errStack
                   else ( arrayOf an [ it / natOf an - 1 ], natOf an )
                end if;
        $$ ↓isnewstack( an ) == natOf an = 0;
           ↓safeStack( an ) == safeArrayNat( an );
           ↓errStack == errArrayNat;
           ↓push( ! an, it ) == ↓errStack;
        ?? ↓pop( an ) == ↓errStack;
        ?? ↓top( an ) == errItem;
           ↓replace( ! an, it ) == ↓errStack;
        ?? ↓isnewstack( an ) == errBool;
        end module ↓Stack;
    end scheme ↓StackScheme;
```

Fig. 8/31

The sort ArrayNat is defined as a Cartesian product (see Section 4.11).
Recall that by default we now have at our disposal the constructor (_ , _),
the selector operations arrayOf _ and natOf _ , and finally the update
operations _ [_ / array] and _ [_ / nat]. The update operations will
not be used in our example. To these default constructor and operations
we add the operation errArrayNat. Recall that the safety function for
ArrayNat objects is as follows (see Section 7.6):

```
operation
   safeArrayNat: ArrayNat -> Bool;
declare an: ArrayNat;
operation axiom
   safeArrayNat( an ) == safeArray( arrayOf an ) and safeNat( natOf an );
```

Fig. 8/32

The error handling in the module ↓Stack (see Fig. 8/31) is closely
related to the one given in the scheme StackScheme (see Fig. 8/30). As an
example, the error handling is such that push, pop and replace on an unsafe
stack, yielding errStack, implies respectively ↓push, ↓pop and ↓replace on
an unsafe arraynat, yielding errArrayNat. As another example, top on an
unsafe stack, yielding errItem, implies ↓top on an unsafe arraynat, yielding
errItem.

Notice the difference between ↓safeStack and safeArrayNat. The operation ↓safeStack is the procedure implementation operation of safeStack. The operation safeStack is defined by the scheme StackScheme as follows:

```
operation
  safeStack: Stack -> Bool;
declare s, s₁: Stack;   it: Item;
  safeStack( s ) ==
    case s of
      newstack: true;
      push( s₁, it ): safeStack( s₁ );
      errStack: false;
    end case;
```

Fig. 8/33

The operation safeArrayNat was given in Fig. 8/32. In the module ↓Stack, we have

```
↓safeStack( an ) == safeArrayNat( an );
```

Fig. 8/34

ArrayScheme

ArrayScheme is defined in Fig. 8/35. It has two requirements Index and Attribute. These requirements are in turn instantiations of respectively IndexRequirementScheme and AttributeRequirementScheme. In ↓StackScheme, ArrayScheme is instantiated with Index being bound to actual parameter Nat and Attribute to actual parameter Item. Notice that Item is itself a formal parameter of ↓StackScheme.

```
scheme AttributeRequirementScheme;
  requirement Attribute;
    export all;
```

```
      sort Attribute;
      operation
        initial, errAttribute: -> Attribute;
    end requirement Attribute;
  end scheme AttributeRequirementScheme;

scheme IndexRequirementScheme;
  requirement Index;
    import Bool, true, _ and _, _ => _ from Bool;
    export all;
    sort Index;
    operation
      _ = _: Index * Index -> Bool;
    declare i, i₁, i₂, i₃: Index;
    theorems
      $i = $i == true;
      $i₁ = $i₂ == $i₂ = $i₁;
      ( $i₁ = $i₂ ) and ( $i₂ = $i₃ ) => ( $i₁ = $i₃ )  ==  true;
  end requirement Index;
end scheme IndexRequirementScheme;


scheme ArrayScheme [
    instantiate AttributeRequirementScheme; end instantiate;
    instantiate IndexRequirementScheme; end instantiate;
  ];

  module Array;
    import Bool, true, false, errBool from Bool;
      all from Attribute, Index;
    export all;
    sort Array;
    constructors
      empty: -> Array $$ ;
      _[ _ / _ ]: $ Array * Attribute * $ Index -> Array $$ ;
      errArray: -> Array ?? ;
    operations
      read: Array * Index -> Attribute;
      isundefined: Array * Index -> Bool;
    declare ar: Array;  i, i₁, i₂: Index;  at, at₁, at₂: Attribute;
    constructor axioms
      not ( i₁ = i₂ ) => $ ( ar [ at₁ / i₁ ][ at₂ / i₂ ]) == $ ( ar [ at₂ / i₂ ][ at₁ / i₁ ]);
      $ ( ar [ at₁ / i ][ at₂ / i ]) == $ ( ar [ at₂ / i ]);
    operation axioms
    $$ isundefined( empty, i ) == true;
    $$ isundefined( ar [ at / i₁ ], i₂ ) ==
          if i₁ = i₂
            then false
            else isundefined( ar, i₂ )
          end if;
    $$ read( empty, i ) == initial;
    $$ read( ar [ at / i₁ ], i₂ ) ==
          if i₁ = i₂
            then at
            else read( ar, i₂ )
          end if;
    ?? isundefined( ar, i ) == errBool;
```

```
  ?? read( ar, i ) == errAttribute;
 end module Array;
end scheme ArrayScheme;
```

Fig. 8/35

Concepts of the Implementation

In Section 8.2 we treated the concepts related to the abstract implementation of module A by module B yielding module ↓A. Notice that in this section each of the modules A and ↓A is the main module of a scheme and, therefore, these modules may contain formal parameters. In our example, we have the implementation of module Stack by means of module ArrayNat yielding module ↓Stack. Unlike the simplified stack in Sections 8.1 and 8.2, Stack and ↓Stack are now the main modules of respectively StackScheme and ↓StackScheme. The formal parameters of StackScheme and ↓StackScheme are errItem and Item. The fact that each of the modules A and ↓A is a main module of a scheme does not affect the concepts and definitions given in Section 8.2.

Recall that the abstract implementation of module A by module B consists of six elements:

1.   the data representation part,

2.   the procedure implementation part,

3.   a representation function ρ^T,

4.   an implementation invariant I,

5.   an abstraction function @ and

6.   an equivalence function $\_ \sim \_$.

Let us return to our example of stacks. The data representation part and the procedure implementation part of the abstract implementation were given in Fig. 8/31. The representation function ρ^T of the abstract implementation is given in Fig. 8/36.

```
operation
  ρᵀ: Tˢᵗᵃᶜᵏ -> T;  -- Tˢᵗᵃᶜᵏ is the set of Stack-terms
declare
  st: Tˢᵗᵃᶜᵏ_Stack;  -- Tˢᵗᵃᶜᵏ_Stack is the set of Stack-terms of sort Stack
  it: T_Item;  -- T_Item is the set of variable-free terms of sort Item
```

operation axioms
$\rho^T(\text{newstack}) == \downarrow\text{newstack};$
$\rho^T(\text{push}(\text{st}, \text{it})) == \downarrow\text{push}(\rho^T(\text{st}), \text{it});$
$\rho^T(\text{errStack}) == \downarrow\text{errStack};$
$\rho^T(\text{pop}(\text{st})) == \downarrow\text{pop}(\rho^T(\text{st}));$
$\rho^T(\text{top}(\text{st})) == \downarrow\text{top}(\rho^T(\text{st}));$
$\rho^T(\text{replace}(\text{st}, \text{it})) == \downarrow\text{replace}(\rho^T(\text{st}), \text{it});$
$\rho^T(\text{isnewstack}(\text{st})) == \downarrow\text{isnewstack}(\rho^T(\text{st}));$
$\rho^T(\text{safeStack}(\text{st})) == \downarrow\text{safeStack}(\rho^T(\text{st}));$

Fig. 8/36

Now follow a few examples, illustrating the application of the representation function ρ^T. The formal parameter it stands for an arbitrary variable–free term of any sort that can be bound to Item.

$\rho^T(\text{push}(\text{pop}(\text{newstack}), \text{it})) ==$
$\downarrow\text{push}(\downarrow\text{pop}(\downarrow\text{newstack}), \text{it}) ==$
$\downarrow\text{push}(\downarrow\text{pop}((\text{empty}, 0)), \text{it}) ==$
$\downarrow\text{push}(\downarrow\text{errStack}, \text{it}) ==$
$\downarrow\text{push}(\text{errArrayNat}, \text{it}) ==$
$\downarrow\text{push}((\text{errArray}, \text{errNat}), \text{it}) ==$
$\downarrow\text{errStack} ==$
$\text{errArrayNat} ==$
$(\text{errArray}, \text{errNat})$
$\rho^T(\text{safeStack}(\text{newstack})) ==$
$\downarrow\text{safeStack}(\downarrow\text{newstack}) ==$
$\downarrow\text{safeStack}((\text{empty}, 0)) ==$
$\text{safeArrayNat}((\text{empty}, 0)) ==$
$\text{safeArray}(\text{empty}) \text{ and } \text{safeNat}(0) ==$
true
$\rho^T(\text{safeStack}(\text{pop}(\text{newstack}))) ==$
$\downarrow\text{safeStack}(\downarrow\text{pop}(\downarrow\text{newstack})) ==$
$\downarrow\text{safeStack}(\downarrow\text{pop}((\text{empty}, 0))) ==$
$\downarrow\text{safeStack}(\downarrow\text{errStack}) ==$
$\downarrow\text{safeStack}(\text{errArrayNat}) ==$
$\downarrow\text{safeStack}((\text{errArray}, \text{errNat})) ==$
$\text{safeArrayNat}((\text{errArray}, \text{errNat})) ==$
$\text{safeArray}(\text{errArray}) \text{ and } \text{safeNat}(\text{errNat}) ==$
false
$\rho^T(\text{top}(\text{push}(\text{newstack}, \text{it}))) ==$
$\downarrow\text{top}(\downarrow\text{push}(\downarrow\text{newstack}, \text{it})) ==$
$\downarrow\text{top}(\downarrow\text{push}((\text{empty}, 0), \text{it})) ==$
$\downarrow\text{top}((\text{empty}[\text{it}/0], 1) ==$
$\text{read}(\text{empty}[\text{it}/0], 0) ==$
1

Fig. 8/37

The implementation invariant I of the abstract implementation can be found in Fig. 8/38.

```
operations
  I: ArrayNat -> Bool;
  alldefined: Array * Nat -> Bool;
declare an: ArrayNat;  a: Array;  n: Nat;
operation axioms
$$ I( an ) == alldefined( arrayOf an, natOf an );
$$ alldefined( a, n ) ==
    if n = 0
      then true
      else
        if isundefined( a, n - 1 )
          then false
          else alldefined( a, n - 1 )
        end if
    end if;
?? I( an ) == true;
?? alldefined( a, n ) == errBool;
```

Fig. 8/38

Notice that the domain is not minimal.

The abstraction function @ of the abstract implementation is shown in Fig. 8/39.

```
operation
  @: ArrayNat -> Stack;
declare a: Array;  n: Nat;
operation axiom
$$ @( ( a, n ) ) ==
    if n = 0
      then newstack
      else push( @( ( a, n - 1 ) ), read( a, n - 1 ) )
    end if;
?? @( ( a, n ) ) == errStack;
```

Fig. 8/39

The equivalence function _ ~ _ of the abstract implementation is given in Fig. 8/40.

```
operation
    _ ~ _: ArrayNat * ArrayNat -> Bool;
declare a₁, a₂: Array;   n₁, n₂: Nat;   an₁, an₂: ArrayNat;
operation axiom
$$ ( ( a₁, n₁ ) ~ ( a₂, n₂ ) ) ==
    if n₁ = n₂
      then
        if n₁ = 0
          then true
          else ( read( a₁, n₁ - 1 ) = read( a₂, n₁ - 1 ) ) and ( ( a₁, n₁ - 1 ) ~ ( a₂, n₂ - 1 ) )
        end if
      else false
    end if;
    ( ! an₁ ~ ! an₂ ) == true;
    ( ! an₁ ~ $ an₂ ) == false;
    ( $ an₁ ~ ! an₂ ) == false;
```

Fig. 8/40

8.5 Example: Scheme of Symbol Tables

In this section the design-implementation structure of the abstract implementation of the symbol table by using a hash coding technique is worked out. This structure was shown in Fig. 8/1. Now follow the specification details of the abstract implementation of the symbol table. Recall that most of the modules in Fig. 8/1 are instantiations of schemes. This is the case for the modules Symboltable, ↓Symboltable, Stack, ↓Stack, Mapping, ↓Mapping, Array, BoundedArray and List. We also use requirement schemes. This high degree of parameterization makes the abstract implementation reusable up to a great extent. A few schemes used in the abstract implementation of the symbol table have been defined elsewhere in the book. This is the case with ListScheme (defined in Fig. 4/6), StackScheme (defined in Fig. 8/30), ↓StackScheme (defined in Fig. 8/31), BoundedArrayScheme (defined in Fig. 7/20), AttributeRequirementScheme (defined in Fig. 8/35). Another aspect, which makes this example interesting, is that error handling and error recovery are systematically included in the modules, requirements and schemes involved in the abstract implementation.

SymboltableScheme

The operations defined on symbol tables are init, enterblock, addid, leaveblock, isinblock and retrieve. Their meaning is as defined in [Guttag77], except for the error handling. The symbol table is a data structure designed for a compiler for a block-structured language. An informal specification may be as follows [Guttag77]. The operation init allocates and initializes the symbol table for the outermost scope. The operation enterblock prepares a new local naming scope. An identifier and its attribute are added to the symbol table by the operation addid. The operation leaveblock discards entries from the most current scope and reestablishes the next outer scope. The operation isinblock checks whether an identifier has already been declared in the current scope. Finally, the operation retrieve returns the attribute associated with the most local definition of a given identifier. Error handling is provided. As soon as an unsafe identifier is added to a naming scope of the symbol table, that scope and the more outer scopes become inaccessible for retrieval as long as the entries from that naming scope have not been discarded. A formal specification is given in Fig. 8/41.

The last theorem of the requirement Identifier (instantiation of IdentificationRequirementScheme) seems a bit peculiar. Following the equality operation for boolean values as defined in Fig. 7/24, this theorem simply requires that the equality operation defined on identifiers must either yield true or false. This property has been used in the formulation of the third constructor axiom of module Symboltable.

The first constructor axiom of module Symboltable indicates that if two equal identifiers have been added in the same block (scope) of the symbol table, only the most recent addition is relevant. The second constructor axiom states that an identifier may be replaced by an equal identifier. The third constructor axiom expresses that the order of addition in a block of the symbol table is irrelevant for identifiers that are not equal. Because the constructor axioms consider safe as well as unsafe identifiers, implementation by means of hash coding (that does not preserve the order of addition) is enabled.

Remember that the safety function for Identifier is imported by the module Symboltable by default, see Section 7.6 (Shorthand Notation and Import Clauses).

```
scheme IdentificationRequirementScheme;

  requirement Identification;
    import Bool, true, false, errBool, _ and _, _ = _ from Bool;
```

```
    export all;
    sort Identification;
    operations
      errIdentification: -> Identification;
      _ = _: Identification * Identification -> Bool;
    declare id, id₁, id₂, id₃: Identification;
    theorems
      (id = id) == true;  -- reflexivity
      (id₁ = id₂) == (id₂ = id₁); -- symmetry
      (id₁ = id₂) and (id₂ = id₃ ) ⇒ (id₁ = id₃) == true; -- transitivity
      (id₁ = id₂) = errBool == false;
        -- the required equality operation yields either true or false
  end requirement Identification;

end scheme IdentificationRequirementScheme;


scheme SymboltableScheme [
    instantiate IdentificationRequirementScheme
      rename Identification as Identifier,
        errIdentification as errIdentifier;
    end instantiate IdentificationRequirementScheme;

    instantiate AttributeRequirementScheme;   -- see Fig. 8/35
    end instantiate AttributeRequirementScheme;
  ];

  module Symboltable;
    import Identifier, _ = _ from Identifier;
      Attribute, initial, errAttribute from Attribute;
      Bool, true, false, errBool from Bool;
    export all;
    constructors
      init: -> Symboltable $$;
      enterblock: Symboltable -> Symboltable $$;
      addid: $ Symboltable * $ Identifier * Attribute -> Symboltable $$;
    operations
      leaveblock: Symboltable -> Symboltable;
      isinblock: Symboltable * Identifier -> Bool;
      retrieve: Symboltable * Identifier -> Attribute;
    declare symtab: Symboltable;   id, id₁, id₂: Identifier;   attr, attr₁, attr₂: Attribute;
    constructor axioms
      id₁ = id₂ ⇒
        addid( addid( symbtab, id₁, attr₁ ), id₂, attr₂ ) ==
        addid( symbtab, id₂, attr₂ );
      id₁ = id₂ ⇒
        addid( symbtab, id₁, attr ) == addid( symbtab, id₂, attr );
      not ( id₁ = id₂ ) ⇒
        addid( addid( symbtab, id₁, attr₁ ), id₂, attr₂ ) ==
        addid( addid( symbtab, id₂, attr₂ ), id₁, attr₁ );
    operation axioms
      leaveblock( init ) == init;
      leaveblock( enterblock( symbtab ) ) == symbtab;
      leaveblock( addid( symbtab, id, attr ) ) == leaveblock( symbtab );
    $$ isinblock( init, id ) == false;
    $$ isinblock( enterblock( symbtab ), id ) == false;
    $$ isinblock( addid( symbtab, id₁, attr ), id₂ ) ==
```

```
            if id₁ = id₂
              then true
              else isinblock( symbtab, id₂ )
            end if;
      $$ retrieve( init, id ) == initial;
      $$ retrieve( enterblock( symbtab ), id ) == retrieve( symbtab, id );
      $$ retrieve( addid( symbtab, id₁, attr ), id₂ ) ==
            if id₁ = id₂
              then attr
              else retrieve( symbtab, id₂ )
            end if;
      ?? isinblock( symbtab, id ) == errBool;
      ?? retrieve( symbtab, id ) == errAttribute;
    end module Symboltable;
  end scheme SymboltableScheme;
```

Fig. 8/41

↓SymboltableScheme

↓SymboltableScheme defines the abstract implementation of symbol tables
in terms of stacks of mappings from identifiers to attributes. Mapping is
instantiated from MappingScheme, which will be discussed later, and Stack
is instantiated from StackScheme, which was defined in Fig. 8/30. The
implementation of stacks in terms of arrays and natural numbers was
discussed in Section 8.4.

```
scheme ↓SymboltableScheme [
    instantiate IdentificationRequirementScheme
      rename Identification as Identifier,
        errIdentification as errIdentifier;
    end instantiate IdentificationRequirementScheme;

    instantiate AttributeRequirementScheme;   -- see Fig. 8/35
    end instantiate AttributeRequirementScheme;
  ];

  instantiate MappingScheme;
    with Domain as Identifier,
      Domain as Identifier,
      errDomain as errIdentifier,
      _ = _ as _ = _;
    with Range as Attribute,
      Range as Attribute,
      errRange as errAttribute;   -- irrelevant
  end instantiate MappingScheme;
```

```
    instantiate StackScheme;   -- see Fig. 8/30
      with Item as Mapping,
        Item as Mapping,
        errItem as newmap;  -- irrelevant
    end instantiate StackScheme;

    module ↓Symboltable;
      import Identifier from Identifier;
        Attribute, initial, errAttribute from Attribute;
        Bool, true, false, errBool, not _ , _ or _ from Bool;
        all from Stack;  all from Mapping;
      operations
        ↓init: -> Stack;
        ↓enterblock: Stack -> Stack;
        ↓addid: Stack * Identifier * Attribute -> Stack;
        ↓leaveblock: Stack -> Stack;
        ↓isinblock: Stack * Identifier -> Bool;
        ↓retrieve: Stack * Identifier -> Attribute;
        ↓safeSymboltable: Stack -> Bool;
      declare s: Stack;  id: Identifier;  attr: Attribute;  map: Mapping;
      operation axioms
        ↓init == push( newstack, newmap );
        ↓enterblock( s ) == push( s, newmap );
        ↓addid( s, id, attr ) == replace( s, addmap( top( s ), id, attr ) );
        ↓leaveblock( s ) ==
          if isnewstack( pop( s ) )
            then ↓init
            else pop( s )
          end if;
        ↓isinblock( s, $ id ) ==
          if ↓safeSymboltable( s )
            then isdefinedmap( top( s ), id )
            else errBool
          end if;
        ↓isinblock( s, ! id ) == errBool;
        ↓retrieve( newstack, $ id ) == initial;
          -- As newstack does not belong to the domain, the value of ↓retrieve is arbitrary.
          -- This may be exploited in the actual implementation by using it as a sentinel
          -- value.
        ↓retrieve( push( s, map ), $ id ) ==
          if ↓safeSymboltable( push( s, map ) )
            then
              if isdefinedmap( s, id )
                then evmap( s, id )
                else ↓retrieve( s, id )
              end if
            else errAttribute
          end if;
        ↓retrieve( errStack, $ id ) == errAttribute;
        ↓retrieve( s, ! id ) == errAttribute;
        ↓safeSymboltable( push( s, map ) ) == safeMapping( map );
        ↓safeSymboltable( newstack ) == true;  -- irrelevant
        ↓safeSymboltable( errStack ) == false; -- irrelevant
    end module ↓Symboltable;
end scheme ↓SymboltableScheme;
```

Fig. 8/42

MappingScheme

The specification of MappingScheme is given in Fig. 8/43.

```
scheme MappingScheme [
    instantiate IdentificationRequirementScheme
      rename Identification as Domain,
        errIdentification as errDomain;
    end instantiate IdentificationRequirementScheme;

    requirement Range;
      export all;
      sort Range;
      operation
        errRange: -> Range;
      end requirement Range;
    ];

module Mapping;
    import Domain, _ = _ from Domain;   Range, errRange from Range;
      Bool, true, false, errBool from Bool;
    export all;
    sort Mapping;
    constructors
      newmap: -> Mapping $$;
      addmap: $ Mapping * $ Domain * Range -> Mapping $$;
    operations
      evmap: mapping * Domain -> Range;
      isdefinedmap: Mapping * Domain -> Bool;
    declare map: Mapping;   dom, dom_1, dom_2: Domain;   ran, ran_1, ran_2: Range;
    constructor axioms
      dom_1 = dom_2 ⇒
        addmap( addmap( map, dom_1, ran_1 ), dom_2, ran_2 ) ==
        addmap( map, dom_2, ran_2 );
      dom_1 = dom_2 ⇒
        addmap( map, dom_1, ran ) == addmap( map, dom_2, ran );
      not ( dom_1 = dom_2 ) ⇒
        addmap( addmap( map, dom_1, ran_1 ), dom_2, ran_2 ) ==
        addmap( addmap( map, dom_2, ran_2 ), dom_1, ran_1 );
    operation axioms
    $$ evmap( newmap, dom ) == errRange;
    $$ evmap( addmap( map, dom_1, ran ), dom_2 ) ==
        if dom_1 = dom_2
          then ran
          else evmap( map, dom_2 )
          end if;
    $$ isdefinedmap( newmap, dom ) == false;
    $$ isdefinedmap( addmap( map, dom_1, ran), dom_2 ) ==
        if dom_1 = dom_2
          then true
          else isdefinedmap( map, dom_2 )
          end if;
    ?? evmap( map, dom ) == errRange;
    ?? isdefinedmap( map, dom ) == errBool;
  end module Mapping;
```

end scheme MappingScheme;

Fig. 8/43

↓MappingScheme

Here, ↓MappingScheme defines the implementation of mappings by means of bounded arrays whose elements are lists of domain-range pairs. For reasons of efficiency (which eventually is the main purpose here), the bounded array is accompanied by a flag (boolean value) indicating whether a domain-range pair has been added of which the domain element (identifier) is unsafe. Due to this flag, the operation ↓safeMapping can be implemented efficiently. Retrieval is implemented by means of hash coding. As mentioned before, implementation by hash coding (that does not preserve the order of addition) is possible because of the constructor axioms in Fig. 8/41 that deal with safe as well as unsafe identifiers.

```
scheme ↓MappingScheme [
    instantiate IdentificationRequirementScheme
      rename Identification as Domain,
        errIdentification as errDomain;
    end instantiate IdentificationRequirementScheme;

    requirement Range;
      import Bool, true, _ and _ from Bool;
      export all;
      sort Range;
      operations
        errRange: -> Range;
        _ = _: Range * Range -> Bool;
      declare ran, ran₁, ran₂, ran₃: Range;
      theorems
        ran = ran == true;
        ran₁ = ran₂ == ran₂ = ran₁;
        ( ran₁ = ran₂ ) and ( ran₂ = ran₃ ) ⇒ ran₁ = ran₃ == true;
    end requirement Range;

    requirement HashDetails;
      import Domain, _ = _ from Domain;  Nat, _ ≤ _ from Nat;  true from Bool;
      export all;
      operations
        minimum, maximum: -> Nat;
        hash: Domain -> Nat;
      declare dom, dom₁, dom₂: Domain;
      theorems
        minimum ≤ maximum == true;
```

```
        minimum ≤ hash( dom ) == true;
        hash( dom ) ≤ maximum == true;
        dom₁ = dom₂ ⇒ hash( dom₁ ) == hash( dom₂ );
    end requirement HashDetails;
];
```

```
module DomainRange;
  import Domain, errDomain, _ = _ from Domain;
    Range, errRange, _ = _ from Range;  Bool, _ and _ from Bool;
  export all;
  sort DomainRange == Domain * Range;
  operations
    errDomainRange: -> DomainRange;
    _ = _: DomainRange * DomainRange -> Bool;
  declare dom₁, dom₂: Domain;  ran₁, ran₂: Range;
  operation axioms
    errDomainRange == ( errDomain, errRange );
    ( dom₁, ran₁ ) = ( dom₂, ran₂ ) == ( dom₁ = dom₂ ) and ( ran₁ = ran₂ );
end module DomainRange;
```

```
instantiate ListScheme;   -- see Fig. 4/6
  with Item as DomainRange,
    Item as DomainRange,
    undefined as errDomainRange,   -- irrelevant
    _ = _ as _ = _;
end instantiate ListScheme;
```

```
instantiate BoundedArrayScheme;   -- see Fig. 7/20
  with Attribute as List,
    Attribute as List,
    initial as nil,
    errAttribute as nil;   -- irrelevant
  with OrderedIndex as Nat,
    Index as Nat,
    _ = _ as _ = _,
    _ ≤ _ as _ ≤ _;
end instantiate BoundedArrayScheme;
```

```
module BoundedArrayBool;
  import BoundedArray from BoundedArray;  Bool from Bool;
  export all;
  sort BoundedArrayBool == BoundedArray * Bool;
end module BoundedArrayBool;
```

```
module ↓Mapping;
  import Domain from Domain;  Range, errRange from Range;
    Bool, true, false from Bool;  all from BoundedArray;
    all from DomainRange;  all from BoundedArrayBool;
    minimum, maximum, hash from HashDetails;
    List, nil, _ | _ from List;
  operations
    ↓newmap: -> BoundedArrayBool;
    ↓addmap: BoundedArrayBool * Domain * Range -> BoundedArrayBool;
    ↓evmap: BoundedArrayBool * Domain -> Range;
    ↓isdefinedmap: BoundedArrayBool * Domain -> Bool;
    ↓safeMapping: BoundedArrayBool -> Bool;
    evlist: List * Domain -> Range;
```

```
        isdefinedlist: List * Domain -> Bool;
    declare ba: BoundedArray;  b: Bool;  dom, dom₁, dom₂: Domain;  ran: Range;
    operation axioms
      ↓newmap == ( empty( minimum, maximum ), true );
      ↓addmap( ( ba, b ), $ dom, ran ) ==
        ( ba [ ( ( dom, ran ) I read( ba, hash( dom ) ) ) / hash( dom ) ], b );
      ↓addmap( ( ba, b ), ! dom, ran ) ==
        ( ba [ ( ( dom, ran ) I read( ba, hash( dom ) ) ) / hash( dom ) ], false ) ;
      ↓evmap( ( ba, b ), $ dom ) ==
        if b   -- ↓safeMapping( ( ba, b ) )
          then evlist( read( ba, hash( dom ) ), dom )
          else errRange
        end if;
      ↓evmap( ( ba, b ), ! dom ) == errRange;
      ↓isdefinedmap( ( ba, b ), $ dom ) ==
        if b   -- ↓safeMapping( ( ba, b ) )
          then  isdefinedlist( read( ba, hash( dom ) ), dom )
          else errBool
        end if;
      ↓isdefinedmap( ( ba, b ), ! dom ) == errBool;
      ↓safeMapping( ( ba, b ) ) == b;
      evlist( nil, dom ) == errRange;
      evlist( ( dom₁, ran ) I list, dom₂ ) ==
        if dom₁ = dom₂
          then ran
          else evlist( list, dom₂ )
        end if;
      isdefinedlist( nil, dom ) == false;
      isdefinedlist( ( dom₁, ran) I list, dom₂ ) ==
        if dom₁ = dom₂
          then true
          else isdefinedlist( list, dom₂ )
        end if;
  end module ↓Mapping;
end scheme ↓MappingScheme;
```

Fig. 8/44

We invite the reader to define explicitly the concepts of the abstract implementations, i.e. data representation parts, procedure implementation parts, representation functions, implementation invariants or domains, abstraction functions, and equivalence relations for the abstract implementations given in this section, as we did for ↓StackScheme in the previous section.

8.6 Properties and Relations

In this section a number of properties that can be derived from the implementation constraints discussed in Section 8.3, is given. The properties are illustrated by the simple example of the stacks, which was also used in Sections 8.1, 8.2 and 8.3. Also, the relations between the different concepts of abstract implementations (see Section 8.2.) are discussed.   Furthermore,   the   natural   composition   of   abstract implementations is studied. The lists of properties and relations are not exhaustive.   No proofs are included. They can be found in [Van Horebeek87b, Van Horebeek88a].

Properties

9. The representation function applied to an A-term of sort A denotes an   object   belonging   to   the   domain   Dom,   i.e.   meeting   the implementation invariant:
    $I(\rho^T(a)) == $ true;

Example

> declare it: T_{Item};
> theorems
> $I(\rho^T($ push(newstack, it))) ==$
> $I(($ empty [it / 0], 1)) ==$
>   not isundefined(empty [it / 0], 0) ==
>   true

Fig. 8/45

10. Two A-terms of sort A whose representations denote equivalent objects, denote the same object:
    $\rho^T(a_1) \sim \rho^T(a_2) \Rightarrow a_1 == a_2$;

Example

> declare it: T_{Item};
> theorem
> $\rho^T($ pop(push(newstack, it))) $\sim \rho^T($ newstack)
>   -- since $\rho^T($ pop(push(newstack, it))) $== ($ empty [it / 0], 0) $\sim$
>   --   (empty, 0) $== \rho^T($ newstack)

> $\Rightarrow$
> pop(push(newstack, it)) == newstack;

Fig. 8/46

11. If two terms of sort B denote objects of the domain Dom and their abstractions denote the same object of A, then the terms obtained by consecutively applying the abstraction and the representation functions to the given terms, denote equivalent objects of B:

  $I(b_1)$ and $I(b_2)$ and $(@(b_1) = @(b_2)) \Rightarrow$
  $\rho^T(@^T(b_1)) \sim \rho^T(@^T(b_2));$

Example

---

declare it_1, it_2: T_{Item};
theorem
  $I((empty [it_1 / 0][it_2 / 1], 1))$ and
  $I((empty [it_1 / 0], 1))$ and
  $@((empty [it_1 / 0][it_2 / 1], 1)) = @((empty [it_1 / 0], 1))$
    -- since $@((empty [it_1 / 0][it_2 / 1], 1)) ==$ push(newstack, it_1) ==
    -- $@((empty [it_1 / 0], 1))$
  $\Rightarrow$
    $\rho^T(@^T((empty [it_1 / 0][it_2 / 1], 1))) \sim \rho^T(@^T((empty [it_1 / 0], 1)));$
    -- since both are equal to (empty [it_1 / 0], 1)

Fig. 8/47

12. If two terms of sort B denote objects of the domain Dom and their abstractions denote the same object of A, then the given terms denote equivalent objects:

  $I(b_1)$ and $I(b_2)$ and $(@(b_1) = @(b_2)) \Rightarrow b_1 \sim b_2;$

Example

---

declare it_1, it_2: Item;
theorem
  $I((empty [it_1 / 0][it_2 / 1], 1))$ and
  $I((empty [it_1 / 0], 1))$ and
  $@((empty [it_1 / 0][it_2 / 1], 1)) = @((empty [it_1 / 0], 1)) \Rightarrow$

$$(\, empty \, [\, it_1 \, / \, 0 \,], 1 \,) \sim (\, empty \, [\, it_1 \, / \, 0 \,][\, it_2 \, / \, 1 \,], 1 \,);$$

Fig. 8/48

13. If two terms of sort B denote objects of the domain Dom that are not equivalent, then the abstractions of the given terms denote distinct objects of A:

$$I(\, b_1 \,) \text{ and } I(\, b_2 \,) \text{ and not } (\, b_1 \sim b_2 \,) \Rightarrow @(\, b_1 \,) \neq\neq @(\, b_2 \,);$$

where

$$s \neq\neq t;$$

means that

$$s == t;$$

does not hold.

Example

declare it: Item;
 theorems
   $I((\, empty, 0 \,)) \text{ and } I((\, empty \, [\, it \, / \, 0 \,], 1 \,)) \text{ and}$
   $not((\, empty, 0 \,) \sim (\, empty \, [\, it \, / \, 0 \,], 1 \,)) \Rightarrow$
     $@((\, empty, 0 \,)) == newstack \neq\neq$
     $push(\, newstack, it \,) == @((\, empty \, [\, it \, / \, 0 \,], 1 \,))$

Fig. 8/49

14. The abstraction function @: B -> A is surjective, i.e. each object of sort A is the abstraction of an object of the domain:

$$\forall a \in A, \exists b \in Dom: @(\, b \,) == a;$$

Example

declare it: Item;

push(errStack, it) denotes a stack and
 $@((\, empty, errNat \,)) == errStack == push(\, errStack, it \,)$

Fig. 8/50

15. If two A-terms of sort A denote the same object, then the terms obtained by consecutively applying the representation and abstraction function to the given terms, denote the same object:

$$a_1 = a_2 \Rightarrow @^T(\rho^T(a_1)) == @^T(\rho^T(a_2));$$

Example

```
declare it: T_Item;
theorems
  pop( push( newstack, it ) ) = newstack ⇒
    @ᵀ( ρᵀ( pop( push( newstack, it ) ) ) ) ==
    @ᵀ( ↓pop( ↓push( ↓newstack, it ) ) ) ==
    @ᵀ( ( empty [ it / 0 ], 0 ) ) == newstack ==
    @ᵀ( ( empty, 0 ) ) == @ᵀ( ↓newstack ) ==
    @ᵀ( ρᵀ( newstack ) )
```

Fig. 8/51

16. If two A-terms that are not of sort A denote the same object, then the terms obtained by applying the representation function to the given terms denote the same object:

$$x_1 = x_2 \Rightarrow \rho^T(x_1) == \rho^T(x_2);$$

Example

```
declare it: T_Item;
theorems
  isnewstack( newstack ) = isnewstack( pop( push( newstack, it ) ) ) ⇒
    ρᵀ( isnewstack( newstack ) ) == ↓isnewstack( ↓newstack ) ==
    ↓isnewstack( empty, 0 ) == true == ↓isnewstack( empty [ it / 0 ], 0 ) ==
    ↓isnewstack( ↓pop( empty [ it / 0 ], 1 ) ) ==
    ↓isnewstack( ↓pop( ↓push( ( empty, 0 ), it ) ) ) ==
    ↓isnewstack( ↓pop( ↓push( ↓newstack, it ) ) ) ==
    ρᵀ( isnewstack( pop( push( newstack, it ) ) ) )
```

Fig. 8/52

17. Over the minimal domain, implementation constraint 7 is redundant with respect to implementation constraints 1 to 6. After reformulation we obtain:

Let s_i be an A-constructor or an A-operation of sort A whose j_1^{th}, ... and j_n^{th} arguments are its only arguments of sort A. As the rank must be preserved, the j_1^{th}, ... and j_n^{th} arguments and the range of the implementation operation $\downarrow s_i$ are of sort B. If a_{j_1} and a'_{j_1}, ... and a_{j_n} and a'_{j_n} are terms of sort A whose representations are pairwise equivalent, then replacing $\rho^T(a_{j_1})$ by $\rho^T(a'_{j_1})$ as j_1^{th} argument of $\downarrow s_i$, ... and $\rho^T(a_{j_n})$ by $\rho^T(a'_{j_n})$ as j_n^{th} argument of $\downarrow s_i$ results in an equivalent object of B:

$$(\rho^T(a_{j_1}) \sim \rho^T(a'_{j_1})) \text{ and } ... \text{ and } (\rho^T(a_{j_n}) \sim \rho^T(a'_{j_n})) \Rightarrow$$
$$\downarrow s_i(..., \rho^T(a_{j_1}), ..., \rho^T(a_{j_n}), ...) \sim$$
$$\downarrow s_i(..., \rho^T(a'_{j_1}), ..., \rho^T(a'_{j_n}), ...);$$

Example

```
declare it₁, it₂, it₃: T_Item;
theorems
    ρᵀ( push( newstack, it₁ ) ) ~ ρᵀ( pop( push( push( newstack, it₁ ), it₂ ) ) )
      -- since ρᵀ( push( newstack, it₁ ) ) == ( empty [ it₁ / 0 ], 1 ) ~
      --        ( empty [ it₁ / 0 ][ it₂ / 1 ], 1 ) ==
      --        ρᵀ( pop( push( push( newstack, it₁ ), it₂ ) ) )
    ⇒
    ↓replace( ( empty [ it₁ / 0 ], 1 ), it₃ ) == ( empty [ it₁ / 0 ][ it₃ / 0 ], 1 ) ==
    ( empty [ it₃ / 0 ], 1 ) ~ ( empty [ it₂ / 1 ][ it₃ / 0 ], 1 ) ==
    ( empty [ it₁ / 0 ][ it₂ / 1 ][ it₃ / 0 ], 1 ) ==
    ↓replace( ( empty [ it₁ / 0 ][ it₂ / 1 ], 1 ), it₃ )
```

Fig. 8/53

18. Over the minimal domain, implementation constraint 8 is redundant with respect to implementation constraints 1 to 6. After reformulation we obtain:

Let s_i be an A-operation not of sort A whose j_1^{th}, ... and j_n^{th} arguments are its only arguments of sort A. As the rank must be preserved, the j_1^{th}, ... and j_n^{th} arguments of the implementation operation $\downarrow s_i$ are of sort B, whereas the range of $\downarrow s_i$ is of the same sort as the range of s_i. If a_{j_1} and a'_{j_1}, ... and a_{j_n} and a'_{j_n} are terms of sort A whose representations are pairwise equivalent, then replacing $\rho^T(a_{j_1})$ by $\rho^T(a'_{j_1})$ as j_1^{th} argument of $\downarrow s_i$, ... and $\rho^T(a_{j_n})$ by $\rho^T(a'_{j_n})$ as j_n^{th} argument of $\downarrow s_i$ results in the same object:

$$(\rho^T(a_{j_1}) \sim \rho^T(a'_{j_1}))\ \text{and} \ldots \text{and}\ (\rho^T(a_{j_n}) \sim \rho^T(a'_{j_n})) \Rightarrow$$
$$\downarrow s_i(\ldots, \rho^T(a_{j_1}), \ldots, \rho^T(a_{j_n}), \ldots) ==$$
$$\downarrow s_i(\ldots, \rho^T(a'_{j_1}), \ldots, \rho^T(a'_{j_n}), \ldots);$$

Example

---

declare it_1, it_2: T_{Item};
theorems
  $\rho^T($ push(newstack, it_1)) $\sim \rho^T($ pop(push(push(newstack, it_1), it_2)))
    -- since $\rho^T($ push(newstack, it_1)) $==$ (empty [it_1 / 0], 1) $\sim$
    --   (empty [it_1 / 0][it_2 / 1], 1) $==$
    -- $\rho^T($ pop(push(push(newstack, it_1), it_2)))
  $\Rightarrow$
    $\downarrow$isnewstack((empty [it_1 / 0], 1)) $==$ false $==$
    $\downarrow$isnewstack((empty [it_1 / 0][it_2 / 1], 1))

Fig. 8/54

19. Let s_i be an A–constructor or an A–operation of sort A whose j_1^{th}, ...
and j_n^{th} arguments are its only arguments of sort A. As the rank
must be preserved, the j_1^{th}, ... and j_n^{th} arguments and the range of the
implementation operation $\downarrow s_i$ are of sort B. If the terms b_{j_1}, ... and b_{j_n}
of sort B denote objects belonging to the domain, then the application
of s_i to the abstractions of b_{j_1}, ... and b_{j_n} denotes the same object as
the abstraction of the application of the implementation operation $\downarrow s_i$
to b_{j_1}, ... and b_{j_n}:
  $I(b_{j_1})$ and ... and $I(b_{j_n}) \Rightarrow$
    $s_i(\ldots, @(b_{j_1}), \ldots, @(b_{j_n}), \ldots) == @(\downarrow s_i(\ldots, b_{j_1}, \ldots, b_{j_n}, \ldots));$

Example

---

declare it: Item;
theorem
  $I($ empty [it / 0], 1) $\Rightarrow$
    pop(@(empty [it / 0], 1)) $==$
    @($\downarrow$pop(empty [it / 0], 1));

Fig. 8/55

Relations Between the Concepts

We discuss the relations between the different concepts for abstract implementations.

A. Given a data representation part, a procedure implementation part (and thus a representation function ρ^T), an implementation invariant I and an abstraction function @ such that the implementation constraints 1 and 2 and property 19 are met. Then, one and only one equivalence relation $\sim$ exists meeting the implementation constraints 3, 4, 5 and 7.

B. Given a data representation part, a procedure implementation part, and an equivalence relation $\sim$ such that implementation constraint 3 and property 10 are met. Then, one and only one minimal domain Dom and abstraction function @ exist such that the implementation constraints 1, 2, 4 and 5 are met. Each other domain and abstraction function are such that the domain contains the minimal domain and the abstraction functions are equal over the minimal domain.

C. Given a domain Dom and an abstraction function @. Then one and only one equivalence relation $\sim$ exists meeting implementation constraint 4 and property 12 (or 13).

D. Given a domain Dom and an abstraction function @ such that property 14 is met. Then at least one data representation part and one procedure implementation part (and thus a representation function ρ^T) exist such that the implementation constraints 1, 2 and 6 are met, and such that, given the equivalence relation $\sim$ defined by relation C, constraints 3, 5, 7 and 8 are met (i.e. Dom, @, ρ^T and $\sim$ form a correct implementation).

E. If a data type A is implemented by a data type B, the initial algebra of B is, in general, not isomorph with the initial algebra of A. This was demonstrated in Fig. 8/21, in which the abstract object newstack has several distinct representations, e.g., (empty, 0) and (empty [it / 0], 0).

   The quotient algebra of the domain with respect to the equivalence relation of the implementation, considering all operations but the implementation operations as hidden operations, is isomorph with the initial algebra of A. Consider in Fig. 8/21 the equivalence classes of $\sim$ in the domain as objects and the nonnullary implementation operations as functions between these objects (the classes are indicated by a dotted line in Fig. 8/21). This algebra is isomorph with the initial algebra of Stack.

Natural Composition of Abstract Implementations

Given a correct abstract implementation of module A by module B, denoted AB. The implementation module $\downarrow$A contains the implementation operations $\downarrow s_{ABi}$. Also for one of the directly imported modules of the implementation module $\downarrow$A, say module X, a correct abstract implementation is given. Furthermore, the latter abstract implementation is extended (as explained in Section 8.2.7) for the implementation operations $\downarrow s_{ABi}$ of AB. Then, the natural composition of these abstract implementations is again a correct abstract implementation.

We will consider the most interesting case, in which the directly imported module X is module B. Thus, an abstract implementation of module B by a module C is given, denoted BC. The implementation BC is extended in a second step for the implementation operations $\downarrow s_{ABi}$. Then, the *natural composition* of these abstract implementations is defined in the following way.

The implementation invariant I of the natural composition is

$$I(\ x\ ) = I_{BC}(\ x\ ) \text{ and } I_{AB}(\ @_{BC}(\ x\ )\ )$$
$$\text{Dom} = \{x \mid x \in \text{Dom}_{BC} \text{ and } @_{BC}(\ x\ ) \in \text{Dom}_{AB}\}$$

with I_{AB} and I_{BC} the implementation invariants of AB and BC respectively, and with Dom_{AB} and Dom_{BC} the respective domains.

The abstraction function @ of the natural composition is defined as

$$@ = @_{AB} \text{ o } @_{BC}$$

with $@_{AB}$ and $@_{BC}$ the abstraction functions of AB and BC respectively.

The equivalence function ~ of the natural composition is defined as

$$c_1 \sim c_2 \ == \ @(\ c_1\ ) = @(\ c_2\ );$$

which is equivalent to

$$c_1 \sim c_2 \ == \ @_{BC}(\ c_1\ ) \sim_{AB} @_{BC}(\ c_2\ );$$

with $\sim_{AB}$ the equivalence function of AB.

The data representation part and the procedure implementation part of the natural composition consist of

1. the additional implementation operations of the second step of the abstract implementation BC, denoted $\downarrow s'_{BCk}$,

2. a mapping m_{data} from A-constructors onto implementation operations $\downarrow s'_{BCk}$, such that $m_{data} = m_{BCproc} \; o \; m_{ABdata}$ with m_{ABdata} and m_{BCproc} the mappings of the data representation part of AB and the (extended) procedure implementation part of BC respectively, and

3. a mapping m_{proc} from A-operations onto implementation operations $\downarrow s'_{BCk}$, such that $m_{proc} = m_{BCproc} \; o \; m_{ABproc}$ with m_{ABproc} and m_{BCproc} the mappings of the procedure implementation parts of AB and BC respectively.

An important property is that the natural composition of two correct abstract implementations invariably yields a correct abstract implementation. Another property is that the natural composition of abstract implementations is an associative operation.

8.7 Bibliographic Notes

John Guttag is undoubtedly one of the pioneers who introduced the ideas of abstract implementations [Guttag77, Guttag78b]. In [Guttag77] the concept of abstract implementations is informally illustrated by means of an example: a symbol table is implemented as a stack of arrays. For each operation f an implementation operation, denoted f', is given. The abstraction function is called *interpretation function* and is denoted Φ. It is emphasized that the inverse of the interpretation function may not exist. Implementation invariants are called *representation invariants*. Nothing is said about equivalence relations.

In [Guttag77] a data type B is considered a correct abstract implementation of data type A if the so-called representation invariants are verified and the *inherent invariants* are proved. An inherent invariant is obtained in the following way. Consider each axiom of data type A

- if the sort of its left(right)-hand side is A, thus the axiom is of the form $a_1 == a_2$, then $@^T(\rho^T(a_1)) == @^T(\rho^T(a_2))$. This is equivalent to our property 15 (see Section 8.6).

- if the sort of its left-hand side is not A, thus the axiom is of the form $x_1 == x_2$, then $\rho^T(x_1) == \rho^T(x_2)$. This is equivalent to our property 16 (see Section 8.6).

The properties required in [Guttag77] from B for being a correct abstract implementation of A, are weaker than our implementation constraints (see Section 8.3). In particular, Guttag allows that the implementation constraint 2, i.e. $@^T(\rho^T(a)) == a$, is not met as far as the representation and inherent invariants are met. This will be illustrated by a small example. Assume that the following conditional axiom is added to the specification of the array (see p. 400 in [Guttag77])

NOT IS_SAME?(id_1, id_2) $\Rightarrow$
  ASSIGN(ASSIGN(arr, id_1, $attrs_1$), id_2, $attrs_2$) ==
  ASSIGN(ASSIGN(arr, id_2, $attrs_2$), id_1, $attrs_1$)

expressing that the order of assigning is irrelevant if the indices (identifiers) are distinct. Assume that no analogous axiom is given for the data type Symboltable. As a consequence

  S == ADD(ADD(INIT, id_1, $attrs_1$), id_2, $attrs_2$)

and

  T == ADD(ADD(INIT, id_2, $attrs_2$), id_1, $attrs_1$)

denote distinct objects (i.e. they cannot be proved equal using equational reasoning) if id_1 and id_2 are distinct. But if we use the same representation as in [Guttag77], then $\rho^T(S) == \rho^T(T)$. The abstraction function $@^T$ can be defined such that either $@^T(\rho^T(S)) == S$ or $@^T(\rho^T(T)) == T$. But both are not possible.

This illustrates that the definition of correct abstract implementation in [Guttag77] is less restrictive than ours. But the drawback of the former is that it is possible that when a new operation is defined, all the previous abstract implementations become useless and have to be designed anew. For instance, if a new operation f: Symboltable -> Bool is defined such that f(S) results in true but f(T) results in false, then the implementation by means of the array (such that $\rho^T(S) == \rho^T(T)$) becomes useless.

Our more restrictive viewpoint is a consequence of a different mathematical foundation. Our specifications are based on initial algebras while the specifications in [Guttag77] are based on observational equivalence (see Section 2.19). The basic idea of initial algebras is that all objects are distinct unless the opposite is specified. The hierarchical constraints guarantee that objects that were equal (or distinct) must not become distinct (equal) when the specification is extended. However, using observational equivalence two objects may be assumed equal as far as their external behaviour is the same. As a consequence two objects that have the same external behaviour may have the same implementation. But if later an operation is added such that their behaviour is no longer equivalent, this implementation becomes useless.

Guttag's second famous article about abstract implementations [Guttag78b] is also based on observational equivalence. Therefore, in his second article as well, his definition of abstract implementation is less restrictive than ours but the price that must be paid is high, as mentioned above.

The concepts of abstract implementations are informally explained by means of examples: a stack is implemented as an array and an integer, a symbol table is implemented as a stack of mappings and, in an appendix, a mapping is implemented using a hash table. In contrast to Guttag's first article, his second one defines an equivalence function (by defining an *equality operator*). He asserts that the use of equivalence functions is a generalization of the use of abstraction functions (p. 1058 [Guttag78b]). But we have shown in this chapter that it is not so: abstraction functions and equivalence relations are equally general concepts for defining abstract implementations.

In [Guttag78b] implementation operations are defined in a rather complicated way using a function SYMT. This function SYMT is the abstraction function although it is not explicitly mentioned in the article. Another confusing notation is the symbol "=" for the equivalence function, called *equality operator*. If $b_1 = b_2$ is written, do b_1 and b_2 denote the same objects or do they denote equivalent objects?

In [Guttag78b] a data type B is considered an implementation of data type B if

1. The *representation invariant* is proved. The representation invariant states that each object of A has a representation (i.e. our property 14).

2. The so-called equality operator (i.e. equivalence function) must be reflexive, symmetric and transitive and must meet the *substitution* property. The substitution property is equivalent to our constraints 7 and 8.

3. The implementation operations must be closed with respect to the implementation invariants (i.e. our implementation constraint 1). This property is formulated in a rather complicated way.

4. Consider each axiom of A

    -   if the sort of its left(right)-hand side is A, thus the axiom is of the form $a_1 == a_2$, then $\rho^T(a_1) \sim \rho^T(a_2)$. This is equivalent to our implementation constraint 3.

    -   otherwise the axiom has the form $x_1 == x_2$, and then $\rho^T(x_1) == \rho^T(x_2)$. This is equivalent to our property 16.

In the first part of [Bernot86a, Bernot86b] abstract implementations are discussed. For the implementation of sort A by sort(s) B_i, he introduces an intermediate sort, called $\overline{A}$, constructed as a product of the lower level sorts B_i, but with an equality superimposed upon. This equality, *la représentation de l'égalité*, corresponds to our equivalence relation. The representation function from A to $\overline{A}$ is called *l'opération de représentation*. In view of the potential problems with conventional equational reasoning, he avoids abstraction functions as such. On the other hand, he does provide a similar function called *l'opération de synthèse* from B_i to $\overline{A}$. An abstraction function, as defined in our context, would have to be defined as a composition of *l'opération de synthèse* and the inverse of *l'opération de représentation*. Many of the properties discussed in this text can be found mutatis mutandis in [Bernot86], e.g., constraints 3 and 4 correspond to *la validité* and *la consistance*. Our idea of correctness corresponds to his *correction forte*.

In [Ehrig82] and [Sannella82] the relation between abstract implementations and categorical theory is emphasized. A critical survey of these works can be found in [Bernot86].

The technique of abstract implementations is not only used for algebraic specifications. In [Fielding82, Bjorner82] the technique is called *data refinement* and applied to VDM specifications. Data refinement is defined as a process in which a less abstract representation is chosen and new operations are defined in terms of the more concrete ones (p. 327 [Fielding82]). Implementation invariants are called *data type invariants* and the abstraction function is called *retrieve function*.

In [Van Horebeek87b, Van Horebeek88a], we distinguished between data implementations and procedural implementations. In this book, a distinction between data representation operations and procedure implementation operations is made. Therefore the formulations of the definitions of the concepts are slightly different. However, the concepts themselves are completely analogous. As a consequence, the proofs that can be found in [Van Horebeek87b, Van Horebeek88a] remain valid. A case that is not considered in this book but that is treated in [Van Horebeek87b, Van Horebeek88a] is the following one. Assume that an abstract implementation of module A by module B is available. If in another module X a constructor s_i of sort X is defined that has one or more arguments of sort A, the original abstract implementation can be extended by providing an implementation operation $\downarrow s_i$.

Equational Reasoning

As demonstrated in [Ehrig82] and later in [Bernot86], conventional equational reasoning as discussed in Section 2.13 is no longer valid for axioms containing abstraction functions. In particular, when the abstraction functions are applied to elements not belonging to the domain. In [Van Gestel88] we claim this is not a problem inherent to the implementation formalism but to an inappropriateness of conventional equational reasoning for dealing with abstraction functions. Based on the approach of Section 2.13 [Goguen81], we propose in [Van Gestel88] an augmented set of deduction rules to take abstraction functions into account. These rules are a proper generalization of those given in Section 2.13 in that they are identical in the absence of abstraction functions.

Imperative Implementations

A topic left open in this book is the issue of an eventual imperative implementation. In fact several options are open. The simplest one would be to use the direct implementation available for any constructive implementation, assuming the refinements are sufficiently tuned towards efficiency. This would often impose a prohibitively large implementation effort. The problem may however be remedied in two different ways.

Obviously, for abstract data types closely resembling the primitive data types available in imperative programming languages, one should directly substitute the corresponding imperative structures, rather than the (synthesized) direct implementation which often will use but a small fraction of the available primitive data types. Likewise, a number of abstract data types are presumably of such usefulness, it may well be worthwhile to handcraft a very efficient implementation for them, e.g., involving many intricate refinements. By making these available as library primitives, the need to dwell too deeply into most implementations is reduced.

Conversely, the strategy for synthesizing the direct implementations itself can and, when producing product quality, should be refined. Several efforts along this line are currently on the way. E.g., [Thomas88a, Thomas88b] present a method for allocating objects optimized with respect to efficient access as determined from an analysis of the operation axioms. The method is only applicable to a limited set of specifications, namely *non-indexed* data types only (e.g., no hash coding), but reduces the need for many handcrafted, special purpose implementations. The method itself is described as a generic abstract implementation.

Conclusions

"To every thing there is a season,
and a time to every purpose under the heaven:
A time to introduce and a time to conclude;
a time to specify, and a time to pluck up that which is specified ..."
Old Testament, Ecclesiastes, III, 1-8 (modified)

A number of important topics treated in the previous chapters will be discussed and evaluated. These topics are the mathematical foundations of algebraic specifications, the role of algebraic specifications in software engineering, the role of software engineering in algebraic specifications, the definition of a specification language, the power and limits of rigorous reasoning, constructivity and abstraction, and the relation between specifications and programs. Several case studies that have been worked out will also be evaluated. Finally, the software tools which have been developed will be discussed.

Mathematical Foundations

An important aspect of algebraic specifications is that they have a rigorous *mathematical foundation*. Thanks to these mathematical concepts, a well-defined and implementation-independent meaning can be given to algebraic specifications and due to the mathematical foundation rigorous mathematical reasoning on algebraic specifications is possible.

In this book, an intuitive understanding of the underlying mathematical concepts have been strived after. Therefore, the book is directed towards *software engineers* rather than mathematicians. Much care has been taken of making the necessary links to references where mathematics is treated in depth.

If we prefer to use one single algebra (possibly up to an isomorphism) as the underlying model of an abstract data type, the *initial algebra* is most appropriate for two reasons. Firstly, initial algebras are termalgebras, i.e. every object can be denoted by a variable-free term. Secondly, axioms enable literally different terms to denote the same object; consequently, it is quite logical to start from a situation where literally different variable-free terms denote different objects. Therefore, we have chosen initial algebras as underlying model.

However, the class of all algebras that are *behaviourally equivalent* with the initial algebra, is more abstract than the initial algebra itself. This class of algebras is in fact a generalization of the theory of many-sorted initial algebras [Sannella87]. The price that must be paid is that rigorous reasoning becomes heavier. E.g., a theorem can be satisfied by one algebra and not by another, even if both algebras are behaviourally equivalent.

Remaining within the mathematical framework of many-sorted initial algebras, we have proposed an *error detection and error handling method*, and the different concepts of *abstract implementations* have been formulated, discussed and compared.

Algebraic Specifications in Software Engineering

The role of algebraic specifications is situated in the design phase of the life cycle of a software system. We see algebraic specifications as a means to describe parts of a software system in an implementation-independent way with mathematical precision. In contrast with what many people claim, algebraic specifications are not a passe-partout to describe any part of the design of a software system. Algebraic specifications as described in this book are well-suited to describe *data* modules of a software system but they are inadequate to describe the design at the level of, e.g., concurrent and communicating processes. Therefore, either algebraic specifications must be extended to deal with concurrency or another description formalism must be used. These topics are part of current research. They fall outside the scope of this book.

Another point that may lead to confusion is that algebraic specifications are more of a formalism and a programming style than of a design method. In that respect, algebraic specifications as a software engineering tool do not suffice. There is a strong need for design methods to work with algebraic specifications. In our case study of the mini-PABX, emphasis is put on the *object-oriented* design method, where the message passing is an intrinsic property of the interface between the objects of the system.

An important software engineering principle is *abstraction*. The specifications of data types are abstract because of two reasons. Firstly, they are defined up to an isomorphism, i.e. abstraction is made from representations. Secondly, because of the mathematical notion of algebras, only the fundamental properties of the objects and the functions are relevant. The *what* can be specified without the *how*. Algebraic specifications can be made at different levels of abstraction. At the highest level, the introduction of extraneous details places unnecessary constraints on the choice of an implementation and may potentially eliminate the best solution. However, if we are interested in implementation details, they can be specified using the same algebraic formalism giving rise to algebraic specifications at a lower level. Another kind of abstraction is abstraction by parameterization. A generic mechanism that allows to define a whole family of analogous specifications was defined. This kind of abstraction promotes the reusability of specifications.

Throughout the text *modularity* as a software engineering principle is present at different levels:

- *at the level of the algebraic specification language*
  Such a module is the smallest unit that encapsulates an abstract data type and on which import and export clauses can be defined.

- *at the level of the design method*
  A number of modules can be grouped to represent a logic feature of the software system being described. This kind of modularity is such that we start with a kernel module covering the behaviour of a small subset of the software system. Then, the description may grow stepwise by adding modules representing one specific system feature. For our PABX example, the kernel module describes a two-party voice call. Then, modules can be added stepwise describing features such as enquiry, user actions, parking or camping, intrusion, transfer, pick up, booking, wake up, conference calls, etc. [Vergauwen87]. This kind of modularity is not explicitly supported by the algebraic specification language. In literature on algebraic specifications little attention has been paid to this important aspect of system design.

- *at the level of error handling*
  As a result of the stepwise design method to treat error detection and error handling, each module consists of two parts: one dealing with the normal situations and one dealing with the exceptional (erroneous) situations.

- *at the level of implementation*
  First, a high level specification of a data type is produced in which abstraction is made from all irrelevant details, only the relevant properties being described. Next, an implementation for the specification can be constructed using specifications of other data types. Then, in turn, for these specifications implementations can be made, and so on.

Software Engineering in Algebraic Specifications

In most literature on algebraic specifications, mathematical foundation has led to a minimal notation to illustrate the mathematical concepts by means of simple examples such as stacks, queues, sets and lists. In order to cope with more complex data types, this notation must be further extended with features supporting software engineering methods and principles. Such features are very helpful to master the complexity and to enhance reliability, extendibility, robustness and continuity. Important issues that are related with software engineering are modules with import and export clauses, hierarchy of modules, information hiding, abstraction by parameterization, distinction between data and procedural abstraction, constraints for constructiveness, uniqueness and completeness, abstract implementations and error handling.

In most algebraic specification languages no explicit distinction is made between *data and procedural abstraction*. In the specification language we designed, the distinction between constructors and operations is supported. The axioms are divided in constructor axioms and operation axioms. Then, it enables us to check the constructiveness, uniqueness and completeness constraints mechanically.

Another direction in which a notation for algebraic specifications must be extended is *error detection and error handling*. Indeed, in a high level specification of a software system it is not sufficient to know exactly in which situations the system will fail to work correctly (error detection), but it must also be specified what will happen next in such situations (error handling). We strongly believe that the specification of error detection and handling must be part of the algebraic specification and not of a lower (implementation) level as suggested by [Liskov86]. The algebraic specification language we designed contains a powerful error detection and error handling mechanism, supporting a design method. The method consists in designing specifications in two steps. In a first step the specification is constructed only for safe objects as arguments, in a second step unsafe objects are dealt with.

A formal specification without any informal documentation is hardly *readable*. All examples given in the previous chapters were commented with informal texts or pictures. Formal and informal specifications must not be seen as competitive but rather as complementary methods. A natural language is very appropriate for a first intuitive introduction and as documentation of a formal specification. Theorems play an important role as formal documentation for better understanding specifications. The readability of the formal specifications has been further enhanced by introducing many syntactic constructs, e.g., ifthenelse, case and let constructs. Moreover, the use of import and export clauses makes it easier to locate the definitions of sorts, constructors and operations.

An Algebraic Specification Language

Using software engineering aspects such as mentioned above, the mathematical notation has been developed towards a practical specification language. During this transformation process, many case studies were performed. These experiments have led to successive improvements of the language.

The result is a formal specification language based on many-sorted initial algebras. In fact, it is a *strongly typed functional programming language*. In contrast with most other algebraic specification languages as OBJ2 and ACT ONE, a strong *constructivity* is explicitly required. This means that we make a distinction between constructors and operations, as well as a distinction between constructor axioms and operation axioms, and we have uniqueness, completeness and constructiveness constraints. Moreover, a module mechanism is provided with import clauses, similar to the import clauses of Modula-2 [Wirth82], and also export clauses. The parameterization concept is analogous to that of OBJ2 [Goguen84] and ACT ONE [Ehrigh85], but instead of parameterizing only one module or one requirement, groups of modules and/or requirements may be parameterized. Another difference is the introduction of a more restricted form of a claimed requirement, namely the claimed module. Finally, the language contains an elegant notation supporting an explicit error detection and error handling mechanism.

The algebraic specification language is used as a *didactic* vehicle to teach software engineering principles and methods, and to learn rigorous reasoning. Even people without professional training in computer science become familiar with the specification language in a few weeks.

Rigorous Reasoning

Due to the existence of a mathematical foundation, algebraic specifications are very suitable for rigorous reasoning. Rigorous reasoning in an early stage of a project is important because design inconsistencies can be detected before the implementation is actually started. By rigorous reasoning we are encouraged to analyze in detail the design decisions made at a given level. Rigorous reasoning is the appropriate means to get insight into the problem area in order to avoid wrong decisions in an early stage of the project. In this way, software production time can be decreased and maintenance becomes easier, but most of all the system is more reliable.

Rigorous reasoning is much concerned with proving a given assertion (theorem) to be correct. Rigorous reasoning is useful for several reasons:

- As we have seen in this book, properties of algebraic specifications can be specified as theorems. If we can prove the theorems, it will increase our confidence that the specification expresses what we have in mind.

- When a scheme is instantiated, the actual parameters must meet the (formal) operation axioms and theorems of the claimed requirements and claimed modules.

- If semi-constructive specifications are used, the first hierarchical constraint may be violated resulting in an inconsistent specification. By means of theorem proving the consistency can be proved as was done in Section 4.9.

- Using the technique of abstract implementations, the implementation constraints must be proved.

- Proving the termination of algebraic specifications considered as term rewriting systems is another interesting application of rigorous reasoning. In general, the termination problem is undecidable [Huet78], but a method for proving termination of constructive specifications that succeeds in most cases [Bevers87] has been developed. With this method the termination of nearly all operations given in the examples of Chapters 3 until 8 have been proved.

Unfortunately, theorem proving is a very hard and tedious job. Although many theorem proving systems exist, their users still need many hours to prove theorems even for small specifications. We believe that still many research and implementation efforts are required for producing theorem provers that can handle industrial examples.

Constructivity and Abstraction

The main characteristic of our specification language is its *constructivity*. Constructivity is an important property since it enables rapid prototyping. In this way, a software system can be tested before it has been implemented. The drawback of constructivity is that sometimes a *less abstract* specification is obtained.

This drawback was illustrated by an example of a very simple robot system. The constructive specification was longer and less abstract than the non-constructive one. The former may be considered as an implementation of the latter. The advantage of the constructive specification is that rapid prototyping is possible. Furthermore, rigorous reasoning is easier. The price that must be paid is a lower level of abstraction. Although our algebraic specification language does only support (semi-)constructive specifications, non-constructive specifications are of great importance in the design phase of a software system. Non-constructive specifications are considered as the highest documentation level of the design. Furthermore, the operation axioms of the non-constructive specification can be used as theorems in the constructive version.

Specifications and Programs

A critical reader may argue that there is still a wide gap between a formal specification and an implementation in a von Neumann language. In Chapter 8 the method of abstract implementations was presented. It is a top-down technique where the top level is the most abstract level and where implementation details are introduced in lower levels. We believe that this technique must be accompanied by a (semi-)automatic *transformation system* that introduces von Neumann concepts (tail recursion must be transformed into loops, sharing must be introduced where possible, etc.) [CIP85]. Moreover, theorem proving techniques and tools are necessary for checking implementation constraints of abstract implementations. As mentioned before, further progress in the field of theorem proving is needed.

The ideal situation would be that an implementation is automatically derived from its specification. Although we are far from this situation, formal specifications are very useful. By making a formal specification we are forced to *probe the matter to the very bottom* in a very precise and complete way. Furthermore, rapid prototyping may be done before any implementation is constructed. In this way, the cost of making specifications is more than compensated and high quality software can be obtained.

Case Studies

The algebraic specification language has been successfully used in several case studies in different application fields. Some of them were specified in an earlier version of the specification language. The general conclusion of these case studies is that algebraic specifications are particularly suitable for *describing the data parts of software systems*.

One of the first case studies we made was the formal specification of a small didactic system, called Karel The Robot [Pattis81]. It was situated in a comparative study of the denotational [Lewi85a] and algebraic [Lewi85b] specification formalisms. The conclusion was that the denotational semantics with its high order functions are very suitable for specifying control structures whereas the algebraic approach with its abstract data types is more appropriate for data structures.

In Chapter 5 and in [Van Horebeek87a], the ferry problem was discussed. It is a nice example of a parameterized specification. The riddle of the farmer, the wolf, the goat and the cabbage, and the riddle of the missionaries and the cannibals are particular instantiations of the ferry problem. Building parameterized specifications requires considerably more time, but this additional effort is justified by the obtained reusability of the specifications.

In [Van Coppenolle86] the Unix-like file system of B. Sufrin [Sufrin84] is algebraically specified. Substantial parts of graphical packages including GKS are specified in [Huyghe87]. An algebraic specification of an interpreter for an earlier version of our language can be found in [Devriendt86], where an implementation in ADA is handcoded from the formal specification. The Knuth-Bendix completion procedure for our algebraic specification language is algebraically specified in [Stroobants87].

Within the context of our project we have been confronted with an industrial problem concerning a call handling system (PABX). As the original informal descriptions of the features of the call handling system often were ambiguous and incomplete, detailed questions about the features could only be answered after these features had been implemented either by looking at the assembler code or by executing the code. As a remedy for this we have built a formal specification of a substantial part of the call handling system. This specification was designed according to the software engineering principles and methods that were advocated in this book, see Chapter 6. However, reducing the call handling system to a single monolithic data structure would have resulted in a less readable specification as the number of states grows out of control very rapidly. Therefore, an object-oriented design method was used. Each logical object is always in a definite state. Furthermore, the logical objects can communicate with each other by sending messages. When an object receives a message, the state of the object can be changed and it can in turn send messages to other objects. Using this object-oriented method the length of the specification grows about linearly with the number of described features. A subset of the specification of the PABX has been used for rapid prototyping. We believe that rapid prototyping has the effect of decreasing the total software development effort and that it results in software of higher quality.

Software Tools

While elaborating the case studies mentioned above, the need for adequate software tools arose. Therefore, we have developed a number of software tools. A parser checks the syntax of the specifications. The import and export clauses enable testing of the interfaces between the modules and requirements. Since it is a strongly typed language, a type controller has been built. Furthermore, the uniqueness, completeness and constructiveness constraints can be checked mechanically. By means of a reductor, rapid prototyping is possible. In this way, formal specifications of software systems can be checked, tested and tuned before an implementation is built. A theorem prover based on explicit induction has been built for an earlier version of the language [Bevers85].

These software tools were written in Ada. We used the syntax-directed compiler generator MIRA [Mira84] and the metaprogramming language ABSYNT [Craeynest87]. The software tools were constructed for the specification language as described in this book except for mixfix notation, overloading, clusters and Cartesian products of sorts. Incorporation of error handling is planned for the near future. All examples of Chapters 3, 4, 5 (the ferry problem) and 6 (the mini-PABX) have been checked and tested. An example of rapid prototyping, concerning the specification of the mini-PABX, can be found in Appendix B. A graphical interface for this mini-PABX has been built [Delva88].

Appendix A: Syntax

> "This is the sort of English up with which I will not put."
> *Winston Churchill*

The syntax notation used to describe the algebraic specification language was explained in the introduction of Chapter 3.

```
<specification> = <element>+

<element> =
  <module> | <cluster> | <scheme> | <instantiation> | <run>

<module> =
  "module" [ <module name> ] ";"
    [ <import clause> ]
    [ <export clause> ]
    [ <sorts part> ]
    [ <constructors part> ]
    [ <operations part> ]
    [ <declarations part> ]
    [ <constructor axioms part> ]
    [ <operation axioms part> ]
    [ <theorems part> ]
  "end" "module" [ <module name> ] ";"

<import clause> =
  "import" ( <item name list> "from" <place name list>
    [ <rename clause> ] ";" )+

<export clause> =
  "export" ( <item name list> [ "from" <place name list> ]
    [ "to" <place name list> ] ";" )+

<item name list> =
    <item name> ( "," <item name> )*
  | "all" [ "except" <item name> ( "," <item name> )* ]

<item name> =
  <sort name> | <constructor name> | <operation name>
```

<place name list> = <place name> ("," <place name>)*

<place name> = <module name> | <requirement name>

<rename clause> = **"rename"**
  (<item name> | <element name>) **"as"** ("identifier" | <pattern>)(","
  (<item name> | <element name>) **"as"** ("identifier" | <pattern>))*

<element name> = <module name> | <cluster name> |
  <scheme name> | <requirement name>

<sorts part> = (**"sort"** | **"sorts"**)
  (<sort name> ["==" <sort name> ("*" <sort name>)*] ";")+

<constructors part> = (**"constructor"** | **"constructors"**)
  (<constructor declaration>)+

<constructor declaration> =
  <constructor name> ("," <constructor name>)* ":"
  [["$"] <sort name> ("*" ["$"] <sort name>)*]
  "->" <sort name> <safety condition> ";"

<safety condition> = "$$" | "??" | "$" <boolean expression> "$"

<operations part> = (**"operation"** | **"operations"**)
  (<operation declaration>)+

<operation declaration> =
  <operation name> ("," <operation name>)* ":"
  [<sort name> ("*" <sort name>)*] "->" <sort name> ";"

<constructor axioms part> =
  (**"constructor" "axiom"** | **"constructor" "axioms"**)
  (<constructor axiom>)+

<constructor axiom> =
  [<boolean expression> "=>"]
  <constr expression> "==" <constr expression> ";"

<operation axioms part> =
  (**"operation" "axiom"** | **"operation" "axioms"**)
    (<operation axiom>)+

<operation axiom> = <left-hand side> "==" <expression> ";"

<theorems part> =
  (**"theorem"** | **"theorems"**)
    (<theorem>)+

<theorem> = [<boolean expression> "=>"]
  <expression> "==" <expression> ";"

<declarations part> = "**declare**" (<declarations>)+

<declarations> = <variable> ("," <variable>)* ":" <sort name> ";"

<cluster> =
  "**cluster**" [<cluster name>] ";"
    (<module> | <requirement> | <instantiation>)+
  "**end**" "**cluster**" [<cluster name>] ";"

<scheme> =
  "**scheme**" <scheme name> [<claimed element list>] ";"
    <scheme element list>
  "**end**" "**scheme**" [<scheme name>] ";"

<claimed element list> = "[" <scheme element list> "]"

<scheme element list> =
  (<module> | <cluster> | <instantiation> | <requirement>)+

<requirement> =
  "**requirement**" [<requirement name>] ";"
    [<import clause>]
    [<export clause>]
    [<sorts part>]
    [<operations part>]
    [<declarations part>]
    [<theorems part>]
  "**end**" "**requirement**" [<requirement name>] ";"

<instantiation> =
  "**instantiate**" <scheme name> [<rename clause>] ";"
    ("**with**" <place name> "**as**" <place name> (","
      <item name> "**as**" <item name>)* ";"
)*
  "**end**" "**instantiate**" [<scheme name>] ";"

<run> =
  "**run**" [<run name>] ";"
    <import clause>
    [<declarations part>]
    [<questions part>]
  "**end**" "**run**" [<run name>] ";"

```
<questions part> =
  ( "question" | "questions" )
    ( <question> )+

<question> = <expression> ";"

<left-hand side> = [ <marker> ]
  ( ( "identifier" | "qualified identifier" )
      [ "(" <constr expression> ( "," <constr expression> )* ")" ]
  | ( <token> | <constr expression> )+ )

<constr expression> = [ <marker> ]
  ( <variable>
  | "(" <constr expression> ")"
  | ( "identifier" | "qualified identifier" )
      [ "(" <constr expression> ( "," <constr expression> )* ")" ]
  | ( <token> | <constr expression> )+ )

<expression> = [ <marker> ] ( <ifthenelse construct> |
  <case construct> | <let construct> | "(" <expression> ")" |
  <prefix> | <mixfix> | <variable> )

<ifthenelse construct> =
  "if" <boolean expression>
    "then" <expression>
    "else" <expression>
  "end" "if"

<case construct> =
  "case" <case index> "of"
    ( <case arm> )+
    [ "otherwise" ":" <expression> ";" ]
  "end" "case"

<case index> = <expression>

<case arm> = <choice> ":" <expression> ";"

<choice> = <constr expression>

<let construct> =
  "let"
    ( <let arm> )+
    "in"
      <let expression>
  "end" "let"

<let arm> = <variable> "==" <expression> ";"
```

<let expression> = <expression>

<prefix> = ("identifier" | "qualified identifier")
  ["(" <expression> ("," <expression>)* ")"]

<mixfix> = (<token> | <expression>)+

<boolean expression> = <expression>

<module name> = "identifier"

<cluster name> = "identifier"

<scheme name> = "identifier"

<requirement name> = "identifier"

<run name> = "identifier"

<sort name> = "identifier" | "qualified identifier"

<constructor name> = "identifier" | "qualified identifier" | <pattern>

<operation name> = "identifier" | "qualified identifier" | <pattern>

<pattern> = (<token> | "_")+

<variable> = "identifier"

<marker> = "$" | "?" | "!" | "$$" | "??"

<token> = "identifier" | "number" | "+" | "-" | "*" | "/" | "." | "%" | "^" | "@" | "&" |
  "[" | "]" | "=" | "," | ";" | ":" | "<" | ">" | "≤" | "≥" | "<=>" | "(" | ")"

Appendix B: Rapid Prototyping, the Mini-PABX

"Saying is one thing, and doing is another."
Montaigne

At the Department of Computer Science, we have developed several prototypes of software tools: a parser, a checker of the import and export clauses, a type controller, a checker of the uniqueness, completeness and constructiveness constraints, and a reductor [Devriendt86]. In this way, formal specifications of software systems can be checked, tested and tuned before an implementation has been built.

To enable rapid prototyping, the specification language is provided with a new construct, namely a *run*. A run contains *questions*, i.e. expressions, that must be reduced. It has the following syntactic form:

```
<run> =
  "run" [ <run name> ] ";"
    <import clause>
    [ <declarations part> ]
    [ <questions part> ]
  "end" "run" [ <run name> ] ";"

<questions part> =
  ( "question" | "questions" )
    ( <question> )+

<question> = <expression> ";"
```

The formal specification of the mini-PABX discussed in Chapter 6 was manually modified. The major modifications were the elimination of overloading and mixfix notation (because they are not yet supported by the reductor). Then, an instantiation of the scheme MiniPABX was made such that the requirement PhoneIdentity is bound with the module Nat:

```
instantiate MiniPABX;
with PhoneIdentity as Nat,
   PhoneIdentity as Nat,
   errPhoneIdentity as zero,
```

```
    eq as eq;
  end instantiate MiniPABX;
```

Finally, a run was added. The question contained in the run describes the following scenario: The user of phone 2 goes off-hook and dials the number of phone 1. Then, the user of phone 1 goes off-hook. Next, the user of phone 2 operates the recall button and dials the number of phone 3. Finally, the user of phone 3 goes off-hook. At that moment we want a snapshot of the situation. This snapshot can be obtained by giving the following run to the reductor:

```
run call2to1enquiry23;
  import all from PhonePool, MessageScheduler, CallStates,
    PhoneStates, EnquiryStates, Phone, MessagePairs, Nat,
    PhoneMessages, UserMessages, Codes, EnquiryMessages;
  declare phpool, newpabx1, newpabx2 , newpabx3, newpabx4,
    newpabx5: PhonePool; ph1, ph2, ph3: Nat;
  question
    let ph1 == succ( zero );
        ph2 == succ( succ( zero ) );
        ph3 == succ( succ( succ( zero ) ) );
    in
        let phpool == addPhone( addPhone( addPhone(
                  emptyPhonePool,
                  newPhone( ph1 ) ),
                  newPhone( ph2 ) ),
                  newPhone( ph3 ) );
        in
            let newpabx1 == transform( send( U( offHook ), ph2 ),
                    phpool );
            in
            let newpabx2 == transform( send( U( dialCode(
                    phoneCode( ph1 ) ) ), ph2 ), newpabx1 );
            in
            let newpabx3 == transform( send( U( offHook ), ph1 ),
                    newpabx2 );
            in
            let newpabx4 == transform( send( U( button ), ph2 ),
                    newpabx3 );
            in
```

```
        let newpabx5 == transform( send( U( dialCode(
                phoneCode( ph3 ) ) ), ph2 ), newpabx4 );
            in
                transform( send( U( offHook ), ph3 ), newpabx5 )
            end let
            end let
            end let
            end let
            end let
        end let
      end let
  end run;
```

The output produced by the reductor is as follows:

```
+----------------------------------------------------+
|                                                    |
|                                                    |
|   Interpreter for Modular Algebraic Specifications |
|                                                    |
|            Ada version 1.0                         |
|                                                    |
|                                                    |
+----------------------------------------------------+

REDUCED: PhonePool.addPhone
    ( PhonePool.addPhone
        ( PhonePool.addPhone
            ( PhonePool.emptyPhonePool,
              Phone.mk
                ( Nat.succ
                    ( Nat.zero ),
                  PhoneStates.E
                    ( EnquiryStates.heldBy
                        ( Nat.succ
                            ( Nat.succ
                                ( Nat.zero ) ) ) ),
                  PhoneModes.normal ) ),
          Phone.mk
            ( Nat.succ
                ( Nat.succ
                    ( Nat.zero ) ),
```

```
          PhoneStates.C
            ( CallStates.connected
                 ( Nat.succ
                     ( Nat.succ
                         ( Nat.succ
                             ( Nat.zero ) ) ) ) ),
          PhoneModes.enquiry
            ( Nat.succ
                ( Nat.zero ) ) ) ),
  Phone.mk
    ( Nat.succ
        ( Nat.succ
            ( Nat.succ
                ( Nat.zero ) ) ),
      PhoneStates.C
        ( CallStates.connected
             ( Nat.succ
                 ( Nat.succ
                     ( Nat.zero ) ) ) ),
      PhoneModes.normal ) )
```

We see that phone 1 is held in a kind of waiting state by phone 2, i.e. the state of ph1 is heldBy(ph2). Communication between phones 2 and 3 is possible, i.e. the state of ph2 is connected(ph3) and the state of ph3 is connected(ph2). This call is an enquiry call activated by phone 2 during a call with phone 1, i.e. the mode of ph2 is enquiry(ph1). Neither phone 1 nor phone 3 have activated an enquiry call, i.e. ph1 as well as ph3 have mode normal.

The output of the reductor as given above is not very readable. Therefore, we have made a graphical interface [Delva88], running on a Sun 3/50 workstation. The output of this interface is similar to the graphical representations of Chapter 6. The input to the interface can be given in a very natural way, e.g., going off-hook is executed by touching the hook of the phone by means of the mouse. Thanks to rapid prototyping, we detected not only several inconsistencies and errors in the formal and informal specifications of the mini–PABX, but we detected also many design errors in the PABX itself.

Bibliography

"A man should keep his little brain attic stocked
with all the furniture that he's likely to use,
and the rest he can put away in the lumber room
of his library, where he can get it if he wants it"
Sir Arthur Conan Doyle

ACT Group [1985]. Material for the working group on *Algebraic Specifications in ACT ONE* during the TAPSOFT Conference at the TU Berlin. March 1985

ADA Joint Program Office [1983]. *Reference Manual for the Ada Programming Language.* Pentagon (U.S.A.) ANSI/MIL-STD 1815 A. January 1983

BACKUS, J. [1978]. Can programming be liberated from the von Neuman style? *Communications of the ACM.* Vol 21. Num 8. 613-641

BELKHOUCHE, B. and URBAN, J. E. [1986]. Direct Implementation of Abstract Data Types from Abstract Specifications. *IEEE Transactions on Software Engineering.* May 1986. Vol SE-12. Num 5. 649-661

BELL TELEPHONE MANUFACTURING COMPANY [1985a]. *The new dimension in digital communications.* ITT 5200 BCS System Description

BELL TELEPHONE MANUFACTURING COMPANY [1985b]. *5400 BCS Digital Business Communication Systems*

BERGHAMMER, R. EHLER, H. and ZIERER, H. [1988]. Towards an algebraic specification of code generation. *Science of Computer Programming.* 11 (1988). 45-63

BERGSTRA, J. A., BROY, M., TUCKER, J. and WIRSING, M. [1981]. On the Power of Algebraic Specifications. *Proceedings 10th International Symposium on Mathematical Foundations of Computer Science.* Lecture Notes in Computer Science 118. Springer-Verlag. Berlin. 193-204

BERGSTRA, J. A. and TUCKER, J. V. [1982]. The completeness of the algebraic specification methods for computable data types. *Information and Control* Vol 54 (1982). Num 3. 186-200

BERGSTRA, J. A., HEERING, J. and KLINT, P. [1985]. *Algebraic definition of a simple programming language.* Centrum voor Wiskunde en Informatica. Amsterdam. Report CS-R8504. February 1985

BERGSTRA, J. A. [1987]. *Terminologie van algebraïsche specificaties.* Kluwer Programmatuurkunde

BERNOT, G., BIDOIT, M. and CHOPPY, C. [1986a]. Abstract Implementations and Correctness Proofs. *Proceedings 3rd Annual Symposium on Theoretical Aspects of Computer Science.* MONIEN, B. and VIDAL-NAQUET, G. (eds). Lecture Notes in Computer Science 210. Springer-Verlag. Berlin. 236-251

BERNOT, G. [1986b]. *Une sémantique algébrique pour une spécification différenciée des exceptions et des erreurs; application à l'implémentation et aux primitives de structuration des spécifications formelles.* Doctoral dissertation. Université de Paris-Sud Centre d'Orsay. February 1986

BERT, D. and ECHAHED, R. [1986]. Design and Implementation of a generic, logic and functional programming language. *European Symposium on Programming 86.* ROBINET, B. and WILHELM, R. (eds). Lecture Notes on Computer Science 213. Springer-Verlag. Berlin. 119-132

BEVERS, E. [1985]. *Een verifikatie- en reduktiesysteem voor algebraïsche specifikaties.* Eindwerk. Departement Computerwetenschappen. K. U. Leuven. Juli 1985

BEVERS, E., VAN HOREBEEK, I., LEWI, J. [1987]. *On Proving Termination of Constructive Algebraic Specifications.* Report CW59. K.U.Leuven (Belgium). Department of Computer Science

BIDOIT, M., CHOPPY, C. and VOISIN, F. [1985a]. The Asspegique specification environment. Motivations and Design. *Recent Trends in Data Type Specification.* KREOWSKI, H.-J. (ed). Informatik-Fachberichte 116. Springer-Verlag. Berlin. 54-72

BIDOIT, M., BIEBOW, B., GAUDEL, M., GRESSE, C. and GUIHO, G. D. [1985b]. Exception Handling: Formal Specification and Systematic Program Construction. *IEEE Transactions on software engineering* March 1985. Vol SE-11. Num 3. 242-252

BIDOIT, M., GAUDEL, M. and MAUBOUSSIN, A. [1987]. *How to make algebraic specifications more understandable? An experiment with the PLUSS specification language.* Université de Paris-Sud. Centre d'Orsay. Rapport de Recherche 343

BIEBOW, B. and HAGELSTEIN, J. [1985]. Algebraic Specification of Synchronisation and Errors: A Telephonic Example. *Formal Methods and Software Development. Proceedings of the International Joint Conference on Theory and Practice of Software Development (TAPSOFT).*

Volume 2: Colloquium on Software Engineering. EHRIG, H. and FLOYD, C. (eds). Berlin. March 1985. Lecture Notes in Computer Science 186. Springer-Verlag. 294-308

BIRKHOFF, G. [1938]. Structure of Abstract Algebras. *Proc. Cambridge Philosophical Society* 31. 433-454

BIRKHOFF, G. and LIPSON, D. [1970]. Heterogeneous Algebras. *Journal of Combinatorial Theory* 8. 115-133

BJORNER, D. [1982]. Stepwise Transformation of Software Architectures. *Formal Specification & Software Development*. BJORNER, D. and JONES, C. (eds). Prentice-Hall International. Chapter 11

BOEHM, B. W., BROWN, J. R., MCLEOD, G., LIPOW, M. and MERRIT, M. [1978]. *Characteristics of Software Quality*. TRW Series of Software Technology. North-Holland Publishing Co. Amsterdam

BOEHM, B. W. [1976]. Software engineering. *IEEE Transactions on Computers*. Vol C-25. Num 12. 1226-1241

BOYER, R. S. and MOORE, J. S. [1979]. *A Computational Logic*. Academic Press. New York.

BROY, M., PEPPER, P. and WIRSING, M. [1981]. On Design Principles for Programming Languages: An Algebraic Approach. *Algorithmic Languages*. DE BAKKER, VAN VLIET (eds). North-Holland. 203-219

BROY, M. and WIRSING, M. [1984]. A systematic study of models of abstract data types. *Theoretical Computer Science*. 33 (1984). North-Holland. 139-174

BROY, M. [1988a]. Equational specification of partial higher-order algebras. *Theoretical Computer Science*. Vol 57. Num 1. April 1988. 3-45

BROY, M. [1988b]. Views of Queues. *Science of Computer Programming*. 11 (1988). 65-86

BUCHBERGER, B. [1985]. Basic Features and Development of the Critical pair/ Completion procedure. *Rewriting Techniques and Applications*. JOUANNAUD, J. P. (ed). Lecture Notes in Computer Science 202. Springer-Verlag. 1-45

BURSTALL, R. and GOGUEN, J. A. [1977]. Putting theories together to make specifications. *Proc. of 5th International Joint Conference on Artificial Intelligence*. Cambridge. MASS (1977). 1045-1058

BURSTALL, R. and GOGUEN, J. A. [1980]. Semantics of CLEAR, a specification language. *Abstract Software Specifications*. BJORNER, D. (ed). Proc. 1979 Copenhagen Winter School. Lecture Notes in Computer Science Vol. 86. Springer-Verlag. 292-332

BURSTALL, R. and GOGUEN, J. A. [1982]. Algebras, Theories and Freeness: an Introduction for Computer Scientists. *Theoretical Foundations of Programming Methodology*. BROY, M. and SCHMIDT, G. (eds). D. Reidel Publishing Company 239-349

BURTON, C. T. P. [1988]. *Verification and Transformation of Simple Recursive Programs - an Algebraic Approach*. Department of Computer Science. Queen Mary College. Report CSL 449. June 1988

CRAEYNEST D., KINNAES, D., DE BISSCHOP, W., DE NIEL, A. and DE VLAMINCK, K. [1987]. *A Metaprogramming Language based on Abstract Syntax - Language Description*. Report CW57. August 1987. K. U. Leuven (Belgium). Department of Computer Science

CHERIFA, A. B. and LESCANNE, P. [1986]. An actual implementation of a procedure that mechanically proves termination of rewriting systems based on inequalities between polynomial interpretations. *8th International Conference on Automated Deduction*. SIEKMANN, J. (ed). Proceedings. Oxford. July 1986. 42-51

CIP Language Group [1985]. *The Munich Project CIP. Volume1: The Wide Spectrum Language CIP-L*. Springer-Verlag. Lecture Notes in Computer Science 183

CLEAVELAND, J. [1980]. Mathematical specifications. *Sigplan Notices* Vol 15. Num 12. 1980

COHN, P. M. [1965]. *Universal algebra*. Harper and Row. New York

COLEMAN, D. and GALLIMORE, R. M. [1985]. *Software Engineering Using Executable Specifications*. Hewlett Packard Labs. Bristol

CULIK, K. [1983]. On formal and informal proofs for program correctness. *Sigplan Notices* Vol 18. Num 1. January 1983

DECLERFAYT, O., DEMEUSE, B., WAUTIER, F., SCHOBBENS, P.-Y. and MILGROM, E. [1989]. *Precise Standards through Formal Specifications: A Case Study: the UNIX File System*. Report. Université Catholique de Louvain. Belgium

DELVA, R. [1988]. *Grafisch grensvlak voor een telefooncentrale*. Eindwerk. Departement Computerwetenschappen. K. U. Leuven

DEMARCO, T. [1978]. *Structured Analysis and System Specification.* Yourdon Press. New York

DE REMER, F. and KRON, H. H. [1976]. Programming-in-the-Large Versus Programming-in-the-Small. *IEEE Transactions on Software Engineering.* Vol SE-2. Num 2. June 1976. 80-86

DERSHOWITZ, N. [1979]. A note on simplification orderings. *Information Processing Letters.* Vol. 9, Num. 5. November 1979. 212-215

DERSHOWITZ, N. [1982]. Orderings for term-rewriting systems. *Theoretical Computer Science.* Vol 17. Num 3. March 1982. 279-301

DERSHOWITZ, N. [1985]. Termination. *Rewriting Techniques and Applications.* JOUANNAUD, J. P. (ed). Lecture Notes in Computer Science 202. Springer New York. 180-224

DEVRIENDT, E. and VAN GESTEL, E. [1986]. *Implementatie van een specificatietaal gebaseerd op abstracte data types.* Eindwerk. Departement Computerwetenschappen. K. U. Leuven. Juli 1986

DIJKSTRA, E. W. [1976]. *A discipline of programming.* Prentice Hall

DUPONCHEEL, L., HEYMAN, J. and VAN PUYMBROECK, W. [1987a]. *Experience with the prototype Software Environment for ADTS.* BTM-RC Report. Bell Telephone Mfg. Co. Antwerp. August 1987

DUPONCHEEL, L., HEYMAN, J., VAN PUYMBROECK, W., LEWI, J. and VAN HOREBEEK, I. [1987b]. The Algebraic Data Type Specification Language. *Microprocessing and Microprogramming.* Vol 21. Num 1-5. Proceedings of EUROMICRO 87. SCHUMNY, H. and MOLGAARD, J. (eds). September 14-17 1987. Portsmouth. North-Holland. 231-240

DUPONCHEEL, L., HEYMAN, J. and VAN PUYMBROECK, W. [1988]. Algebraic Data Type Specifications. A Language, Method and Tools. To appear in the proceedings of *CompEuro 88.* Brussels. April 11-14 1988

EHRIG, H., KREOWSKI, H. and WEBER, H. [1978]. Algebraic specification schemes for data base systems. *Proc. 4th Int. Conf. Very Large Data Bases.* 1978

EHRIG, H., KREOWSKI, H., MAHR, B. and PADAWITZ, P. [1982]. Algebraic Implementation of Abstract Data Types. *Theoretical Computer Science.* Vol 20. July 1982. 209-263

EHRIG, H., KREOWSKI, H., THATCHER, J., WAGNER, E. and WRIGHT, J. [1984]. Parameter Passing in Algebraic Specification Languages. *Theoretical Computer Science.* 28 (1984). North Holland. 45-81

EHRIG, H. and MAHR, B. [1985]. *Fundamentals of algebraic specifications 1. Equations and Initial Semantics.* EATCS Monographs on Theoretical Computer Science. Springer-Verlag. Berlin

EVANS, T. [1978]. Word Problems. *Bulletin of the AMS.* Num 84-5. 789-802

FIELDING, E. and JONES, C. [1982]. Program Design by Data Refinement. *Formal Specification & Software Development.* BJORNER, D. and JONES, C. (eds). Prentice-Hall International. Chapter 10

FLOYD, R. W. [1967]. Assigning meaning to programs. *Mathematical aspects of computer science.* American Mathematical Society. SCHARTZ, J. T. (ed). 19-31

FUTATSUGI, K., GOGUEN, J. A., JOUANNAUD, J. and MESEGUER, J. [1985]. Principles of OBJ2. *Proceedings of the Annual Symposium on Principles of Programming Languages 1985.* ACM. 52-66

GANZINGER, H. [1981]. *Parameterized specifications: parameter passing and optimizing implementation.* TUM-I8110

GIARRATANA, V., GIMONA, F. and MONTANARI, U. [1976]. Observability concepts in abstract data type specifications. *5th MFCS.* Lecture Notes in Computer Science 45. 1976. 576-587

GOBEL, R. [1987]. Ground Confluence. *Proceedings of the Second International Conference on Rewriting Techniques and Applications.* LESCANNE, P. (ed). Bordeaux. May 1987. Lecture Notes in Computer Science 256. Springer Berlin. 156-167

GOGOLLA, M., DROSTEN, K., LIPECK, U. and EHRICH, H. [1984a]. Algebraic and Operational Semantics of Specifications allowing exceptions and errors. *Theoretical Computer Science.* 34 (1984). 289-313

GOGOLLA, M. [1984b]. Partially ordered sorts in algebraic specifications. *Ninth Colloquium on Trees in Algebra and Programming.* COURCELLE, B. (ed). Bordeaux. March 5-7 1984. 139-153

GOGUEN, J. A. [1974]. Semantics of Computation. *Proceedings of the First International Symposium on Category Theory Applied to Computation and Control.* University of Massachusetts at Amherst. 1974. 234-249 Also in: Lecture Notes in Computer Science Vol 25. Springer-Verlag. 1975. 151-163

GOGUEN, J. A., THATCHER, J. and WAGNER, E. [1978]. An initial algebra approach to the specification, correctness, and implementation of abstract data types. *Current trends in programming methodology.* YEH, R., (ed). Prentice Hall. 80-149

GOGUEN, J. A. and TARDO, J. [1979]. An Introduction to OBJ: A Language for Writing and Testing Software Specifications. *Specification of Reliable Software.* IEEE Press. 1979. 170-189

GOGUEN, J. A. [1980]. How to prove algebraic inductive hypotheses without induction, with applications to the correctness of date type implementations. *Proceedings of the 5th Conference on Automated Deduction.* BIBEL, W. and KOWALSKI, R. (eds). Lecture Notes in Computer Science 87. Springer-Verlag. 356-373

GOGUEN, J. A. and MESEGUER, J. [1981]. Completeness of many-sorted equational logic. *Sigplan Notices* Vol 16. Num 7. 24-32

GOGUEN, J. A. and MESEGUER, J. [1982]. Rapid prototyping in the OBJ executable specification language. ACM *Sigsoft software engineering notes* Vol 7. Num 5 (1982) 75-84

GOGUEN, J.A., MESEGUER, J. and PLAISTED, D. [1983]. Programming with Parameterized Abstract Objects in OBJ. *Theory and Practice of Software Technology.* FERRARI, D., BOLOGNANI, M. and GOGUEN, J. (eds). North-Holland. 1983. 163-193

GOGUEN, J. A. and BURSTALL, R. [1984a]. Some Fundamental Algebraic Tools for the Semantics of computation. Part1: Comma Categories, Colimits, Signatures and Theories. *Theoretical Computer Science.* 31 (1984) 175-209

GOGUEN, J. A. and BURSTALL, R. [1984b]. Some Fundamental Algebraic Tools for the Semantics of computation. Part2: Signed and Abstract Theories. *Theoretical Computer Science* 31 (1984) 263-295

GOGUEN, J. A. [1984c]. Parameterized Programming. *IEEE Transactions on software engineering.* Vol SE-10. Num 5. September 1984. 528-543

GOGUEN, J. A. and MESEGUER, J. [1984d]. Equality, Types, Modules and (Why not?) Generics for Logic Programming. *The Journal of Logic Programming* Vol 1 Num 2. 1984. 179-210. Appeared also in *Proceedings 1984 Logic Programming Symposium.* Upsala. Sweden. 115-125

GOGUEN, J. A. and MESEGUER, J. [1985]. Order-Sorted Algebra I: Partial and Overloaded Operators, Errors and Inheritance. *Working Material of the International Summer School on Advanced Programming Methodologies.* San Sebastian. September 2-6 1985

GOGUEN, J. A. and MESEGUER, J. [1986]. Extensions and Foundations of Object-Oriented Programming. *Sigplan Notices* Vol 21. Num 10. October 1986

GOGUEN, J. A. [1987a]. Modular Algebraic Specification of Some Basic Geometrical Constructions. *AI Journal, Special Issue on Computational Geometry*. MUNDY, J. (ed). 1987. To appear

GOGUEN, J. A. and MESEGUER, J. [1987b]. Order-Sorted Algebra Solves the Constructor-Selector, Multiple Representation and Coercion Problems. To appear in *Logic in Computer Science*. Cornell

GOGUEN, J. A. [1987c]. Private Communication about error handling

GOGUEN, J. A. and MESEGUER, J. [1987d]. Remarks on Remarks on Many-Sorted Equational Logic. *Sigplan Notices*. Vol 22. Num 4. 41-48

GOLDBERG, A. and ROBSON, D. [1983]. *Smalltalk-80: The Language and its Implementation*. Addison-Wesley. Reading

GOLDBLATT, R. [1979]. *TOPOI The Categorical Analysis of Logic*. North-Holland Publishing Company. Amsterdam

GOOVAERS, S. [1986]. *ADTS in een PABX. Specificatie voor call-handling faciliteit*. Eindwerk. Hoger Instituut der Kempen 1985-1986

GOOVAERTS, V. and VAN PUYMBROECK, W. [1983]. Int. Rep. (EA4/VGWVP/583) Bell Telephone M. C. Antwerp

GOOVAERTS, V. and VAN PUYMBROECK, W. [1984]. Executable algebraic specifications. *Advances in Microprocessing and Microprogramming*. MYHRHAUG, B., WILSON, D. R. (eds). Elsevier 1984. 99-103

GORDON, M. J. C. [1979]. *The denotational description of programming languages*. Springer-Verlag. New York

GRAETZER, G. [1968 or 1969]. *Universal Algebra*. Van Nostrand. Princeton.

GRIES, D. [1981]. *The Science of Programming*. Springer-Verlag. New York

GUTTAG, J. V. [1975]. *The Specification and Application to Programming of Abstract Data Types*. PhD thesis. University of Toronto. Computer Science Department. Report CSRG-59

GUTTAG, J. V. [1977]. Abstract Data Types and the Development of Data Structures. *Communications of the ACM*. June 1977. Vol 20. Num 6. 396-404

GUTTAG, J. V., HOROWITZ, E. and MUSSER, D. [1978a]. The design of data type specifications. *Current trends in programming methodology.* Vol 4. YEH, R., (ed). Prentice Hall. 60–79

GUTTAG, J. V., HOROWITZ, E. and MUSSER, D. [1978b]. Abstract Data Types and Software Validation. *Communications of the ACM* Dec 1978. Vol 21. Num 12

GUTTAG, J. V. and HORNING, J. J. [1978c]. The Algebraic Specification of Abstract Data Types. *Acta Informatica* 10. 27–52

GUTTAG, J. V., HORNING, J. J. and WING, J. M. [1982]. Some notes on putting formal specifications to productive use. *Science of Computer Programming.* 2 (1984). North-Holland Publishing Company. 53–68

GUTTAG, J. V., HORNING, J. J. and WING, J. M. [1985]. *Larch in Five Easy Pieces.* Digital Systems Research Center. Report 5. July 1985

HAYES, I. J. [1986]. Specification Directed Module Testing. *IEEE Transactions on Software Engineering.* January 1986. Vol SE-12. Num 1. 124–133

HEYMAN, J., DUPONCHEEL, L. and VAN PUYMBROECK, W. [1986]. *The Algebraic Data Type Specification language.* Bell Telephone Mfg. Co. Antwerp. Working Report. October 1986

HIGGINS, P. J. [1963]. Algebras With a Scheme of Operators. *Mathematische Nachrichten* 27. 115–132

HILTON, P. and WU, Y-C. [1974]. *A Course in Modern Algebra.* Wiley. New-York

HOARE, C. A. R. [1972]. Proof of Correctness of Data Representations. *Acta Informatica.* 1.

HORNUNG, G. and RAULEFS, P. [1980]. Terminal algebra semantics and retractions for abstract data types. *7th Int. Coll. Automata, Languages, and Programming.* Springer-Verlag. Lecture Notes in Computer Science 85. 310–323

HUET, G., LANKFORD, D.S. [1978]. *On the uniform halting problem for term rewriting systems.* Rapport Laboria 359. INRIA. Le Chesnay. France. August 1979

HUET, G. and OPPEN, D. C. [1980] Equations and Rewrite Rules. A Survey. *Formal Language Theory. Perspectives and Open Problems.* BOOK, R. V. (ed). Academic Press. 1980

HUET, G. and HULLOT, J. M. [1982]. Proofs by induction in equational theories with constructors. *21st IEEE Symposium on Foundations of Computer Science*. 96-107

HUYGHE, D. [1987]. *Algebraïsche specificatie van een grafische taal.* Eindwerk. Departement Computerwetenschappen. K. U. Leuven. Juli 1987

JACKSON, M. A. [1975]. *Principles of Program Design*. Academic Press. London

JACKSON, M. A. [1983]. *System Development*. Prentice-Hall International. Hemel Hempstead

JACOBS, J. [1986]. Lecture about the specification of call handling facilities in the PABX. Geel. November 1986

JOUANNAUD, J.P., LESCANNE, P. and REINIG, F. [1982]. Recursive decomposition ordering. *Proceedings of the second IFIP Workshop on Formal Description of Programming Concepts*. Garmisch-Partenkirchen West-Germany. 331-348

KAMIN, S. and LEVY, J. J. [1980]. *Two generalizations of the recursive path ordering*. Unpublished note. Department of Computer Science. University of Illinois. February 1980

KAPLAN, S. [1984]. Conditional rewrite rules. *Theoretical Computer Science*. 33 (1984). North-Holland. 175-193

KAPUR, D., NARENDRAN, P., SIVAKUMAR, G. [1985]. A path ordering for proving termination of term rewriting systems. *Proceedings of the Tenth Colloquium on Trees in Algebra and Programming*. EHRIG, H., FLOYD, C., NIVAT, M., THATCHER, J. (eds). Lecture Notes in Computer Science 185. Springer Berlin. 173-187

KLAEREN, H. A. [1983]. *Algebraische Spezifikation. Eine Einführung*. Springer-Verlag. Berlin

KLAEREN, H. A. [1984]. A constructive method for abstract algebraic software specification. *Theoretical Computer Science*. Vol 30. Num 2. August 1984. 139-204

KLAEREN, H. A. [1985]. *Bibliography on Algebraic Software Specification*. Unpublished

KLUZNIAK, F. and SZPAKOWICZ, S. [1985]. *Prolog for Programmers*. Academic Press. London

KNUTH, D. E. and BENDIX, P. B. [1970]. Simple word problems in universal algebras. *Computational Problems in Abstract Algebra*. LEECH, J. (ed). Pergamon Press. 1970. 263-297

KOWALSKI, R. [1982]. Logic as a Computer Language. *Logic Programming*. CLARK. K. L. and TARNLUND, S. A. (eds). Academic Press. 3-16

KUTZLER, B. and LICHTENBERGER, F. [1983]. *Bibliography on Abstract Data Types*. Informatik-Fachberichte 68. Springer-Verlag. Berlin

LAUT, A. [1980]. Safe procedural implementations of algebraic types. *Information Processing Letters*. Vol 11. Num 4

LAUT, A. [1983]. An algebraic specification of Pascal's file type. *Sigplan Notices* Vol 18. Num 4. April 1983

LESCANNE, P. [1984]. Uniform termination of term rewriting systems: Recursive Decomposition Ordering with Status. *Proceedings of the Ninth Colloquium on Trees in Algebra and Programming*. COURCELLE, B. (ed). Cambridge University Press. 181-194

LESCANNE, P. [1985]. *An introduction to term rewriting*. Working Material at the International Summer School on Advanced Programming Technologies. San Sebastian. September 2-6, 1985

LEWI, J. and VAN HOREBEEK, I. [1985a]. *Denotational Semantics. A case study: Karel The Robot*. Report CW36. June 1985. K.U. Leuven (Belgium). Department of Computer Science

LEWI, J. and VAN HOREBEEK, I. [1985b]. *Algebraic Specifications. A case study: Karel The Robot*. Report CW37. June 1985. K.U. Leuven (Belgium). Department of Computer Science

LEWI, J. and PAREDAENS, J. [1986]. *Data structures of Pascal, Algol 68, PL/1 and Ada*. Springer-Verlag.

LIENTZ, B. P. and SWANSON, E. B. [1980]. *Software Maintenance Management*. Addison Wesley

LISKOV, B. and ZILLES, S. N. [1974]. Programming with abstract data types. *Sigplan Notices* Vol 9. Num 4. 50-59

LISKOV, B. and GUTTAG, J. V. [1986]. *Abstraction and Specification in Program Development*. MIT Press. Cambridge

MALLGREN, W. [1982]. *Formal Specification of Interactive Graphics Programming Languages*. An ACM Distinguished Dissertation 1982

MANNA, Z. and NESS, S. [1970]. On the termination of Markov algorithms. *Proceedings of the Third Hawaii International Conference on System Science.* Honolulu. January 1970. 789-792

MARTIN, U. [1987]. How to choose the weights in the Knuth Bendix ordering. *Rewriting Techniques and Applications.* Lescanne, P. (ed). Proceedings. Bordeaux. May 1987. 42-53

MAJSTER, M. E. [1977]. Limits of the Algebraic Specification of Abstract Data Types. *Sigplan Notices.* Vol 12. Num 10. 37-41

MCNULTY, G. [1976]. The Decision Problem for Equational Bases of Algebras. *Annals of Mathematical Logic.* Num 11. 193-259

MESEGUER, J. and GOGUEN, J. A. [1985a]. Initiality, Induction and Computability. *Algebraic Methods in Semantics.* Cambridge University Press. 1985. NIVAT, M. and REYNOLDS, J. (eds) 459-540

MESEGUER, J. and GOGUEN, J. A. [1985b]. *Deduction with Many-Sorted Rewrite Rules* Technical Report, SRI International, Computer Science Lab. 1985

MEYER, B. [1988]. *Object-Oriented Software Construction.* Prentice Hall. New York

MILGROM, E., DARIMONT, R., DECLERFAYT, O., DEMEUSE, B., SCHOBBENS, P.-Y. and WAUTIER, F. [1988]. A Guided Tour among Specification Tools and Languages. *International workshop on Software Engineering and its Applications.* Toulouse. December 1988

MIRA Development Group [1984]. *MIRA / Pascal, C, Ada User's Manual.* Version 3. Expert Software Systems N. V. Gent

MONTEYNE, M. [1988]. *Specificatie van implementaties m. b. v. abstracte data types.* Eindwerk. Departement Computerwetenschappen. K. U. Leuven

MUSSER, D. R. [1980]. On proving inductive properties of abstract data types. *Proceedings 7th Symposium on Principles of Programming Languages.* ACM Sigplan. 154-162

NAKAJIMA, R., HONDA, M. and NAKAHARA, H. [1980]. Hierarchical Program Specification and Verification - a Many-sorted Logical Approach. *Acta Informatica* 14. 135-155

NOLAN G. [1979]. Dasim1: a practical exercise in data abstraction. *Proceedings of the symposium on language design and programming methodology. Sydney.* September 10-11 1979

OYAMAGUCHI, M. [1985]. On the data type extension problem for algebraic specifications. *Theoretical Computer Science.* 35 (1985). North-Holland. 329-336

PARNAS, D. L. [1972a]. A Technique for Software Module Specification. *Communications of the Association for Computing Machinery.* 15 (1972)

PARNAS, D. L. [1972b]. On the Criteria to Be Used in Decomposing Systems in Modules. *Communications of the Association for Computing Machinery.* Vol 5. Num 12. December 1972. 1053-1058

PARTSCH, H. and BROY, M. [1978]. Examples for Change of Types And Object Structures. Proceedings Symposium *Program Construction.* Lecture Notes in Computer Science 69. Springer-Verlag. Berlin. 421-463

PATTIS, R. E. [1981]. *Karel The Robot. A Gentle Introduction to the Art of Programming.* John Wiley & Sons. New York

PETER, R. [1967]. *Recursive Functions.* Academic Press. New York

PHILLIPS, N. [1984]. Safe Data Type Specifications. *IEEE Transactions on software engineering* Vol SE-10. Num 3. May 1984

PLAISTED, D. A. [1978]. *A recursively defined ordering for proving termination of term rewriting systems.* Report R-78-943. Department of Computer Science. University of Illinois. September 1978

ROBERTS, W. T. [1988]. A Formal Specification of the QMC Message System: The Underlying Abstract Model. *The Computer Journal.* Vol 31. Num 4. August 1988. 313-324

RUSINOWITCH, M. [1985]. Path of Subterm Ordering and Recursive Decomposition Ordering Revisited. *Rewriting Techniques and Applications.* JOUANNAUD, J. P. (ed). Lecture Notes in Computer Science 202. Springer-Verlag. New York. 225-240

SANNELLA, D. and WIRSING, M. [1982]. *Implementation of parameterized specifications.* Report CSR-103-82. Department of Computer Science. University of Edinburgh

SANNELLA, D. and TARLECKI, A. [1985a]. On observational equivalence and algebraic specification. *Mathematical Foundations of Software Development. Volume 1: Colloquium on Trees in Algebra and Programming.* Proceedings TAPSOFT, CAAP'85, Berlin, March 1985. EHRIG, H., FLOYD, C., NIVAT, M. and THATCHER, J. (eds). Lecture Notes in Computer Science 185. Springer-Verlag. 308-322

SANNELLA, D. and TARLECKI A. [1985b]. Some Thoughts on Algebraic Specification. *Recent Trends in Data Type Specification*. Proceedings of the 3rd Workshop on Theory and Applications of Abstract Data Types. KREOWSKI (ed). Informatik Fachberichte 116. Springer-Verlag. Berlin. 31-38

SANNELLA D., and TARLECKI A. [1987]. *Lecture Notes on Categories, specifications and institutions*. Draft version

SCHOBBENS, P.-Y. [1989]. *A bibliography of algebraic specifications*. Université Catholique de Louvain. Belgium. Unpublished

STEEGMANS, V. [1984]. *Two Party voice calls*. ITT 5400 BCS. Feature Implementation. International Telephone and Telegraph Corporation. New York

STEEGMANS, V. [1985]. *Enquiry and Transfer*. ITT 5400 BCS. Feature Implementation. International Telephone and Telegraph corporation. New York

STOY, J. E. [1977]. *Denotational Semantics: The Scott-Strachey Approach to Programming Language Theory*. MIT Press. Cambridge

STROOBANTS, S. [1987]. *Implementatie van het Knuth-Bendix vervolledigingsalgoritme voor een algebraïsche specificatietaal*. Eindwerk. Departement Computerwetenschappen. K. U. Leuven. September 1987

SUFRIN, B. and MORGAN, C. [1984]. Specification of the Unix Filing System. *IEEE Transactions on software engineering*. March 1984. Vol SE-10. Num 2

SUNSHINE, C., THOMPSON, D., ERICKSON, R., GERHART, S. and SCHWABE, D. [1982]. Specification and Verification of Communication Protocols in AFFIRM Using State Transition Models. *IEEE Transactions on Software Engineering*. Vol. SE-8. Num 5. September 1982. 460-489

TARSKI, A. [1968]. Equational Logic. *Contributions to Mathematical Logic*. SCHUTTE (ed). North-Holland

THATCHER, J. W., WAGNER, E., EHRIG, H. and WRIGHT, J. B. [1978]. Data Type Specification: Parameterization and the Power of the Specification Techniques. *Proc. 10th Symp. Theory of Computing*. May 1978. 119-132

THOMAS, M. [1988a]. *Implementing Algebraically Specified Abstract Data Types in an Imperative Programming Language*. Research Report

CSC/88/R3. Department of Computing Science. University of Glasgow. May 1988
also appeared in *Proceedings TapSoft '87*. Pisa. Lecture Notes in Computer Science 250. Springer-Verlag. Berlin

THOMAS, M. [1988b]. *The Imperative Implementation of Algebraic Data Types*. Research Report (PhD) CSC/88/R4. Department of Computing Science. University of Glasgow. May 1988

THOMPSON, J. [1983]. The use and abuse of formal proofs. *Sigplan Notices* Vol 18. Num 7. July 1983

TOMPA, F. [1980]. A Practical Example of the Specification of Abstract Data Types. *Acta Informatica* 13 (1980) 205-224

VAN COPPENOLLE, G. [1986]. *Bestandenbeheer: een modelvoorbeeld van algebraïsche specificaties*. Departement Computerwetenschappen. K. U. Leuven. Eindwerk. Juli 1986

VAN GESTEL, E., VAN HOREBEEK, I. and LEWI, J. [1988]. Remarks on Many-Sorted Equational Logic with respect to Algebraic Implementations. *Sigplan Notices* Vol 23. Num 1. January 1988. 120-126

VAN HOREBEEK, I. and LEWI, J. [1986a]. *An Introduction to Algebraic Specifications: From initial algebras to constructive specifications*. Report CW49. December 1986. K.U.Leuven (Belgium). Department of Computer Science

VAN HOREBEEK, I., LEWI, J., VAN PUYMBROECK, W. and BEVERS, E. [1986b]. *Error Handling in Algebraic Specifications*. Report CW52. December 1986. K.U.Leuven (Belgium). Department of Computer Science

VAN HOREBEEK, I., VAN GESTEL, E. and LEWI, J. [1987a]. *A constructive Algebraic Specification of the Ferry Problem*. Report CW54. January 1987. K.U.Leuven (Belgium). Department of Computer Science

VAN HOREBEEK, I., VAN GESTEL, E., LEWI, J. and MONTEYNE, M. [1987b]. *Abstract Implementations for Constructive Algebraic Specifications*. Report CW63. November 1987. K. U. Leuven (Belgium). Department of Computer Science

VAN HOREBEEK, I. [1988a]. *Formal specifications based on many-sorted initial algebras and their applications to software engineering*. Ph. D. Thesis. Department of Computer Science. K. U. Leuven. February 1988

VAN HOREBEEK, I., VERGAUWEN, B. and LEWI, J. [1988b]. Formal Specifications: an Industrial Case Study. *System Design: Concepts Methods and Tools*. Proceedings of CompEuro 88. Brussels. April 11-14 1988. Computer Society Press of the IEEE. 240-252

VAN HOREBEEK, I., LEWI, J., BEVERS, E., DUPONCHEEL, L. and VAN PUYMBROECK, W. [1988c]. An Exception Handling Method for Constructive Algebraic Specifications. *Software - Practice and Experience*. Vol 18. Num 5. May 1988. 443-458

VAN PUYMBROECK, W. and GOOVAERTS, V. [1984]. A translator for algebraic specifications. *Advances in Microprocessing and Microprogramming*. MYHRHAUG, B. and WILSON, D. R. (eds). Elsevier 1984. 105-109

VERGAUWEN, B. [1987]. *Een modelvoorbeeld van algebraische specificaties: een telefooncentrale*. Eindwerk. Departement Computerwetenschappen. K. U. Leuven 1986-1987

VAN VLIET, J. C. [1984]. *Software engineering*. H. E. Stenfert Kroese B.V. Leiden

WAND, M. [1979]. Final algebra semantics and data type extensions. *Journal of Computer and System Science* 19 (1979) 27-44

WARREN, D. H. D [1974]. *WARPLAN - a System for Generating Plans*. DGL Memo 76. University of Edinburgh

WARREN, D. H. D [1976]. Generating Conditional Plans and Programs. *Proceedings of the AISB Summer Conference*. Edinburgh. 344-354

WIRSING, M. and BROY, M. [1982]. An Analysis of Semantic Models for Algebraic Specifications. *Theoretical Foundations of Programming Methodology*. BROY, M. and SCHMIDT, G. (eds)

WIRTH, N. [1982]. *Programming in Modula-2*. Springer-Verlag. New York

YOURDON, E. N. and CONSTANTINE, L. L. [1979]. *Structured Design: Fundamentals of a Discipline of Computer Program and Systems Design*. Prentice-Hall. Englewood Cliffs

YUASA, T. and NAKAJIMA, R. [1985]. IOTA: A Modular Programming System. *IEEE Transactions on Software Engineering*. Vol. SE-11. Num 2. February 1985. 179-187

ZILLES, S. N. [1974]. *Algebraic specificaton of data types*. Project MAC Progress Report 11. MIT 1974. 28-52

Index

"Speak English!" said the Eaglet,
"I don't know the meaning of half those long words,
and what's more, I don't believe you do either!"
'Alice in Wonderland', Lewis Carroll

abnormal situation, 215
abstract data type (ADT), 3, 7, 8,
    10, 14-65, 27, 38, 55, 69, 92, 309
abstract data type Mini-PABX, 184
abstract data type Phone, 182-184
abstract implementation, 10, 12,
    13, 246-308, 314, 315
abstraction, 33
abstraction by parameterization,
    10, 164, 312
abstraction function, 254, 265-268,
    274, 284, 302, 308
abstract machine, 64
ABSYNT, 317
A-constructor, 255
ACT ONE, 13, 116, 159, 313
actualization, 117
actual module, 85
Ada, 1, 66, 85, 140, 316, 317
ADJ-group, 12, 58
algebra denoted by a presentation,
    31
algebraic specification, 7-10
algebraic specification language,
    66-119, 313
A-operation, 255
assignment, 29, 59
A-term, 259
automatic theorem proving, 6
axiom, 8-10, 30-31
axiomatic method, 7

basic generator, 159

behavioural abstraction, 64
behavioural equivalence, 12, 64,
    309
Bell, 11, 176
Bergstra, 13, 63, 114
Bernot, 245, 307, 308
Bert, 13
Bevers, 61, 125, 163, 314, 317
Bidoit, 13
Biebow, 176
Birkhoff, 58
Bloom, 58
Boehm, 1, 3
booking feature, 212
bottom-up, 74
bottom-up design, 75
Boyer, 43, 61, 125
Buchberger, 59
built-in operation, 116
Burstall, 13, 58, 59, 116, 118

call handling system, 11, 176, 316
camping feature, 212
carrier, 59
cartesian product of sorts, 155, 241
case construct, 81, 241
category, 26, 35
category theory, 59, 116
Cherifa, 162
Church-Rosser property, 160
CIP, 315
CIP-group, 12, 13
claimed requirement, 85, 314

claimed module, 151–155, 314
class, 1
CLEAR, 13, 118
closed set of axioms, 59
closed under substitution, 163
closure, 59
CLU, 2, 66
cluster, 2, 111–113
Cohn, 58
Coleman, 160
combination, 116
compatible with rewriting, 162
completeness, 120, 126, 317
completeness constraint, 124, 152,
    159, 213, 216, 224, 242
complete hierarchy, 114
composition of schemes, 107
computable total function, 61
concretion, 34
conditional axiom, 80, 116
conditional error axiom, 244
conference call, 212
confluence, 160
congruence class, 36
consistency, 314
consistency property, 142–144
consistent, 114
constant term, 24
constructing requirements, 140
constructive, 12, 63
constructive formal specification,
    6, 7
constructiveness, 126
constructiveness constraint, 123,
    213, 317
constructive specification, 15,
    123–134, 139, 159, 212, 314
constructivity, 10, 39, 125, 157,
    313, 314
constructivity constraint, 271
constructor, 123
constructor axiom, 121, 130–134,

139, 160, 216, 288
continuity, 3, 246
correctness, 1, 6, 13, 32, 120, 246,
    249, 271, 273
correctness proof, 61
Craeynest, 317
critical pair completion method, 59

data abstraction, 120, 123, 159,
    312
data implementation, 307
data refinement, 246, 307
data representation, 4, 38
data representation operation, 256,
    307
data representation part, 254, 256,
    284
data type invariant, 307
Declerfayt, 13
Delva, 317, 326
De Man, 176
De Marco, 3
denotation function, 16
denotational semantics, 7, 58, 315
De Remer, 1
Dershowitz, 162, 163
design-implementation structure,
    246
design phase, 2
Devriendt, 316, 323
Dijkstra, 7
direct implementation, 7, 169, 308
documentation, 120, 212, 312, 315
domain, 262, 286, 302

efficiency, 1
Ehrig, 13, 26, 27, 34, 35, 36, 37,
    58, 59, 61, 107, 114, 116, 159,
    307, 308, 313
enquiry call, 176, 198–206
enrichment, 114
Eqlog, 13, 118

equality operation, 128
equality operator, 306
equation, 59
equational reasoning, 14, 32, 39,
  43–55, 59, 60, 125
equivalence function, 254,
  268–270, 284, 286, 306, 306
equivalence relation, 268–270
equivalent module, 92
equivalent specification, 92, 123
error detection, 10, 11, 310, 312,
  313
error handler, 244
error handling, 11, 13, 184, 215–
  245, 278, 287, 310, 311, 312, 313
error object, 244
error propagation, 243
error recovery, 9, 10, 243, 287
evaluation, 59
example Array, 39, 79, 92
example ArrayScheme, 88, 127,
  137, 282–284
example Bag, 63, 64
example BlueRedIntegers, 50–51
example Bool, 69, 78, 126, 238–239
example BoundedArrayScheme,
  232–235
example BoundedStack, 228–231
example CircularList, 52–55
example ExtendedNat, 70
example ExtendedStack, 74
example FarmerWolfGoatCabbage,
  40–42, 165, 169
example FerryProblem, 154,
  166–169, 316
example GeomFScheme, 149–150
example INT, 118–119
example Integer, 43–50
example KarelTheRobot, 111, 113,
  157, 315
example ListScheme, 129–130
example MappingScheme, 292,
  293–295
example MissionariesCannibals,
  165, 171–173
example Nat, 18, 21, 22, 23, 26,
  117, 128, 216, 217–218, 219,
  223, 239–240
example NatArrayScheme, 102
example Numbertable, 99
example Orientation, 38
example PABX, 156
example Peekstack, 55
example PeekstackScheme, 237
example PrimitiveSet, 70
example Queue, 75, 78
example Robot, 158
example Set, 64
example SetScheme, 131–133, 135,
  160–161
example SomeOperationRequirementScheme, 107–108
example Stack, 3–4, 7–8, 8, 9, 10,
  15, 16, 17, 24, 25, 28, 29, 30,
  31, 34, 35, 37, 73, 75, 81, 87,
  117, 224–226, 250–254,
  260–262, 263, 266, 269, 271,
  284–287
example StackArrayScheme,
  103–105, 105–107, 109–111
example StackScheme, 86, 94, 99,
  100, 121–122, 278, 279
example Symboltable, 247–249
example SymboltableScheme,
  288–295
example ThreeThings, 153
exception algebra, 245
exhaustiveness constraint, 159
export, 9, 11, 66, 71–73, 115, 312,
  313, 317
export of import, 73
expression, 59
extended recursive path ordering
  with status, 163

extendibility, 1, 176, 180, 246
extending module, 114
extension, 114

ferry problem, 11, 164-175
field, 151
final algebra, 12, 62-63, 116
Floyd, 7
FOOPS, 118
formal module, 85
formal specification, 3, 5-7, 212
formula, 59
free algebra, 59
free functor, 116
fundamental type, 114
Futatsugi, 13, 58, 114, 116, 118,
    119, 136, 159, 162, 244

Ganzinger, 116
generated termalgebra, 58
generator, 159
generic package, 140
GeomF, 138-139, 141
Giarratana, 12, 64
Gipe, 13
Gobel, 160
Goguen, 12, 13, 26, 27, 32, 35, 36,
    37, 58, 59, 60, 61, 114, 116,
    118, 119, 136, 164, 244, 308
Goldberg, 2
Goldblatt, 59, 116
Gordon, 7
Goovaers, 176, 214
Goovaerts, 58, 59, 63, 159
Graetzer, 58
graphical programming language,
    13
ground confluence, 135-139, 160
ground confluence property,
    144-145
ground confluent specification,
    134-139

ground substitution, 28, 29
group, 149
Guttag, 12, 13, 58, 59, 64, 116,
    159, 164, 243, 304, 305, 306

Herbrand universe, 59
heterogeneous algebra, 58
hidden function, 10
hidden operation, 55, 61, 160
hidden sort, 55
hierarchical constraint, 66, 75,
    94-99, 95, 114, 139, 255,
    271, 305, 314
hierarchical specification, 10, 67,
    74, 94, 114
Higgens, 58
Hilton, 59, 116
Hoare, 7
homogeneous algebra, 58
homomorphism, 20-23
Hope, 13
Horn clause logic, 13
Hornung, 63, 64
Huet, 13, 50, 59, 61, 135, 160, 162,
    314
Huyghe, 316

identity, 59
ifthenelse construct, 76-78, 240
implementation constraint,
    271-278, 295, 302, 304, 314
implementation invariant, 254,
    262-264, 273, 284, 286, 302, 306
implementation of the ferry
    problem, 173-175
implementation operation, 258
implementation module, 247
implementation of module A by
    module B, 254
implementation phase, 2
import, 9, 11, 66, 68, 71-73, 115,
    116, 242, 312, 313, 317

inconsistent, 63
inconsistent specification, 139
induction, 14, 39, 43–55, 61, 93,
   125
inductionless induction, 61
induction without induction, 61
information hiding, 312
informal specification, 5, 6, 212
inherent invariant, 304
initial algebra, 12, 13, 14–65, 26,
   35–37, 58, 62–63, 309
instantiation, 85, 91–93
instantiation constraint, 91
intermodule dependency, 66
interpretation, 59
interpretation function, 304
intrusion feature, 212
iota, 114, 116
isomorphic, 58
isomorphism, 20–23, 64

Jackson, 1, 3
Jacobs, 212, 214
Jouannaud, 162

Kamin, 63, 162
Klaeren, 12
Kluzniak, 175
Knuth, 59, 162
Knuth–Bendix algorithm, 59, 61,
   162, 316
Kowalski, 164
Kreowski, 58
Kutzler, 13

Larch, 13
Laut, 59, 61, 116
law, 59
left-to-right term rewriting
   system, 120, 123, 124, 159, 160
Lescanne, 59, 160, 163
let construct, 82

Lewi, 61, 111, 115, 159, 315
Lientz, 3
Lipson, 58
Liskov, 1, 2, 58, 312
LISP, 61
LPG, 13

Mahr, 58, 116
maintenance, 2, 3, 5
maintenance phase, 2
Majster, 13
Mallgren, 13, 61, 138, 140, 141,
   150, 159
Manna, 162
many-sorted algebra, 7, 12, 15–20
many-sorted initial algebra, 14–65,
   310, 313
Martin, 162
Meseguer, 12, 27, 32, 34, 59, 64, 65
Meteor, 13
Meyer, 1, 2
Milgrom, 7
mini-PABX, 176–214, 310,
   323–326
MIRA, 317
mixfix notation, 78–80, 116
modularity, 1–2, 5, 10, 14, 66,
   68–74, 91, 114, 176, 180–182,
   215, 246, 311
Modula-2, 2, 66, 71, 115, 313
module, 2, 3, 4, 66, 68–71, 74, 91,
   92, 111
module Array, 252
module ArrayNat, 252
module NextPhone, 196–197,
   205–206, 208–209
module OutPhone, 197–198, 206,
   210–212
module Phone, 190, 199–200
module PhoneMessages, 191–196,
   201–204, 207–208
module Stack, 250, 251

monotonic, 162
Monteyne, 273
multi-target algebra, 245
multi-target operator, 245
Musser, 61

Nakajima, 114, 116
natural composition, 303
Ness, 162
no confusion, 58, 75
no junk, 58, 75
Nolan, 55
non-constructive specification, 14,
    120, 157, 159, 315
non-constructivity, 10
non-constructor operation, 123
non-hierarchical specification, 94
non-indexed data type, 308
nonnullary operation, 15
normal situation, 215
nullary operation, 15

OBJ, 116, 118, 159, 244
object-oriented design, 176, 177,
    212, 214, 310
OBJT, 136
OBJ2, 162, 313
observable sort, 64
observational equivalence, 64, 305
ok object, 244
ok function, 244
one-sorted algebra, 58
operation, 7, 123
operation axiom, 123
order-sorted algebra approach, 119,
    244

PABX, 311, 316
package, 1
parameter binding mechanism, 85
parameterization, 13, 66, 313
parameterized parameter passing,
    103, 116
parameterized requirement,
    107–111
parameterized specification, 11,
    12–13, 66, 85–111, 116, 117,
    150, 175, 232, 243,246, 287
parameterized theory, 118
parameter morphism, 85, 90–91,
    103, 153
Parnas, 1, 2, 64
partial function, 59
partial instantiation, 101–103
partial parameter morphism, 101
Partsch, 12
path of subterm ordering, 162
path ordering of Kapur, Narendran
    and Sivakumar, 163
Pattis, 315
phyllum, 59
pick-up feature, 212
Plaisted, 162
post-condition, 7
precedence, 162
precedence ordering, 162
pre-condition, 7
presentation, 30–31, 32, 35–37, 38
problem analysis phase, 2
procedural abstraction, 120, 123,
    159, 312
procedure implementation, 4, 254,
    307
procedure implementation
    operation, 257, 307
procedure implementation part,
    257, 284, 302
procedure module, 114
program correctness proof, 6
program documentation, 4, 32
program validation, 5
Prolog, 118
propagation, 220
protected, 114

protecting module, 114

qualified name, 84, 99
question construct, 323
quotient, 114
quotient algebra, 36, 37

rank, 16
rapid prototyping, 6, 11, 12, 63,
    120, 134, 169, 212, 215, 225,
    255, 270, 316, 317, 323-326
reachable termalgebra, 58
readability, 67, 111, 176, 180, 214,
    215, 253
recursion, 125
recursive, 162
recursive decomposition ordering,
    162
recursive decomposition ordering
    with status, 163
recursive path ordering, 162
recursive path ordering with
    status, 162
reliability, 1, 32, 67
reflexivity, 32
rename clause, 100
renaming, 84, 99, 253
replacement property, 162
representation function, 254, 258-
    262, 265, 274, 284, 285, 302
representation invariant, 304, 306
representation part, 302
requirement, 85, 93
requirements definition, 2
retrieve function, 307
reusability, 1, 3, 246, 278, 311
rewrite rule languages, 13
rigorous (mathematical) reasoning,
    6, 10, 14, 32, 273, 309, 313
robustness, 1, 66
run construct, 323
run with memory, 136

Rusinowitch, 163

safe object, 217, 220, 224
safety condition, 227-237
safety function, 217, 220
safety marker, 221-224
Sannella, 12, 58, 64, 307, 310
scheduling of the message, 187-188
scheme, 85
Schobbens, 12
search strategy, 173-175
semi-constructive, 11
semi-constructive specification,
    134-139, 157, 160, 314
semi-contructivity, 160
semi-constructivity constraint,
    134, 139
side-effect, 8
signature, 8, 15-20, 26, 27
simplification ordering, 162
skeleton of the mini-PABX,
    188-189
Smalltalk, 80, 2
software development, 4, 5
software engineering, 1-2, 10, 310,
    311
software life cycle, 2-3, 4, 5, 7,
    120, 310
sort, 7, 61
sort constraint, 244
specification, 2, 4-5, 123
standard parameter, 116
state explosion, 176
Steegmans, 189, 199, 212
Stoy, 7
Stroobants, 316
structural recursion, 125
structured diagram, 114
subsort, 118, 244
substitution, 28
substitution property, 306
substitutivity, 33

subterm property, 162
sufficiently complete, 63
Sufrin, 316
Sunshine, 176
symmetry, 32
syntax, 318-322

Tarlecki, 12
term, 28
termalgebra, 26, 32, 43
terminal algebra, 64
terminating specification, 124-125
termination, 162
termination of algebraic
    specifications, 314
termlanguage, 27-28, 69
term rewriting system, 11, 162
test phase, 2
Thatcher, 12, 13, 55, 56, 58, 116
theorem, 14, 32, 125, 142, 159,
    310, 312, 313, 315
theorem of the scheme, 145-149
theorem proving, 13
theory, 59, 118
Thomas, 308
time-out, 212
top-down, 6, 12, 66
top-down design, 6, 246
top-down testing, 6, 246
top-down verification, 6, 246
transfer feature, 212
transitivity, 33
tupling of types, 114
two-party voice call, 176, 189-198
type module, 114
type of interest TOI, 59
typical algebra of a category, 58

unbounded array, 39
undecidable, 114, 160, 162, 314
uniqueness, 120, 126, 317
uniqueness constraint, 124, 152,

159, 213, 217, 242
universal algebra, 58
unix file system, 13
unsafe function, 244
unsafe object, 217, 220
unsafety marker, 221-224
user action, 206-212
using module, 114

validation suite, 5
Van Coppenolle, 316
Van Gestel, 308
Van Horebeek, 296, 307, 316
Van Puymbroeck, 58, 159
variable, 27-28
variable-free term, 24
variable-free termlanguage, 23-24
variety, 26, 32, 43
VDM specification, 307
Vergauwen, 176, 180, 199,
    206-212, 311
verification, 6
view, 118
visible sort, 64

Wagner, 58
wake-up service, 212
Wand, 12, 63
Warren, 175
well-founded ordering, 162
wide spectrum language, 13
Wirsing, 59, 64
Wirth, 2, 71, 115, 313
word algebra, 24-25, 36, 59
word problem, 59
Wright, 58

Yourdon, 2, 3

Zilles, 12, 58